CBT + DBT + ACT
WORKBOOK
7 BOOKS IN 1
Cognitive Behavioral Therapy, Dialectical Behavior Therapy, Acceptance and Commitment Therapy, Complex PTSD, Vagus Nerve, EMDR Therapy and Somatic Psychotherapy

EMILY JEFFERSON

First printing edition 2021 in the United States.
The content of this book is published in the United States of America, and persons who access it agree to do so in accordance with applicable U.S. law. All opinions expressed by Emily in this book are solely Emily's opinions. You shouldn't take any of Emily's opinions as specific encouragement to follow a particular course of action or make a particular decision, but rather as an expression of his opinion. Strategies or opinions mentioned in this book may not be suitable for you.
This material does not take into account your individual objectives, situation, or needs and is not intended.
The information in the " CBT + DBT + ACT Workbook" is provided for informational purposes only. Readers are advised to consult a qualified health professional regarding specific health concerns or treatment.
The author and publisher make no representations or warranties with respect to the contents of this book and specifically disclaim all implied warranties, including for merchantability or fitness for a particular purpose. Readers should be aware that the information provided in this book is not intended as a substitute for consultation with a professional healthcare or legal advisor. The information in the " CBT + DBT + ACT Workbook " should not be considered complete and does not cover all issues, topics, or facts that may be relevant to individual circumstances.

CONTENTS

Dear Fellow Traveler,
With immense joy and a profound sense of responsibility, I welcome you to our transformative journey within the pages of the **"CBT + DBT + ACT Workbook."** I'm Emily Torres, and this collection is more than just a set of texts; it's a beacon of hope, understanding, and transformation for you, ready to embark on the profound path of self-healing and mental wellness.

My stance has always been unambiguous: self-compassion, practice, and knowledge are the three pillars of true healing. Each section of this workbook represents a unique thread of therapeutic wisdom, carefully selected and woven to offer you a holistic view of mental health from diverse therapeutic perspectives. I aim to equip you with the tools and insights necessary to navigate the complexities of your mental landscape, fostering resilience, healing, and personal growth.

Our journey begins with "Cognitive Behavioral Therapy," where I explore the intricate connection between thoughts, feelings, and behaviors. This section offers practical strategies to identify and challenge cognitive distortions, laying the foundation for positive change in your life.

Following this, "Dialectical Behavior Therapy" introduces you to the art of living in balance. It emphasizes the importance of mindfulness, emotional regulation, distress tolerance, and interpersonal effectiveness as pillars for building a life worth living.

In "Acceptance and Commitment Therapy," I invite you to embrace your thoughts and feelings rather than fighting or feeling guilty for them. It encourages commitment to actions that align with your values, fostering a rich and meaningful life.

Additionally, we delve into specific areas with "The Complex PTSD," providing insights and strategies for those dealing with the aftermath of prolonged exposure to highly stressful situations.

"Vagus Nerve" uncovers the pivotal role of this crucial nerve in regulating our body's response to stress and trauma, offering practical exercises to harness its power for healing and balance.

For people who have felt trapped by their past, "EMDR Therapy" offers a ground-breaking approach to processing and recovering from traumatic experiences.

Lastly, "Somatic Psychotherapy" focuses on the body-mind connection, emphasizing the importance of integrating physical and emotional awareness into the healing process.

This workbook is designed to be your companion on a path of self-discovery. It includes not just information, but interactive exercises and reflections designed to actively engage you in your healing process. My deepest hope is that the **"CBT + DBT + ACT Workbook"** serves as a trusted guide, empowering you to navigate mental health challenges with courage, knowledge, and hope.

Warmest regards,

Emily Jefferson

BOOK 1

COGNITIVE

BEHAVIORAL

THERAPY

How to Break Free from Anxious Attachment -
Empowering Yourself with Tools for Building Resilience
and Nurturing Secure, Positive Bonds

Reflection Page

This area is exclusively yours. Utilize it for monitoring your growth or expressing your thoughts and emotions.

INTRODUCTION

Welcome to the first step in your journey through Cognitive Behavioral Therapy (CBT), a path that promises not just insight, but transformation. As we embark on this exploration together, we delve into a therapy that's not just about understanding the patterns of your mind but about embarking on a journey of change that's both profound and personally empowering.

CBT is more than a set of techniques; it's a collaboration between you and your thoughts, a dialogue where your beliefs, feelings, and actions come together to script a new narrative for your life. This book is your guide, your companion, as you navigate this transformative journey.

Let's step into the world of CBT, understanding its roots, appreciating its evolution, and embracing the empowerment it offers.

Understanding the value behind Cognitive Behavior Therapy, referred to as CBT, is important. This powerful tool can open the pathway for someone to modify behaviors that aren't working with them. The goal is to replace them with behaviors that help them achieve their desired outcome. It takes time to see positive changes and to re-train the mind to think that way.

The length of time for such therapy depends on the individual and their needs. Typically, the person will see their therapist once a week for up to 20 sessions. In dire circumstances, they will see them twice a week to combat a crisis, then see them once a week.

For serious issues, it can take a year or longer with CBT for someone to no longer need therapy sessions. Everyone moves along at their own pace, but they should be working hard to see positive changes. CBT works best for those that are interested in learning and reach out because they want to end cycles that aren't productive for them.

Sometimes, individuals are forced into therapy, and it is harder to convince them this can help them live a better life. For example, parents may take their children to see a therapist if they believe they have a mental health concern, they have an eating disorder, or they struggle with anxiety.

Each patient is carefully assessed to help ensure nothing falls through the cracks. CBT works well when it is focused, guided, and specific to the goals of the individual. They must know what they are working towards and why it is to their benefit to do so. Only so much can be done in an hour of a therapy session. The rest is done outside of that environment.

The therapist will make sure they have all the tools and concepts they need to do this outside of the sessions. Then the patient will report back how they felt and what they experienced. Often, a journal is kept that the patient brings to those sessions. They also discuss any triggers or setbacks they experienced between the sessions.

Being mindful of triggers and other concepts is also important. Otherwise, a person can easily slip back into old behaviors due to stress or certain triggers. Taking control of your responses can help you feel in control. It can help you break the cycle of behaviors and actions that aren't serving you well.

Understanding the history and theory behind CBT is a good place to start. This helps create a strong foundation for the techniques and strategies CBT can be used for. All of this will be covered as you continue to reach through the materials in this book. It is important to realize CBT can be a successful tool for controlling various mental health concerns too.

Using CBT techniques, an individual can rely on these coping mechanisms to help them improve their overall quality of life. They can rely on them to help them end behaviors that aren't helping them live their life the way they want to. Chipping away at those barriers is an important path to empowerment. CBT techniques are the most successful when introduced by a professional.

Such experts can complete an assessment and determine the diagnosis for a patient. With that information, they can create a custom treatment plan for them that includes CBT techniques. Certain techniques work better for mental health concerns or personal needs than others. There aren't a one-size fits all concept with the use of CBT.

As you read the materials in this book, you can see how CBT techniques could improve your life. Perhaps you have a loved one struggling in one or more of the areas included in this book. Encourage them to seek professional help and ask specifically about CBT techniques that could assist them with their diagnosis. This can be a wonderful gift you deliver to yourself or someone you care about!

What is CBT?

Cognitive Behavior Techniques are typically referred to as CBT. This type of treatment is designed to change the way a person thinks about something. Our perceptions, subconscious, and conscious can be misleading. The distorted thoughts we have can cause problems for us. When the situation is re-evaluated from a new point of view, a better understanding comes to light.

CBT involves changing the way you see something so that it presents a positive outcome. The way you thought about it before was holding you back due to poor behaviors and outcomes. The goal of the new way of thinking is to present a positive mindset and desired outcomes. It can be challenging to make such changes, and you must be patient. It takes time to re-train your mind to think the way you want it to.

There are 5 key areas involved in CBT. Some patients will explore all these areas. For others, it will be focused on one or two of them. It depends on the coping situation or the mental health issue that is diagnosed. The expert will take all of this into consideration when they create the treatment plan. For dual diagnosis, they will focus on the key issues first. These 5 areas include:

- **Actions**
- **Emotions**
- **Physical state**
- **Situations**
- **Thoughts**

How does CBT work?

CBT methods work best when you work with a professional. They have the right information, tools, and techniques to help you modify your way of thinking. They can help you peel back the layers of what you think now and dissect it. What has happened in your life to make you think or feel that way about the subject?

They can introduce you to facts and information to help you see the subject in a better frame of mind. We tend to overlook what we are exposed to throughout our lives will shape the way we think and perceive situations. Yet that doesn't mean the way we see the is true or fact-based. Accepting this is important so you can let go of those previous thought patterns and replace them with ones that serve a purpose for you.

For CBT to work, a structured and detailed action plan is created for the individual by the expert. This is based on an assessment that identifies any underlying concerns and/or mental health issues. This form of talk therapy can involve several steps all intertwining with each other. They may include:

- **Activity planning**
- **Analysis of success**
- **Assignments**
- **Journaling**
- **Positive affirmations**
- **Therapy sessions**
- **Skill training**
- **Specific exercises introduced by the therapist**

Patients are encouraged to take an active role in their treatment plan. This includes showing up for all scheduled therapy sessions. It involves completing homework assignments and documenting how you feel in a journal. Being open and honest with yourself and with your therapist can help you gain the most value from CBT techniques.

The History and Evolution of CBT

Today, CBT is highly regarded as a powerful and effective way to change behaviors and beliefs. It is successfully implemented in a wide variety of coping situations including grief and anxiety. It is used for various types of mental health concerns including depression and personality disorders. Understanding the history of CBT and how it has evolved with time can give you a grand appreciation of all it entails.

It is believed the core of the treatment with CBT in its infancy began in the 1940s. It was a way to help those coping with what they had seen during World War II return to a normal life.

Psychiatrist Aaron T. Beck dove into the idea of CBT in the 1960s. His basis for doing so was observing many of his patients were having internal dialogues with themselves. The goal was to help change that dialogue to make it positive for those patients instead of holding them back.

This type of behavioral therapy has continued to evolve due to additional learning and seeing the success CBT offers to patients. This included cognitive models focused on changing the way a person thinks about a subject and strategies for helping them think in ways that are good for them. Testing in controlled environments, reviews of data, and introducing individualized concepts have helped CBT use to evolve and grow.

It is hard to argue with the facts, and there is plenty of proof in the statistics about the value CBT can deliver. One of the biggest evolutions is creating a specific plan for the individual. Rather than an umbrella type of treatment plan, it is defined for the unique needs of the individual. This increases the probability of someone gaining value from CBT. Each person has specific goals with CBT and objectives to help them achieve those goals.

Therapists rely on feedback from their patients to help them grow and evolve. That information shares with them what someone gained through CBT and where they thought it may fall short. They share with them their comfort level with the therapist and even how they felt about the assessments. Honest feedback ensures that therapists can make positive changes on their end. Their goal is always to offer a safe space and the best treatment possible for every single patient they work with.

Why is CBT Important in the Field of Mental Health?

Getting to the core of mental health issues isn't easy. The goal is to educate the public and break down the thought that it is taboo to talk about it. When people know it is okay to reach out for help, they are more likely to do so. When they see there are options for successful treatment, including CBT, they are encouraged to find out more about it. They want to live their best life possible!

Everyone faces challenging situations in their lives. Some of them are more difficult to deal with than others. When a person doesn't have adequate skills and techniques to cope with what is taking place, they can get locked into a cycle. They can end up on a downward spiral. It can be hard for them to do well in any area of their life until those core concepts are corrected.

CBT is important within the realm of mental health because it allows someone an opportunity to change their patterns of thinking. They can address it clearly and respond in a way that helps them get their desired outcome. As they see the benefit of doing so, they will continue on that path. In time, that new behavior will become an automatic response for them.

The National Alliance of Mental Illness (NAMI) has identified CBT as an important part of helping people have a good quality of life despite mental health concerns. CBT can be the core part of treatment as it helps someone engage in positive behaviors and actions rather than those that are self-destructive. A person may need CBT combined with medication to get the best outcome. It all depends on their diagnosis.

CBT is proven to offer many benefits in the field of mental health. They include:
- **Avoiding relapse to harmful behaviors and actions**
- **Learn coping and communication techniques**
- **Conflict resolution**
- **Controlling emotions**
- **Coping with loss and grief**
- **Coping with trauma**
- **Dealing with physical ailments and illness**
- **Managing mental health symptoms**
- **Reduced need for medication to control mental health concerns**

Effective treatment for mental health is important, but it can also prove to be difficult. Each patient has something different they face, but the CBT methods work well for all types of mental health concerns. That is encouraging because without such treatment, a person can struggle in all aspects of their life.

The amount of time it takes for them to benefit to the fullest from CBT varies. It depends on the type of mental health concern they are diagnosed with. It also depends on the severity of it. Some people dealing with situational depression, and as they learn coping skills and problem-solving skills, they move through their treatment plan.

Some patients have a harder time with the concepts and the changes. It can take them a year or two in therapy with CBT for them to have the skills and techniques they need to be happy and to live a good quality of life. Progress is progress – no matter how slowly it takes.

There can be some guesswork involved with treatment plans for those with mental health concerns. The therapist will do their best to pinpoint the key concepts to work on. However, the original treatment plan may require modification to continue to help the patient to the fullest. It often needs to be changed when additional goals are added in.

It can be scary to learn you have a mental health concern, but you aren't alone. The best thing you can do is seek effective treatment with a therapist. Understanding the mental health symptoms, you experience and how to offset them will change your life. It can help you with a job, relationships, feeling happy, and reaching your goals in life. Mental health concerns don't have to hold you back or be an excuse that gets in your way!

CHAPTER ONE

UNDERSTANDING CBT

Cognitive Behavioral Therapy involves replacing harmful thoughts and actions with positive ways of thinking and positive actions. It involves a variety of steps and techniques to create a mindset that enables the best outcome. For many patients, it involves eliminating old behaviors and replacing them with new ones.

They must understand why it is important to do so. Taking an analytical look at why you feel a certain way about something or why you be afraid you can't control in other scenarios has an impact. Often, such behaviors and actions are repetitive. While you may know they aren't working for you, that is the pattern you are familiar with.

Changing that involves identifying the underlying reason why you were making that decision to begin with. What is behind those behaviors and actions? What is behind those thoughts and beliefs? Many of us just take them at face value, and we see that as just the way things are. In therapy, you must be open and receptive to the facts and new realities. Changing your mindset can be empowering and bring with it a better quality of life.

The work of Psychologist B.F. Skinner has helped shape the way we see CBT today. His early work involved patients at a mental hospital located in Massachusetts. He had previously worked with animals and remembered the power that positive reinforcement and the rewards system had with them.

He decided to incorporate this idea by changing the ideas and thought patterns of patients. By persuading them to change their perceptions based on the rewards and the benefits of a positive outcome, he was able to accomplish this. At the same time, this process eliminates the negative thinking and negative actions that get in the way of success.

Beck is also credited with his procedures involving the evolution of CBT. He is identified as the father of Cognitive Behavior Therapy. He published his manual of treatment processing in 1979. While it has been modified and updated since then, the core concepts remain in place today.

Why is CBT so successful? Many experts believe it can be applied to a wide range of coping needs and mental health concerns. Yet it is effective because we all have the power to change our thoughts and perceptions. The way we see the world is through our past experiences, yet it isn't always true to reality. CBT brings that reality to the forefront, and it gives everyone the chance to have a better way of thinking.

CBT is also powerful because it is customized to fit the needs of the patient. Everyone has their own traumas, coping situations, and mental health concerns to work through. With this type of treatment, it focuses on those specific elements for each person. The treatment plan for one person is very different than that of the next. It is this focus on individualized needs that helps so many people incorporate the benefits of CBT into their lives.

Core Principles of CBT

Even though each treatment plan is unique, there are core principles within the CBT framework. There are two sides to this – the cognitions which are thoughts and the behaviors which are actions. The treatment plan should continue to evolve as the needs of the patient change. If they have several issues, the one with the most impact is the priority.

For CBT to work, the patient and therapist must form a strong bond. The patient must trust the methods of the therapist. They must be open and honest and take an active role in their treatment plan. While CBT does involve therapy sessions, a great deal of the changes stem from what a patient does on their own time between those sessions.

CBT is goal-oriented and that is important to grasp. There can be several steppingstones though along the road to reaching an established goal. Identifying the problem and then creating a solution is a partnership between the therapist and the patient. Identifying thoughts and behaviors in the way of that goal and removing them is a vital part of being successful with this form of treatment.

Education is at the core of CBT. This ensures the patient can learn and grow. Education allows them to see facts and realize some of their perceptions aren't true. The result of such learning is the patient learns better ways to cope with anything that comes along. They develop skills, communication concepts, and the ability to feel in control. They have a choice in their actions, and they choose wisely before they react.

The timeframe for CBT to work for someone depends on the coping they need or their mental health concerns. Some make tremendous progress in a few weeks or over a few months. Others require a year or longer to see the best results. There is no rush with this type of treatment. The goal is to keep moving forward, even if the progress is slow moving.

Through CBT, a patient can analyze their thoughts and make a conscious choice to change how they act and how they think. This is a powerful tool designed to help them gain confidence and feel empowered. Problem-solving skills are introduced that can be applied to a variety of scenarios.

Each interaction with a CBT expert is structured. This makes it different from other forms of therapy. At the beginning of the session, there is a discussion of what has occurred since the last session. The middle of the session involves going over any exercises or homework assignments that were asked to be completed before this appointment.

Before the appointment ends, feedback on progress and the treatment plan is given. It is also a chance for the patient to ask questions or comment on what they feel is working or not working. Your thoughts, feelings, and beliefs constantly influence each other. When you can identify each of those parts and the role they play in your life, you regain control.

CBT doesn't mean you will never have problems or trauma in your life again. Instead, it means you have tools and techniques to help you better cope and better work through them. Your thinking is solution-oriented and serves you in a positive manner.

The ABC Model

When the CBT concept is discussed, the ABC Model is often something people think about. This model is at the core of changing your way of thinking. Initially, you will have to focus your awareness on your thoughts and actions. You will have to stop the negative in their tracks and replace them with positive. This takes a conscious effort.

Over time, you will discover that your new thinking and new positive outcomes become part of who you are and how you think. It will be incorporated into your subconscious, serving your best interests. You should always strive for the best outcome. If your current behaviors don't reflect that, it is time for some positive changes to take shape!

 A. Activating Event – Any event that triggers dysfunctional ways of thinking or emotional distress.
 B. Belief – Negative thoughts that stem from the activating event.
 C. Consequences – Negative behaviors and feelings that are the result of the activating event.

The ABC Model opens our eyes to see that our beliefs are what create behaviors and emotions about subjects or events. Working through this method, a patient can see their irrational thoughts and behaviors about a certain subject. Once they are identified, they can work with the therapist to identify better thoughts and behaviors to associate with that subject.

It isn't always easy; the human mind is complex. The guided structure with the ABC Model though helps to simplify it in therapy sessions. The goal is to provide each patient with tools where they can analyze a situation in their life. They can ask themselves what is true based on facts and not perceptions.

Identifying triggers that are part of your thought process is a big step with this type of therapy. The world isn't going to tiptoe around you, and there will be triggers that emerge from many variables. Understanding them and identifying better ways to handle such triggers is the key to feeling your best physically and emotionally.

We don't always have control over situations and what takes place around us. However, we do have control over how we respond to those triggers. We can also recognize people or situations that aren't ideal for us. You may have to change your lifestyle and even set boundaries with people you are currently associated with to get the most value from CBT.

Thoughts, Emotions, and Behaviors

Think of thoughts, emotions, and behaviors as a triangle. At the pointed top, you have your thoughts. On the right-hand side, you have your emotions and that leads you to the left side which is your emotions. When these thoughts, emotions, and behaviors aren't parallel with your goals, it is time to implement changes.

Cognitive restructuring involves the process of re-training your mind. When negative thoughts enter your mind, you stop them and redirect them to something positive. In time, your mind will automatically go to the positive thinking when future triggers or situations emerge. You can't bury your emotions; you must come to terms with them. They can become larger than life if you are trying to ignore them or self-medicate so you don't have to deal with them.

At times, exploring the depths of our emotions can be hard. What you may discover is you act in ways that aren't parallel with your emotions. For example, when you are hurt or upset you may come across as being angry instead. What can you do to change that, so you properly convey the right emotion to fit that scenario?

Being mindful brings awareness to your choices of emotions and behaviors. You have the ability and the power to change things. You don't have to continue to act and react as you always have. Understanding why you have done so is a learning experience. As you see things differently, you can use that education as a tool to help you decide how you will best serve yourself through actions and behaviors.

Not everyone has the same skills, and that influences how they act and react to situations. This is why some people remain calm and others tend to be a mess pertaining to the same situation. Take the time to develop skills to help you fill in those gaps. If your skills are weak in areas such as communication, make a conscious effort to improve them.

CBT techniques can help you with day-to-day situations, work-related interactions, relationships, and more. They aren't just tied into mental health issues or crisis situations. When CBT methods are part of your core being, they flow outward into all you do and all you experience.

Evidence-Based Practice with CBT

Studies and other evidence hold CBT in high regard when it comes to effectively helping patients to be the best version of themselves. Since it can be personalized, it can be used in a wide variety of situations. The commitment to using science to help modify and improve CBT practices continues to be a driving force behind such methods.

This is also the underlying reason why CBT has been identified as a successful therapy for various forms of trauma, lack of self-confidence, and many mental health concerns. Such research includes unbiased data and clinical trials. While there are variables including patient backgrounds, personalities, and cultures, CBT has proven time and again to be backed by science to change behaviors and emotions.

Therapists are accountable to use evidence-based practices with each patient. They must clearly outline and define goals in their individual treatment plans. They must identify the diagnosis, all elements of the treatment for that patient, and the goals for such treatment. They also document after each therapy session any concerns or improvements to help show the progress someone is making with CBT.

Therapists have a responsibility to identify the best treatment for each patient. They must guide them in a structured manner to achieve positive changes. This ensures each patient has the optimum opportunity to use these learning experiences, tools, and techniques to improve their life.

There is another element of evidence-based practices with CBT too. Insurance companies often pay for these therapy sessions. They want to know if the patient gets a good return on that investment of time and money. The cost of the delivered treatment must be reasonable. The individual treatment plans also ensure the least amount of risk is involved with offering CBT treatment to a client.

How is CBT Different from Other Types of Psychotherapy?

It is important to know there are other types of Psychotherapy offered. CBT is a common one therapist recommend. They believe based on science and studies that such positive changes can help someone in all aspects of their lives. There is plenty of room for improvement and that is encouraging.

One of the biggest differences is CBT focuses on what a person feels and thinks at the present time. It doesn't reflect on the past. Of course, there are times when subconsciously a person thinks and acts in certain ways due to perceptions formed from past experiences. Yet it continues to reflect how they feel now, and that is why it is still deemed as a current issue and not a previous one.

CBT focuses on the concept that cognitions are tied to behaviors and thoughts. They all play a role together, like that triangle example given previously. This means the therapist has to offer a treatment plan that takes all into consideration at the same time.

Another significant difference is CBT focuses on effective problem-solving. We can all agree that influences many aspects of a person's life. To get to this point, a patient must look at what they are currently doing that isn't working for them. Learning new ways to communicate and better ways to react can prevent problems from getting worse. They are solution-driven, with the focus on a positive outcome.

CBT is the only type of Psychotherapy that focuses on learning new skills. A person isn't just told to act or think a certain way. Instead, they are encouraged at all points and levels to identify the truth and change their perception based on that truth and information.

CHAPTER TWO

BEHAVIORAL TECHNIQUES IN CBT

There are several amazing behavioral techniques involved in CBT. The ones implemented depend on the needs of the client and the expertise of the therapist. It isn't uncommon for several of these techniques to be used for someone's treatment plan. When the therapist can see they are making progress, they are encouraged to continue down that path.

What happens when treatment isn't working? The therapist will have a discussion with the client. Are they truly implementing the treatment plan in their day-to-day activities? Are they completing homework exercises and journaling? If the client isn't giving it 100%, it holds back the value from CBT methods.

The therapist can lead and guide them, but in the end, they must decide whether to dive in and benefit or not. Most people that seek CBT are interested in seeing what it can do for them. They realize many of their thoughts and behaviors aren't serving their best interests. They want help to change all of that, and they are thrilled to find a therapist offering CBT they can trust and rely on.

Exposure Therapy

Reducing anxiety is a common goal for those going through CBT. To do this, they often must be exposed to the stimuli they are afraid of. They must engage in situations that normally would cause anxiety. This gives them opportunities to try the new behaviors and remove the old ones.

For example, a person with anxiety in public settings may have a goal to go to one event a week. While they are there, they will try the various techniques and use the tools given to them in therapy. They can change how they react and their thoughts during those social gatherings. They can journal how they faced this fear and the outcome. As they see the value of doing so, they will notice they are less fearful. They also have fewer anxiety attacks.

Confronting the actual fear in a controlled way gives someone power over it. Rather than feeling helpless as the event unfolds, they are aware of their thoughts and their feelings. They can have control, such as deciding where they will go and how long they will stay. Typically, a person is going to avoid triggers and elements that cause them to feel anxious. With exposure therapy, they are asked to confront it and deal with it rather than hide it.

Why is this a good idea? When we are fearful of something, it takes on a life of its own. It gets larger and larger, and we feel overwhelmed by it. We get comfortable with our poor actions and reactions to them. We get used to our cycle of fear and the emotions linked to it. Yet we also realize that these feelings and behaviors aren't serving us in a positive way.

Breaking the pattern by facing the fear head-on reduces the size of it. The fear is identified, isolated, and broken down. Exposure therapy takes patience, dedication, and determination. The therapist helps the patient find safe environments where they can expose themselves to that fear.

There are different levels of exposure involved in this type of therapy. Someone struggling with PTSD may not feel safe in certain environments, so it isn't wise to try to expose them to it. In a controlled office setting though the goal can be to try to desensitize them against that scenario.

The pace of exposure therapy is important too. It doesn't have to be a sink or swim effort. It can be touched on around the edges and eased into. Then they take more control and put forth more effort to engage in that fear in a controlled manner. The therapist must measure it based on the situation, the patient, and many other variables. This allows them to create the best way to combat anxiety and other issues through this type of CBT.

Systematic Desensitization

While Systematic Desensitization falls under the category of Exposure Therapy, it warrants its own section here. It involves gradual exposure to fear in a controlled environment. At regular intervals, the level of exposure is increased and increased. The pace for the increases depends on how well the patient is doing with that exposure.

The goal is for them to remain calm and in control, despite the increased exposure to the fearful stimuli. Armed with various techniques and methods, they can focus on changing their thoughts and emotions about that stimulus. This in turn will help them to have a better response and reaction. When they realize the value of the better choices, it will help them go this route from that point forward when they fill triggers that bring on that fear. That fear is going to get smaller and smaller the more they feel the empowerment from the better choices.

Behavioral Activation

It is human nature to respond well to positive stimuli and rewards. Part of the success with CBT is to create goals and a reward system. Increasing the rewards for certain activities can help to boost a person's mood. It can motivate them to continue working with CBT because of the positive benefits they gain with it. At the same time, the more they engage in the positive behaviors, the fewer symptoms of the underlying issue will be present.

Behavioral activation is one of the best skills to master when engaging in CBT. Let's go back to that triangle again with the emotions, behaviors, and then actions. This is a type of treatment method that is often incorporated for those struggling with depression.

The goal is for the patient to place themselves into situations that evoke positive feelings and outcomes. This will boost a person's mood because it releases more of the feel-good chemicals in the brain. Our choice of behaviors influences our emotions. When we make a conscious effort to select behaviors and emotions that work to our benefit, we restructure our brain and the way it is wired.

A common exercise with behavioral activation is writing down the trigger or life event. Next, write down the emotions you feel. What do you typically do when you feel like that? Once you have that all written down, the goal is to identify what you can do differently when you feel like that. Don't underestimate how this change will influence your mood and help you break those negative cycles of behavior.

Another great activity is writing down your values. Next, decide how you can incorporate them into goals and activities that bring your personal satisfaction. For example, you may decide one of your values is giving back to your community. Writing down what you can do to help such as volunteering at the homeless shelter and the library are good places to start. Next, you can put that into action by reaching out to those locations to see how you sign up and what hours you can volunteer that fit into your schedule.

Skills Training

CBT offers value because it involves learning skills you can use for a lifetime. Rather than focusing on what you didn't know, the idea is to make positive changes based on what you know now! CBT treatment plans often include learning specified skills that the therapist believes will help the patient in areas of their life. This includes:

- Assertiveness
- Improved communication skills
- Problem-solving

Such skills take time to learn, and many patients don't have the right methods. Role-playing with the therapist with certain scenarios is a common way to help with these areas. The therapist will put a challenge out there and work with the patient to identify the best way to resolve it.

During this process, they must break down the barriers and change the behaviors that aren't working well. Removing them and introducing effective tools to be assertive, for better communication, and to effectively analyze a situation and problem-solve are skills that can be used in all aspects of someone's life. As a person gets comfortable with these new skills, they can apply them in real-life settings.

They see the value they bring to their career, personal relationships, and feeling heard on various topics. These interactions boost self-esteem and they become part of that person's methods for handling situations because the rewards they gain with these better alternatives are noticeable.

Coping techniques are a skill that may offer value to a patient. Perhaps they don't do well under stress and difficult situations. They may regress to old behaviors or struggle with anxiety due to what is taking place at that time. Situational depression is also a real concept and one that benefits from CBT.

Skills training helps build a strong foundation to build on through CBT. It helps reduce the risk of someone losing their self-confidence. It also reduces the risk of someone regressing to old habits when they face a challenging situation. When a person has great skills to fall back on during a crisis or challenge, they can get through it.

Relaxation Techniques

Too much on your plate and the stress can take a toll quickly. With relaxation techniques, you can learn to take a step back and analyze what is taking place. You can take your time to evaluate rather than emotionally reacting now. Such techniques through CBT help reduce stress and encourage remaining calm.

Some of them are very simple such as focusing on slowly breathing in and out. This can help with anxiety because you are focusing on your breathing instead of what is going on around you. Other methods involve visualizing each of your muscle groups relaxing one at a time.

Meditation and yoga are often encouraged to help with relaxation. They can be a great routine to incorporate into your day. Starting and ending the day with positive affirmations that motivate you and encourage you to stay positive is also part of such CBT treatment options.

The therapist will practice such relaxation techniques with a patient in a controlled setting. The goal is for them to feel comfortable enough with these techniques that they can apply them anywhere they need to. They can identify triggers and dive into using these relaxation options to help them regain control and focus.

It is a good idea to practice such techniques when you are calm and relaxed. This verifies you know what to do and the correct way to do them. When you are in a stressful situation or you are triggered, you can rely on those skills to help you get through it. You won't be able to do that if you haven't practiced because you will struggle to remember the steps.

The goal is to make those techniques second-nature for you to use when you need to. The faster you implement them, the sooner you can offset any serious problems. For example, when they are put in motion as soon as a panic attack starts, it can end almost immediately rather than becoming full-blown.

A person must explore several of these techniques to find those that work best for them. What works well for one person may not be enough relief for someone else. Also, certain techniques can work well in one scenario, but they aren't the best solution for another. Put yourself out there and experiment with the options.

Write down what happened, what you tried, and how you felt. Explore the emotions and if you felt in control. Continue with what works well for you as that is your chance to transform what has been holding you in a cycle that isn't producing positive outcomes.

CHAPTER THREE

CBT FOR ANXIETY DISORDERS

There are several different forms of anxiety disorders. The severity of them and the way in which they affect the person depend on the category they fall under. Some people don't do well in large crowds. Most of us get anxious when it comes to public speaking. For others, they can't leave the house without feeling anxious and it causes problems for them in all aspects of their lives.

Studies show CBT can be an effective tool for helping someone cope with an anxiety disorder. Often, such individuals feel out of control and helpless. They worry about anxiety getting the best of them. When they are fearful of it, the anxiety tends to get worse. The panic attacks and fear they feel increase. The frequency of these issues increases too.

It is hard to have a good quality of life when you are faced with an anxiety disorder. Ordinary things most people take for granted are a challenge when you add anxiety to the mix. Many people feel isolated as they struggle to maintain friendships and intimate relationships because of their anxiety. Others find it impossible to have the career they desire due to bouts of anxiety.

CBT for anxiety is a powerful resource, and it can help someone regain control over their thoughts, feelings, and emotions. It can help them address the underlying fear that has cast a shadow over them for far too long. CBT brings a sense of empowerment and reduces the anxiety a person experiences. The specific treatment depends on the type of anxiety disorder a person is deal with.

Cognitive Restructuring

With CBT and cognitive restructuring, the goal of therapy and the exercises is to change the negative thoughts surrounding anxiety. Replacing them with positive thoughts can help someone feel at ease in a social situation or with life in general. It can help them to calm down, slow down, and stay focused.

This type of treatment works because the negative thoughts are self-sabotaging. When a person can become aware of them, stop them in their tracks, and replace them with positive thoughts, they re-train the brain to think in a certain way. They can let go of those old patterns of behavior that aren't working for them. Many therapists discuss the 3 Cs with their patients to help them remember the steps and actions to take with their thoughts through cognitive restructuring. The 3 Cs are:

- **Catch**
- **Check**
- **Change**

Positive affirmations are important with cognitive restructuring. Identify the sayings that inspire you on a personal level. Say them as you start your day, during the day, and especially when you feel triggers bringing on anxiety. It takes time to develop this skill and put it into motion. When used correctly, it can be a powerful way to combat anxiety with the use of CBT.

Exposure Therapy

Facing fears and the triggers that cause anxiety can reduce and eliminate those symptoms. Exposure therapy is widely used by therapists to help reduce anxiety. What often happens is people with anxiety avoid situations and other people. They isolate themselves rather than dealing with the problem.

The goal of CBT through exposure therapy is to start small and work your way up to more exposure. For example, the patient may be asked to go to a small gathering of about 10 people for 1 hour. Next, they may be asked to go to a gathering that has up to 50 people for 2 hours. As they face the fear through exposure and change their mindset, that fear disappears. With it, the anxiety starts to disappear too.

A person isn't just thrown to the wolves to hope for the best. Exposure therapy is controlled and specific. The therapist will help them select a place to go, who will be with them, and other elements they can control. They can give them relaxation techniques and other tools to help them. Often, role-playing in the therapist's office takes place. What do they visualize? How do they feel? All of this prepares them for an actual outing.

Generalized Anxiety Disorder

Generalized Anxiety Disorder is often referred to as GAD. It is common in children as well as in adults. Sometimes, a traumatic experience can trigger it for someone that never had it before.
Symptoms of GAD include:

- **Difficulty concentrating**
- **Going over worst-case scenarios**
- **Overly emotional as a response to situations**
- **Overthinking**
- **Perceiving situations as threats when no threat exists**
- **Persistent worry**
- **Struggles with uncertainty**

A complete assessment is conducted to identify and diagnose someone with GAD. Blood work and other tests may be conducted to rule out medical conditions. If a person takes medications, they are evaluated to ensure the feelings and emotions aren't part of the side effects from that medication.

CBT helps with GAD through guided treatment and a specific treatment plan. Changing thoughts and using breathing techniques are very common ways to help reduce this type of anxiety. Relaxation techniques and coping skills are often part of the detailed treatment plan for someone with General Anxiety Disorder.

Panic Disorder

When someone struggles with a panic disorder, they have an overwhelming feeling of fear and anxiety. It can come on suddenly and it can last for a few seconds or several minutes. It can cause someone to feel pain in the chest, sweat, and not be able to focus on what is going on around them. It is very scary, and this fear can cause the problem to escalate.

It is hard to explain this gripping feeling of fear that someone has with a panic disorder. Many people tell them to just get over it. Others may feel they are trying to get attention. To the person experiencing this, it is life-altering and very scary. CBT is a wonderful tool to help someone overcome such situations.

Identifying the triggers is a big part of controlling a panic disorder. The patient must pay attention to what is going on around them. Are there certain places, smells, people, etc. that trigger them? Practicing breathing techniques and positive thinking can help someone talk themselves through a panic attack.

When they feel they are in control, the situation isn't as scary to them. They can de-escalate it. They face it head-on rather than avoiding situations where they may have a panic attack. This type of therapy is very detailed and in-depth. It is important for the patient to commit to sessions 1 or 2 times per week. The treatment often continues for several months. Then it may be possible for them to go in once a week or once every 2 weeks.

Social Anxiety Disorder

We all have times when we are nervous walking into a room. It can be difficult to make the first move and break the ice with someone new. There are people struggling with social anxiety disorder. They are afraid when they are around other people because they feel they are being judged.

If they hear people laughing in one area, they assume they are being laughed at. They often perceive threats in the room, but there isn't anything threatening going on. Others worry they are being watched and their every move is scrutinized. When someone does smile or talk to them, they wonder what their underlying motive is.

Social anxiety disorder can make it a challenge to go to school, maintain a job, or enjoy social gatherings. It can make it impossible to create strong bonds with others and develop meaningful relationships. CBT can help someone evaluate their core values. What is preventing them from feeling worthy when they are around other people? It tends to be much more than just low self-esteem.

Cognitive restructuring is introduced, encouraging them to change their mindset when they walk into a room. Taking those negative thoughts and feelings and turning them into something positive. Being assertive and learning to problem solve effectively are techniques to assist with social situations.

Role-playing with the therapist is often incorporated into this type of therapy. Often, the person lacks effective social skills. They don't know how to approach someone. They feel on the hot seat or interrogated when someone is trying to engage them in small talk. Learning social skills is a wonderful way to boost self-confidence and feel relaxed in a social setting.

Children can struggle with anxiety disorders, and it is helpful for them to get therapy when they do so. Learning how to cope with them and how to regain control can help them with school, relationships, and being healthy adults. Some therapists work exclusively with children and CBT.

CHAPTER FOUR

CBT FOR STRESS MANAGEMENT

Each of us encounters stress for various reasons in our lives. However, chronic stress can take a toll on the mind and the body. It can make it hard to focus, make decisions, and feel good about the direction life is taking. You may feel like you are just going through the motions rather than experiencing the emotions of anything in your life.

Sometimes, stress is just too much for someone to handle. It piles on and on, with no end in sight. They haven't learned how to cope with stress, so they become angry, or they may throw in the towel. Others become depressed and they feel like they don't measure up compared to everyone around them.

CBT for stress management is a good idea. It doesn't mean you will never experience stress again. What this type of treatment offers though is a way to cope with it. Learning important problem-solving skills and communication skills can reduce stress. It can help someone become assertive and feel like they are being heard.

The specific treatment plan for stress management with CBT depends on the patient and their needs. The therapist will explore the options, create the treatment plan, and modify it as necessary while the treatment progresses. The assessment reviews the thoughts, actions, and circumstances someone is involved with.

Once that is identified, CBT can be introduced to give the person control over their thoughts. It can be a way for them to stop feeling overwhelmed by stress when it happens. Instead, they can formulate a method to successfully break it down and move forward.

Chronic stress often means changes need to happen in a person's life. Perhaps they have too much on their plate. Burning the candle at both ends will catch up with you and wear you down. Chronic stress due to work or relationships can mean those are toxic elements and it is time to sever ties and bring peace and balance back into your life.

Intense feelings physically and mentally can develop due to stress, and it isn't good for a person. Learning effective strategies to analyze the situation, cope, and problem-solve helps reduce stress. It also gets a person out of the cycle of the same stress happening to them again and again. With confidence and a positive mindset, you can talk about how you feel and not feel obligated to people please or let others take advantage of you.

It isn't uncommon for a treatment plan with CBT for stress management to include:

- **Coping strategies**
- **Problem-solving skills**
- **Relaxation techniques**
- **Time management skills**

Coping Strategies

We all get tossed curve balls in life. Things don't go as planned or we failed to plan and now we are out of time. There are many reasons why stress occurs, but you can't let the entire world crumble around you because of it. Understanding the core of the situation, evaluating options, and moving on from it will help you reduce the negative impact from stress.

Your therapist will introduce various coping strategies and ask you to implement them. You will be asked to journal about what you did, how that felt, and the outcome. Look for common patterns in your stress too. Are there certain people or situations where it peaks? If so, what can you do to de-escalate that?

Is your lack of commitment or your lack of preparation to blame? If so, it is time to stop making excuses and get organized. If you have too much on your plate, you must prioritize and then take a step back from the rest of it. Sometimes, we create our own stress by not speaking up or not being able to say no to what others ask of us.

Your therapist will ask you to evaluate your lifestyle habits with them. They will encourage you to get enough sleep each night, avoid drugs and alcohol use, and engage in at least 30 minutes of exercise each day. You will be encouraged to eat healthy meals and not skip meals.

Problem-Solving Skills

You can't get upset every time you experience stress. You must learn effective problem-solving skills to get you through the situation. If you expend all your energy on negative thoughts and feelings, you aren't accomplishing anything. Instead, you must take a good look at the problem without letting your emotions run the show.

What is the main concern? Why is it causing you stress? What options do you have to alleviate the problem? If you typically put off dealing with stress or avoid confrontation, you must change those behaviors as you learn to problem-solve. You can have discussions with people and set boundaries without arguing. You can be open-minded about possible solutions and look closely at the pros and cons each option offers.

Problem-solving to reduce stress involves identifying the outcome you want. You can't control other people and how they feel or think. What you can control is how you will react to them. You may have to remove some people from your life to get the stress to end. If you are in a toxic cycle with them, you must be the one to initiate change.

Relaxation Techniques

Ongoing stress creates problems of its own. A person often doesn't sleep well, and they are irritable because of it. That compounded with the stress can cause you to snap at the smallest of things. Instead of letting them roll off your back, you are defensive and now you have more stress to deal with.

Relaxation techniques are a big part of CBT, and they work well with stress. They give you a chance to calm down and not respond now when your emotions are high. Your therapist will ask you to practice deep breathing in and out so you can focus on steady breathing to help the moment pass. This can help you regain your composure.

Progressive muscle relaxation is another common tool they can share with you. This technique involves focusing all your attention on one muscle group at a time. Feel it relaxing and the tension leaving your body. Move on to the next segment of the body and continue this process from head to toe. Take as much time as you need for everything to loosen up.

Yoga and meditation are wonderful ways to relax the mind and body. These activities will help them get in sync with each other. Starting your day with such an activity can improve your mood, lower stress, and help you get through your day with a positive outlook.

Time Management Skills

One of the biggest reasons for ongoing stress is trying to take on too much. You may wear many hats – a spouse, a parent, an employee, a friend, and so many more. Make your own needs a priority so you have energy, and you are rejuvenated for what you face out there. We all have the same 24 hours a day to work with. The question is, what matters to you the most to spend that time on?

Getting organized will help you manage your time. A routine at home will ensure everyone living there knows what to expect. Ask your partner and older children to help with chores or hire someone to come in and do them for you. Find a job that is meaningful to you, not just a place to earn a paycheck.

Break down larger projects and deadlines into smaller pieces and smaller timeframes. Hold yourself accountable to keep up with those established commitments. If you feel like you have too much work on your plate to reasonably get done, it is time to speak with your boss. Share with them what you feel should be delegated and why. If you don't speak up, they will continue to pile it on!

Don't be afraid to say no when people ask you to do things you don't have time for. You don't have to give them a lengthy explanation either. Simply share with them that you don't have the time to take part in that right now. If they press the issue, stand firm in your decision that it isn't a good fit for you right now.

You don't have to fill every day with activities and being productive either. Slow down and take some time to just relax and enjoy what is going on around you. Find daily activities you like that also get your body moving. This will improve your mood and help you reduce the risk of health issues.

Your therapist can guide you through time management and developing such skills to fit your own lifestyle. There are times when you will have to juggle schedules, but don't let it get the best of you. Being assertive with other people and not worrying about their expectations will help you see things clearer than before.

Effectively handling stress will help you with all aspects of your life. It will help you remain focused and in control when things are out of the ordinary. You can be a leader and a role model with your decision making and how you handle adversity. If you have children, your behaviors can influence how they handle conflict and decisions too.

Show them the path that will help them take care of their needs and guide them. As you learn better concepts and methods, you can share them with others in your household. It will improve communication and bonding among all of you. Don't be afraid to admit you have made mistakes in the past with how you handled things.

CHAPTER FIVE

CBT FOR DEPRESSION

One of the most common mental health concerns in our society is depression. Not everyone with it has been properly diagnosed. Some don't like the idea of treatment and they try to self-medicate. Such efforts often include the use of drugs and/or alcohol. Others don't realize they have an issue because it is just the way they have always felt and always functioned. They don't realize there is a better life possible.

Depression can be mild, moderate, or severe. It is a misconception that depressed people don't try to find joy or happiness in their lives. It is a misconception that they can just snap out of it. For many of them, it is due to the chemicals in their brain. The goal is to get more of the feel-good chemicals flowing.

This is why therapy for depression often includes self-care and daily exercise. It isn't selfish to focus on your needs. It isn't selfish to do what you can to feel your best physically and mentally. CBT is a good option for the treatment of depression. It may be enough on its own but for many patients, it is offered in conjunction with the use of daily medication.

It is true some people go through what is coined situational depression. For example, they struggle with the loss of a loved one and that brings on symptoms of depression. Being hit with a major life change or stress can trigger depression. For those that already struggle with it, such factors can cause it to worsen. As you talk with a therapist, they can determine if it is situational or ongoing depression you have.

A complete assessment and diagnosis are the starting points for a therapist. If the diagnosis is depression, it also must be identified in terms of the severity. CBT works well for mild to moderate depression. It can be part of a treatment plan for someone with severe depression, but the sessions should be closer together. They will likely be taking medication at the same time they go through the therapy.

There are several approaches taken when CBT is introduced to treat depression. The focus area depends on the patient, what is taking place in their life, and their overall circumstances. The plan must be detailed and personalized so it can target the behaviors and emotions that are the result of a depressive state. Such approaches can include:

- **Behavioral activation**
- **Graded exposure**
- **Identify negative thoughts**
- **IPT**
- **MBCT**

Behavioral Activation

The brain responds well to rewarding activities. This boosts mood because it increases the amount of Serotonin in the brain. Through behavioral activation, a person engages in more of the type of activities that bring on this type of reward feeling for the mind and the body. However, the activities of choice must be positive for them. They can't be harmful or a form of self-sabotage.

This is important because many people turn to drugs and/or alcohol to cope with depression and other mental health concerns. The mind and body feel rewarded with the way they feel due to the drugs and/or alcohol. While this gives the feeling they are after, both entities are harmful and addictive. It is important to be on a path that promotes the best version of yourself possible.

There can be cycles a person goes through relating to their depression. For behavioral activation to work with CBT, they must understand their cycle. This involves working closely with the therapist to identify that cycle. Where does it start? What is the step-by-step process for them?

Monitoring daily activities, no matter how routine, is important for this type of treatment to be successful. The therapist will expect a detailed report of what you do and how you respond to it. This gives them a chance to discuss with you places where you can change your daily activities to make them more rewarding to the mind and body.

Specific goals and values must be identified for the person to use as their platform. It helps them choose behaviors that give them rewarding feelings. At the same time, it will increase energy levels and motivation. This is all accomplished through pleasure and personal satisfaction. Scheduled activities should have a purpose of fulfilling such a role. They should be enjoyable to the patient and meaningful to their quest for personal satisfaction.

It takes time and commitment working with a therapist for CBT to work with depression. Identifying barriers to success can help break them down. Anything that is being avoided must be dealt with. Learning skills for improved communication and better problem-solving will help to make this is possible. The changes are going to be gradual, and the focus is on that progress. The changes won't occur quickly but the more the ideals are implemented, the more the brain changes.

Graded Exposure

The process of graded exposure involves gradually placing yourself into activities or situations that you previously avoided due to your depression. It isn't uncommon for people to withdraw from family, friends, and hobbies when they struggle with depression. This method of CBT involves making a conscious effort to avoid those people or those situations no longer.

It can be challenging at first to find joy in what you are used to. Things change due to depression, and it is hard to put your finger on it. You may have to have some difficult conversations with those you care about. Sharing with them you have depression is a good place to start. It isn't something to hide or be ashamed of.

Such therapy involves sharing with the therapist what you are the most afraid of. They will help you rank your fears and anxiety relating to people and situations from the worst to the best. Typically, the treatment plan starts with those items at the lower end of the list. As a person makes progress and positive changes, those toward the middle and top of the list are discussed.

Graded exposure is detailed and focused. The client must work closely with the therapist for this type of treatment to work. It requires being accountable for actions and making a conscious effort to change things for the better. This is usually a lengthy type of treatment. The more the person repeats the behaviors though the easier it is for them to become an ingrained part of their actions and thoughts. This will reduce symptoms of depression, but it does take time.

Identify Negative Thoughts

Ongoing negative thoughts can make depression worse. Often, a person gets into a pattern of thinking that way. They may struggle with self-esteem. They may feel like there isn't much to look forward to so each day is just something they go through on auto-pilot. CBT involves recognizing those negative thoughts and challenging yourself to replace them with positive thoughts.

As this pattern continues, you will find it gets easier and easier to think positively from the start. Studies show positive thinking reduces the symptoms and negative effects from depression. It can help someone feel appreciative, give them things to look forward to in the day, and help them to improve their mood. A therapist will often ask the patient to journal each day how they feel and their emotions during this type of treatment. It helps to identify the cycle of negative thoughts and then a plan is put in place to start eliminating them.

IPT

Interpersonal therapy is often known as IPT. This is short-term therapy with a focus on improving social functioning and interpersonal relationships. Many people struggle with depression because they don't have close ties to others, They struggle to forge relationships and maintain them. They lack the social skills to feel at ease in settings where they must introduce themselves and get to know new people.

IPT involves discussing with the therapist what you feel are the biggest challenges you face with relationships. Identifying the cycles of behavior that get in the way of creating healthy relationships is important. Once those behaviors are identified they can be replaced with better options. Changing how you interact with people can help you feel more confident and at ease with them.

Depression can cause people to put up walls instead of boundaries. The difference is walls keep everyone out. Boundaries let people in, but only the people you choose. Boundaries also share with them the behaviors and actions you are willing to accept. Keeping everyone out is isolation and it can be a lonely place to spend your time!

People often have patterns of behavior in relationships, and this can carry over to when they end too. For example, IPT can be a good CBT for someone seeking therapy after a breakup. They may feel like this always happens or that they always date the same type of person. What they fail to see is their actions often play a role in that outcome playing out again and again.

IPT requires digging deep and being objective about what you see. It is an eye-opening quest that can put someone on a path to self-discovery. Often, a therapist will discourage such patients from getting involved with a new partner until after the treatment ends. During treatment, they will learn various techniques and skills that help them socially and with relationships. A person must be willing to change their thoughts and behaviors for IPT to work.

MBCT

An amazing option for depression is MBCT, short for Mindful-Based Cognitive Therapy. This treatment for depression involves mindful techniques along with CBT. Typically, such therapy is reserved for those struggling with ongoing depression categorized as severe.

Such individuals are chronically unhappy, and they struggle to change such behaviors. It requires many sessions with a therapist and carefully exploring various elements of their thinking process. Everything must be out in the open for it to be evaluated and the therapist to create the treatment plan. The individual must commit to doing exercises and daily journaling.

The more information shared with the therapist, the better the outcome with MBCT. Such individuals often need medication to help them with depression along with the therapy. One or the other isn't enough due to the severity of the problem.

In addition to CBT, the person's attitude is evaluated. Such individuals can be labeled as hard to get along with or hard to work with. They tend to lack social skills and don't have much self-esteem. They are hard to approach as they don't know how to interact well with others. They often feel isolated and alone, but they find that better than the awkwardness of interacting with others. Their attitude and behaviors though can leave others puzzled. They may not respond when they should, or they may not respond in a way that others deem as normal. This further isolate them from others. With MBCT, part of the focus is on meditation. This helps to calm the mind so the person can stay focused.

The goal of MBCT is to encourage someone to become aware of how they act and how they interact. Removing behaviors that aren't helping them find their place in the world is important. Yet such behaviors can be hard to change due to the amount of time the person has engaged in them. Awareness is the start of change, and once the person knows what they are doing isn't helping them, they have the choice to go another route. They can choose to incorporate techniques the therapist has introduced. This type of therapy is often used with getting rid of negative thoughts and a reward system.

Focusing on breathing is also part of MBCT. Often, individuals with this level of depression feel on the spot to respond. That stress can cause them to say something completely off the beaten path for the topic being discussed. Breathing techniques encourage them to slow down, focus, and listen to what is being shared by others. They can take a moment or two before they respond rather than blurting out something.

Slowing down and focusing on what is presently taking place is important. When your mind is in all directions at once, you only get bits and pieces of all of it. While people do successfully multi-task, a person with this level of depression fails to complete most of what they start. This can create tension in personal relationships and work environments.

Through this type of therapy, a person is going to analyze their behaviors but not judge them. They are going to let go of what isn't working well for them and try new options. It is an opportunity to find acceptance with themselves and how they behave. This isn't about the acceptance of others, but about feeling confident in who you are.

Therapy involving MBCT involves exploring and being curious about the world. The challenge is getting someone to see themselves in a new light. Why do they do what they do? Why do they react a certain way? How do they wish they could respond? In what situations do they regret how they acted or what they said? Such information can identify patterns that have to be addressed.

Re-training the brain takes time, and MBCT works very slowly. It takes months of sessions for a person to start bringing it all together. It takes small changes in thought processing and actions. Yet those small steps along the way are going to add up to some huge improvements as time goes by. Changing the thinking process and improving the mood is going to reduce depression symptoms. It also takes time to regulate the right medication and the correct dose of it. All of that is being evaluated at the same time the MBCT is going forward. The treatments must align with each other, and the patient has to give 100% commitment to what they are asked to take part in with this form of therapy.

CHAPTER SIX

CBT FOR INSOMNIA

How well you sleep each night and the amount of sleep you get impact your thought process. These factors influence your mood. If you often get out of bed because your alarm goes off or a child wakes you up rather than you are ready to get up, you may be struggling from a lack of sleep.

For many, they do strive to get enough sleep. However, they find the hours they spend in bed aren't effective. They often toss and turn due to insomnia. They can't sleep during the time they have allocated, and then they are tired all day because of it. Relying on sleeping aids to get enough sleep is difficult.

The body can build up a tolerance to them. This means over time; it takes a higher dose than before to sleep the same. They can become habit forming, especially when a person is taking prescription strength medications to sleep. Such products often come with harsh side effects. It isn't uncommon for someone to wake up feeling groggy.

A lack of sleep isn't something a person can handle for very long. It has a negative effect on both the mind and the body. CBT for insomnia is common, and often where people turn when they feel they have tried all other options. For others, they don't want to try medications, so they go this route instead.

The amount of time it takes to see results through therapy for insomnia depends on the patient. It also depends on any underlying concerns that must be addressed. The benefits tend to start emerging after just a few sessions. This encourages patients to continue with the therapy until they are sleeping better than they have in a long time.

Cognitive Restructuring

Nothing increases the problems with insomnia like thinking about them all the time. If you are full of dread before you go to sleep because you already know it isn't going to be a restful night, you are increasing the odds of it happening. This cycle must be broken for you to find peace and rest well.

Replace those adverse thoughts about not sleeping well with positive ones. For example, tell yourself "Tonight I am going to drift off to sleep quickly and have wonderful dreams". If you do wake up, quickly reassure yourself with positive thoughts and strive to go right back to sleep.

Cognitive restructuring works well because many people quickly become frustrated due to insomnia. Positive thinking helps a person to drift off in less time and to remain asleep longer. You can sleep for fewer hours and feel better rested when you are in deeper levels of sleep.

If your last thoughts when you try to sleep are about how tired you will be at the big meeting tomorrow because you couldn't sleep, you are engaging in self-sabotaging behaviors. Focus on what you envision that meeting to be like. Who will be there? What emotions will you feel? Gently remind yourself you need to relax and get a good night of rest.

Relaxation Techniques

Stress and anxiety are key factors for insomnia. Relaxation techniques can help you to let go of both elements. Focus on deep breaths in and out to help you find a rhythm between your mind and your body. Think about the positive things that you engaged in that day and what you will do the following day. The goal is to boost your mood and be excited for what is ahead.

Bedtime shouldn't be when you worry about bills or the kids. It shouldn't be where you try to think of a clever marketing pitch to take to your boss the next day. If your mind is going, going, and going, you will be stricken with insomnia because you aren't turning your mind off. Get into the habit of slowing down in the hours before bed. This will train your mind to sleep and reach deeper levels of sleep.

Sleep Hygiene

Good sleep habits are important, and when you don't engage in them, it can cause insomnia. Limit the intake of food and drinks after a certain time each night. This will help you sleep better as you aren't dealing with the need to urinate throughout the night or acid reflux.

Keep the room at a comfortable temperature so you can sleep well. If you are too hot or too cold, you will wake up frequently. Your mattress and pillow should offer the best comfort. You may need to experiment to find the firmness of a mattress and a pillow that works best for your preferences.

Strive to go to bed at the same time each night and get up at the same time each day. A bedtime routine will help your mind and body get ready for sleep. You can't make up the sleep you missed by staying in bed longer on your days off from work. Set limits for household chores, work you take home, and other tasks. Don't interrupt your sleep time to get more done than you reasonably should.

Avoid exercise and caffeine close to bedtime. They will stimulate the mind and body, keeping you awake rather than letting you rest. Meditation before bed or some quiet time to journal where you can reflect on the day and calm your mind are recommended activities.

Stimulus Control

Technology is a huge part of the world we live in today. Computers, smart phones, tablets, and other devices are commonly used. However, they can overstimulate the mind before bedtime. They can contribute to insomnia for this reason. Avoid using your phone or computer for at least two hours before you go to bed at night.

TV can have the same outcome. It is fine to have a TV in your bedroom, but don't get into the habit of watching it before you go to sleep. Watch a movie here and there or even during the day on a rainy day. Keeping the TV on while you try to fall asleep can increase the risk of insomnia.

Avoid eating in your bed because that can stimulate your mind and body. If you do keep something to drink in the room, it should be water. You don't want your mind or body to associate going to bed with anything that it will use to perk up. Instead, you want it to be calm and ready to shut down.

Sleep Restriction

A good night of sleep isn't about the hours you spend in bed, it is the quality of that time. Make sure your room is quiet, comfortable, and your mind and body know the bed is for sleep. Don't spend time in bed doing other things such as reading, watching the TV often, or conducting work. It should be a space that is specifically for sleeping.

Some people do well with 6 hours of sleep each night. Others need up to 10. Listen to your body. Your age, overall health, type of work you do, and other variables can influence how many hours you need to be fully rested. Most therapists will tell you to only use the bed for sleep and sex. They will ask you to keep a journal of your activities too so they can work with you to change anything that is hindering a good night of sleep.

CHAPTER SEVEN

CBT FOR PERSONALITY DISORDERS

Proper diagnosis and proper treatment are essential for someone with a personality disorder to live their best life possible. Such mental health issues are complex, but it doesn't mean the individual can't live a great life. It doesn't mean they can't have intimate relationships or ongoing friendships. A personality disorder doesn't have to stop someone from a career they love or enjoying life to the fullest.

With the assistance and guidance of a trained therapist, CBT can be a wonderful way to reduce the symptoms of a personality disorder. There are several different ones a person can be diagnosed with. The treatment has to fit that diagnosis as well as the needs of the patient. The treatment has to be closely monitored and modified when necessary to keep it moving toward the goals of that individual.

There are several options for the therapist to consider when treating someone with a personality disorder. After they complete the assessment and look at all the variables, they may implement DBT and/or Schema Therapy.

Borderline Personality Disorder

One of the common mental health ailments CBT is used for is the treatment of borderline personality disorder. When someone has this diagnosis, the way they think and feel about themselves is negative. They also have negative thoughts and feelings about other people around them.

This projects into everything they experience daily. As a result, they struggle to keep a job or maintain relationships. Individuals with Borderline Personality Disorder often experience the following symptoms:

- **Difficulty managing emotions**
- **Impulsive behaviors**
- **Patterns of unhealthy relationships**

DIALECTICAL BEHAVIOR THERAPY

- **Poor self-esteem**

Until they seek professional help and follow a treatment plan that can introduce new ways of thinking and behaving, the cycles will continue. They may feel isolated and alone because they can't form long-term relationships with others. They may have abandonment issues too because they feel everyone, they try to get close to pushes them away or leaves in the end.

It can be difficult to be around someone with borderline personality disorder. The smallest thing can create an emotional outburst of anger or destructive behaviors. It is a challenge to have a discussion with them about it because they lack problem-solving skills, and they lack effective communication skills.

Often, individuals with borderline personality disorder allow others to treat them poorly. Since they lack a good self-image, they don't think they deserve better. They are also desensitized to it since they have had this pattern with other people. There is no one side to blame, but relationships like this are toxic.

A therapist understands these changes in behaviors and emotions, and they know how to directly talk to someone with borderline personality disorder. Part of the sessions involves assessing and analyzing behaviors that are creating problems for them, without making them feel bad about it. The therapist strives to do this objectively, and asks them to view it from an outsider's perspective looking in.

CBT is one of the most successful treatment options for someone with borderline personality disorder. The outcome with such therapy is to promote a better quality of life and to help the individual learn effective coping skills. The process involves reducing the symptoms by changing the behaviors and actions of the individual. It starts with teaching a person how to interpret situations differently.

A typical treatment plan includes both Dialect Behavior Therapy and Schema-Focused Therapy. If someone is engaging in self-harm such as cutting or attempted suicide, emergency treatment and intervention may be required. If they report to their therapist they have suicidal thoughts, an in-house treatment facility may be recommended for their own safety.

Cognitive-Behavior Avoidance Model

While there are many variables involved in personality disorders, avoidance is a common thread among them. Rather than dealing with situations and people and trying to resolve conflicts, they tend to just find an escape route. Yet the core of the problem is never dealt with that way. It isn't until they engage in CBT and have the guidance of a therapist that they focus their attention on dealing with issues rather than continuing to avoid them.

Avoidance behaviors contribute to personality disorders. A person isn't happy with who they are or what they are doing. They aren't themselves in relationships and they tend to fly off the handle as an emotion. Rather than showing they are upset or hurt, it still comes across as anger. The avoidance can ruin self-esteem and it can increase the risk of someone engaging in self-harm.

Some of the symptoms that indicate avoidance as part of a personality disorder include:

- **Abusing drugs and/or alcohol**
- **Avoid eye contact**
- **Avoiding social gatherings or attending but leaving early**
- **Excessive daydreaming**
- **Isolation**
- **Low self-esteem**
- **Poor relationships with others**
- **Poor social skills**
- **Unable to explore or cope with emotions**

When someone has avoidance issues, it may be combined with other concerns. For example, anxiety or depression. This can cause the avoidance to be worse because the person is using it as a means of some control over their situation. They know that the outcome isn't helping, but it is what they know, and it is what gets them through the situation in the moment.

It isn't uncommon for childhood factors to be identified at the core of such avoidance and concerns. It may be related to child abuse, neglect, or some form of trauma. If it happened when someone was very young, they likely won't remember it. The memories are locked in their subconscious and affect behaviors and actions.

A proper assessment is vital to the success of treatment when it comes to avoidance issues and any other ailments the person may have. The therapist must use this information to create the ideal treatment plan for them. That is one of the reasons why CBT is so successful, it isn't generic. It is designed for that person to gain the most value from.

Dialect Behavior Therapy

Combining CBT with techniques that promote both mindfulness and acceptance is known as DBT, or Dialect Behavior Therapy. This is one of the treatment plans that often include both individual and group therapy sessions. The individual will meet with their therapist as scheduled. They will also be asked to join a group of their peers that share similar needs. The groups are small to ensure everyone gets a chance to participate in the guided exercises.

The focus of DBT is on behavioral skills and identifying the right way to act and react to situations. The key aspects of this learning and development include:

- **Coping with stress and conflict**
- **Creating healthy relationships with others**
- **Eliminating thoughts and actions that lead to self-harm**
- **Living in the moment**
- **Regulating emotions to match the situation**
- **Staying motivated to continue learning and exploring better behaviors and actions**

Not everyone feels emotions the same way. When someone feels them very intensely, it can be overwhelming. Think about a toddler that engages in a tantrum over something we think isn't important. To them, it is worth the meltdown and that is all they can focus on now. This is what it is like for an older child or an adult with certain personality disorders.

They haven't learned how to successfully cope with various feelings and ranges of emotions. Their behaviors are viewed as odd or upsetting by those around them. Others may feel intimidated or threatened when someone acts with such outward anger.

DBT helps individuals learn to understand and cope with their emotions in a positive manner. They are taught how to analyze the situation and use problem-solving skills to work through it. This helps them at work, with relationships, and it improves their self-image. Therapists work on a treatment plan that includes methods for self-soothing. Learning how to remain calm while exploring emotions is an important part of self-control.

What can be done to improve the situation and reduce the stress? Often, just slowing down and focusing on breathing can help. A problem can feel out of control and larger than life when that is all you think about. When you perceive it as a bigger deal than it really is, it can get the best of you. Rather than avoiding dealing with it, the focus is on looking at the pros and cons of the possible solutions.

Focusing on the present situation is part of DBT, and that is where being mindful comes into the equation. It takes time to train the brain to think in such a way if you haven't been doing so. Patients are taught to tune into their senses and use them to help them work through the emotions they feel at that time.

Developing healthy coping skills reduces the power a situation has over someone with a personality disorder. They feel in control even though they are facing a challenge, or they have conflict to resolve. They can remain positive and think of a good way to resolve the issue even though they feel stressed by the situation.

Emotional pain can be very hard to explain to someone else. Using the senses and using coping skills reduce that emotional pain so it is controlled. This doesn't mean the person doesn't identify the emotions they have. It means that they aren't explosive and over the top with them like they used to be.

Learning to think positively when you are in emotional pain can be a challenge. It is hard not to let the negative thoughts flow because that is what you are used to doing. This can lead to impulsive actions and negative behaviors. When those negative thoughts are replaced with positive ones, the decisions are the result of evaluating the pros and cons before acting or reacting.

With DBT, the most important issues are addressed first in treatment. It isn't possible to address all of it at once. The first issue to resolve is any concerns over self-harm or suicidal thoughts. Next, the focus is on what is holding someone back from a better quality of life.

Once those two areas are addressed, the therapist is going to move it in the direction of improving self-esteem. Along the same lines, they are going to discuss behaviors to improve interpersonal relationships. Changing actions and behaviors to ensure boundaries aren't being overstepped is a good learning lesson.

How can the individual be happier? What can they do to have stronger relationships? What are their life goals? These are the questions the therapist will help the patient answer as the DBT treatment moves into the final stages. The patient will have the foundation they built earlier in the therapy to help them continue to move forward.

Schema Therapy

Long-term therapy for personality disorders often includes Schema Therapy. This focuses on changes which are the result of changing a person's core beliefs. It takes time for them to accept what they have always known as truth wasn't the reality of it. Changing perceptions can help someone see situations and people in a new way than they used to.

Many of those perceptions are deeply rooted in the subconscious. They are the result of what may have occurred when someone was very young. The therapist often must point out these concerns because a person doesn't even realize they are creating problems for them.

The person has learned how to cope with such issues, such by avoiding them. In other scenarios, they are desensitized to it because of all that exposure. They behave the same way and believe it is normal to do so. They don't understand that other people aren't viewing it as normal behavior.

There are triggers and thought patterns to identify and then Schema Therapy is used to change them. It takes time for such therapy to work, the person must focus on what they know and what they believe. They must come to terms with what they have done before isn't working for them and they must decide to change that cycle.

Schema Therapy is focused on the emotions of the individual. The treatment is flexible, and it changes as a person's emotions change. Someone involved in this type of treatment should expect to remain in therapy for several years. The progress is going to be worth it!

The purpose of Schema is to give someone the tools they need to make healthier decisions for actions and behaviors. They must address their core needs and values. Breaking the patterns that haven't served them well and replacing them with new concepts changes that cycle for the future.

Uncovering and discovering what has led to dysfunction in relationships and behaviors is essential. This is the only way it can be evaluated, dissected, and then a new plan for moving forward can be put in the works. The downside to Schema Therapy is the time involved. It can become expensive if you need to see the therapist ongoing for a long time.

CHAPTER EIGHT

CBT FOR EATING DISORDERS

We hear so much in society about obesity and the health issues relating to it, but there is more to look at. Many people suffer from the effects of eating disorders. They adversely affect someone both physically and mentally. Some eating disorders cause someone to overeat due to an emotional need that isn't being met as it should.

In other scenarios, a person is not eating enough, and they have an unrealistic idea of how their body should look. CBT can be a wonderful form of treatment for someone struggling with an eating disorder. It may surprise you to learn there are plenty of children out there with such concerns. Getting them into treatment early in life can increase the chance of a healthy lifestyle as an adult.

CBT also reduces the risk of someone regressing and relapsing back into the pattern of an eating disorder. Stress, anxiety, and other variables can influence the severity of an eating disorder. Providing the individual with educational information about healthy eating, daily exercise, and coping skills can get them headed in the right direction.

There is never going to be a life free from stress or challenges. Understanding you have options is important. Learning to let go of what you can't control and focusing on what you can is part of effective problem-solving. Exploring your emotions, identifying triggers, and setting boundaries in your life can help you overcome an eating disorder.

Individuals receiving help from a professional have the highest rate of success. It isn't uncommon for there to be other underlying concerns or mental health ailments present for someone with an eating disorder. A complete assessment and detailed treatment plan can help them come to terms with those issues and make positive changes to more than just their eating habits.

Cognitive Model of Eating Disorders

It is important to take a closer look at the cognitive model of eating disorders to see the clear picture. The core of all eating disorders, even though they have different characteristics and symptoms, has to do with body shape and body weight. Patients get into a cycle with this type of behavior, and they go to great lengths to hide it from others. This includes hiding food, exercising without other people knowing how much time they put into it, and vomiting food or taking laxatives.

There are often intense feelings of guilt and shame associated with eating disorders. This makes it harder for someone to share the cycle they go through with someone else. Their body can suffer due to the cycle, and that takes a toll on them physically too.

The cognitive model of eating disorders requires a therapist to challenge the thoughts and beliefs the person perceives to be true. The facts must be presented, and the patient must agree to them as being true so they will work to change those behaviors and concepts in their mind.

A food diary is often part of CBT-E treatment for eating disorders. The patient is asked to write down everything they eat including the time and the amount. They are also asked to write down how they felt after they ate that food. What behaviors did they engage in? This is important as it shows the cycle, and it can also show they are breaking old habits and patterns when they change what they do after they eat.

Many people with eating disorders see it as an all or nothing effort. With the therapy, they can start to understand eating is essential for the body and mind to be healthy. Yet food doesn't have to be something you depend on for emotions to flow. Some people eat when they are happy, and others eat when they are sad. There are those that eat to fill a void in their life. They aren't eating or avoiding eating because of nutritional value.

For those with an eating disorder, food can be something they fear. They worry about eating too much and gaining weight. Others worry about overeating and then having to compensate for doing so. Avoiding those topics will result in the cycles continuing. In therapy, there are discussions about food and what fears they may have. Addressing them and facing them head-on is part of the success with this form of treatment.

Addressing Body Image

While most individuals with eating disorders are female, that isn't always the case. Both genders are influenced by society and the image out there of the perfect body. So much attention is given to celebrities and what they wear and how they look! Body shaming is common on social media, both of celebrities and common people.

No one wants to be on the receiving end of such comments. For many people with eating disorders, the way they perceive their own shape and body weight influences their eating decisions. They don't set out to have an eating disorder, but that is what develops as the cycle of adverse behaviors continues without treatment.

It is a misconception that everyone with an eating disorder has been body shamed by their family or other people in their lives. It is true, some people grew up in a situation where weight was something they were embarrassed by or teased about. That factor doesn't always have to be there for someone to struggle with an eating disorder though.

Developing a realistic and healthy body shape and weight in the mind of the patient is essential for success. Changing those negative thoughts with positive ones will help them stop obsessing about food and their size. Introducing them to ideals that are realistic rather than focused on society manifestations is also important. They may need to limit viewing celebrity photos and even limit social media access during treatment.

Exposure and Response Prevention

Breaking the cycle of adverse behavior is necessary for combating any eating disorder. Exposure and response prevention is a big part of that because it prevents the cycle from going and going. Identifying the trigger and then modifying the response is important.

The therapist will talk to the patient about what they feel and what triggers them to behave a certain way. It is often tied to body image and emotions they experience. Changing the response and helping them face challenges instead of avoiding the issues is important.

Accountability is a big part of this too, and that is why journaling is important. The patient is asked to share what they eat, when they eat, and what they feel when they do so as part of this treatment plan. As they see their responses changing, it is going to reflect in how they eat and how they feel.

OCD is a common ailment that exposure and response prevention are used for. When you think about it though, the formulated thoughts and cycle with someone struggling with an eating disorder are like OCD. Their thought process is if they eat, they will gain weight. If they are binge eating their thought is that they will get a positive high when they eat all that extra food, but then the low hits them and they feel guilty and ashamed.

Therapy helps identify the specific cycle someone is experiencing. When the therapist sees that information, they can introduce coping methods, new behaviors, and healthy thoughts to offset that cycle. Interrupting that cycle so it doesn't continue to be part of a person's lifestyle is important when treating any eating disorder.

CBT-Enhanced for Eating Disorders

CBT-Enhanced for eating disorders is often referred to as CBT-E. It is considered one of the best treatments for individuals with an eating disorder. It seems to work well regardless of which type of eating disorder someone is diagnosed with. This includes:
- **Anorexia**

- **Binge eating cycles**
- **Bulimia**

For extreme eating disorders, a patient may be advised to enter an in-house treatment option where CBT-E can be part of the treatment plan. If it is deemed the patient can see a therapist on an out-patient basis this type of treatment will be at the core of the plan for everyone. It typically involves 20 sessions, at weekly intervals.

More sessions may be added if the therapist feels it will help the patient to be successful and reduce the risk of relapse. This determination will be made as the patient approaches the end of the 20 weekly sessions. If they are on track and doing well, there may not be a need to continue. It is determined on a case-by-case basis.

In situations where someone is drastically underweight due to anorexia; it may be advised for treatment in therapy to last up to 40 weeks. This additional time encourages them to put on weight and strive to reach a healthy weight. The therapist encourages weight gain, but the patient must see the value in doing so. They aren't going to work for it if their therapist and doctor are telling them they must. They will only do so when they can perceive their body differently than they did before.

CBT-E involves 4 stages, and the therapist will give each one the time it needs before they introduce the next. As is the case with all CBT, the treatment plan is customized. The assessment will tell the therapist what the key focal points for treatment are. From there, they can expand to the other areas once a foundation is in place.

Stage 1

This is the starting point and assessing the overall health and mental state of the patient. If they are in dire need of nutrition, that is the primary concern. The assessment should offer a clear picture of the type of eating disorder and how long it has been affecting the patient. The focus is on normalizing eating patterns and helping them adhere to them. If they aren't eating enough, they must start eating regular meals each day.

If they vomit after eating that must come to a halt. For those that binge eats due to emotions, they must find other ways to deal with those triggers. Introducing coping skills can be a wonderful way for them to stop that cycle from repeating itself. This stage is one where education is introduced about healthy weight and how we all have different body shapes. For severe cases, it may be advised for the patient to see the therapist twice a week instead of once during stage 1.

Stage 2

Many therapists refer to stage 1 as the crisis mode. They take care of the immediate problem and danger to the patient. Once they feel this is stabilized, they can discuss the main elements of the eating disorder. They can discuss triggers, body image concerns, and listen to the mindset the patient has.

All this information will help the therapist work with the patient to create a detailed treatment plan. It is vital the patient is on board with this treatment, and they do their part. For minors, parents are encouraged to be part of the treatment plan. They often must monitor what their child is eating and verify they are following through with what the therapist recommends.

Stage 3

Weekly sessions take place during stage 3. Education continues about positive body image. It is important for the patient to see their body for what it is. If they need to gain weight or lose weight, then that can be part of the treatment plan. It isn't uncommon for a medical doctor to be involved. They can work parallel with the therapist so that everyone is on the same page regarding goals and how to achieve them.

Dietary planning is discussed in stage 3 of CBT-E for eating disorders. Planning menus, discussing calorie intake, and talking about daily exercise are all part of the learning objectives. Someone trying to lose weight can't excessively restrict calories or exercise for hours on end.

Identifying foods that taste good but offer the body fuel without empty calories must be discussed. For those trying to lose weight, it can be done through eating healthier foods and increasing daily activity. Eating well-balanced meals will offer additional energy which can be used to motivate someone to exercise more. Finding activities, they like is important too so the exercise doesn't feel like a punishment. Instead, it is something they look forward to.

There is a pattern of moods, emotions, and eating/not eating that takes place when someone struggles with an eating disorder. The image they have of themselves isn't reality. Learning to deal with day-to-day events and stressors that could trigger the symptoms of their eating disorder is essential for success with the treatment plan.

Otherwise, someone will regress back to old habits any time they face stressors or challenges. Treatment involves education and learning for better coping and better problem-solving skills. Often, improved communication and better self-esteem are ways to motivate someone to move in the right direction with this type of treatment plan.

Stage 4

In stage 4 the focus is on maintaining a positive mindset and the future goals. What will the individual do when they feel a setback or a trigger coming on? What support system do they have in place? What tools and techniques have they learned that will help them make better decisions?

Anyone that has been through CBT-E for an eating disorder needs support in place. They need a place to turn if they feel a crisis mode emerging. This can be a family member, a friend, or reaching out to the therapist for an emergency session. The end goal of such treatment is for the patient to move forward with methods they can count on to help them avoid future concerns with an eating disorder.

Family Based Treatment

Family based treatment is common with eating disorders due to the dynamics involved. The typical patient is a child or adolescent, and they still live with their parents. Often, their parents are upset when they realize this has been going on. They can feel upset that they didn't see the symptoms or that their child didn't feel comfortable coming to them about it.

Accountability is important with the treatment for eating disorders. There are triggers that can cause the person to regress to old habits. They can start to skip meals, exercise too much, or eat too much again. The family can oversee those actions and intervene when possible. They can also encourage the person to eat healthy and the entire family can often learn about meal planning and meal preparation tips.

A support system is essential for overcoming an eating disorder. When a person can rely on their family to help them eat better and be accountable, it makes an impact. Parents often don't know what to do to help their child recover. The treatment plan educates them so they can take steps to offer support, offer healthy foods, and monitor progress.

This is also an opportunity to educate the entire family on the situation and what took place. It isn't something that should be hidden from other family members. Instead, it can shed some light on the subject for them and become a learning experience. It can help the family bond and feel comfortable sharing information with each other.

Proper nutrition is important for anyone recovering from an eating disorder. They shouldn't feel alone or isolated in their efforts. Adults can also benefit from family-based treatment. They may have a spouse or close friend that is going to be their support through the recovery. That person must know what to look for as symptoms, how to encourage them, and even when to reach out to the therapist for help.

Family based treatment doesn't just focus on the eating disorder though. In many situations, the learning involves extends to coping skills. It includes problem-solving and communication methods. It can help the relationships of all involved become healthier with those new techniques and skills in the mix.

CHAPTER NINE

MINDFULNESS AND ACCEPTANCE BASED APPROACHES FOR CBT

A relevant and effective area of CBT involves exploring the mindful and acceptance-based approaches. They offer a variety of concepts, and they can help in an array of situations. They are often included in mental health treatment such as personality disorders and anxiety. They work well to improve social skills and interpersonal relationships.

The complexity with mindful and acceptance-based approaches to CBT is identifying which of them to apply to a particular treatment plan. There can be shifts in the mindset and needs of the patient. When that occurs, the therapist may have to add some concepts from a different approach. The same is true if a patient isn't responding positively like the therapist thought they would. Trying a new concept can be something they relate to and work well with instead.

As shared several times in this book, CBT is so widely used and successful because of the customization. Each of these mindfulness and acceptance-based approaches has something unique to present to the patient. Each of them can help someone focus on the here and now and not be stuck in previous cycles or worried about the future.

Each of these concepts is created upon the belief that distress is caused by how a person responds to an experience or situation. This is different from what most people believe. They tend to think that due to an experience or situation, they must respond in each way. They don't realize until they seek therapy that there are better alternatives.

Mindfulness is associated with awareness, but not with what you perceive. Instead, it has to do with being aware of what is real and what is true. We tend to accept what we think at face value, not questioning why we think that way or why we respond that way. It is just part of who we are.

When we break it down and analyze it though, we can see that our methods often don't serve us well. The cycle can be the same, but the outcome isn't what we wish it was. Our thoughts, actions, and behaviors can prevent us from living the life we desire. They can prevent us from being happy and appreciative. A positive attitude and a calm mind help with mindfulness. Meditation and journaling help to reach these concepts and apply them in day-to-day events.

Accepting what is going on around you doesn't mean you just let life happen. Instead, it means you focus on changing what you have control over. You must learn to let the rest of it go. If you let other people and their actions adversely trigger you again and again, that is your responsibility and not theirs. You must be assertive and set those boundaries in place.

Of course, that is easier said than done for many individuals. There are many underlying reasons why someone struggles, and they need CBT. The good news is you are never too old to change how you think and explore your emotional reactions. It is never too late to make positive changes in a quest to have peace of mind and a better life.

The outcome with mindful therapy is it changes the attitude someone has about certain things because their perception has changed. The thought process and mindset have been restructured from what they used to be. The new methods incorporate better outcomes as they are solution oriented. They give a person coping skills to work with and a way to see the world around them that is no longer categorized as dysfunctional.

These approaches with CBT include:

ACT
DBT
MBCT
MBSR

ACT

The emphasis on Acceptance and Commitment Therapy, commonly known as ACT, is accepting thoughts and emotions. The goal is to accept them without any type of judgment. By doing so, you can stay in the moment and move beyond any previous trauma or difficulties. You aren't reflecting on those times; you are focused on the healing process.

It is a chance to shift your energy from dwelling on the negative to embracing the positive. We all face challenges and disappointments in our lives, but it is how we learn to cope with them that matters. What we learn from those experiences will help shape us into the person we are today. If you aren't happy with that person, it is time to explore why. Sometimes, we must accept we will never get the love or apology from someone that we deserve. The problem is on their shoulders, and not the result of anything you did or didn't do.

Letting go of perceptions of how we think life should be is a big part of ACT. Seeing it for what it really is and accepting that reality is a life-changing way of thinking. We tend to see the good in someone else or a situation because that is what we want it to be. We don't take it at face value, but that concept is just pulling us down and making it harder to have a quality of life that you are happy with.

Changing negative thought patterns and replacing them with positive ones is a big part of ACT. You can do this with help from a therapist who has done their best to create the ideal treatment plan for your needs. If you often feel you aren't good enough, it is time to focus on your strengths and what you offer. Seeing yourself in a new light can help you gain confidence and change what you think.

Positive affirmations can help you start the day on a positive note. They can help you see the good all-around you rather than the negative. There is always so much to be thankful for, don't let the little things be taken for granted because you spent your energy on things outside of your control.

Pay attention to triggers that create anxiety or stress for you. What can be done to de-escalate the situation? Facing issues directly instead of avoiding them is a skill you can learn through this type of CBT. It can prevent you from going through the same issue and the same adverse feelings towards it repeatedly.

When you think in new ways and you rely on effective problem-solving skills, you can try new options. You can look at the pros and cons of the choices you have and decide how you will approach the situation. If you don't get the desired outcome, think about what you can do the next time to improve upon it. Understanding you don't have to go through the same situation and the same outcome again and again is refreshing.

Improving your flexibility when it comes to options is part of ACT. If you often see things as black or white, it is time to embrace the many shades of gray on both sides of that equation. Listening to others and educating yourself on topics before you make decisions can help you feel more in control over what you do. It can give you the confidence to make a choice too rather than depending on luck for a successful outcome.

Stop the dead-end processes that have taken place in your mind. You already know where they lead. You already know you don't like being backed into that corner. With a new path, you can embrace the possibilities. Rather than a doom and gloom cloud over you, there is light at the end of the tunnel!

With change comes empowerment and control over your decisions. For some, this can cause them more stress or anxiety. It is important to discuss this with a therapist, so that the treatment plan reflects this. Stress and anxiety can cause a person to regress, even though they know that path isn't right for them. They do so though because it is familiar to them.

Facing the fear is going to reduce the stress and anxiety. Often, the perception of what could happen is worse than what really takes shape.

Avoiding the situation though is always going to lead to more anxiety and stress. Select the path that brings you the most value.

Don't be afraid to make a mistake. If you try a strategy and it doesn't work, what did you learn from it? How did you feel about trying it? Talk to your therapist about this so that you aren't beating yourself up over the decision. It is better to try something and then realize it doesn't work for you than to continue with methods you already know don't work for you. Keep trying and keep moving forward and you will find what DOES work well for you!

The goal with ACT is to give the patient the confidence and the skills to get through any situation in a positive way. They can focus on self-talk, they can use coping skills, and they can rely on problem-solving methods that help them find the best solution for a given scenario. All this learning leads to personal growth and personal satisfaction.

DBT

Commonly referred to as DBT, Dialect Behavior Therapy is a type of treatment that works well for those with borderline personality disorder. It is often part of the treatment plan with CBT. At the same time, it incorporates both mindfulness and acceptance. A person can get overwhelmed with too many changes at once. This is why the therapist will identify the key points to work on first.

Once the patient is doing well with those, they will add to the process. They will continue to do so, knowing each step forward gives the patient more tools and techniques they can rely on. Most patients are encouraged to continue with the therapy too once they see the value it brings into their lives.

Due to the intense nature of how someone with this mental health concern experiences emotions, they are over the top. They tend to overreact, and they tend to be impulsive with decisions. The way they act doesn't appeal to most people because it is so far away from the norm. This can cause friction within relationships and cause people to even end relationships with such individuals.

Such individuals often have a hard time maintaining employment. They don't deal well with management, other employees, or customers. They tend to have emotions such as anger or being rude which is their reaction to situations. They lack effective skills for communication, coping, and problem-solving.

DBT involves helping a person control their emotions and behaviors in ways that are solution oriented. This doesn't mean they can't get angry, but it does mean that they handle that and work through it in different ways than they have been. They already know those negative behaviors aren't helping them live the life they desire. Yet they are stuck in a cycle of them occurring again and again.

Often, the cycle is due to past experiences and negative thoughts. They have tunnel vision when it comes to how they should act or react in each scenario. With DBT, they are encouraged to focus on the current situation. Not draw from any previous experiences and let go of the negative feelings of distrust or abandonment that may accompany it.

With most feelings of anger, it is sadness or being upset that someone is experiencing. They just never learned how to successfully work through those types of emotions. They don't have the skills to tell someone they have upset them or hurt their feelings. Learning better techniques for communication can help change that around. It can strengthen relationships and help the individual find happiness within themselves.

This type of therapy is structured, more so than any of the other CBT options. This gives the framework for someone to grow and challenge their perceptions. It gives them a chance to explore the truth and learn the facts. Armed with new information they can change how they think and the actions they take part in.

DBT is in-depth, and for good reason. Many patients that require such therapy for borderline personality disorder are self-harming or having suicidal thoughts. Helping them through that crisis is the first order of business. Some people don't see a therapist until they have attempted suicide, or the self-harm has gotten out of control. That is the turning point when they reach out for help.

This is also one of the few types of CBT where the patient is asked to take part in both individual therapy sessions and group therapy sessions on a weekly basis. This is a long-term type of treatment plan, not something that moves along quickly. The relationship between the therapist and the patient takes time to develop.

There are challenges with DBT, but it has been proven to be extremely successful for people with borderline personality disorder. That information helps set the tone for the therapy and gives the patient hope that their future can be better than where they are at that point.

The other challenge is conveying the message that life is full of challenges. That can't be downplayed to the patient. On the other hand, they must be taught their methods of dealing with situations are just making them worse. They never solve the problem; they just compound them. With the right mindset and the right skill set, that doesn't have to be the path they remain on.

Finding the balance between the appropriate way to express emotions and the proper way to problem-solve is where the success begins. Letting go of negative emotions and poor choices of behaviors is empowering. As the patient sees the positive outcome of their better decisions and actions, they are encouraged to continue them. The personal satisfaction they gain is rewarding and they want to feel that way often.

Recognizing situations change, life has scenarios we didn't plan for, and being flexible is part of the treatment with DBT. The goal is to deal with the situation for what it is and move on from it. Of course, some situations are more complex and messier. They require more time and more decision-making to resolve them.

Both science and social aspects play a part in DBT being a good way to treat borderline personality disorder. Mindfulness and acceptance techniques are structured to appeal to the emotional needs of the individual. It takes patience and commitment for this type of treatment to work, but it can completely transform someone's life when it is done well.

MBCT

Mindfulness-Based Cognitive Therapy, known as MBCT, is a good option for someone with depression. It is combined with CBT to help them feel better, improve mood, and remove negative thoughts. It is often part of the treatment plan for someone with ongoing bouts of depression. It is also a good choice for those that struggle to be happy.

Depression isn't a choice, and so many people don't realize that individuals struggle to feel their best. This is why so many try to hide their depression; they are embarrassed by it. Others don't know enough about it to realize there is a mental health issue. They just go through the motions day to day until someone recommends therapy to them.

Being mindful with MBCT involves meditation, journaling, and envisioning positive outcomes. Letting go of the worst-case scenario is important. This type of therapy often focuses on self-esteem and interpersonal relationships. Identifying situations, people, and events the person feels happy engaging in is important.

Being aware of what is taking shape now is important. Being detached from reality is a symptom of depression that must be focused on for treatment to work. Redirecting attention and staying in the moment takes practice. Avoidance is often part of depression, so it is important to select activities to take part in.

The therapist will include this as part of the exercises and homework for the treatment plan. The number of activities and the amount of time spent engaging in them will increase as the treatment plan progresses. Increasing skills in the areas of communication and breathing techniques are often included in MBCT.

Being aware and mindful of all thoughts coming in and their category is important. How many of those thoughts are negative? How are they tied to the emotions and behaviors of that person? Quickly turning those negative thoughts into positive ones will help retain the mind to be happier. It will also improve the emotions and behaviors a person takes part in due to their thoughts.

Changing the attachment and reaction to certain thoughts is taught in this form of therapy. A person has the power to change how they think and how they feel, but they must focus on it. They can't let their mind wander and the subconscious take over. It must be mindful, precise, and there has to be accountability.

Journaling is useful because it can tie together stressors, triggers, and other variables that may influence negative behaviors. When a person thinks about something or experiences something they are automatically going to feel how they have before. This is until they have a new mindset and new perceptions. It is a way to repave the road so to speak!

Paying attention to how you feel and how you react is important. Document what you felt and what you said. Document why that wasn't the best decision and identify any triggers you remember. As you start to incorporate the concepts of mindfulness and the other aspects of your treatment plan, you will notice those triggers have less control.

They don't cause you to think or react negatively anymore. Eventually, you can get to the point where you work through those triggers rather than avoiding them like you did before. MBCT takes time to work, and it also depends on the level of the depression. It tends to work best for individuals with mild to moderate depression. For others, they may need medication along with MBCT to help improve their mood and feel their best.

Engaging in daily physical activity is encouraged with this type of treatment too. It naturally increases the amount of serotonin in the brain, creating feel good emotions. Taking a walk, going to the gym, or engaging in something you like for a hobby can help you to create more of those chemicals in the brain.

Reducing stress, avoiding isolation, and not depending on drugs and/or alcohol can also help reduce depression symptoms. These factors tend to cause a person to focus more on negative concepts because of how they influence the brain. MBCT is complex but it is also solution-oriented and based on the needs of the patient.

It is also useful for anxiety disorders because it helps someone feel in control of their emotions and their moods. It can be a way for the patient to focus on what is within their control and let go of what isn't. Learning better ways to manage thoughts and techniques for breathing and staying focused are also introduced with MBCT for anxiety.

MBSR

Too much stress can take a toll on a person, causing them to struggle mentally and physically. MBSR is a technique to teach mindfulness skills. It will assist with promoting well-being and reducing stress. MBSR stands for Mindful-Based Stress Reduction. Such individuals are often people pleasers at home and work. They will go the extra mile for anyone but put their own needs on hold.

The stress they put on themselves comes in many forms. They may try to be the perfect partner and the perfect parent. They may be afraid to fail at work or other aspects of their lives. As a result, they suffer from insomnia because they can't shut down their mind when they go to bed.

MBSR is designed to help someone identify their self-worth too. Such patients tend to see themselves through the eyes of others. They don't want to disappoint anyone, but they are often taken advantage of. The treatment plan helps them make their own needs a top priority. Self-care is the key to happiness and living the life you really want!

This type of treatment plan teaches people to set boundaries. It is hard to learn to say no when you usually say yes to everyone. Yet there is a sense of relief when you can let go of doing so. You don't have to worry about what other people think of you if you are being genuine and doing all you can to live a life with integrity.

Slowing down is encouraged with MBSR, you don't have to fill your calendar to the brim. You don't have to feel guilty for relaxing with a good book or getting some exercise. It doesn't matter if your house is spotless or if you decline an invitation to an event that you don't really wish to be involved with.

Being selective with how you spend your time is a good way to ensure you are happy. There are times when responsibilities come first, but what are you going to do with the time you have left? Make sure you get plenty of sleep and you eat properly. Engage in hobbies and activities you find satisfying. Spend time with people that support you and fill you with positive energy.

Being assertive helps with setting boundaries and working through difficult emotions. For patients that avoid speaking up and they let things go just to keep the peace, MBSR will help them to clarify how they feel and to set some parameters in place. People can't take advantage of you or treat you poorly if you shut that door on them!

Focusing on what has gone right and what you accomplished is important with MBSR therapy. Changing the mindset from what didn't get done to what did is going to help with gratitude. Daily meditation is encouraged to enhance focus and clarify what is important. Feeling good about your choices, what you learned from mistakes, and accepting no one is perfect does help a person feel happier and more fulfilled.

The goal with MBSR is to give the patient a sense of belonging and purpose. It gives them realistic goals and limits they can adhere to with their daily routine. It involves being selective about where time and attention are spent. What will bring joy and good energy? Awareness of surroundings and behaviors is encouraged so they can be changed. Letting go of negative thoughts and perceptions while replacing them with positive ones is a great way to see changes that reflect the lifestyle you want.

Mindfulness Exercises
There is a long list of mindful exercises that can be used in CBT sessions. Which ones a therapist selects depends on the treatment plan and the method or methods incorporated. The structure is designed to ensure the patient has every opportunity to learn, grow, and change based on the materials presented to them. CBT offers plenty of learning and development for coping, problem-solving, and communication if the patient is receptive to it.

Below are some examples of mindfulness exercises that may be incorporated into CBT Sessions:
- **Awareness**
- **Being present in the moment**

- **Breathing techniques**
- **Meditation**
- **Self-acceptance**

Awareness

Slowing down and taking in what is going on around you is important. Too often, a person rushes and rushes. They may be in one place but their mind wanders to other things they must get done. They try to take on too much, way beyond the normal realm of simply multi-tasking. Using your senses, pay attention to everything around you.

What do you see? What do you smell? What do you hear? What do items and objects feel like? If you are eating or drinking, what does it taste like? As you answer such questions, think about the emotions they create for you too. Hopefully, you are slowing down and taking time for things and foods you really enjoy!

Being Present in the Moment

You can physically be present in a location, but are you there? Are you focused on the people with you and the event taking place? If your mind is wandering, you must retain it to stay present in the moment. This is important to help you with forming interpersonal relationships. It is important for you to recognize your energy and be in tune with your thoughts and behaviors. As you do this, you will find you enjoy moments and events more than you ever did. You will also enhance the bond you have with people in your life.

Breathing Techniques

Any time you feel anxious, or you have negative thoughts enter your mind, calm down and focus on your breathing. Slowing breath in, hold it to the count of 10 and exhale. Change the negative thoughts to a positive one so you can influence the energy created with those thoughts.

When you experience emotions that trigger stress or anxiety, breathing techniques will help you regain control. You can engage in self-talk to help de-escalate the situation. Doing this for just a few minutes can change your mindset and help you stay in control. You don't want to fly off the handle because your emotions got the best of you.

Meditation

There are several types of meditation that can be great exercises to take part in. The most common is sitting meditation. Carve out 15 to 30 minutes each day to focus on yourself and your thoughts. Your back should be straight and your feet flat on the floor. Fold your hands in your lap. Focus on breathing slowly in and out through your nose.

Focus on releasing your mind and body so they flow together and get in sync. If you have something distracting you, remove the distraction and start again. The more you practice this, the easier it is going to be for you to make it happen without anything interrupting you.

Walking meditation can be an alternative if you prefer to stand up. It is also a good choice for someone that struggles to keep their body still for sitting down meditation. You need about 20 feet where you can walk back and forth without being interrupted. Focus on your balance and nothing else. Focus on the sensations you feel so that you can tune into your thoughts.

You may decide to try lying down meditation. Find a comfortable spot such as your couch or a spot on the floor and close your eyes. This is also referred to as body scan meditation. Place your arms at your sides and put your palms downward. Focus on your breathing with this process too. Don't let anything interrupt your chance to relax and calm your mind and body.

Self-Acceptance

You don't have to be perfect to excel in your life! You don't have to compromise your integrity or your values for others to like you. Be true to yourself and the rest will fall into place. Be kind and forgiving to yourself too, just like you would to your friends and family. Loving yourself is a great investment to make!

Self-acceptance also means you accept your body for the way it looks. We are all different shapes and sizes. We are all different skin tones and have various flaws. Focus on the areas of your body you love the most and don't make a big deal about the others. Wear clothing that makes you feel comfortable and confident in all you do!

CHAPTER TEN

ASSESSMENT IN CBT

Offering CBT services to clients in need is an exceptional opportunity for a therapist to give back to their community. It is a challenge on many levels, but one they graciously take on. They know CBT can work and they confidently introduce the various methods mentioned in this book to help people overcome fear, handle mental health issues, and become the best version of themselves they can.

There is no judgment by any therapist when they implement CBT for treatment. They don't rush anyone through the treatment either. What they ask for is trust, communication, and assistance with the treatment goals. They can only guide someone so far. It must be up to the individual to embrace the opportunity and make the most of it.

There can setbacks along the way, but many of the resources offered with CBT are designed to prevent relapses and regressing to old behaviors. Being accountable for actions and behaviors based on facts and not perceptions is a game changer that opens many doors. Anyone that feels they could benefit from such services is encouraged to find a qualified therapist in their area.

What can you Expect?

Reaching out for help for yourself or someone you care about is the first step toward a better future. Understanding the process is important. The commitment to work with the therapist makes an impact. Take your time to find someone that is available during the hours you can see them. If transportation is a concern, make sure you can get to and from those scheduled appointments without any barriers.

If you prefer gender, look into this before you schedule a consultation. Some people are only comfortable talking to a therapist that is a man or one that is a woman. This can be the result of some type of trauma or preconceptions they have before they enter therapy. Don't put up additional barriers when you need treatment, seek a person that fits your criteria.

The same is true for age. You may not feel comfortable seeing someone for therapy that is younger than you. Instead, you may prefer an older individual with plenty of experience in CBT. Find out the education and the training the person has before you see them. It will help you feel confident they can assist you with the best treatment possible. Being able to trust them and communicate with them openly influences the treatment plan and the outcome. If you hide anything, you are self-sabotaging your services with them from the start!

Clinical Assessment

A clinical assessment is an objective tool the therapist uses to correctly determine the symptoms a patient has, their history, and the context. This session typically lasts from an hour to an hour and a half. A series of questions are asked, and the patient is strongly encouraged to answer them correctly and honestly. Half-truths or not fully disclosing symptoms is going to reduce the efficiency of the treatment plan.

Each client is treated with respect and all the information is confidential. The diagnosis ensures the therapist can create the right CBT treatment plan. Questions will explore anxiety, stress, depression, lifestyle habits, and more. Share information about your sleep habits, the use of drugs and/or alcohol, and your diet.

A clear picture of your life and what you are up against will start to emerge as you go through the clinical assessment. Try to remain calm during the assessment and to worry about your answers. If you have concerns about self-doubt or negativity, it is going to show in that assessment. Don't worry, it lets the therapist know what they need to work with you to change.

A proper assessment is at the core of success with CBT. Anyone seeking such services needs to understand that the therapist can't do their job well if they don't have accurate information to work from. Trust the process to work for you by giving all the details.

If the initial assessment determines CBT is a good match for treatment, another session will be scheduled. If it isn't a good match, the therapist will explain why they feel that way. They may have other recommendations for you to consider. Since CBT is a viable treatment option for many concerns though, there is a good chance they can assist you with getting a treatment plan in place.

Identify Goals and Objectives

At your second appointment, you will share your goals and objectives with the therapist. It can be useful to make a list of things you wish to share with them at that appointment, so you don't forget anything. They may have some questions for you based on the information you provide. The purpose is for them to help you get on track to reach your goals. What is the best course of action to make that happen? What is stopping you right now from doing so?

Don't worry if you don't have all the answers, they will guide and direct you. Sometimes, it isn't what you share but what you can't share that helps them the most. For example, if they ask you what makes you happy and you can't think of anything, that can indicate they need to look at symptoms of depression you may be struggling with.

As you explore your thoughts, behaviors, and feelings with them, they can help you connect the dots. Remember, you should always feel involved in your treatment plan. If you don't agree with the goals and objectives of your treatment, speak up. Voice your opinions and any concerns you have so that they can address them with you. The more you are involved, the better success you can achieve with CBT.

At the end of your session, you should have clear and precise goals in place. How will they be measured? What steps are you going to take to achieve them? Is there an estimated timeframe for you to achieve them? Ask questions if anything isn't clear. Your therapist wants you to be informed and to know what you are agreeing to work on.

Goals can only be achieved if they are smart and realistic. The patient has the right to share what they want to achieve. The therapist can chime in and let them know if that is realistic or not. They may ask questions of the client including how they think they are going to achieve that goal and in what amount of time.

The more detailed a goal is, the more likely it becomes someone can achieve it. They aren't reaching for something that is just dangling out there. Instead, they are searching for and working hard to achieve something that is realistic and possible. This doesn't mean there isn't plenty of effort and hard work that will go into making it happen. The effort is worth it though, because with each CBT goal achieved, a person is closer to living the quality of life they truly desire.

To eliminate discouragement with goal setting, therapists help with breaking it down into smaller pieces. This is especially helpful when the forecast for the patient is long-term treatment of a year or longer to reach their goal or goals. The smaller piece also helps someone see the progress they have made. Such rewards along the way help them stay motivated because they know the methods they incorporated are working.

Should there be a setback or an unforeseen roadblock to a goal, the patient and therapist work as a team to find a way around it. They may have to change the plan of action to make it happen, but this possible. Sometimes, the greatest learning comes from those setbacks or roadblocks, and they aren't in vain. Instead, they serve as a reminder that life is unpredictable. Yet armed with the right skills and techniques just about anything can be overcome.

Cognitive and Behavioral Assessments

With clear goals in place, the therapist can look into further assessments to identify cognitive and behavioral information. Such assessments give them insight into your thoughts, behaviors, and actions. It also gives them an opportunity to explore your emotions and your belief system.

There are no right or wrong answers as you take these assessments. Don't tell them what you think they want to hear. Tell them what you really feel and how you process information. Their job is to help you change what isn't working, but they can't do that if your assessments aren't accurate. Don't try to cheat the system, you will only be cheating yourself.

The specific assessments used to gather such details depend on the therapist and the initial assessment. They will use those tools they believe gives them an objective look at what is going on. They want the facts and the details, but they also know there isn't a one size fits all assessment. This is why some patients require more assessing than others.

A therapist isn't going to rush to make their diagnosis or to determine a treatment plan. They know they have a huge responsibility on their shoulders to provide exceptional service. There are times when treatment must be modified along the way. This can be due to new facts emerging or because of some of the changes the patient has made that weren't expected.

Any such changes to the treatment plan will be discussed with the patient. The idea is to keep everyone on the same page with the direction it is taking. Sometimes, a treatment plan has CBT techniques and methods that aren't serving their intended purpose. The therapist may try something new to see if that is a better fit for that patient.

The Therapeutic Alliance

A strong therapeutic relationship between the therapist and the client is essential for CBT to work as it was intended. This is a strong bond that is professional but also personable. The therapist is responsible for offering a safe and supportive place to explore treatment options and complete them.

The patient has a responsibility to show up to scheduled appointments, complete exercises, challenge themselves to learn new skills, and benefit as much as they can from the assigned treatment plan. Both are working on ways for those shared goals to be reached. The relationship is based on mutual trust and respect.

The therapist is encouraging but also holds the patient accountable. As a result, they continue to be motivated and work hard. They don't let challenges along the way sabotage their success. A quality relationship between the therapist and the patient increases the benefits a person gains from the sessions too.

When the therapist determines treatment can end, they hope the patient can continue with learning and changing perceptions. They feel confident they have given them adequate tools, techniques, and learning materials for them to make better choices and feel empowered.

Detailed Treatment Plan

A great deal of time and planning goes into each CBT, and for good reason. What helps one person on the path to success isn't going to help the next. There are too many variables in place. The emotions of someone, their behaviors, and their motivation all influence what goes into those goals and the treatment plan.

It must be structured and precise. The patient must see the value in the treatment plan and the methods in place. When they can embrace the why behind all of it, they are encouraged to dive in and give a 100% commitment to see those changes materialize.

As a patient completes the most vital parts of their learning and modification, the next part of the goals can be put in place. A wise therapist doesn't put all the goals out there at once. Trying to change too many concepts at the same time sets a person up for failure. Instead, the focus is on the main issues and that can serve as a solid foundation to build upon.

Patients are urged to share their treatment plan with medical doctors and others they may be working with. This ensures everyone can be working towards the same types of goals for the patient. A unified effort is a good idea. Typically, the therapist will ask for a release to share information with your doctor and any other specialists you may like for them to work with on your behalf.

For minors, parents can be informed of the treatment plan. Parents need this information to support a child and provide an environment that is helpful for those goals to be reached. Specifics of what is shared in therapy sessions though will remain confidential. The exception is when someone is at risk of harming themselves or harming someone else.

Feedback and Monitoring

A therapist must believe in what they are doing, in the services they offer. One way for them to stay focused and motivated is through feedback from their patients. How do they feel? What is helping them the most in their treatment plan? What isn't working for them?

Discussions about progress and any barriers in the way are a big piece of feedback and monitoring. A patient has the right to speak up about what they love with their treatment or what isn't working. It isn't uncommon for them to show up for a session eager to share the outcome of an exercise they tried!

Therapists are known to say they learn just as much from their patients as they share with them! They love the feedback because it helps them grow and learn new things. It helps them find the balance between the science of CBT and the human elements that are involved with it. This keeps them humble, and it also helps them press on when they are challenged.

Not all therapy sessions are easy, and that can take a toll on someone offering those services. Yet when they know what they do has helped others, and they hear those stories, they feel rejuvenated and inspired. They are patient and they are motivated to give all they can to every single client because they know they are planting seeds for beautiful changes to emerge!

CONCLUSION

Cognitive Behavior Therapy has been proven time and time again to be a successful way to treat various concerns and mental health ailments. Numerous studies, clinical trials, and data all come to the same conclusion. While some methods of CBT are more widely used than others, the options ensure therapists have an arsenal of tools to put into action with any treatment plan they create.

That treatment plan can be updated and modified as many times as necessary throughout the therapy. As someone makes progress, it may be time to incorporate another tactic. If they aren't responding well to a certain technique, the therapist can switch gears and ask them to try something else.

The customized treatment plan is at the core of working with the therapist. This ensures treatment is moving in the right direction for the individual to reach the established goals. The progress depends on the type of treatment, what the person is being treated for, and other variables.

Creating these treatment plans shouldn't be taken lightly. They can't be vague either. Instead, they must be detailed with precise steps. They should have timeframes assigned, when possible, for accountability. The therapist should encourage the patient to have a say in that treatment plan too, within reason. They may not know what is best for their diagnosis, that is for the professionals to determine.

It isn't uncommon for individuals to specifically ask a therapist if CBT is right for them. It all comes down to the assessment and the diagnosis. It is a good idea to schedule an appointment to talk to someone about what is taking place and why you wish to make positive changes. Carefully select the therapist you reach out to. Verify their credentials and their background with CBT.

One of the wonderful elements of CBT is the patient is involved in their treatment. They share details with the therapist after they engage in exercises and use tools in their day to day lives. They work hard to change behaviors and to face challenges they used to avoid.

There are certainly plenty of variables involved with CBT, but that is what makes it customizable. People from all walks of life and with all types of concerns have gone down this path. They have found CBT offers them a way to have a better quality of life. This ranges from assistance with insomnia, eating disorders, stress, and anxiety. It also includes various mental health conditions such as depression and personality disorders.

At the core of CBT is the assessment because each person has their own needs they must address. It is remarkable that this umbrella of techniques and methods can help so many people with such a wide spectrum of concerns. When someone puts these techniques and methods into play, so many areas of their life improve. It doesn't just influence that one reason they decided to embark on this journey.

CBT is a rewarding type of therapy because it opens the door for learning. It encourages new skill sets in the areas of coping mechanisms and problem-solving. It also encourages effective communication skills and interpersonal skills. None of us are perfect by any means, but doing our best to live a life that is fulfilling and reflective of our goals is important.

It is extremely difficult to do all of this on your own. Working with an expert, you can work as a team to identify your goals and those barriers in your way. Through their eyes, you can identify your cycles of behavior that stand in your way. Together, you can work to break down those barriers by replacing poor behaviors and negative thoughts with those that serve you better.

How to Remain Motivated

There will be times when you run into barriers, and you are ready to give up. That is when you need your therapist the most. That is when you need to look to your tools and the skills you learned to pull you up and move you forward. You only fail if you completely give up, not if something comes along that makes the path a bit more difficult to maneuver. If you continue to learn and value what life can offer to you, there are wonderful opportunities to improve and find happiness!

Do your best to stay motivated! These tips can help you stay on track. Always keep your scheduled appointments with the therapist. If you need something more due to a crisis, reach out to them immediately for an extra session. Don't hold it all in until your next scheduled appointment.

- **Accountability for your actions and behaviors**
- **Be assertive and let your boundaries and emotions be heard by others. Share information respectfully.**
- **Be present and focus your attention on what is taking place.**
- **Break larger goals into smaller steps and pieces you can achieve along the way**
- **Challenge yourself to end negative thinking**
- **Change what you can control that isn't bringing you positive energy and healing**
- **Commit to making decisions based on facts and not on emotions**
- **Create a reward system for your efforts and healthy choices**
- **Eliminate distractions that zap your energy and your time**

- **Engage in meditation methods**
- **Focus on long-term benefits and reaching your goals**
- **Journal your thoughts and activities**
- **Keep it simple and straightforward so you know what to work on**
- **Learn from setbacks, don't let them define you**
- **Practice self-love and compassion**
- **Reflect on where you started and where you are now**
- **Schedule activities you enjoy taking part in**
- **Schedule your life in a manner that gives you free time**
- **Visual reminders and positive affirmations can help you remain focused.**

Embrace the Chance to Learn and Grow

There is so much room for growth and such opportunities to develop skills that were lacking before. We don't know what is missing or what we are doing on repeat that we shouldn't until it is pointed out to us. There is no judging by your therapist. They are there to guide you, to show you, and to help you eliminate perceptions. They will help you dig deep to find facts and get to the core of what is on your plate.

The length of time it takes to complete CBT depends on the treatment plan. The result is what matters, not how long it takes to get there. If you can honestly say you gave it your all and you did what your treatment plan asked, then you should be proud of those efforts. Each step of the way was a chance for change and a chance to learn. Personal growth is amazing, and you won't know how far you have come until you reflect on where you started.

Analyze

When you embrace CBT, you are in for a challenge! Yet you are in for a great reward because you are undoing what is harming you and holding you back in life. It can be uncomfortable at times to follow the exercises or to grow through learning new skills. You may feel like you failed but be forgiving that you didn't have the information you have now to work with.

Once you have that information though, you must decide whether to use it or not do anything. It is a shame to see that opportunity go down the drain because you didn't want to put forth the effort or you worried about failure. We all have the right to be happy, and negative thoughts or depression shouldn't prevent you from that experience.

When you remove the negative thoughts and perceptions, you are left with the truth. This will set you free and it will empower you. It will help you see your value and appreciate what life has to offer to you. Take one step at a time, even baby steps if you are unsure. Retraining your mind is a complex process but worth the investment of your time and your conscious effort.

Negative thinking can be a dark shadow that lurks in your life right now. When you remove it and the sun shines though, it is a brand-new perspective that covers all of your days as you move forward. Life will still be difficult at times, but with better ways to cope and react, you can handle it all. You won't feel alone or isolated and you won't feel like you aren't as worthy as those around you.

Developing compassion for yourself is a gift that no one else can offer to you. Don't gauge the success in your life on what others think of you. Don't compare your journey to that of anyone else. We are all fighting battles that most others around us don't know anything about. Be kind to others, but don't forget to be kind to yourself in the process!

Monitor your behaviors and mood so you can pinpoint any triggers or unresolved issues. Bring them to the attention of your therapist so they can be addressed and part of your treatment plan. Spend your time wisely on activities you love and with people that bring out the best in you. Those activities should align with your core values to bring you true happiness.

What to Expect from CBT Treatment

If you and your therapist believe CBT treatment is a good fit for you, it is a good idea to get it in progress. There are 4 core expectations you should have going into this form of treatment:

- **Commitment from your therapist to help you overcome challenges and reach your established goals.**
- **Defining your core values and changing your perceptions to ensure you can feel good about them.**
- **Structured treatment plan and educational development to help you gather important skills.**
- **Timeframes for treatment based on your assessment so you understand how long your CBT is expected to take to obtain the most value from it.**

Give it your All!

When you fully commit to your CBT plan, you will see great results! Time is going to pass by. Are you going to continue doing the same things you are now that aren't working or try something new? You can expect to learn many things through CBT, and it all comes down to your specific treatment plan. Such growth can include:

- **Building awareness of negative behaviors and thoughts**
- **Challenge yourself to remove dysfunctional thoughts and behaviors**
- **Develop a positive outlook**
- **Distinguish between facts and opinions**
- **Establish realistic goals**
- **Feel in control of your decisions and problem-solving skills**
- **Focus on the present**
- **Identify problem areas that you can focus on and change**
- **Prevent the risk of relapse by relying on tools and educational skills learned**
- **Practice being kind and forgiveness towards yourself**

Thank you!

I would like to thank you for taking the time to read this book. The information is helpful and can put you on the path to seeking the help of a therapist. Perhaps you have a loved one you feel could benefit from CBT, and you are encouraged to talk to them about the options after reading these materials.

Thank you for taking the time to explore the concepts and strategies involved with Cognitive Behavior Therapy. I hope it leaves a lasting impression on you and how you see the world. I hope it gives you the feeling that it is safe to reach out for help, therapy isn't something to hide from the rest of the world!

Kindly share your thoughts on the book, your feedback is encouraged. If you leave a review about this book, it can help others decide if it is the right material for them to learn from.

BOOK 2

DIALECTICAL
BEHAVIOR
THERAPY

Turning Life's Darkest Moments into Your Greatest
Strength: A Journey of Transformation and
Empowerment

Reflection Page

This area is exclusively yours. Utilize it for monitoring your growth or expressing your thoughts and emotions.

....

....

....

....

....

....

....

....

....

INTRODUCTION

Dialectical Behavior Therapy is widely known as DBT. It is a powerful resource because it is part of successful treatment plans for a variety of concerns and ailments. In this book, you will learn about the origins of DBT, its core elements, and how it is used for specific needs a patient may have.

Dr. Marsha Linhan introduced DBT in the 1970s. It has been modified and updated over the years, but the core concepts remain the same. The modifications and updates are the results of data and analysis of treatment plans. The goal has always been to use DBT to create the best chance of success for each patient.

This process is unique because it is implemented with objectives that meet the specific needs and goals of the patient. There aren't a one size fits all concept with the use of it. Therapists complete an assessment with the patient to determine if they would benefit from DBT. If so, it is included in their treatment plan. It is widely used in connection with other forms of treatment.

One of the fascinating facts about Dr. Linhan is her own experiences she brings with DBT. She shared early on that she struggled with mental illness. She successfully used DBT methods to help her cope with her mental health concerns and live the best life possible.

When DBT is used, there is a balance in place with the treatment. It looks at the beliefs and the perceptions someone has. At the same time, it takes the human elements and the complexities of the brain and factors them into the mix. DBT can be a good resource for patients with mild, moderate, or severe concerns.

What is DBT used for?

Borderline personality disorder is one of the largest realms where DBT is introduced to assist the patient. This was the first treatment to introduce the concept of mindfulness. It is at the foundation of the techniques, and it continues to be a driving force in these treatment plans today.

However, that is just one of the areas where DBT can be valuable. The list of them includes:

- **Anxiety**
- **Borderline Personality Disorder**
- **Depression**
- **Eating disorders**
- **PTSD**
- **Self-harm**
- **Substance use disorders**
- **Suicidal thoughts and attempts**

Studies indicate DBT is a powerful way for therapists to connect with patients and give them tools/resources to help them improve. Only a small amount of actual treatment is conducted at the sessions. This is where the patient forms a bond with the therapist and shares information.

Most of the treatment takes place in the day-to-day life of each patient. They take the tools and resources given to them and apply them to their daily life. They use this information to change thought patterns and behavior. Studies prove DBT can work for both genders. It can work for adolescents and adults. Individuals from all ethnic groups and all economic backgrounds can gain value through DBT.

Studies also show fewer patients with the above concerns must be hospitalized for treatment when DBT is successfully implemented into the treatment plan. When a person does have to be hospitalized, the length of the stay can be reduced once a concrete treatment plan is in place for them.

The same patients aren't in a cycle of being hospitalized repeatedly when DBT is part of the treatment. They learn to use those skills to help them with their needs and concerns.

Behavioral Therapy isn't Always Enough

Linhan began her studies with individuals experiencing suicidal thoughts and self-harm. She was one of the few professionals handling such cases, so she often saw the most extreme cases. Through her research and observations, she found Cognitive Behavioral Therapy (CBT) wasn't enough for patients that had such a diagnosis.

In fact, she noticed in many of those cases CBT could make the situation worse for the patients. Today, it isn't uncommon for CBT and DBT to be combined in the same treatment plan for someone. Therapists are trained to watch for changes in the patient. If they aren't improving, CBT should be removed from the treatment plan.

The key difference with DBT is it introduces dialects to the mix with the treatment. This is not included in CBT or the Humanism approach. Encouraging patients to accept the reality of their life and behavior was a turning point. This approach is empowering and uplifting. It doesn't give the patient the feeling that the therapist is saying they are to blame. Instead, they are saying this is what is going on, how can we change it?

Thanks to her own circumstances, Linhan understands all too well how mental health can consume you if you don't get adequate treatment. She shared that her only goal with creating DBT was to offer a form of treatment to get someone out of the personal hell they were experiencing.

Zen Influence

If you are into Zen, you will notice the strong influence it has with DBT concepts. Zen believes everything has a balance, and with that balance in place, you can find inner peace. It incorporates being present in the moment, relaxation methods such as meditation, and letting go of what you can't control.

It relates to DBT because the thought with Zen and DBT is that you can't avoid what is going on. If you do so, it will lead you down a path of long-term suffering. It is only when you face what is taking place in your life and work through it that you find inner peace.

Goals of DBT

While each treatment plan with DBT is different, there are three goals in mind when they are created.

- Eliminate self-harm and any life-threatening concerns
- Reduce behaviors that interfere with therapy
- Reduce behaviors that interfere with the quality of life

Nobody wants to just get through life, and that is what often happens when a person is struggling. DBT is designed to help each person have a life they feel is worth living! At times, it is a challenge to help a patient stay motivated. The therapist must incorporate various tools and concepts to keep someone on track and fully invested in their treatment plan.

Individual and Group Therapy

Patients start with individual therapy, but that isn't the end of it. Typically, they will dive into skills training in a group setting. They will also take part in group therapy with their peers weekly. Each of these elements of DBT provides them with resources, reinforcement, and guides to help them live a better lifestyle.

Individuals work closely with their therapist at least once a week. In a group setting, everyone is encouraged to participate. The groups are small so that people don't feel overwhelmed. There are rules for the groups too. For example, everything discussed is confidential. Patients can share their feelings and discuss topics, but they can't be hostile toward each other.

Group members are discouraged from contacting each other outside of the group therapy sessions. They shouldn't exchange contact information or meet outside of the group.

For skills, there are usually handouts or workbooks the patients can write in, and they can take home. This gives them the information at their fingertips so they can review it again and again as they desire. They can also take the materials to their individual therapy sessions.

Skills training is detailed, and the classes give patients plenty of time to ask questions and interact with the learning materials. There are examples, role-playing exercises, and other techniques mixed in to keep it interesting and ensure those in attendance take away valuable information.

Sometimes, what takes place in individual therapy will influence discussions that emerge in group sessions. At other times, what is shared in group therapy will trigger something a person wishes to discuss further in their individual sessions.

Validation

At the center of DBT is validation, and this is why it can benefit each patient. Validation encourages a patient to continue the path using that type of treatment because they find personal value within it. There are 3 types of validation I person can experience with DBT. The type depends on their thought process and the problem they are approaching.

- **Emotional:** validates without escalating that emotion. The goal is to not judge and to explore both the primary and secondary emotions of a situation.
- **Behavioral:** It shares the message that your behaviors are based on what is taking place in your life at that time.
- **Cognitive:** recognizing the underlying reasons for behaviors. This includes exploring the beliefs and assumptions a person has about a situation or topic. It also includes awareness of thought patterns.

Validation isn't going to occur immediately when you incorporate problem-solving skills for a situation. You don't want to validate everything in your life, but you need to choose what you give weight to. A therapist can teach a patient how to use validation to help them when they feel challenged, and they are ready to give up.

However, the use of it should start to fade as a person becomes more confident in their choices and behaviors. The validation isn't to justify the behavior, it is to help the person feel there is value in what they think, how they feel, and the emotions they go through because of it.

As they put the tools and techniques of DBT in motion, they will change how they think and how they behave. This is going to change the dynamics of the emotions they go through too. As they go through such changes, the need for validation should lessen. When used correctly, validation can be a useful tool on the path to positive change.

The Role of the Therapist with Validation

The therapist has the responsibility of introducing validation into the treatment process. They can show the patient how to identify the type of validation and how to use it to urge changes. The therapist has a role to support the patient as they go through the validation process. They can do this by engaging in the following:

- Treat them with respect and talk to them like you would a friend (Radical Genius)
- Try to see it from their point of view
- Reflect on what they shared to ensure you heard it accurately
- Show interest and listen intently
- Validate based on the current situation
- Validate with them based on consistency and their history

Radical Genius Concept

While the roles are defined in therapy between patient and therapist, the term Radical Genius can help with the validation process. This involves the therapist treating the patient as an equal.

CHAPTER ONE

WHAT IS DIALECTICAL BEHAVIOR THERAPY?

With DBT, opposites are brought together to cause positive change. What is being left out? That is what the therapist and patient must find. Then they must create an action plan to incorporate that missing link. Behavioral patterns can be identified as the therapy progresses. Often, patients are unaware of their patterns until they start to write them down or discuss them with an expert.

They are such a normal part of their life that they don't focus on them. They don't analyze why they think, feel, or behave a certain way. They just roll with it, even when it isn't serving them well. Some patients reach out to a therapist because they do notice those patterns. They want a better life, but they need help identifying how to make the changes.

There are two ends with each thought, and the patient can go from one end or the next. They can also choose a decision in between. When they look at each end objectively, they can decide which behavior, emotion, or action best serves them. Balancing this dilemma isn't easy, and it takes lots of practice and patience. DBT is powerful but a person must commit to using those tools and techniques to make changes.

Understanding Dialects

Regarding DBT, dialects help the patient handle and resolve inner conflicts. Typically, the methods introduced help them resolve conflicts within themselves. As they find value with these skills, they can move into using them to resolve conflicts with others too. DBT can have a positive impact on every aspect of a person's life. This includes how they view themselves, how they view the world, their relationships with others, and their career.

We don't all see the same thing, and that is why conflicts arise. It is more than a difference of opinion. Have you ever seen those pictures where you have to identify what you see? You may see a pair of birds while someone else sees a tall trophy. One of the popular scenarios on social media a few years ago was a dress. Some people saw it as purple, and others saw it as blue. It was phenomenal!

Remembering such differences can help us strive for facts and information without being judgmental. Remember, 2+2 = 4 but so does 3+1! There is more than one way to arrive at the same conclusion. There are also reasons why people arrive at different conclusions or behave differently with the same scenario.

When it comes to dialects and emotions, DBT is useful for regulating emotions. Some people have very little regulation and others have too much. That influences how they think and react. It influences decisions and even communication styles. Finding mutual ground with emotions where they find middle ground is the goal.

Key Principles and Components of DBT

There are several principles and components that create DBT. They are effective tools and methods, proven time and time again. Numerous studies show how effective this type of treatment has been for patients. In future chapters, we will address some specific ailments DBT is used to treat.

The unique components of DBT include each treatment plan is individualized to ensure the patient has what they need to attain their goals. The dialect component helps a patient to accept what they feel and how they behave, and then look at what they can do on the opposite end of that to transpose negative thoughts and behaviors into positive ones.

DBT focuses on several areas including:

- Distress tolerance
- Emotion Regulation
- Interpersonal effectiveness
- Mindfulness
- Training Skills

Each of these areas creates a great foundation for a person to change their life with. The information and skills they learn in each of these areas can help them stay focused on the present. Instead of avoiding issues, they have the information and methods they need to find a solution that helps rather than making the situation worse.

Each of these elements adds a new layer to the DBT benefits, and they will be discussed in detail in this book in later chapters. The therapist works hard to give the patient the tools they need and information about how to use them in their day to day lives. This includes how to use certain techniques to help them through a crisis. The goal is for them to make better decisions and be in control of their emotions because of these DBT concepts they have learned.

Desired Outcomes

The treatment plan with DBT is structured with these core areas in place. At the same time, specific goals for the patient are addressed. The therapist and patient work as a team to identify any barriers and the best way to resolve them. They work together to create a powerful treatment plan to help the patient achieve their goals and live the life they want.

There are several desired outcomes, and the therapist incorporates them into the treatment for each patient. Understanding the result when they use DBT methods will help with motivation. The therapist has a limited amount of time in sessions to assist each patient. The growth and development with DBT mainly happen outside of the individual and group sessions.

This can only occur if the patient is committed to the treatment plan. It can only work if they are promoting the skills and techniques they have learned through exercises and skill classes. They need a solid understanding of them and even when to implement them so that they don't relapse back to old behaviors. The desired outcomes discussed and used to help keep patients motivated include:

- Acceptance and change
- Behavior identification and modification
- Collaboration
- Cognitive changes
- Skill sets
- Support

No one can force an individual to change! They can point out why they should and how it will improve their life. The choice is always up to the patient. When they can accept reality and are motivated to change, DBT opens many opportunities for them. People do have a desire to change, to get better results. The problem is they often don't know how to do it.

DBT involves therapy to teach them how to do it. The goal is to give them enough education and skill sets that they no longer need therapy. No one is rushed to identify behaviors that don't work for them. Instead, they are encouraged to be mindful of them and that is what leads them to modify them. When you feel like A what can you do differently with B to get a better result? These questions and formats are discussed in therapy.

Collaboration is important because a person needs to know they aren't alone in their efforts. It is scary to go through such changes, and DBT can open some wounds too. For example, when someone is discussing a childhood trauma or PTSD. Using the available resources can help a person work through anything that has negatively affected them.

Teaching skill sets is a wonderful benefit from DBT, and they are often taught in small groups. Such skills include coping methods, relaxation techniques, and problem-solving methods. Exploring emotions and how to control them rather than being controlled by them is a valuable skill.

Individuals going through DBT need support. They will get it from their therapist and be treated as an equal. They will get it from their peers in the group sessions. Hopefully, they receive it from friends and family too.

The Importance of Mindfulness in DBT

One of the concepts that set DBT apart from other concepts is the idea of mindfulness. Being present and accepting the reality of what is going on is important for a patient to grasp. They aren't doing themselves any favors by avoiding the issues or making them worse. Due to the importance of mindfulness, it is the first skill a person is taught with this type of treatment. Once therapist feels there is no risk of self-harm or suicide, they can start teaching this important part of DBT.

Mindfulness is important because it is a huge challenge for anyone to change their perceptions, thought process, and how they behave in certain situations. Those are patterns of behavior they engage in. It may be due to trauma, mental health, or many other variables. Even though those outcomes often don't serve them well, they continue the pattern because it is familiar to them.

With DBT and therapy, they start to understand there are better ways. They can change their thought patterns and carefully choose behaviors rather than being impulsive. They can evaluate a situation in the moment rather than avoiding it and letting it get out of control. They can explore their emotions and strive to create experiences in their lives where they feel positive emotions. Mindfulness is at the center of these types of changes. They can only happen with awareness.

Regulating emotions is key to success with DBT, and mindfulness is the way to do this. Getting through day-to-day situations and dealing with a crisis are skills a person is taught. They are exposed to coping skills, relaxation techniques, and problem-solving skills. They are encouraged to talk in individual therapy sessions and group therapy about the changes they implemented and how they worked out.

Resolving interpersonal conflicts is important for healthy relationships to be established. A relationship can't grow if both people aren't able to deal with emotions and communication effectively. The relationship could continue, but it will be toxic in many areas. When a person is mindful, they can use skills and techniques to help them resolve interpersonal conflicts without destroying the relationship. They learn to be assertive and set boundaries.

Studies show mindfulness is an excellent skill for someone to possess. It can help them reduce stress and improve their mood. It can prevent a basic situation from moving into a crisis mode. It can help someone with mild to moderate depression reduce their symptoms.

Mindfulness helps a person relax and remain calm. They feel they can focus easier, and they aren't anxious. They feel a boost in their self-esteem, and they are excited about life and what it offers. They aren't just going through the motions. The benefits a person gains with mindfulness depend on their situation, but the outcomes are positive and encouraging.

The Role of a DBT Therapist
Any therapist incorporating DBT into their practice doesn't decide to do so lightly. They know it is going to be difficult and many of their patients will need therapy for a year or longer. They know they are taking on the huge task of creating a custom treatment plan for each patient. Yet they have the desire to help people be their best and live the best life. They truly believe in DBT and the doors it can unlock when it is used properly!

A DBT therapist treats the patient as an equal, which is an important concept involved in this type of treatment. They hold the patient accountable and address any concerns if they are missing appointments or creating other barriers to avoid working on what they should be. The therapist offers solutions through skills training, role-playing, and other forms of exercise to help the patient learn and use those tools effectively.

It is a balancing act for a DBT therapist to validate how someone feels, but also hold them accountable for changes. They must guide someone and not let them make excuses. They must help them learn to be mindful and process their emotions effectively.

Any time a patient is involved in self-harm or may have suicidal thoughts, that is the priority of a DBT therapist. They must work to de-escalate the situation and help the person get on track. They must help them find better ways to cope with situations rather than avoiding them.

Such a therapist also changes the treatment plan when necessary to ensure it is still offering the patient the best outcome. They must help them set goals and continue to encourage them to reach them. Offering inspiration and motivation are all part of the DBT therapist role. Teaching emotional relation is on the list of skills because it is such a crucial learning experience for someone to change their behavior.

The 4 Models of DBT
There are 4 models offered with DBT. It is common for a patient to have a combination of the models incorporated into their treatment plan. The goal is for them to receive treatment to best help them reach the established goals. Not everyone is ready to dive into the models of DBT right away.

For example, someone with self-harm concerns has to be treated differently. Every part of the treatment is designed to de-escalate that element and help them by promoting self-care. Resources are offered to reduce risks and coping skills are explored. Crisis intervention required depends on the assessment the therapist completes.

Typically, DBT works best when a patient is involved in individual counseling sessions, group counseling sessions, and they are mindful in their daily activities. Everything they learn in their therapy sessions is implemented to help them become aware and focus on necessary changes.

The 4 models of DBT are:
- Mindfulness
- Distress tolerance
- Emotion regulation
- Interpersonal effectiveness

Mindfulness

Being aware of what is going on in the moment and awareness of how you feel and how you behave is the first model of DBT. This is one of the most crucial parts that a patient can take part in with this type of therapy. It can help them to change various aspects of their life to reach their goals.

Being non-judgmental is also part of mindfulness. Many patients find incorporating meditation into their daily routine helps them focus. It can prevent their mind from wandering when they try to be present in the moment. They must retrain their mind to stay present.

This model of DBT involves analyzing, observing, and describing what is taking place in a person's life. It also involves identifying and working through the various emotions the individual experiences. Working towards better emotions and better behaviors for their circumstances can promote positive changes. It can help to break the cycle of behaviors and feelings that aren't helping that person be successful.

A person can experience a different state of mind depending on the day. Sometimes, their state of mind can change several times in a single day. It depends on what is going on. It depends on how they process their emotions. The goal of DBT with mindfulness is observing without overreacting. Identifying problems and solving them before they spiral out of control is empowering.

DBT offers skills and problem-solving concepts a person may not have had before. Such information gives them resources they can rely on when they have a situation they need to work through. The coping skills they learn in therapy can help them stay focused and work through the problem rather than avoiding it.

Distress Tolerance

It is human nature to regress to old habits when they feel stressed. Individuals in a cycle of constant stress must deal with the underlying issues and problems. Others seem to do well with DBT treatment until they have a difficult event arise in their life. The goal of distress tolerance is to arm someone with skills and techniques so that they can effectively work through the situation.

None of us live a perfect life. There will always be variables around us at work, with personal relationships, and in society that we can't control. When we feel that they are bigger than life, that can cause us to regress into old habits. DBT teaches distress tolerance so a patient can identify when they are starting to feel that way.

Rather than regressing though, they use what they have learned in therapy to help them through it. They can evaluate the situation, identify their emotions, and make decisions based on facts. This can help them remain calm and in control of their emotions and their behaviors while they work to resolve the situation.

When they see the value that brings to such a situation, they will remember it. The brain will remember how that felt and why it was a better outcome than avoidance or how they used to deal with things. This sets the stage for a person to continue to use those skills and techniques when they have a challenge in their life. It will eventually become the thought pattern they rely on, and they won't regress to old ways in the face of stress or crisis situations.

One of the main reasons people overreact both emotionally and with their behaviors to a crisis is they feel desperate. They feel that they have no control, everything is a mess in their life, and they give up hope. DBT helps them to see the situation differently. They don't take it personally, they are objective. They don't judge, they look at the possible solutions. Such changes can reduce the likelihood of someone turning to self-harm, drugs, or alcohol to get some temporary relief and control back.

Staying on track and striving for those goals is essential. When a person regresses to old habits, they often feel ashamed. They don't want to ask for help because they know they didn't make the best choice. DBT also shares with them how to reach out for help in crisis situations. Support from loved ones and their therapist helps them push forward.

Many individuals with mental health concerns struggle with impulsive behaviors. They act before they think it through. Then they create additional problems for themselves on top of the situation that triggered the impulsive outcome. Preventing that outcome is a huge step with DBT.

One of the effective ways that is done is by creating a list. Writing down the pros and cons of acting a certain way can help a patient see they aren't helping themselves by being impulsive. The time it takes for them to do that helps them to slow down and calm down. They don't react in the moment, and they can choose a better behavior to follow.

They think through the possible consequences of what they will do or what they won't do. Hopefully, the knowledge of the consequences involved if they impulsively react a certain way will help them go a different route. It is a conscious effort to do so, they aren't relying on the subconscious cycle of behavior they used to engage in.

It takes plenty of practice and discipline to implement DBT and all that is learned through therapy into the equation. Yet making a mistake doesn't mean the treatment has failed. Often, a patient can learn from that mistake as they continue toward their goals. They can identify why they did what they did and why it wasn't the best decision. They can discuss what they will do differently next time.

That level of awareness IS progress. It didn't get them the desired outcome with that issue. However, it did gain them plenty of awareness and being mindful of the situation. That is something to be proud of, and the therapist will share that with them.

That fight or flight response is hard to change for many individuals. When they are aware of it, they can do something else. It is common for a therapist to provide such patients with different options they can explore so that they don't engage in the fight or flight response. Some of these options include:

- Accepting the reality of the situation for what it is
- Created a pros and cons list of possible behaviors
- Exercising
- Distraction skills (this is very different from avoidance) where you focus on what you can control and let go of the rest
- Placing the hands in cold water
- Practicing forgiveness while keeping boundaries in place

Emotion Regulation
We will cover emotion regulation in depth in a later chapter. This model of DBT involves identifying emotions and understanding them. What is their connection to how you feel and how you act? Next, it involves trying to identify the opposite of emotions that don't serve you well. How can you transform how you feel and reach that other end?

Emotions are identified as primary and secondary. We all have triggers that cause us to react and feel things that don't serve us well. They can cause us to overreact, or they can hold us back because they hamper our self-esteem. The focus of DBT is exploring the value emotions bring to our lives. Without them, we wouldn't exist!

We get more benefits from positive emotions, and that is important to identify. The more you have positive moods and emotions, the less you are deeply affected by negative emotions. They do affect you, but they don't take control over you. It is important to understand DBT doesn't try to eliminate emotions or your feelings. However, some people don't feel them enough and others feel them too much. Finding that middle ground and being mindful of them makes a world of difference.

Exercises with coping skills are common in DBT therapy. They are practiced again and again so the patient has that information when they need it the most. They feel comfortable using those skills to help them through the situation. Physical health is promoted through this model too. The mind and body function best when they are both taken care of and in sync.

Getting enough sleep, eating well, and taking part in activities that help you feel good is all part of emotion regulation. Self-care is a big part of the education piece for this DBT element. Effective coping skills and problem-solving skills, both for the short term and long term are explored with the patient.

All of this promotes positive change and feeling in control over emotions rather than at their mercy. Learning how to effectively navigate through emotionally charged experiences is a skill someone can use for the rest of their life when they learn it through DBT. Those skills continue to serve them well long after therapy ends.

Interpersonal Effectiveness
DBT also promotes healthy interpersonal skills. Learning to ask for help when you need it is important. If you try to tackle everything on your own, you feel overwhelmed and isolated. The problems often spiral out of control and then you feel like there is just no solution to take care of them.

If you struggle to say no to people, you may have too much on your plate. You try to please everyone at home, in your personal life, and at work. Yet you suffer when you go this route because you aren't happy, and you can't realistically get it done. It is a juggling act and eventually, something falls through the cracks.

DBT promotes effective interpersonal skills including healthy communication skills, time management, and self-care. Establishing firm boundaries while reducing conflict is a skill that takes time to master. It is a learning process, and it starts with identifying emotions. Rather than getting mad and avoiding the issue, share emotions about how that made you feel and why you aren't content to let that behavior continue.

It feels good to hold others accountable, but you must remember not everyone will be receptive to it. When you have healthy boundaries, some relationships will get better. The communication opens and you can discuss issues respectfully. In other scenarios, you may have to limit interactions with that person or end your relationship with them. It can be tough, but it can be part of your steps to living the best life possible. You aren't responsible for the choices others make.

Targeting social skills and relationships, this model of DBT has a big impact on a person's life. It can help someone feel more involved at work. It can help them feel confident to strike up a conversation with a new person at a gathering. It can help them stop the patterns of behaviors that aren't helping their personal relationships to thrive.

In therapy, the discussion involves talking about areas where a person feels they struggle. The therapist may use assessment tools to help them pinpoint the areas to target with this type of discussion. Skills to help with being assertive, managing relationships, and being aware of how decisions affect you personally can help you put these DBT skills into play.

The result of this is less conflict because you are defusing situations before they get out of control. You also break the cycle of certain behaviors and problems arising with the same person again and again. Your choice to change will affect the dynamics of that cycle.

Learning about boundaries and how to maintain them is an important move forward with DBT. If you don't follow through with them, it can cause more problems and more negative emotions. Setting clear boundaries that are fair for the circumstances will help you feel empowered. It will help you build healthy relationships and stop being so invested in those that are toxic.

CHAPTER TWO

UNDERSTANDING ANXIETY AND DBT

Individuals with anxiety can struggle to maintain relationships. They often find it hard to take part in social gatherings or hobbies. Even going to work each day can prove to be difficult for them. The level of anxiety can influence how much of a hold it has on them. It can feel like invisible chains around them that prevent them from finding joy in their life.

When anxiety has a hold on someone like that, it continues to manifest and get worse and worse. Avoiding the issue can make it hard to get it under control. DBT is a good tool offering therapeutic methods to manage anxiety. Feeling in control can help someone have a better life. They aren't going to feel their anxiety has the upper hand anymore.

What is an anxiety disorder?

There are several definitions tossed around out there when it comes to anxiety disorders. This is because they can be different from each other. There is GAD, which is Generalized Anxiety Disorder. There are also those relating to certain phobias.

PTSD is often overlapped with anxiety disorders. A therapist can complete assessments to determine the specific anxiety disorder someone has. This helps guide them to create the perfect treatment plan. The level of anxiety someone struggles with is also factored in for the treatment plan.

Social Anxiety Disorder is one many people are identified as experiencing. This can make it hard to be part of social events. Even small gatherings can be stressful for them. While most people will attend that event and be excited about it and enjoy it, someone with this type of anxiety disorder struggles to even show up. Once they are there, they can struggle to find anything positive about it.

With DBT, their thoughts, emotions, and behaviors can change. This can give them a new lease for enjoying the company of other people. Instead of avoiding social events or struggling while there, they can find good things about it and dive in and be part of the fun!

Separation anxiety disorder is another type people can have. It can be difficult to explain, especially in adults. It is typically tied to childhood trauma. For example, feeling unloved or being abandoned by a parent can cause this type of anxiety to manifest. Sometimes, adolescents or adults experience it due to the loss of a loved one or a failed relationship with a love interest.

All anxiety disorders can cause negative emotions for someone. They can cause distress and create crisis situations for that individual. The worry they feel can be irrational, but it is real to them. A person can't just let go of that worry without effective therapy such as DBT. Many people try to hide it because others around them don't understand it.

Any anxiety disorder can affect someone negatively on many levels. It touches each aspect of their life. This includes:

- Daily activities
- Personal relationships
- School or work interactions
- Socializing

In therapy, underlying triggers of anxiety are discussed. Some people know what they are. For example, they experienced physical or emotional abuse growing up. Others aren't sure where it manifested, it is locked in their subconscious.

However, they may start to come to some realizations through the therapy. Understanding the triggers is important if they can be identified. However, DBT can be a successful treatment for anxiety disorders even if the underlying triggers remain unknown.

This is because the therapist gives them skills and techniques to help them identify emotions. Focusing on what they feel, why they feel it, and how to change it is all part of moving forward with DBT. It can change the life someone has because they feel happier. They gain self-confidence and they can find solutions to problems that create anxiety.

Breaking the cycle of anxiety includes being mindful and using coping skills to work through the situation. Selecting behaviors to engage in rather than allowing them to impulsively flow because that is what you have done before is a game changer. It can give someone calmness and inner peace that was lacking before.

How does Anxiety Affect the Mind and the Body?

Anxiety has a negative effect on both the mind and the body. It can create issues for someone the longer it continues. Early intervention with therapy is recommended, but not everyone gets a diagnosis early on.

Others don't understand that anxiety is a mental health concern that millions of people struggle with. They try to handle it on their own but finally reach out for help.

One of the huge risks of anxiety is the concept of self-medicating. It isn't uncommon for people to turn to drugs and/or alcohol to help them cope with anxiety. They feel it gives them courage in social situations. They can use it to help them numb the emotions they feel, but they don't know how to work through them correctly yet. DBT can help them do so without the use of drugs and/or alcohol.

The other risk is self-harm due to anxiety. Suicidal thoughts, cutting, and other forms of self-harm increase when a person has severe anxiety. Frequent panic attacks can take them down this road too. The self-harm gives them control that is missing. DBT gives them control but in healthy ways, so they don't feel the urge to engage in self-harm.

If they do have that urge, they can rely on the skills and techniques they were taught to find a safer alternative. They can also reach out to their therapist and other support in their network to help them overcome those feelings and urges.

When a person is anxious, the body doesn't relax. They can feel physical pain due to the tension. It can be hard to breathe because of the anxiety until the patient learns to control it with breathing techniques. Some people feel nauseous or get a headache when they experience anxiety due to the intensity of it. Trembling isn't uncommon due to the anxiety and the change in body temperature.

It often feels like the heart is beating too fast when anxiety takes over. Some people have thought they were having a heart attack, or a stroke and it was anxiety or panic attacks they experienced. Pain or bloating around the abdomen has also been linked to chronic anxiety.

Bouts of fatigue can be associated with fatigue because they take so much energy from the body. Insomnia can also be brought on by anxiety. Anyone not getting enough rest regularly is going to find it harder to concentrate. They will also be irritable and find it harder to rationally handle day to day conflicts.

The mind doesn't get a free pass either with anxiety. It can be thinking in all directions at a fast pace, and it is overwhelming. A feeling of dread can take over the mind and body, and that is hard to shake. It makes it almost impossible to focus the mind on anything with clarity.

The Connection Between Anxiety and Emotion Dysregulation

Emotion Dysregulation often results in someone experiencing outbursts showing anger. This can make it difficult for them to maintain healthy relationships with other people. It can cost them their job too if they can't get along with others and people are afraid of them. Individuals with anxiety tend to experience Emotion Dysregulation at a higher rate than other people.

They may come across as impulsive and a ticking time bomb. Other people may feel like they must tiptoe around them. They don't feel they can approach the individual to discuss anything. It always ends up explosive and with lots of tension, but nothing gets resolved. DBT strives to help someone with controlling emotions and identifying them. They are taught skills that reduce impulsive behaviors or outbursts of anger.

They are encouraged to look at the pros and cons of possible behaviors. If they react in such a manner, how will it help them? The reality is it won't. In fact, there is a good chance it will make the situation worse than it already is. Armed with positive options for problem-solving and coping, they can work through issues and not create additional problems for themselves or others.

Individuals struggling with anxiety due to a traumatic experience often feel emotions full of intensity. They are overly sensitive to them, and that can cause them to react in ways that others wouldn't. They can turn a regular event into a crisis because of their emotional response to it. They may feel intense fear or anger. Sometimes, they feel intense sadness.

Emotional Regulation gives the patient skills through DBT to change how they handle situations. They use mindfulness to consciously become aware of what they feel and how they think. They have the power to change their emotions and work through them. They also have the power to accept their emotions for what they are but also deal with the situation instead of avoiding it.

How can DBT Help with Managing Anxiety?

Changing the thought process and the behavior is how DVT helps with managing anxiety. Helping the person to see the situation for what it is and feel in control of it is the goal of the therapist. They teach this through various skills and practice role-playing what to do in various circumstances.

Promoting a positive lifestyle is part of the treatment plan. This includes self-care and eating right. Daily exercise and taking part in activities that evoke positive emotions are all part of how to effectively manage anxiety. Identifying any underlying triggers and learning to cope with them as well as implementing problem-solving skills help reduce impulsive behaviors like angry outbursts due to anxiety.

The skills and techniques taught with DBT improve the mind and the body, so they are less affected by anxiety. It feels good to the patient to experience those positive elements. That is what they strive to repeat through their thoughts and actions. They see clearly, they have to be mindful and fight to change so that they can let go of the hold anxiety has over them.

Acceptance and change are a big part of success with DBT for anxiety. By identifying the opposite emotion, they can work with the therapist to achieve it. This gives someone the chance to rewrite the ending rather than going through the same ineffective cycle.

Specific DBT Techniques for Treating Anxiety

The therapist will select specific DBT techniques to help a patient with their anxiety. This often starts with skills training so they can put them in motion when they feel anxiety coming on. This includes being mindful, awareness of emotions, and relaxation techniques. Breathing exercises can help someone stay in control when they feel anxious.

Distress tolerance skills are taught to help someone with anxiety through DBT. Such skills are typically taught to those that experience anxiety often and/or they experience it very deeply. Individuals that struggle with panic attacks tend to benefit the most from these skills. They can rely on them when they identify a trigger. It can reduce the frequency and severity of panic attacks.

Emotion regulation skills are put in motion. They can help a patient stop the anxiety and prevent a panic attack before it gets started. They learn to identify the triggers and their emotions. They can use skills and techniques to help them change those negative emotions and replace them with positive emotions.

Learning to accept the situation for what it is may sound harsh for someone with anxiety, but it isn't. In therapy sessions, they will talk about what anxiety is and why it manifests. They will try to remove the power it has over someone and give them back control. Once a person understands there are times they will experience undesirable emotions, they can accept that and use the tools they must work through the experience.

Awareness is taught with DBT for anxiety. Sometimes, it is the place a person is at or the people they are around that triggers it. Changing where you go and being selective about who you spend time with can reduce anxiety. Being comfortable with what you feel because you have coping skills and problem-solving skills changes the balance of things.

Interpersonal effectiveness skills are great for treating anxiety with DBT. Many people feel anxious in crowds. They don't know how to interact well with others. They don't have effective communication skills. A lack of self-esteem can also trigger anxiety when it comes to these types of relationships. As a person learns these skills in therapy, they can feel better about how they interact with others and the outcome.

Setting boundaries and enforcing them is part of these interpersonal effectiveness skills. How you deal with conflict can help a relationship get stronger or it can ruin it. When you can look at the possible solutions and calmly come to a decision about how to behave, it influences the future of that relationship. If you are a people pleaser, it can lead to anxiety.

You don't want to do something, but you do it because you wish to avoid conflict with the other party. They are taking advantage of you, but you haven't set any boundaries with them. Challenging this without being impulsive or disrespectful is empowering. It also helps you resolve problems instead of creating additional issues.

CHAPTER THREE

TREATING DEPRESSION WITH DBT

A comprehensive approach can work well for individuals battling depression. DBT can be a viable part of treatment, especially for those with chronic depression or severe depression. The longer someone has suffered from depression, the more intense it becomes. Sometimes, it is triggered due to trauma or PTSD.

With the use of DBT, a patient is exposed to various methods and techniques to help them cope with and overcome depression. Mindfulness is a big part of this type of treatment. The patient must identify the triggers, the behaviors, and use methods to help them turn it around. Part of the treatment plan likely includes engaging in activities the patient finds joy with so that they boost their mood.

Daily exercise, getting enough rest, and a balanced diet are also encouraged. All these elements can help the brain produce more serotonin. This chemical helps boost the brain and reduces stress and anxiety. Thinking clearly and calmly can help someone with depression identify the reality of it and how they can consciously change their focus and change their mindset.

Depression is complex, and every therapist understands that. They do know studies show DBT can help reduce the symptoms and improve a person's quality of life. Depressed individuals can isolate themselves from others. They may self-medicate with the use of drugs and/or alcohol. They are also at a higher risk of self-harm, including suicidal thoughts.

The therapist works with them to assess their level of depression and identify any symptoms of self-harm. Once that has been deemed not a high risk for them or successfully de-escalated, other forms of treatment can be implemented. Teaching new skills including coping methods, problem-solving skills, and identifying emotions as you work through are often part of DBT for someone with depression.

Behavioral based therapy works well for depression, and often incorporates CBT. However, not all patients respond well to CBT and that is where DBT can be effective. It can be used instead of CBT or along with it. The therapist must evaluate the patient and decide which path is best to put into that treatment plan. If they don't see improvements, they may modify it in future sessions to promote the best service to that patient.

DBT is often a method used to treat depression when other methods on their own have failed. This is encouraging because some patients think there is no hope for them. DBT may be combined with medications to provide the patient with the best outcome. Everything is carefully decided based on the needs and behaviors of the patient.

Understanding Depression

It can be difficult to get a grasp on what depression is and how it affects people. Not everyone has the same symptoms. Not everyone has the same severity of symptoms. Sadly, society tends to make people feel ashamed to ask for help with depression. Uneducated individuals about the topic often don't understand it. They may ask what does that person have to be depressed about? They may take it personally when a loved one is withdrawn from them.

Offering support to someone with depression means learning the basics of it and helping them where you can. Encouraging them to work with a therapist and sharing with them you are proud of their efforts is important. Millions of people struggle with some form of depression, it is very common. It is time to open those discussions and provide awareness. Each of us either struggles with depression or knows someone who is.

A person with depression may be viewed as difficult or a pessimist. They may focus on the worst-case scenario for just about everything. This can cause people to keep their distance, they don't want to be around someone that zaps their energy from them. Depression can cause both physical and mental symptoms. It can also cause someone to behave irrationally and impulsively as they struggle to regain some control.

Depression is classified as a mood disorder. It creates frequent feelings of sadness and a loss of interest in activities a person used to enjoy. It can affect every aspect of a person's life because depression affects how a person feels, reacts, thinks, and behaves. If it isn't treated it can cause additional problems for the mind and the body.

Not everyone knows why they are depressed, that is just the way they feel. The therapist will explore possibilities with them. Sometimes, it is linked to a traumatic event or chronic stress. Depression can be tied to an illness too. For example, someone that used to be very active is now in pain due to Rheumatoid Arthritis. They experience fatigue each day and it prevents them from the lifestyle they once knew. This can trigger depression because they haven't found a way to cope with their illness.

Research indicates depression can be genetic in some instances. There may be a family history of it. However, this can be hard to identify because many generations either didn't identify depression because they didn't have information available now or they tried to hide it. The use of drugs and/or alcohol can alter a person's mood and cause depression. Others start to use those products to self-medicate and offset symptoms of depression. It is a temporary fix though and it makes the symptoms of depression worse.

Common symptoms of depression include:

- Anxiety
- Changes in appetite
- Changes in sleep habits
- Digestive concerns
- Difficulty concentrating
- Fatigue
- Feeling hopeless or worried about everything
- Impulsive or radical behaviors
- Irritability
- Loss of interest in people, hobbies, job, etc.
- Physical aches and pains
- Sexual dysfunction or loss of interest in sex
- Suicidal thoughts or self-harm

Depression is treatable, but it takes the right information and education for someone to benefit from that treatment. DBT can be a viable solution to help someone get on track and regain control rather than depression ruling their behaviors and lifestyle. Therapists offer many tools, including those that help someone avoid relapsing should they experience a trigger or crisis.

The Connection Between Depression and Emotion Dysregulation

There is a connection between depression and Emotion Dysregulation. When a person continually has adverse thoughts or mood patterns, it may become all too normal for them. That norm isn't healthy though, and they struggle mentally and emotionally.

A big part of DBT for depression involves identifying emotions and accepting them. The next step is to work on changing how they feel so that it is a positive emotion rather than a negative one. Some of these exercises in therapy involve identifying the opposite emotion through role-playing.

All mood disorders, including depression, have a common denominator. There aren't enough positive emotions taking place. The patient has to become aware of this and focus their attention on striving for better emotional releases. What can they take part in that will help them feel happier? What triggers do they identify which cause them to feel worse? How can they cope with those negative emotions or change them, so they don't continue to have such a profound effect on their quality of life?

Moods that change often but tend to go back to negative are common for those with chronic depression. They swing back and forth, and that accounts for the impulsive and irrational behaviors. They may have days where they are upbeat and dive in with vigor. The next day they are disinterested and emotionally unattached to the same topic.

Emotion Dysregulation can make someone appear irresponsible and uncaring at times. They tend to fail to follow through when they say they will do something. They struggle with deadlines, and they struggle with change. Routine is important to them, even when what they take part in isn't serving their best interests. It is familiar to them, and they find solace in that.

How can DBT Help Manage Depression?

Regaining control over emotions and changing the negative is the best way DBT can help manage depression. A person will have support instead of feeling all along as they go through the process. It provides the patient with skills, techniques, and tools so they can best handle situations and reduce triggers. Mindfulness is a huge part of success with DBT for depression.

Irregularities in mood caused by depression affect each element of a person's life. When they learn valuable skills to regulate their emotions, they can be balanced. This isn't to say there won't be rough days or times when they feel sad or down due to circumstances taking place. However, they will have coping skills and problem-solving skills to help them through that. They are less likely to relapse when they have such resources in place.

Learning such skills helps a person understand emotions and other intangible aspects that influence depression. They learn to regulate their moods and modify ineffective behaviors. It isn't practical to think all treatment can occur in the therapy sessions. The therapist must give the patient an arsenal of tools they can carry with them to use as they need to for their day-to-day life.

They also teach identifying symptoms of depression and how to offset them before they get worse again. Breaking that cycle and intervening early on can help someone make healthy choices and regulate mood in practical and sustainable ways. As the symptoms of depression are less intense and occur less frequently, a person can see the value of being happier and engaging in a positive lifestyle.

In group therapy sessions, the patient can understand they aren't alone. They are in discussions with peers that also have depression. It is a guided group therapy and a way for someone to gain self-esteem and stay motivated with their treatment plan. These group sessions are non-judgmental and that can help a patient see that they don't have to go through it alone.

Dealing with depression can make a person feel isolated. They don't think others understand what they are going through. The group sessions are typically once a week. The patient will also see their therapist individually once or twice per week too.

DBT can help someone start the healing process. While the therapist encourages being mindful and accepting reality, they also encourage patients to be kind to themselves. It takes time to heal, time to change behaviors. As the patient learns new skills, they can begin to identify what works for them best. Everything is discussed in therapy and that helps to modify the treatment plan when necessary to help the patient reach their goals.

DBT Techniques to Help Treat Depression

There are several DBT techniques incorporated to help someone with depression. Those included in the treatment plan depend on their needs. The therapist will start with the most important techniques first. As the patient understands them and how to incorporate them, they will continue to add more techniques. In the therapy sessions, they will discuss which DBT techniques seem to help the most and which help the least. This can help with modifying the treatment plan.

Mindfulness is typically the first DBT technique the therapist will introduce. Learning how to be present in the moment means the patient must face the depression and they can't ignore it or avoid it. This helps a patient focus on the current circumstances. They are taught to identify emotions and their current state of mind.

This information helps identify patterns of thoughts and behaviors that seem to get in the way of a positive mood and positive mindset. Once the patient can do this consciously, the focus is on how to make healthier thoughts and boost mood. All this effort helps the patient have more control over their mind. They no longer feel like depression is in charge.

Mindfulness can be a transformation process for patients in therapy for depression. It is this DBT technique that stands apart from other treatments that may have failed to work for them. It is important to be mindful without judging. When you judge, you increase the amount of emotional distress associated with the symptoms of depression.

Distress Tolerance is a great DBT technique to treat depression. It gives the patient skills to accept emotions, including those that are uncomfortable. It assists with regulating moods. Teaching coping skills and problem-solving skills encourages the patient to find better ways to handle situations, so they don't get worse.

Identifying triggers that tend to lead a person to self-harm or negative behaviors is part of Distress Tolerance. When a patient engages in this type of technique, they work through the problem. They look at the pros and cons of acting a certain way. If that behavior won't help them resolve the situation in a healthy way, they don't engage in it.

Patients often respond well to Distress Tolerance because it is empowering. They recognize they have ways to help them change the outcome of situations they once thought was out of their control. This also reduces stress and anxiety.

Emotion Regulation

While we can't control all the things going on around us, we can control how we respond to them. Emotion Regulation is a piece of DBT treatment a patient can use day to day. They can also use it in crisis situations. Once you accept your emotions, you can focus on changing them. Learning how to be in control of emotions rather than feeling controlled by emotions is a huge benefit to anyone with depression.

Regulating emotions isn't always an easy task. It takes mindfulness and awareness to focus on what you are feeling. It requires taking a step back to identify what you feel with those emotions and why. The goal is to stop emotions from raging out of control from the start.

Interpersonal Effectiveness is a part of DBT techniques to treat depression, it is important to have healthy relationships with others. Depression may have caused a person to lose relationships or withdraw from people in general. As they learn methods to cope with depression and improve their mood, it can be a new chance to create better personal relationships.

These relationships should have boundaries in place and preserve a person's self-respect. Effective tools for social interactions may be required with treatment to help someone feel comfortable spending time with other people. Otherwise, problems with anxiety can develop. Sharing common interests, good communication skills, and even letting go of toxic relationships are all discussed with the therapist. The goal is healthy relationships built on trust.

Combining DBT with Medication for Depression Treatment

Studies show about 75% of patients that follow DBT and take medication show significant improvement with depression in six months or less. This can transform their lives for the better in that window of time. It can help someone see the value of life and focus on living rather than just struggling to get through each day.

It takes time to regulate DBT with medication for depression treatment. The lowest possible dose of medication is given and then it may be increased if necessary. The patient must agree to take the medication as prescribed every single day. If they change the dose or skip doses, it won't work like it was intended.

For severe depression, a higher level of medication may be necessary. Combined with DBT, the dose can be tapered down as the patient benefits from DBT. They may no longer require the same level of medication they did when they entered therapy. A discussion about DBT and medication and how they can work together should be completed early on in treatment when the therapist feels this is a good mix for the patient.

Many patients hesitate to take medications for depression. They worry about the cost and side effects. Education about what to expect and how medication can help them gain value from DBT in less time may encourage them to give it a try. The medication can help calm the mind and increase the feel-good chemicals the brain naturally creates.

CHAPTER FOUR

ALLEVIATING STRESS WITH DBT

Stress is something everyone experiences. Sometimes, it can be a strong motivator to get things completed. Living with ongoing stress can take a harsh toll on a person both mentally and physically. Learning how to let go of the stress and replace it with positive emotions and behaviors is important.

Learning to get out of your head and out of your way is important to understand. With DBT for stress, a person can learn how to cope with situations, how to communicate effectively, and ways to problem-solve. They can replace behaviors that don't bring them positive results with these new skills and techniques.

Ongoing stress can be self-induced by taking on too much at once. It can be the result of a job, finances, and even toxic relationships with other people. The therapist will help by assessing the situation. Introducing a variety of skills to help someone reduce stress is important.

Once triggers are identified, these tools can be used to stop a situation early on. Then it doesn't escalate and turn into a crisis. Too often, small issues become big ones due to avoidance or negative behaviors. Effective interpersonal skills can help with every aspect of life and reduce stress. When there is less stress, a person can focus, and they sleep better. They tend to be happier, and their mood is stable rather than extreme highs and lows all the time.

How does Stress Impact a Person's Mental Health?

Too much stress or chronic stress can cause a person to be irritable. It can also cause them to be aggressive. It is hard to focus or remain calm when you have such levels of stress. It can make a person behave impulsively or fly off the handle due to something small. That issue may be small, but it was the straw that broke the camel's back so to speak.

Reacting in such a manner can make the situation worse for the individual. They may struggle with personal relationships because people can't predict how they will act. They don't share information or feelings with them because they don't want to anger the person. When you have to walk around on eggshells around someone the relationship is crumbling. Such behaviors can make it hard to maintain employment. Disciplinary action at work or losing a job can add to the stress factor.

When a person deals with too much stress, they often feel they have lost control. They are fearful and they may think about worst case outcomes. The fight or flight feelings are common. A person is going to make the situation worse by how they react, or they will ignore the issue completely. Stress is going to get bigger and bigger if it isn't dealt with.

Difficulty focusing and concentrating are often the result of too much stress. This can make it hard for someone to complete daily tasks as they should. It increases the risk of errors and mistakes. It can be a challenge to make important decisions when you are dealing with stress.

A person can become burned out or struggle with anxiety when they have ongoing stress. It can also trigger depression due to mood changes that aren't good for a person. All of this will take a toll on someone mentally. It can carry over to the physical aspects too. It isn't uncommon for someone with high stress to suffer from aches and pains. Abdominal issues are often reported too.

The Connection Between Stress and Emotion Dysregulation

Search indicates when a person experiences Emotion Dysregulation the pre-frontal part of the brain doesn't have control for successful control over emotions. A person tends to experience emotions intensely when they struggle with stress. They feel completely out of control. They can't focus on the situation or work through solutions.

Instead, they make the situation worse. That increases their level of stress. It is a repetitive cycle until they find an outlet. This can be an outburst of anger, crying, or even self-harm. Some individuals indulge in the use of drugs and/or alcohol due to the connection between stress and Emotion Dysregulation.

They haven't learned effective tools to cope with the situation or effective ways to problem-solve. Through DBT therapy they can learn those skills and change their behaviors. They can also regain control over their emotions and situations.

Individuals diagnosed with PTSD tend to have high levels of stress and anxiety. Experts agree this is trauma induced and causes Emotion Dysregulation due to the experiences the person has been exposed to. Such individuals often experience irrational fear, high levels of stress and anxiety, and they may show sadness as their primary emotion.

How can DBT Help with Managing Stress?

DBT can help with managing stress because the patient learns to live in the moment and identify emotions. They learn ways to change their thinking, so they don't continue with adverse thoughts or behaviors that aren't promoting the life they want. Patients use their 5 senses to help them identify what they see and feel around them. This awareness then gives them the option to change their mood and focus on a positive outcome.

Most therapists teach patients how to use breathing techniques and relaxation methods to assist them. These coping skills go a long way toward reducing the stress a person experiences. This can help them to remain calm and focused. Many individuals are hypersensitive to their environment. DBT can help them identify emotions without being held captive by them.

Individuals can easily be overwhelmed by emotions, especially in a crisis. That can cause them to act impulsively and act aggressively. Objectively identifying and working through those emotions as they emerge prevents them from hitting their peak levels. This gives the person a chance to evaluate the situation. They can use their coping methods and problem-solving skills to assist them with a better outcome.

The goal of DBT with stress management is to help someone remain in a calm state. Even when they have a situation they are dealing with, they don't have to feel like everything is out of their control. They can focus on that one situation at that moment and move on. The methods taught through DBT help a person return to their calm state if stress has gotten too high.

Specific DBT Techniques for Reducing Stress

The specific DBT techniques used for someone to reduce stress depend on their circumstances and their self-esteem. A therapist is often going to work to boost self-confidence. They guide the patient through scenarios to set boundaries and resolve conflict in a healthy way. It isn't a good idea to keep emotions bottled up, but you can't just explode with them either.

Teaching interpersonal skills helps a patient reduce stress by establishing boundaries and enforcing them. It may require them to end relationships that bring on stress all the time. They can be toxic and if both parties can't change that outcome, it may be best to sever the ties. In therapy, discussions about what is taking place in the patient's life is important. This helps the therapist identify patterns and triggers where stress develops.

For example, it may be due to a certain job, person, or tied to a specific place. Rather than avoiding the feelings of stress, the patient is encouraged to talk about them and work through them in therapy. What can they control about that situation to reduce the stress? It may include telling the boss you have too much work and it is time to hire another person to take on part of it.

Mindfulness helps with reducing stress because the individual can focus on what is taking place right now. They don't have to worry about what has already happened or what will take place later. This reduces the sensation of being overwhelmed and feeling helpless. Mindfulness is part of all DBT efforts and one of the main differences of this type of treatment.

Regulating emotions help the patient feel empowered and in control. It is when they lose control over what they think and what they feel that the stress and anxiety get worse. Regulating emotions through DBT involves validation but not using that as an excuse or the end of the line. It is the starting point for some positive changes.

Role-playing about regulating emotions is part of both individual and group therapy for stress with DBT. The patient practices how they will identify their emotions during the moment. Next, they will explore how they can get those emotions in check and even put a positive spin on them.

Distress tolerance is found in DBT treatment, and it prevents a crisis from causing someone to relapse to behaviors that don't work well for them. With proper tools and skills, a person doesn't have to get to the point where they feel they are in distress. They can start tackling their feelings and situations long before it gets to that point.

Practicing positive feelings and emotions reduces stress. Naturally, we just feel better when we are happy and in a good mood. When we are regulated like that, the changes in our lives don't cause us to go from one extreme to the next. We can experience emotions and accept them, but they don't cause us to be impulsive or aggressive in our behaviors.

Interpersonal Effectiveness is important with DBT and stress management. People will take advantage if you allow them to. Don't feel like there is something wrong with you when they do. Therapy teaches healthy boundaries and role-playing explores how to have tough conversations with someone so that they don't continue to create stress for you. Share with them what is going on, why it makes you feel a certain way, and the outcome you desire.

Incorporating Self-Care Practices in DBT

It isn't self-fish or self-centered to practice good self-care habits. In fact, a person struggles emotionally and physically when they don't take care of their own needs. A lack of self-esteem often results in a person being taken advantage of. They may be doing too much at home for everyone in the household. They may be taking on too much at work.

They try to juggle it all in silence though because they don't want to let anyone down. They don't want to fail, but they spread themselves so thin they can't get it all done. They don't enjoy activities either because their mind jumps to what they have to do later or what they need to still get done that day.

Sleeping enough each night is a wonderful way to start self-care. Listen to your mind and body, some people can get by with 6 hours of sleep. Others need up to 10. Get enough rest so you don't wake up tired and irritable. That is a terrible way to start the day. If you struggle with insomnia, self-care practices can help you sleep easier too.

Time management skills are part of DBT for self-care. Carve out time to complete your responsibilities without rushing or cutting corners. Create time to get enough sleep and take care of routine household chores. Identify time for exercise and activities you like to enjoy. Learn to tell people no when you are overextended, or you simply don't want to spend time taking part in what they have to offer.

CHAPTER FIVE

COMBATING INSOMNIA WITH DBT

Difficulties sleeping on a regular basis will harm your mental health and physical well-being. Getting to the core of insomnia isn't always an easy feat. Often, there are underlying concerns including anxiety and stress that make it hard for the mind to shut down when you try to sleep.

As a result, you struggle to fall into a slumber. You may wake up often, and you start your day tired out. This type of fatigue can make a person irritable, and it makes it hard to function all day long.

Insomnia can be treated with DBT and working closely with a therapist. Identifying the reasons why you don't sleep well can help you change it around. Many people don't want to take medications for insomnia. They don't like the harsh side effects. They don't like that the body builds up a tolerance, so they must increase the dose over time. They also don't like the groggy feeling it creates.

Breaking the cycle of insomnia is important. Your mind and body need adequate rest for overall well-being. Sleeping well helps boost your mood and fight depression and fatigue. It can help the body recover from injuries and feel rejuvenated. If you struggle with insomnia, don't overlook the benefits of DBT to fight it.

Frequently, individuals with borderline personality disorder struggle with insomnia. It has to do with their mind racing all the time and they can't focus and calm down. Some will try to fix this with self-medicating options such as the use of drugs or alcohol.

Marijuana strains are often promoted to sleep better, but they just mask the problem. DBT can help reduce and eliminate insomnia and other sleep disorders. Individuals that struggle with anxiety or paranoia also have insomnia. They can't determine the difference between reality and fantasy. They often have an escalated feeling of fear. It is hard to sleep when you are afraid, or you are worried.

Understanding Insomnia and Sleep Disorders

Everyone has nights when they don't sleep their best. If you have small children or someone is sick, your night may be interrupted to help them get comfortable and back to sleep. Most people with insomnia and sleep disorders are tired, and they desperately want to rest! They simply find it hard to fall asleep and stay asleep. It is important to break that cycle so you can be healthy.

Insomnia is a specific type of sleep disorder. Your therapist can help confirm that diagnosis. There are other types of sleep disorders, but they have different symptoms associated with them. They include:

- Narcolepsy
- Restless Leg Syndrome
- Sleep Apnea

For a diagnosis of insomnia to be founded, the patient has to struggle with falling asleep and staying asleep for at least six months. The sooner the patient seeks DBT treatment the faster they can get back on track with deep sleep and plenty of it each night! Insomnia can be short-term (less than 6 months) if it is brought on by trauma. The patient is urged to seek therapy for the traumatic event and to bring insomnia to the attention of the therapist.

What is the Connection Between Insomnia and Emotion Dysregulation?

Sleep studies performed show a connection between insomnia and Emotion Dysregulation. Difficulties controlling emotions, controlling behaviors, and identifying how they feel about situations can all prevent someone from getting into the deeper REM sleep cycles. As a result, they toss and turn, they wake up easily, and they struggle to fall asleep. They may be in bed for hours before they finally drift off for a little bit.

The situation gets into a perpetual cycle because a lack of sleep increases Emotion Dysregulation. A person can't think clearly or concentrate when they continually don't get enough sleep. A person can't be in a good mood, and they are often irrational and irritable due to the lack of sleep. Small things may evoke behaviors that make problems worse. They don't have the mindset to deal with things well because they are on edge from a lack of sleep.

How can DBT Help Manage Insomnia?

DBT can help patients to sleep better. The goal of such therapy is to rule out any underlying diagnosis. This includes health issues and mental health concerns. If they are diagnosed, DBT will be implemented for that along with insomnia. As the patient works on the treatment plan, they typically start to sleep better.

DBT for insomnia works by focusing on awareness, both at the physical and mental levels. Focusing on breathing exercises to relax the mind and body are important. Practicing starting at the top of the head and only focusing on one muscle group at a time is a common exercise practiced in therapy sessions. Visualizing each of the areas being removed of stress and anxiety so they are fully relaxed.

Breathing exercises where the patient focuses on counting in their breath, holding it, and counting out the release can help them relax for sleep. When the mind is focused on not sleeping and how it will affect them in the morning, it can make the situation worse. It can create anxiety too.

Individuals with insomnia may feel angry, alone, scared, or nervous to name a few of the common emotions. With DBT they can learn to identify those emotions and get a handle on them. They can focus on being mindful and dealing with how they feel in the moment. Identifying those emotions and trying to eliminate the negative with a positive can help them manage insomnia.

Specific DBT Techniques for Improving Sleep Patterns

Being mindful is the best DBT technique to improve sleep patterns. It helps someone accept the situation without their emotions getting the best of them. Learning to problem-solve, communication skills, and coping skills can help someone feel better about what took place that day. When stress and anxiety are reduced, it is common to sleep better.

Breathing exercises are often taught in therapy for insomnia. This is different than just counting sheep when you can't drift off! With DBT, the focus is on controlling your thoughts and relaxing. When you must count your breath in, hold it for 10 seconds, and count it back out, your mind can't wander to various thoughts or emotions. You will be surprised how much faster you fall asleep with the use of breathing exercises in the mix.

Developing a Sleep Hygiene Routine with DBT

Strive to get the best night of sleep you can. Creating a positive routine with DBT can help train your mind and body for sleep. Remove stimulation from the bedroom including electronic devices. Don't play on your phone or watch TV when it is time for bed.

Before you get into bed, practice mediation and positive affirmations. This will help the mind and body relax. It can get them in sync, so you rest better. Focusing on what you accomplished that day and not what didn't get done helps you feel appreciative. Focus on what you have to be thankful for as you get ready to sleep. It will help you drift off with a smile! Journaling before you get ready for bed can also help clear the mind and relax the body.

Avoid eating, consuming drinks with caffeine, or exercising in the hours before bed. They can overstimulate the body and mind, keeping you awake when you really need to sleep. Make sure your mattress and pillows are comfortable so you can sleep well. Changing the setup may be necessary for you to get the best night of sleep. The room needs to be at a comfortable temperature too.

Noise levels in your bedroom should be evaluated. If your partner snores and it keeps you awake, consider wearing earplugs. If you can hear your neighbors in the apartments around you, get a white noise machine to drown them out. If you have anxiety, consider a weighted blanket to help you feel at ease.

Strive to go to bed at the same time each night and get up at the same time each morning. Your mind and body will get used to that routine and identify those hours as time to be asleep. Soon, you won't have to look at the clock to determine it is time to go catch some ZZZs. You will find you wake up automatically around the time your alarm is set to go off. You will wake up well-rested and ready to enjoy the day ahead!

CHAPTER SIX

BALANCING CHANGE AND ACCEPTANCE

A complete assessment and various types of testing must be conducted for a therapist to offer a diagnosis. Based on that diagnosis, they can decide if they feel DBT would be a good match for that patient. A detailed and individualized treatment plan is essential for success. The therapist must design it with the needs and the current situation of the patient in mind.

The patient should be part of the treatment plan for it to work. They must understand what it includes. They must know why this treatment is recommended for them. They need an understanding of the steps involved with DBT and what they specifically will do to obtain the established goals.

The initial focus of any such therapist and patient relationship is to reduce and eliminate any behaviors that implicate self-harm or the risk of suicide. If the situation can be handled on an outpatient basis that will be done. If the therapist feels further intervention is necessary, hospitalization may be recommended.

It isn't fair or realistic to expect any patient to work with DBT and work towards positive change when they are handling the internal struggle of self-harm. That is why this must be completely under control before anything further is discussed. It has the utmost importance.

Pre-Treatment

All patients begin in what is referred to as pre-treatment. The therapist will review the results of the assessment and the diagnosis with the patient. They will talk to them about the recommended treatment plan. This is a time for the patient to ask questions and give their input.

One of the discussions that will take place with the patient is what motivates them to take part in this plan. What is causing them to commit to the agreed upon treatment plan? While all of this is conducted verbally, it plays a role in what goes into writing. The complete treatment plan and all it entails should be put into writing.

The patient has the freedom to express their feelings about treatment or about the action plan. Perhaps they have worked with a therapist before and didn't get the results they desired. Maybe they have tried to deal with things on their own and didn't get anywhere. Such thoughts are manifesting that they are afraid of change.

Understanding what is expected from them and what they can gain through DBT can help them feel comfortable giving it a try. They don't have to commit long-term in the beginning. Getting them to agree to 3 sessions and some homework assignments they complete between those sessions is a good starting point.

The sessions may be twice per week in the beginning, especially if there are concerns about self-harm. If that isn't an issue or once those issues are under control, the sessions are typically going to be once per week. Yet there is plenty that the patient works on between those sessions. They implement tools and techniques into their daily lives. They bring the outcome of doing so back to the meetings for discussion.

While the patient does have the ultimate choice about treatment, the therapist will encourage them to do so. They will let them know what can happen if they continue their current path without therapy. The focus of these therapy sessions will shift with time. This is because the hierarchy of issues and needs will change the more sessions a person attends.

A feeling of success is important for anyone in DBT. Larger goals are broken down to make them achievable. When a person can see the small pieces, they have accomplished and how it fits into the big picture, they are encouraged to continue. When the therapist praises the patient for achieving something they committed to, it can encourage them to try the next thing the therapist asks them to engage in.

Both the therapist and the patient should be on the same page regarding the treatment plan. They should discuss it and agree to it. A patient has the right to tell the therapist at any time that a part of that treatment plan isn't working well for them. The therapist should ask questions about what isn't working and modify the treatment plan accordingly.

At each session, the therapist should assess the commitment of the patient and their progress. Even if the progress is very slow, it is successful if they remain committed and they continue to do the best they can.

Commitment

Adults can expect a commitment of at least 1 year with DBT. It isn't a rapid solution, but it may be the best solution. The patient can see great results over that timeframe. After the year ends, the therapist can evaluate the progress with them They can decide if it is recommended to end the sessions or continue them. Therapy should continue until the patient has a firm grasp on all the tools and techniques provided to help them with a better quality of life.

For adolescent treatment, the commitment should be at least 6 months. It all depends on what they are seen for. It also depends on the amount of progress they make as they continue with therapy. Each patient will move through DBT at a different pace due to the variables.

Following the Treatment Plan

It can be hard for a patient to grasp the importance of sticking to their treatment plan. They must acknowledge the balance of change and acceptance. This means they are encouraged to change but they also see the reality of where they are right now. They can work with the therapist to identify what should be changed and then how to change it.

Clear goals with a timeframe assigned to them are necessary with patients and DBT. Otherwise, the "someday I will do that" mentality sits in. They must be aware and mindful every single day. Initially, it can be exhausting both physically and mentally to do this. As they make positive changes though, it gets easier.

The therapist must identify the main elements for the patient to focus on. If they are given too much to do, they will fail. They will become overwhelmed by it and give up. It is reasonable when they have one or two major concepts to work with. As they do well with them, they learn better skills that carry over into the other areas they need to work on.

The therapist will evaluate the progress of each patient. The treatment plan will be modified as they see fit to continue to help the patient. The amount of time someone spends in DT therapy depends on their assessment, their situation, and how much progress they make with their treatment plan.

While most patients are willing to work on things to feel better and behave better, they can get in their own way. It is hard to break old habits, even when a person knows those habits aren't in their best interest.

Identifying and breaking down TIBs

The best way a therapist can help someone get out of their comfort zone and break poor habits is to hold them accountable. TIBs must be addressed between the therapist and the patient, or they will continue. TIBs are Treatment Interfering Behaviors. They must be eliminated for someone to gain the most value from DBT. A TIB is anything that directly prevents a patient from successfully participating 100% in their treatment plan.

Common TIBs

The list of TIBs is endless, and some patients are creative when it comes to the excuses they present or the barriers they identify. These are common ones that therapists frequently deal with:

- Demanding solutions without working through the process
- Disrespect towards the therapist or other staff
- Failure to complete assignments between sessions
- Frequently late to appointments
- Lying or withholding information
- Missing scheduled appointments
- Not participating in sessions
- Rescheduling appointments at the last minute
- Resisting the treatment plan and the components it entails

As a general practice, therapists identify TIBs as soon as they see them appearing as a pattern of behavior with a patient. For example, if a patient is late to one session due to traffic it isn't a big deal. However, if they are chronically late for their sessions, that behavior must be addressed. They may intentionally show up late because they know the session must end on time. There will be less time for them to focus on it with the therapist. It is a form of avoidance that is very common.

Therapists don't like addressing TIBs, but it is necessary. They know without that discussion the problems will continue. They strive to hold patients accountable and reduce barriers that lower the chance of DBT working successfully for them. Addressing TIBs can make the bond stronger with a therapist. It can also save someone's life!

Discussion about the behavior tied into a TIB is the best place to start. The therapist will share the reality of what they see taking place. Next, they will talk to the patient about why they behave that way and the emotions they experience. The next part of the discussion is how they can change that behavior. A plan to reduce or eliminate each TIB as soon as possible is a huge step with a treatment plan.

Moving Forward after Discussing TIBs

This is a learning opportunity too for patients. They gain the chance to explore their emotions and articulate them. They need the guidance of the therapist to do this. As their treatment progresses, they become increasingly comfortable with this process. This can be a learning process for the therapist too. They may get information about what the patient is experiencing and dealing with through this type of discussion to end TIBs.

The therapist uses words like "we" to share with the patient that they are going to help them through this. For example, they may ask the question "what are we going to do so that this behavior doesn't continue?" Presenting the information this way helps to keep the patient engaged.

As the patient improves the behaviors, the therapist will reinforce those changes. They will share they notice the difference in behavior and that they appreciate the effort put forth to make that happen.

Ending Treatment

A therapist is dedicated to giving the best treatment with DBT to someone. They can't make it work though if the patient isn't dedicated to the process. If a therapist can't get them to commit to a treatment plan, they may have to be firm and tell them they can't see them anymore.

If a patient is self-sabotaging treatment due to TIBs, the therapist may have to go that route with them. Every possible option to get them on track and keep them as a patient is explored before that decision is made. They can't help a patient that won't try any of the DBT methods. If they aren't showing up for appointments, they prevent other patients from being seen in those allocated slots.

CHAPTER SEVEN

MINDFULNESS IN DBT

In many of the previous chapters, we touched on the topic of mindfulness. The numerous references to it are important because they are a key element of successful DBT treatment. Once a patient is found not at risk of self-harm or suicide, this is typically the first technique introduced to them It carries over into all the other techniques and skills provided to the patient. It is part of the foundation toward a better life!

When a person is being mindful, they focus on each moment and don't let their mind wander to anything else. They objectively look at situations, as if they were watching someone else through a lens. This awareness includes focusing on how you feel, what you think, what your body is experiencing, and the variables within the environment around you at that moment.

Mindfulness helps a person feel alive and gives them a zest for living their best life. They aren't going through the motions, trying to hide from situations anymore. They aren't being impulsive because they feel out of control and some type of action or behavior helps them feel in control again. Mindfulness can reduce stress and anxiety because a person accepts reality and then works through it.

When most of us think about meditation, we think about a quiet place at home where we focus on relaxing our mind and body. Mindfulness is a type of meditation, but you take part in it everywhere you go. It doesn't matter if you are alone or with a group of friends. It doesn't matter if you are at work or a social event. Training your mind to be in this state is an important part of the benefits with DBT.

While you are aware in the moment, there may be times when you feel overwhelmed, and you must regain control of your emotions. Implementing techniques introduced in therapy including breathing exercises, guided imagery, and relaxation methods can help a person work through it and not let the situation get worse.

Understanding Mindfulness and all it Entails

Mindfulness is the centralized idea behind DBT. The purpose of it is to create thinking in a manner that identifies emotions and promotes reasonable actions. Mindfulness is about being aware and being in the moment. Sometimes, it is believed to be the same as guided imagery or relaxation, but they are different concepts.

If a person isn't engaged in self-harm, mindfulness is often the first concept a therapist will introduce to them. They need this skill to guide them and assist them as they work through their concerns. It is essential with DBT and that is why the educational piece with it is so imperative early in the therapy sessions.

Patients are encouraged to find the desire to stop a certain thought pattern or behavior when they are mindful. What can they do in that moment to change how they will think or how they will act? Relying on the senses and the thought process, mindfulness can help bring a calm feeling to a situation. It can help a person feel in control, even though the circumstances before them are out of their control.

There are three states of mind:

- Emotional mind
- Reasonable mind
- Wise mind

Emotional Mind

When your emotions are in control of what you do and how you behave, you are in emotional mind. This is something DBT helps with eliminating. You always want to feel in control of your thoughts and actions, no matter what the scenario is. Don't make rash decisions or take part in impulsive behaviors. The goal is to move from emotional mind to reasonable mind or wise mind before you do anything.

Before DBT, many patients would act and behave while in emotional mind. They may show anger, aggression, or take part in self-harm. Emotions are valuable, but they should be something you feel and explore, not something that dictates behaviors. DBT helps patients to see this and make the necessary changes within their thought process.

Emotional mind can be beneficial when it is evaluated and processed correctly. It can help a person decide they need to deal with a situation. It can promote looking at the pros and cons of given options. It can help someone set boundaries and be assertive with communication, so those negative emotions don't continue to manifest.

Reasonable Mind

When a person is in reasonable mind, they can objectively look at the situation and focus on what is taking place. The emotions are felt, but they aren't in control. The sense of urgency to act and behavior NOW are removed, and a person isn't going to be impulsive. Instead, they will look for information and separate that from perceptions. They will evaluate the options and use both coping skills and problem-solving skills to help them make decisions.

This doesn't mean someone ever decides they didn't like. It means they carefully look at the consequences and outcomes before they do anything. They can feel confident their decision is the best choice for them in that moment. If they learn later, it wasn't, they know they did the best they could with the information they had. There are fewer feelings of regret. In emotional mind, a person is often going to make the situation worse. That isn't typically the outcome with reasonable mind.

Wise Mind
With wise mind, a person uses the positive elements of both emotional mind and reasonable mind. Think about two parents and they have a child. Genetically, that child gets all the best DNA elements from each parent with none of the weaker elements in place. Of course, that isn't how it really works with genetics, but in this example, you can see how taking the best of both of those concepts and combining them would create the best, which is wise mind.

The goal of DBT is for someone to reach their wise mind. This is where they just know that they should behave or feel a certain way based on what is going on. Sometimes, it is called intuition, but it is a much deeper concept than that. Wise mind involves all three of the mind concepts. It means a person is confident that something they think, or feel is valid. They don't doubt it for a second!

Mindfulness Techniques used in DBT
Objectively identifying emotions and working through them is a common technique from DBT used for mindfulness. This prevents emotions from taking control, which leads to impulsive behaviors. Getting used to being uncomfortable due to certain emotions is important. Rather than allowing that to create anxiety and fear, it is used to evoke the patient to search for answers and make decisions. They no longer avoid situations that are uncomfortable to them. This gives them the freedom to be assertive and set boundaries while remaining calm.

Problem-solving skills and communication skills learned through therapy help someone talk about how they feel and why they feel that way. It isn't fair to assume someone knows how their actions or what they say makes us feel. When you can share that with them, you open effective lines of communication. When you approach the situation with the goal to find a solution, you can make relationships stronger.

Exploring emotions makes us vulnerable, but we must feel them to get our minds and bodies to respond. Emotions are a way for us to process and they give us a chance to heal. They also give us a chance to make positive changes, so we don't continue to feel the negative emotions we don't like. Don't get too comfortable feeling angry, sad, or alone.

Breathing techniques are often used with mindfulness. People use it to help them remain calm when stress or anxiety starts to climb. They are tuned into their mind and body, and they can identify triggers. Stopping the problem early on so it doesn't get worse is a great way to get a handle on the situation. The breathing techniques help the mind focus and they help a person stay calm. It decreases the chance of acting on impulse.

Guided imagery may be a tool the therapist offers. It is a type of relaxation technique in DBT that involves concentrating on certain objects or sounds to remain calm and collected. While you are focusing on that, you are encouraged to clear your mind and think peaceful thoughts. This brings you back into balance instead of struggling with stress or anxiety at that moment.

Accepting yourself and accepting relationships are part of DBT techniques. This can boost self-esteem. When you know your self-worth, you tolerate less from others that may be toxic or taking advantage of you. With self-esteem, you can focus on the life you want and what you must do to achieve it. Individuals are less likely to engage in self-harm when they accept themselves and have self-confidence.

The Benefits of Practicing Mindfulness

The benefits with mindfulness are plentiful, and that is why therapists tend to start with it when it comes to ways to implement change. A person can go through their day and not focus on anything around them. They simply are thinking of everything under the sun. Mindfulness puts someone in the present and it helps them use their senses to experience life instead of it just taking place. This boosts a person's mood and that helps create a mind that is calmer and happier.

Mindfulness gives someone the ability to explore their emotions and get comfortable with them. It gives them the opportunity to base responses and behaviors based on facts and information rather than doing so impulsively. Being mindful can help situations get taken care of rather than being avoided or made worse.

Self-harm is typically the result of feeling out of control. With mindfulness, a person is less likely to relapse to those behaviors. They use the tools and coping skills they must work through the emotions and the situation. Being mindful boosts self-esteem because the person is objective and non-judgmental.

Both depression and anxiety are reduced when a person is mindful. This can help them feel better mentally and physically. The practice helps a person reduce stress too, especially chronic stressors. It can reduce insomnia and help a person sleep better than before. Waking up refreshed after a great night of sleep can help someone start the day with a positive attitude.

Physical pain including headaches and abdominal pain can be reduced with mindfulness. Studies indicate it can play a role in controlling the risk of high blood pressure and heart disease too.

Incorporating Mindfulness into Daily Life

Practicing mindfulness as often as you can makes it part of your thinking process and behaviors. It soon gets incorporated not your daily routine and what you take part in with your life. Being in the present moment brings focus to what is taking place. Focusing on feeling good and being in the best mood possible is encouraged.

Use the senses to pay attention to the body. How do you feel in certain locations or around certain people? Your goal should be to find people and places that boost your mood, and you feel secure. If there are triggers, working through them and perhaps even ending relationships that are toxic can help you focus on the better aspects in your life.

Accepting and exploring emotions is a great way to incorporate mindfulness into daily life. The goal is to use reasonable mind and wise mind to help you through all scenarios. Emotional mind is a good resource if you don't let the emotions take control. If you feel like they are, use the techniques and tools taught in treatment to take that control. Skills are going to help you change the way you react and behave versus how you used to. The positive reinforcement of those better actions and behaviors will motivate you to continue with them.

Separate your perceptions from reality. There is a huge difference between the two, and you must draw a line in the road. Question WHY You think a certain way. What facts do you have to back that up? You will discover concepts you always accepted as truth were merely perceptions. Changing what you accept at face value will help you remain in control of emotions, set boundaries, and make decisions.

Observe yourself through the lens of objectivity. What did you do well? What can you do better next time? When you analyze, hold yourself accountable but also be forgiving. There is no judging with mindfulness. Don't get caught up in the cycle of beating yourself up for doing this instead of that. Use the situations as learning experiences and move on.

The 5 senses can be used to help someone stay focused and use mindfulness. You can't explore all the senses if your mind is racing all over the place. Being present in the moment and using those senses to help you explore the situation and environment can be a great resource.

DBT is a work in progress and any movement forward should be seen as a victory. If you feel like you didn't rely on your skills and techniques enough, practice through role-playing so you can put them into play when you need to next time.

CHAPTER EIGHT

EMOTION REGULATION IN DBT

Controlling and understanding emotions is a big part of DBT and how successful it is for treatment. Each of us has an array of emotions. How we identify them, respond to them, and convey them varies. Some people have healthy ways of working through emotions. Others are in a cycle of behaviors that isn't good for them physically or mentally.

DBT works on validating emotions but also identifying those that need to change. In therapy, this is referred to as emotion regulation. Not all emotions are healthy, or they aren't shared properly. For example, a person may be upset but they are behaving in a way that says they are angry instead. Someone that doesn't want to argue may agree when they are feeling anxious and letdown.

DBT teaches patients the value of emotions and that they do have a place. It gives them the security to explore the emotions they feel and then dig into why they feel a certain way. Next, they are challenged to remove emotions from their behavior that doesn't serve them well.

We don't all feel emotions the same way. For those with mental health concerns and other ailments, they can feel them intensely. This is why they struggle when there is a challenging situation taking place. The therapist will use DBT to help a patient identify and label the emotions they feel.

Understanding Emotion Regulation

With Emotion Regulation, a person learns how to identify and work through their emotions using health skills and techniques taught with DBT. Emotional responses tend to be subconscious, but they don't always serve our best interests. When a person is mindful, they learn to be aware of emotions and use them effectively.

Emotions can help someone feel happy and content. They can also tell someone that situations or certain people aren't healthy for them based on the emotions they create. It isn't a sign of weakness if you identify your emotions and share them with others to set boundaries or have open communication.

Bringing mindfulness and awareness to the equation, a person can regulate their emotions throughout the day. The small things beyond their control such as traffic or a rude customer don't ruin the day for them. They don't respond hastily and get angry which only makes those types of situations worse.

Being in control of emotions rather than controlled by them is the opposite outcome for many going through DBT. They use Emotion Regulation to help end impulsive thoughts and behaviors. They use it to reduce stress, anxiety, and depression.

Education

Through therapy, patients learn that emotions are a part of humans. They are part of survival, and they are linked to evolution over time. We wouldn't be able to survive if we didn't experience emotions. Why is it hard to change our emotions and behaviors to them? They are hardwired into our brains.

We act and react in certain ways due to what we have learned and what we have experienced. Some of those experiences and teachings we remember. Others are locked away in our subconscious. We struggle to know the "why" behind them, but they do influence our emotions.

Finding the balance with emotions is essential. If you are void of them, you don't express how you feel or what you are going through. If you are too sensitive, everything can turn into a big ordeal for you to handle. From a social impact perspective, you must find a way to share what you need to without letting it overwhelm you. That can be taught through DBT.

Mindfulness and Emotions

We have talked about mindfulness, but it warrants adding here too about emotions specifically. Learning to identify and label our emotions gives us power over them. It gives us a chance to evaluate before we react. As we are identifying and evaluating them, we can reduce the effects they have on us.

It isn't uncommon to experience a variety of emotions at the same time over a given situation. When you break them down, try to identify them as primary or secondary. For example, anger can be the primary emotion you feel now. Some of the secondary emotions that may coincide with anger include hurt and disappointment.

Being mindful of emotions reduces the amount of control they have over us. You don't want to feel like you have tunnel vision, you can't focus on anything but those emotions because of it. Self-care is a big part of reducing the power emotions have over you, especially the negative ones.

Studies indicate taking care of the following can assist you with changing emotions and replacing them with positive ones. Self-care can help you have more positive emotions in your life than negative ones. We all have situations that will make us sad or angry. We can't be happy and upbeat all the time. The level the negative emotions affect a person depends on how well they take care of themselves and their perceptions.

Areas of self-care to focus on include:

• Avoid using substances that can alter your mood and emotions. This includes drugs and alcohol.
• Eat healthy meals and focus on reasonable portions of food
• Engage in daily exercise to feel good physically and mentally.
• Get enough sleep each night.
• Treat any physical illnesses or pain with the help of your primary care physician.

Studies also show when we take part in activities we enjoy and positive experiences, it inflates our mood. It reduces the risk of negative emotions being a dark shadow over us. DBT teaches you to deliberately target activities that bring out the best emotions for you. This includes being selective of the people you spent time around.

Certain people may evoke negative emotions for you based on the relationship you have with them. Other people may evoke positive emotions because of how much you enjoy being around them. Don't let people that zap you of feeling good take up your time. Set boundaries and decide if those relationships are worth salvaging or if it is time for them to end.

Coping Skills

DBT teaches coping skills to help you keep your emotions under control when you are in a stressful situation. This doesn't mean you don't feel them or explore them. What it means is you don't base your behaviors off of those emotions. Such coping skills can help you change your behavior and focus on better ways to handle that situation.

In therapy, you may be asked to role play and use those coping skills. You may be given a scenario, and you share how you can respond better than you used to. The reason behind this is to arm you with valuable skills and techniques you can use when you are under stress. Reaching for those coping skills and putting them in place rather than regressing is important.

Engaging in problem-solving behaviors rather than emotion-based behaviors is a sign of success with DBT. You must learn to go from emotional mind to reasonable mind with very little time in between the two concepts.

Emotion Regulation Module

Educating patients about emotions and how to deal with them in a healthy way is part of the Emotion Regulation Module. Not only does it teach how to change emotions, but it also focuses on reducing how vulnerable someone is to certain emotions or triggers that cause that specific emotion.

The module teaches how emotions work, why we feel them, and how to accept them. It discusses both primary and secondary emotions and what they mean. Correctly identifying emotions and categorizing them gives a person a chance to reflect and be objective. It also gives them control over emotions rather than being vulnerable and at a loss with them.

When a person experiences emotional distress, they have two choices. They can either be mindful with it or they can be judgmental. When they are mindful, they are aware of their feelings, and they pay attention to their 5 senses. They look at facts and use that information to help them accept what is going on at that moment. This is the process we aim for with DBT.

When someone is judgmental, there is no value from it. They are relying on how they perceive something and their assumptions. They may be comparing it to other situations based on triggers. They are assessing value through perceptions or what they think other people will think. This can increase anxiety and stress and make the problem worse.

Judgment often makes a person feel ashamed of how they feel and what they think. This is where the fight or flight comes in, and they may act aggressively or strive to avoid the situation rather than deal with it. When a person shuts down like that, it alters the mood for the worst.

With mindfulness in the works, Emotion Regulation helps the individual work through the situation and remain in control. Sometimes, it involves radical acceptance, even when the person doesn't like the facts or the way it makes them feel. Considering the opposite action and how to flip it around to something positive is a great part of this module that therapists teach their patients. Breathing techniques and staying in the moment help a person work through it, not avoid it.

Action Steps

Through DBT, a patient should address and act steps. They are part of the overall goals within the treatment plan. These actions encourage them to be aware and mindful of their emotions and work through them. Opposite Action is an activity designed to help someone switch their emotions around.

For example, when a patient is feeling anxious, what activity can they choose to engage in that will cause them to experience calming emotions? If a patient is sad, what activities can they engage in that will make them happy? The goal of this is to replace negative emotions with positive emotions.

Self-care is often discussed in therapy relating to action steps and Emotion Regulation. Too many people feel self-care isn't necessary. They don't make time for it because they are too busy doing things for everyone else. Others feel guilty for taking part in it, they think it is selfish. Understanding the value self-care brings for a person's mind and body is important to discuss in therapy.

The Role of Emotion Regulation in DBT

The role of emotion regulation in DBT aids to empower people so they can make healthier choices with actions and behaviors. It is designed to boost mood through awareness. Once a person realizes the negative emotions take away from the life they want, they can accept them and work to change them.

A loss of control can cause someone's mind to spin. They can't focus and they either fight or flight and that doesn't resolve anything. That may be the cycle they have known their entire life. With Emotion Regulation in DBT, that stops in its tracks and no longer negatively affects that person in all aspects of their life. Instead, they look for solutions with positive consequences.

We all experience negative emotions, and that can cause irritability and sadness. When those negative emotions are allowed to manifest, it can be hard to pull yourself out of that hole. You may not recognize what is happening because it is such a part of your daily routine. Through Emotional Regulation in DBT, reducing the negative emotions and their impact makes room for boosting a person's mood and positive emotions.

Building positive emotional experiences changes the dynamics in a person's world. It often means changing the script through awareness. Which people make you feel supported and safe? Which people do you have relationships with that seem to always evoke negative emotions for you? The triggers of people, places, and more must be identified.

Being mindful of your behaviors and the impact they have on how you feel and what you do is important. You can't make decisions in the heat of the moment. You can make decisions based on your fears or perceptions. This form of DBT helps with exploring facts and looking at problem-solving options.

With Emotion Regulation, a person can rely on the skills and techniques provided in therapy. They can use DBT to self-regulate thoughts and behaviors based on these proven methods. By doing so, they reduce the risk of self-harm or making destructive choices.

Emotion Regulation Techniques used in DBT

A therapist will introduce various Emotion Regulation techniques when DBT is part of treatment. Each of them helps a person understand and work through their emotions for better decisions and behaviors. Identifying and naming emotions as well as dividing them into primary and secondary emotions is a good place for many to start. It introduces the concept and provides the patient with simple exercises.

The therapist may ask the patient to journal their emotions and put them into categories for the following week. They can discuss them at the next session. This can help the therapist see any emerging patterns of emotions too. This can open up the discussion of what is going on in their life that is bringing on each of the emotions they experienced.

Descriptive terms are encouraged with Emotion Regulation techniques to identify the emotions. The therapist will give examples because it is very important to really know what the emotion is and then examine what is behind it.

Coping skills are introduced because now you have identified these emotions, and you need to know what to do with them. Mindfulness in the moment and identifying emotions give you time to explore options instead of being impulsive. Problem-solving skills and interpersonal skills are techniques of DBT through skills learning that help a patient move through these steps.

Identifying triggers and why they create positive or negative emotions for the person is important. Trauma and other variables can make certain locations, situations, or people a trigger. The goal of DBT is to recognize how you feel and accept it, but also to see what you can do to change it. Reducing negative emotions and replacing them with positive ones means changing how you think and how you behave.

What is the story you tell yourself? Is that aligning with the truth and the facts? One of the realizations with Emotion Regulation techniques is so much of what we think, and feel is based on perceptions or what we have been exposed to rather than the truth. Mindfulness makes questioning everything a process your mind goes through and that helps to weed out anything that isn't based on fact.

Self-talk and self-soothing are taught in DBT to guide someone through scenarios, so they don't turn into a crisis. Ask questions, focus on breathing techniques, and visualize an image or sound that makes you calm are all techniques a person can implement as they need to. These skills are important and a great way to pave the path to healthier thinking and better moods.

Therapists encourage situation selection, choosing events and locations that encourage positive moods and emotions. Where you go and who you spend time with should be selected carefully. You can't always make that choice though. For example, if traffic is crawling and that is the only route, you must deal with the slow-moving process.

There can be people around you or a work environment you aren't thrilled with. You may have to be around those people, but you can limit that exposure and how they affect you emotionally. It may be time to have a discussion with your employer about how you feel. If they won't make changes to help with improvements, it may be time to find a different place to work. Your mental and physical well-being is worth far more than a paycheck!

Situation modification is a technique you can put in motion too with DBT and Emotion Regulation. If you feel there is tension building when you talk to someone, tell them that you want to take a break and have some time to think about it and you will discuss it with them later. You can set boundaries and be assertive without being disrespectful. You don't want it to escalate to a heated argument, that isn't going to resolve anything.

Attention deployment is a technique that can work in certain situations. Some feel this contradicts DBT which tells you to be mindful and be present. That isn't what attention deployment is about though. For example, you may avoid going to the gym for exercise because you are focused on others watching you or your weight. With this technique, you can focus on your health, boosting your mood, and the benefits you get from the gym and not the negative you were initially thinking about.

Cognitive reappraisal helps you change the way you see a situation. There is always something to be thankful for. There is always a silver lining. Retrain your mind with DBT to think about the positive. What opportunity does it present? What freedom does it bring? What did you learn from that experience? Remove the negative thoughts of what is in the way and focus on what you will do to accomplish your goals!

Response modulation is how you express your emotions and then let them go. You don't give them the power to control you. Don't be judgmental so you can forgive yourself and others where you need to. Everyone makes mistakes and you can discuss them and move on. If someone has hurt you or upset you, they need to know that. You don't have to keep that information to yourself. If they make the choice to continue once they know how they make you feel, it may be time to end that relationship or drastically reduce the interactions with them.

The Benefits of Mastering Emotion Regulation

There are amazing benefits of mastering Emotion Regulation. Most people that have this type of DBT feel that it has changed how they see themselves and how they interact with others. It gives them the freedom to explore their emotions and they work through them. They are proud that they no longer act impulsively or avoid situations. They like the positive outcomes, and they can let go of fear and feelings of shame associated with emotions.

Feeling in control over decisions and knowing that they are based on proven problem-solving methods and facts is a great feeling. A person can feel confident in the decisions and choices they made. They are consciously focused on a solution, and they don't make the problem worse.

With effective Emotion Regulation, a person is happier. Symptoms of depression, insomnia, stress, and anxiety are reduced or eliminated. Experiencing a better mood and positive emotions gives a person the chance to be their genuine self. They often experience more self-confidence, and they take part in self-care activities more than they used to.

The overall well-being of a person improves with these types of skills. They experience less conflict and less stress in their life. They have the tools they need to handle any situation as it comes along. They are establishing boundaries in a healthy way too instead of being mad or upset with other people each time there is a conflict.

Being satisfied at work is a big part of life, and with these skills, a person can interact better. They don't have to be friends with each person they work with, but they don't take differences in personality personally.

They can work out conflicts with the boss, other employees, and customers without being impulsive or engaging in behaviors that will get them into trouble.

Enriched relationships with others are a great outcome from mastering Emotion Regulation. Individuals can use DBT to end the cycle of relationships that aren't healthy for them to be involved with. They can clearly share their feelings and thoughts. They can also set boundaries and focus on facts rather than perceptions. All of this helps them create strong bonds with people they want to have long-term relationships with.

Developing an Emotion Regulation Plan with DBT

The Emotion Regulation plan with DBT created for someone is specific to their needs and the cycle of behaviors. The therapist will give them specific exercises to take part in. They will schedule certain skill training to give them tools assessments and discussions show they may lack. This includes those relating to coping, problem-solving, and communication.

Focusing on positive emotions and working to reduce or eliminate the negative ones is part of this plan. When a person thinks positively and feels positive emotions, they are happier and have fewer issues mentally and physically. Focusing on mindfulness and identifying the facts of a situation are involved with this plan.

For those that tend to be impulsive, the therapist will ask them to make a list of their emotions and why they feel that way. Next, they will create a list of possible pros and cons for selected options on the table. The goal is to get them to see the best behavior and the best possible outcome rather than acting impulsively with self-harm, being angry, and other negative possibilities.

Encouraging a healthy lifestyle including getting enough sleep, organizing time, and self-care are part of an Emotion Regulation plan. Being mindful of taking part in events and being around people that bring out the best emotions is encouraged. Eating a balanced diet and daily exercise are part of this treatment plan. The mind and body will be calmer and healthier by doing so.

Staying organized reduces stress and anxiety, and that encourages positive emotions Being realistic about what is going to get done and what isn't is important. Too many things on your to do list is setting yourself up to fail, and that brings negative emotions with it. Positive affirmations and focusing on the good things improve a person's mindset. It gives them the motivation to keep going when they face challenges.

When a person is often influenced by negative emotions, the therapist may implement a technique into the treatment plan with DBT to transpose this. It is known as Opposite to Emotion Action, and it is designed to help someone see the opposite emotion of what they feel. What can then be done to change that to reach that opposite? How can a harmful emotion become helpful?

Anger is one of the emotions that fall into this category. Someone that reacts in anger to situations is going to isolate themselves from relationships. They may struggle to keep a job. People don't like to be around someone that can fly off the handle over small things. What is the path the patient can take to turn that anger into something they can work through to reach a positive emotion? That specific path they follow is created with the therapist.

What can you do more of that you know will bring you positive emotions? A common exercise is for the therapist to ask the patient to make a list of things that make them feel good. This can include anything healthy for them such as taking a walk after dinner and spending time with their children. The therapist will encourage them to take part in items on that list each week to help promote positive emotions and a better mood.

Sometimes, a patient must learn to ride the wave with their emotions. This means that positive emotions aren't going to last every single day. It also means that a negative emotion isn't the end of the world. It will pass and things can get back in balance. There are twists and turns every single day with emotions and the circumstances that evoke them. We don't have control over what all goes on, but we can strive to consciously control how we react to it and the behaviors we engage in.

Releasing negative emotions takes place once we accept them. We don't have to like them, but we do have to work through them. That is a part of a treatment plan with DBT. Being present in the moment and working through it based on facts and not perceptions prevent emotions from taking control. Negative emotions are an opportunity to change what we engage in to reduce them.

Not all of the pieces of Emotion Regulation may be in the treatment plan to start with. The therapist doesn't want the patient to get overwhelmed. As they learn skills and practice the techniques, additional options may be added to the treatment plan. If certain techniques aren't working for someone, the therapist may swap them in the treatment plan to see if a positive outcome is created by doing so. It all depends on the specific needs of the patient and what they respond best with using DBT.

CHAPTER NINE

INTERPERSONAL EFFECTIVENESS IN DBT

Great relationships based on trust, understanding, and boundaries should be the cornerstone of who you interact with. DBT teaches how to enhance your relationships and let go of cycles that get in the way of creating them. Low self-esteem, poor communication skills, and a lack of problem-solving skills get in the way of great relationships. This type of therapy offers skills and techniques to help change all of that.

Healthy relationships give people a chance to ask questions, share information, and safely discuss their emotions. They don't have to hide things or avoid conversations because they worry about how the other party will react. For many patients in DBT, they haven't always faced relationship issues head-on. They may be the one that acts out in anger or shuts down and that puts up a wall between themselves and others.

With interpersonal effectiveness methods in the DBT plan for treatment, a person can replace behaviors that don't serve them well with those that will. This is part of what makes someone a great leader. Keep will do what you ask when you do so in a respectful manner. They aren't afraid to make mistakes or ask questions because they know they have supported no matter what.

Understanding Interpersonal Effectiveness

Social skills help someone feel a sense of belonging when they interact with others. They don't want to feel out of place when they show up for an event or they approach someone. They want to feel that they have just as much value as anyone else in that room. DBT can help someone overcome feelings and behaviors that could be socially unacceptable.

The ability to communicate clearly and honestly is important. It affects your relationships with your family, friends, people you work with, and how people feel about you when they meet you. It is fine to express your opinion on topics if you also listen and respect the opinions of others.

There is a difference between opinion and fact so being mindful of that is important.

Being aware of what you want from a relationship and what the other person wants from it is important. Don't worry if that changes with time though. For example, you both may wish to be friends. As you spend more time together though, it could move into a romantic relationship.

Caring about other people is a part of sharing emotions. Through DBT, a person can learn how to express that. We should never assume other people know how we feel about them. We should take the time to tell them. It does mean being vulnerable at times, but it is the healthy way to progress in relationships.

The ability to collaborate with others and work with them is essential and a lifestyle to strive for. Everyone has strengths and weaknesses they bring with them. In a group effort, how can you promote your strengths, and everyone benefits from them? Where can you work to improve so your weaknesses aren't holding anything back?

Effective skills for conflict management and resolution are a healthy part of relationships. You aren't always going to agree with someone you live with. You aren't always going to agree with your romantic partner. There will be times at work when you don't get along with someone. How you use the interpersonal skills you have learned in DBT will guide you to find the best solution to resolve them without anger, fear, or anxiety.

The Role of Interpersonal Effectiveness in DBT

The role of interpersonal effectiveness in DBT is to create healthy relationships. People have different thoughts, ideals, and concepts that shape who they are. Being able to see the world through the eyes of someone else is a great experience. When they feel comfortable opening to you, it can be a learning moment! Boundaries must be in place by both parties and enforced for the relationship to be healthy. If one party is taking advantage of the other or being toxic, the relationship won't grow.

With DBT, a person gets to objectively examine both sides of this coin. Are they being respectful in relationships of the thoughts and feelings of others? Do they listen when someone shares their thoughts and emotions? Do they work to resolve conflict or just try to get their own way?

On the flip side of that, someone must evaluate relationships. Is it mutually beneficial? Does it create a feeling of safety and belonging with that person? Sometimes, the decision is made in therapy that some relationships must come to an end for the well-being of the patient. The therapist can help them to come to this conclusion and process the loss.

There are 3 goals with interpersonal effectiveness:

- Objective effectiveness
- Relationship effectiveness
- Self-respect effectiveness

The role of the therapist is to teach each element and share with the patient how they can implement DBT into their own life. A pattern of failed relationships is a sign something must change in one or more of these areas to engage in better relationships.

Being a great listener and being flexible will go a long way with interpersonal relationships. DBT shows a person how to do this and still maintain their values. Too often, we only partially listen because we want to dive in and share what we think or what we want to say. Give the other party the chance to talk without being interrupted. This is a great skill to master, and you can often learn plenty by doing so.

Life is rarely black and white when it comes to relationships. Try to be flexible and see how well that works out. The other party can benefit from it, and they will respect you seeing it from their point of view and finding some middle ground. They will do the same for you when an issue arises later, and you need them to be flexible. Relationships are about give and take.

Interpersonal Effectiveness Techniques used in DBT

There are plenty of interpersonal effectiveness techniques a person can gain through DBT. They can be used for all types of relationships and help someone feel more confident socially.

Learning to empathize with others is a great technique. This doesn't mean you give people a free pass to treat you how they desire. Instead, it means you try to see where they are coming from. Rather than taking it personally that they behaved a certain way, you give them a chance to explain and work through their issues.

Mindfulness is a great technique of DBT to use for interpersonal effectiveness. Being in the moment and sharing information or just having a good laugh with someone is a way to boost your mood and relax. Learning to describe how you feel and share your emotions can help other people see where you are coming from.

How you treat people and how you behave set the tone for the relationship. If they can't trust you to remain calm and cool when there is a conflict, it can destroy the relationship. They may choose not to be around you. In DBT, a person learns how to effectively share emotions and that helps prevent small problems from being blown out of proportion.

The Benefits of Improving Interpersonal Skills

There are several benefits of improving interpersonal skills through DBT. It gives people a chance to stop putting up walls that destroy their relationships. It is an opportunity to communicate better and think before you speak. It gives someone a chance to practice empathy and that can salvage a relationship.

A person using effective interpersonal skills through DBT will have a feeling of pride and self-respect in the relationships they take part in.

They find ways to balance the wants and needs of the relationship with priorities.

Ineffective communication is a barrier, and it creates a ripple effect. So many conflicts can be avoided with proper communication skills and problem-solving skills. Understanding what the other person is sharing and what they need from the relationship is important. We must see it from our point of view but also from theirs for it to work.

It is important to understand effective interpersonal skills is more than just what you say. Your verbal communication skills should be powerful, but make sure you aren't lagging when it comes to your non-verbal communication skills too. Do you make eye contact with people? Do you smile at them when you walk by and say hello? Don't wait for someone else to always make that first move, be confident in your actions to be the one to engage with them!

Developing an Interpersonal Effectiveness Plan with DBT

The interpersonal effectiveness plan with DBT created for someone depends on many variables. Their communication style and any concerns must be addressed. The therapist would like to set specific goals with this and make sure the behaviors and actions of the person will align with those goals. Teaching someone coping skills, how to explore their emotions, and how to problem-solve are often part of such a treatment plan with DBT.

Creating a positive outlook for life and a solution for problems as they arise is often part of an interpersonal effectiveness plan with DBT. Those that look at the positive options instead of the negative ones tend to get people gravitating toward them. They like that energy and they like the motivation behind it. This also helps someone feel in control because they are working towards a goal that brings a positive outcome with it.

Some patients need to be more assertive in their relationships. People tend to take advantage of them and walk all over them. They tend to take on too many tasks because they don't want to tell anyone no. Role-playing in the sessions can help them feel better about saying no and setting boundaries without getting into an argument. Such tools will help someone feel empowered and boosts self-esteem.

Since a lack of effective skills holds a person back socially, the focus of the treatment will always be to fill in the gaps they have. The therapist can gather this information through discussions and assessments. They can help them stop avoiding interactions or feeling uneasy about themselves through DBT methods.

Some of the questions a person is encouraged to ask themselves and reflect upon when it comes to relationships include:

- **What do you want in this relationship?**
- **How do you ask for what you want and convey your emotions?**

- How do you negotiate conflicts to promote an outcome all involved accept?
- Are you gathering information and relying on facts instead of perceptions?
- Are you saying no in a way that protects the relationship?

Are you behaving ethically and in conjunction with your core values?

CHAPTER TEN

DISTRESS TOLERANCE IN DBT

Distress tolerance is a huge piece for changes in behavior through DBT. This model involves identifying the difference between something that makes them uncomfortable and an actual crisis. The skills a person uses when they feel they are in crisis mode ensure the situation doesn't get worse.

The situation is seen at face value, objectively. Emotions aren't going to run the show! What is defined as a crisis vs. an uncomfortable situation? A crisis has certain elements:

- Induces high amounts of stress
- Possibility of dire outcomes
- Short-term situation
- Urge to find an immediate solution to reduce the stress

Understanding Distress Tolerance

The concept of Distress Tolerance takes time to wrap your head around. In therapy, the therapist will offer various exercises and learning methods where this can be applied. In simplest terms, it is the ability a person must manage their emotions during times of distress.

When a person can't do that, they often struggle with impulses and behaviors that could get them into trouble or make a problem worse. They may experience insomnia, issues with anxiety, or stress. They may experience depression if they can't find a way to boost their mood.

DBT promotes healthy Distress Tolerance so a person can accept how they feel but not allow it to control them. Being mindful of the situation and working through emotions can help someone remain in control no matter what is going on around them. When uncomfortable emotions arise, a person may decide to fight, or they may avoid it altogether. DBT encourages them to assess what is really going on and get the facts, not just perceptions.

The 3 main emotions when a person doesn't do well with distress are being:

- **Mad**
- **Sad**
- **Scared**

Identifying triggers and emotions but putting them in perspective helps to control distress. With Distress Intolerance skills learned from DBT, a person can still move forward when they face uncomfortable situations. They don't let sadness or anger or fear control what they will do next.

The Role of Distress Tolerance in DBT
The overall role of distress tolerance in DBT is to handle a crisis. Learning to accept reality rather than distorting it helps a person regain control. Relying on coping skills and problem-solving skills, they can look at the pros and cons of a situation and their choices for how to react. They can also explore and identify their emotions tied to that crisis.

When a person is in a crisis, they tend to regress to previous behaviors. This can include self-harm or suicidal thoughts. With DBT, and specifically the element of distress tolerance, a person is less likely to slip back into those negative behaviors. Instead, they have the skills and techniques they need to handle it better.

Distress Tolerance Techniques used in DBT
The role of the therapist is to give the patient several techniques they can incorporate when they are in crisis mode. Practicing these techniques in role-playing exercises means the patient can recall them when they need them. Such techniques include:

- ACCEPTS
- STOP
- TIPS

ACCEPTS
A- Activities, engage in what makes you happy
C – Contributing, do something for others or your community
C- Comparisons, remember when things were worse for you than they are now
E – Emotions, identify your emotions and focus on the positive ones
P- Push it away, visualize putting the problem on a shelf
T – Thoughts, focus on thoughts that are helpful and encourage positive behaviors
S – Sensations, use the 5 senses and focus on how you feel with each of them
STOP
S- Stop what you are doing and try to be calm and relaxed, use breathing techniques
T – Take a step away from the situation, analyze it for what it is objectively
O – Observe, what is going on around you
P – Proceed in a mindful fashion, be aware

TIP

T – Tip the temperature of your face, slash it with cold water
I – Intense exercise, for at least 20 minutes
P – Paced breathing, focus on your breathing and focus on relaxing your muscle groups

The Benefits of Mastering Distress Tolerance

There are many benefits a person can gain when they master distress tolerance. They won't make a situation worse due to their behaviors or the actions they took. They will feel in control, despite the crisis at hand. They will gain confidence using their tools and skills to help them work through the situation.

Their emotions won't take over and cause them to regress to behaviors that aren't positive. Instead, they can identify those emotions and work through them. Even though they have a crisis going on, they can face it head-on and tackle it with a solution that works best and helps them with a healthy outcome.

Mastering distress tolerance helps reduce the stress involved with a crisis. A person can gain some relief as they work through the process using proper skills and techniques. The risk of them acting impulsively or engaging in self-harm is significantly reduced. The person can accept reality for what it is, even if they don't like it.

Rather than ignoring the problem or avoiding dealing with it, they put their knowledge into play. They rely on DBT to help them work through the crisis to de-escalate it. They don't give it room to grow, they put out the fire. Often, they can start to put it out when there is just smoke, no flames yet! Following this module means the person isn't going to struggle and suffer, they are solution-driven.

Developing a Distress Tolerance Plan with DBT

Creating a specific Distress Tolerance Plan with DBT and your therapist is a big step forward. Following that plan and implementing it everywhere you can in your life is going to help you change your outlook on life. It is going to help you improve physically and mentally.

Each of these concepts must be included in a quality Distress Tolerance plan relying on DBT.

- ACCEPTS
- STOP
- TIPS

Each of them is fully described earlier in this chapter. To take it to the next level, each component of those concepts must be discussed in therapy. The patient should give input about what they feel each of them means and how they can apply them. The therapist can guide and encourage them, but they should give the patient an opportunity to come to conclusions on what to do and the way to do it for their goals.

Decision-making and problem-solving are part of this type of plan too. The therapist should work with the patient to learn how to make pro and con lists before making decisions. They should be detailed and apply to the specific situation taking place. This tool reduces the risk of someone acting impulsively and making the problem worse than it was. The time it takes to create those lists involves thinking and calming down.

Using the senses is something most of us take for granted. We hear, see, smell, taste, and touch. If we aren't mindful though, we can do those things on autopilot and not gain value from them. Tuning into the senses is a wonderful concept to include in a Distress Tolerance plan. Not only does it give you depth with your thinking, but it helps the mind and body relax.

CONCLUSION

Dialect Behavior Therapy has proven to help patients in areas where other forms of therapy couldn't get them to the finish line. It can be used alone, or it can be combined with other forms of therapy. It is a challenge to work with such patients as they often need plenty of encouragement, support, and the therapy continues for quite some time.

The speed of progress depends on the patient and their needs. The role of the therapist is to encourage them but to also give them the security they need and the time they need to move at a pace they are comfortable with.

DBT offers powerful skills and techniques a patient can use for the remainder of their life. So many patients wish they had received DBT years before they did because of the value it brought to their quality of life. It is an effective form of therapy and includes individual sessions, group sessions, and skills training.

The biggest difference with DBT and other forms of therapy is the dialect. This is the piece that help so many patients get over the humps and see the view on the other side. They enjoy life to the fullest when they can control their emotions and behaviors. Instead of avoiding situations and avoiding social outings, they can embrace those connections.

DBT explores 4 stages. They often overlap, and there is no set timeframe for each of them it all depends on the needs of the patient. The therapist is aware of the stage the patient is in, and that influences the treatment plan and other variables.

- Behavior Stabilization
- Reduce trauma-related symptoms
- Day to day behaviors
- Deeper exploration

Behavior Stabilization

The first order of business in therapy is to stabilize behavior. The safety of the patient is a priority. Any signs or symptoms of self-harm or suicidal thoughts must be addressed. They are taken seriously as these can be life-threatening behaviors with dire consequences. If the therapist doesn't think outpatient services are enough, they may encourage hospitalization for the patient.

Skills are introduced in this first stage of DBT. They include coping skills to help someone work through feelings and a crisis. Problem-solving skills are also taught to give them options for future decisions.

Reduce Trauma-Related Symptoms

Stage 2 is a time for discussions about any trauma a person remembers. It may be resent, or it may be childhood issues they are struggling with. Traumatic emotional events and PTSD may require some additional steps for the therapist to go through with the patient.

As the discussions continue about the trauma and the details involved, it can cause emotions to escalate. The patient is encouraged to talk about how they feel and why they feel that way. They are encouraged to discuss how they can change those negatively charged emotions and replace them with a better option.

Day to Day Behaviors

Stage 3 focuses on day-to-day behaviors. How are they implementing the skills and techniques they have learned in therapy to their situation? What is improving? What are they still struggling with? How are they going to reach the established goals? Their daily behaviors are evaluated when they come in for therapy sessions.

The goal is living life to the fullest and being happy. The focus is on positive choices that promote healthy emotions. Learning to trust yourself and the decisions you make is important. It boosts confidence and helps with establishing boundaries. Reaching individual goals is satisfying and it shows personal growth.

Deeper Exploration

In stage 4, a patient is ready to end therapy. They have reached goals, and they feel confident with how to use skills and resources. They have changed behaviors and explored their emotions. They understand the value these methods bring to the lifestyle they desire.

A deeper understanding of who they are as a person and where they plan to be in the future is explored. They still focus on being mindful and in the moment, but also how what they do today is going to assist them in the future. It can be a breath of fresh air when you can rely on your intuition because you can take what you feel and know it is true and not just a perception.

It is important to understand these stages of DBT aren't always chronological. If a patient needs to repeat a stage, there is no judgment and it is implemented. For example, if a patient is in stage 2 but then starts to exhibit symptoms of self-harm, the shift is back to stage one. Once the behavior is stabilized again, the stages can progress forward.

Why DBT?

Many therapists include DBT in treatment plans for patients. They understand CBT isn't always enough for someone to thrive. They have the desire to collaborate and teach because they want people to have a chance to change their lives. They take on the challenges of working with people from all walks of life and with various concerns. This includes mental health situations and self-harm crisis situations.

A therapist understands with encouragement and the right tools/techniques, a person can transform things in their life. They know DBT is proven to work, and they are dedicated to using their experience and training to reach individuals and help them successfully achieve the goals of their treatment plan.

There is plenty to juggle when offering DBT therapy. The stages a person goes through often intertwine. Validating feelings, emotions, and behaviors is a big part of helping them see the reality of the situation. Encouraging them to be mindful in each aspect of what they think and do is an important skill to teach. DBT is worth it, and most therapists find personal gratification in using it to promote a healthy life for their patients.

The bond between a patient and therapist is strong, they trust each other. Often, therapy lasts at least 6 months, but it can be a year or longer. This amount of time together creates a relationship of mutual trust and respect. The therapist wears many hats, and they are designed to keep the patient interacting and motivated. Treating them as an equal is a big part of the DBT modules and methods.

Lessons Learned from DBT

When the techniques and ideas of DBT are successfully incorporated into the lifestyle and thought patterns of a person, everything changes. They can see things objectively and weigh their options. They can think about how their behaviors influence the outcome, and that encourages them to slow down and think about the options they have before they react.

One of the lessons with DBT is feelings aren't facts. Feelings can be validated but they aren't an excuse for behaviors. They are a conscious choice, and you must choose the choice that serves the best outcome for you. Don't burn bridges everywhere you go because then you end up on a dead end with no options of where to go!

Exploring facts is a big part of DBT and it gives people the security to make decisions and not second-guess themselves. They are confident what they are basing their decisions upon are facts and not perceptions Feelings have value, but you have to use them in a way that helps you through situations instead of you being thrown into the fire when the heat turns up!

Another great lesson, it is encouraged to self-indulge now and then as long as there is value from it. Relax on the weekend instead of filling up your schedule with activities. Save time by planning meals, ordering groceries online, and more! This frees up time for you to do what you enjoy the most!

Self-care is a gift only you can provide, and it can help create a strong foundation for your mental and physical health. You don't want cracks around that foundation to let issues seep through because you didn't pay attention to that foundation! Never feel guilty for taking care of yourself.

Pain and discomfort are part of life, and we all deal with them. However, if you avoid the issue or behave poorly then you can prolong that suffering. This can be a tough lesson for someone with mental health concerns or even poor-self-esteem to grasp and accept. In therapy and through DBT, you will get techniques to help you apply this successfully.

One of the best lessons is therapy is a journey, there is no end destination. Your time seeing a therapist is going to end at some point, but that doesn't mean your therapy does. Self-care, talking to friends or family members, journaling, and using the DBT techniques are all part of therapy. You can rely on them each day and especially in a crisis!

Thank you so much for taking the time to read this book about Dialect Behavior Therapy. This method of treatment may be the best option for someone with a mental health concern, eating disorder, and many other ailments. Working closely with a therapist, they can decide if DBT is a good route to consider. The goal of DBT is to offer the best life possible for each patient.

I encourage you to share your feedback about this book. Doing so will help others decide to read it. I am confident there is plenty of wonderful information in this book about DBT. It may encourage people to get treatment or recommend treatment to a loved one. It is inspiring to know DBT techniques can help transform lives. That is why it is frequently incorporated as a part of effective therapy.

BOOK 3

ACCEPTANCE AND COMMITMENT THERAPY

Emotional Tethers and Psychological Anchors:
Addressing the Deep-Seated Underlying Triggers and
Traumas at the Heart of Addiction

Reflection Page

This area is exclusively yours. Utilize it for monitoring your growth or expressing your thoughts and emotions.

....

....

....

....

....

....

....

....

....

INTRODUCTION

You don't need fame and fortune to live a great life! Most people don't think they do, but they struggle to be as happy as they want to be. They may worry that they aren't living the life they want or being the person they truly would like to be. There are basic human needs that influence us including food, air, and water. Beyond that, though is the desire to be happy and have pleasurable experiences.

None of us are perfect, not even close, but we should be forgiving of our shortcomings and mistakes. If you can look at the person in the mirror and agree you have done your best, then that is worth celebrating. As you learn new concepts and coping skills, you can see your behaviors and thoughts shift in a better direction. You don't have to feel broken or let something that happened before defining who you will be today.

To change all of this and reach your potential with happiness and pleasure, you first must let go of what isn't serving you well. Being bogged down with negative thoughts and behaviors that don't get your desired results will continue to hold you back. Think of these elements as clutter in a room. You must sort through it all and keep what works and discard what doesn't so the room is the way you want it to be! For many individuals, they have no idea where to start to get to their desired goal. Many of us don't know the behaviors and thoughts that hold us back. They are such a part of what we do and how we think, we overlook them. We need an outside person with special training to help us identify them and then create a plan to change them. That is where a therapist can introduce you to new ways of thinking and behaving!

Acceptance and Commitment Therapy is commonly referred to as ACT. This type of psychotherapy involves being mindful and staying focused on what is taking place in the moment. It also involves accepting the feelings and thoughts taking place in the moment. A person using this type of tool must learn to be non-judgmental with what they think and how they feel.

Therapy sessions introduce a variety of coping skills and concepts a person can put into place in their daily life. Role-playing is part of learning, and it is often conducted in the sessions with the therapist. This ensures the patient can implement those tools and concepts in each situation when they need them.

As a person does this, they break cycles of negative thoughts and behaviors that are preventing them from living the life they desire. They can replace those thoughts and behaviors with positive ones. They can determine their actions and thoughts based on the outcome they want.

There is no analysis of life events with ACT. Instead, the focus is on accepting it for what it is. In therapy, patients explore the difference between reality and perceptions. A situation must be accepted for what it is, but misconceptions and distortions must be removed from that equation. The patient must objectively see what is going on at that moment in time.

All of us have difficult experiences in our past that still influence us. This often takes place subconsciously. Facing those experiences and seeing how they shape your thoughts and actions can give you the power you need to change them. At the same time, ACT is designed to help a person be compassionate and forgiving towards themselves.

When we continue to obsess and think about situations outside of our control, they prevent us from being happy. They prevent us from being present in the moment and creating happy memories. They can prevent us from finding peace of mind or joy in much of anything we do.

Mindfully accepting experiences, even those that aren't the most pleasant, helps a person regain control. When a person commits to ACT, they agree to stop living in the past and start living in the moment. This is the only way to have the future you want and a happy life!

ACT involves a conscious decision to override what we feel subconsciously. The therapist will provide the tools to do this. However, only a fraction of the changes occurs in the therapy sessions. Instead, they give you the tools and guidance to apply to your life. When you do so, you become positive. You have the strength and resilience to move forward no matter what life brings your way.

The purpose of ACT is to encourage patients to use it to work through challenging emotions. When those negative emotions continue to control them, they may experience high levels of stress and anxiety. They may avoid situations, or they may engage in behaviors that are impulsive.

Negative thoughts and emotions can make a person fatigued and cause insomnia. ACT helps a person work through their emotions rather than feeling like they are held captive by them the desired outcome is for the patient to use the tools and techniques they learn with ACT to help them heal and focus on the positive.

We can't control all that goes on in our lives or around us. It is how we handle it that influences the quality of life we have. Childhood trauma, PTSD, and other concerns can contribute to mental health issues and many other ailments. ACT is guided by a trained professional to help people come to terms with what is outside of their control and change patterns of behavior that aren't beneficial to them.

The Importance of ACT in Mental Health Treatment

Research indicates ACT can help with mental health treatment. It can reduce the severity of chronic stress and anxiety. It can boost mood, reduce symptoms of depression, and promote healthy sleep patterns.

From a statistical point of view, ACT can reduce relapsing to behaviors that a person was trying to eliminate. When they face a difficult situation, they can rely on the skills and techniques they learned in ACT rather than regressing to their old behaviors. Hospitalization is reduced for those with this type of treatment too because they are less likely to engage in self-harm or continue substance abuse as a form of self-medicating.

Many experts believe ACT can help reduce severe symptoms of many types of mental illness. This means that despite such a diagnosis, the individual still has the means to control their thoughts and behaviors so they can promote a healthy lifestyle through those choices.

From an employer's point of view, ACT can help people focus and have a positive attitude. They are less likely to call off work or quit. They are satisfied with their job, and they aren't going to suffer from burnout because they are taking care of their needs.

Effective treatment with ACT does more than just offer therapy to someone with mental illness. It gives them the tools and skills they need to integrate into society and do well. Through treatment, they can heal and have a better outlook for the future. They can let go of things that are beyond their control and take so much energy from them.

ACT can help people with a variety of mental health concerns. Such issues may be brought on by traumatic events, PTSD, genetics, the environment a person is exposed to, and more. It has been proven to be beneficial for those struggling with:

- Anxiety
- Depression
- Phobias
- Stress
- Substance abuse

A therapist specializing in ACT has advanced training and expertise. It is a good idea to ask about their qualifications if you are specifically interested in ACT. If you have tried other forms of therapy, let them know what didn't work for you and what did. The use of ACT for substance abuse is limited, but it is growing.

There is more research that must be conducted to confirm how much it can help. Often, ACT is introduced when other programs including 12-step programs have failed. Perhaps the person has relapsed several times, and it isn't going to be worth it to go down that same path again. When someone is abusing drugs and/or alcohol to self-medicate, they go to that same scenario and issue again and again.

That is why ACT may help them, it can be a way for them to accept things and move forward rather than compounding the problems by not healing from what has already happened. When you add drug and/or alcohol problems on top of that, it can cause a person to feel alone and miserable. Nobody deserves that quality of life!

Mindful exercises are a huge part of success with ACT. Later in this book, you will view such exercises and see how they can help you change your mindset and change your behaviors.

ACT includes distinct parts that work together to help a patient be positive, accept events and scenarios, and focus on what they can change. In this book, we will explore each of the six processes of ACT and how they work together to help someone accomplish their goals. This type of therapy is exciting because there is scientific proof to back up claims that it works. For many patients, other forms of treatment and therapy didn't create the results they desired. It wasn't until ACT was part of their treatment plan that they noticed they were moving in the right direction.

It takes time for someone to incorporate the concept and processes of ACT to help them. Therapists offering this type of treatment are determined to help each patient reach their full potential. They willingly address the difficult challenges because they know the outcome it can deliver to someone once they reach the other side.

Learning such skills and methods is something a person can carry with them for the remainder of their life. They can use those techniques and coping skills to help them get through any hardship or situation. It helps them keep their eyes on what is taking place now and work for the life they want. They aren't held back by invisible chains due to circumstances beyond their control or events that happened to them in the past.

CHAPTER ONE

WHAT IS ACT AND WHAT VALUE DOES IT OFFER?

While ACT isn't as widely known as other forms of therapy, it doesn't give this concept any less value. A therapist that has training in this area understands what it can bring to a patient. They carefully assess the patient in sessions and with assessment tools to confirm a diagnosis and decide on the treatment plan.

Something that often stands out for patients that talk to a therapist about ACT is they haven't had success with other forms of therapy. They may be skeptical that this time something will work. They may be at their wits end trying to find a solution. Sometimes, these individuals have heard about ACT from someone they know or through their own research.

They specifically looked for a therapist in their area offering ACT so they could inquire about it. For others, luck is on their side because they make an appointment with a therapist who just so happens to be trained in ACT. The therapist sees the value this process could bring to that individual, so they discuss it as a means of treatment.

There are times when a therapist will refer a patient to another therapist. While the first one doesn't have ACT certification, they are aware of what the treatment offers. When they have a patient that isn't responding well to other therapies or one, they feel would really do well with ACT, they aren't going to waste precious time. They will likely give them a referral to the therapist that can help them the most.

Information about ACT continues to spread, and the outcome is exciting. The various scientific studies and testing have concluded ACT can offer tremendous value to certain patients. It can be a way for them to see the world in a different light than they did before.

Think about a CD that freezes up at a certain scene when you are engrossed in watching a movie. This is distracting and the CD isn't going to do anything different for you. Even when you rewind it a bit, it gets to that same spot and the same scenario happens. That is like the way of thinking for some patients. With ACT they can stop reenacting that scene over and over in their head from a time in their life.

Definition and Principles of ACT

The definition of ACT involves understanding that by nature, we all experience suffering on a psychological level. It is part of survival, and it often helps us to become more compassionate individuals. This isn't to say it is fun to go through or it isn't hard to handle. It simply means none of us are alone with that experience, it is a common thread.

It doesn't matter where you were born, your skin color, gender, economic status, or other variables. Hard experiences will happen to all of us, and the way we deal with them determines how happy we are and how we rebound from hardships. Some of us had a difficult life from the start. We had to fight for attention, survival, and our self-esteem suffered as a child.

For others, the home was loving and full of support. The struggles and adverse events people go through vary. Some are in an environment where they can thrive, and others are barely getting by. Sometimes, there are unfair circumstances such as the death of a parent or a traumatic event that a person hasn't dealt with in a healthy manner. Life goes on, but their quality of life is lower than they would like it to be.

In addition to the struggles of the external world, we all deal with internal struggles. The thoughts and feelings that go through our mind can hold us back due to fear of failure or they can give us the courage to take steps forward. When a person doesn't successfully deal with a situation that happened, it is referred to as situational avoidance.

Ironically, a person thinks that if they don't talk about it or try not to think about it, they can move on. They are thinking about it more than they realize. Often, they think about it both consciously and subconsciously. They avoid working through that thought process and they avoid expressing how they feel about it. This is like running in place and never getting to move forward.

ACT ends that repetition and that is important. It is exhausting to think about trauma and other unpleasant scenarios again and again. It takes your energy mentally and physically. It can make it hard to sleep and hard to focus. It can make it a challenge to find happiness around other people or in hobbies.

It is often said that we can't truly embrace love from others until we accept and love ourselves. This is a valid statement, and ACT gives patients the skills and tools they need to begin healing. That often begins with forgiving themselves for past behaviors and thoughts. It includes accepting themselves and seeing situations as they truly are without letting them hold their thoughts and feelings hostage.

When you no longer feel guilty about your thoughts and feelings it is a release you won't forget. The weight that is lifted from your heart and off your shoulders is hard to describe. At times, ACT can seem confusing.

You are focusing on the present and not the past. You are still exploring feelings and emotions, but you are trying to make them positive.

I will share a story with you. As a child, I spent a lot of time with my grandma. When I was 6, she fell to the floor and couldn't get back up. I was there alone with her, and I wasn't sure what to do. About 15 minutes later my dad came to pick me up and he immediately called 911. The next day I was told my grandma had a heart attack and she had died.

My parents were very loving and comforting during this time. I remember my dad telling me again and again how much she enjoyed spending time with me. From the time I was a child though, I felt guilty that my grandma died, and I blamed myself. What if I hadn't asked her to play that day? What if I had known to call 911 as a child?

It wasn't until I was an adult and had children of my own that I could finally let go of those feelings and thoughts. They held me back for a long time from being happy and from being the person I wanted to be. Through no fault of my own I had created trauma in my mind from losing the grandma I had dearly loved.

From that moment forward, I decided that any time I thought about the day of her death I would immediately think of two good things I did with my grandma. It took some time for me to do this and to redirect my thoughts to positive ones. I may have only been six when my beloved grandma passed away, but we shared a wonderful bond. We had so many fun moments and the memories I have of my time with her will always be a treasure close to my heart.

The core principle of ACT is to create a meaningful life that you love! At the same time, you must accept that pain is an inevitable part of all we experience. Do I wish I had never had to go through that loss of my grandma? Absolutely, but I wouldn't trade that pain and sadness because it would also mean losing all the great memories and feelings of love created in her presence.

This type of therapy doesn't attempt to reduce symptoms of a mental illness or other issues. Instead, the coping skills, learning, and techniques offered help the individual think differently and feel differently. It is a way to successfully handle the hardships of life without becoming overwhelmed and victimized by them. As a result, the symptoms of many ailments often are reduced or eliminated through ACT.

Evolution of ACT and its Relevance to Mental Health
It is important to take a close look at the early introduction of ACT and how it has evolved. Specifically, how it is relevant to the success of mental health treatment. ACT uses mindfulness and awareness, but it is also a paradox of sorts.

While ACT isn't the only therapy focused on mindfulness, there are enough differences for it to be in a category of its own. It is considered a 3rd wave therapy, given life in 1986 by Steve Hayes. The 1st wave is those introduced in the 50s and 60s focusing on changing behaviors.

2nd wave therapy refers to cognitive interventions that were introduced in the 70s. ACT seems to have more flexibility and versatility than DBT. While it is mainly used for individual therapy, it can be used for couples as well as in group therapy. In some situations, it is used for families when they have all been affected by the same trauma.

Hayes liked the fact that this self-talk dialect gave the patient the power and control to seek out positive changes. It wasn't realistic to think it could all be done in those short sessions with the therapist. By giving the patient proper tools, they could apply each day to their life, it was a way for them to see the benefits and work toward creating those behaviors and thought patterns.

It is interesting to learn that Hayes used himself as a study for ACT and the elements of it. His experiences with pain helped him realize suffering is a part of life, but it shouldn't be the anchors that hold you in place or that drag you down. He explored what happened when he faced his fears and found it brought him a sense of personal fulfillment.

The time in treatment can be brief or it can be long-term. It all depends on the needs of the patient and their progress. A therapist is never going to rush someone through the process to end therapy. It is a natural progression, but the therapist should feel the patient is putting in the effort to reach the established goals and change how they feel and think.

Therapists have far more freedom with ACT than they do with DBT and other techniques. While DBT and CBT both include unique treatment plans, ACT takes it a step further. The therapist has the authority to create mindfulness techniques and methods specific to that person. They often incorporate the help of the patient with this creation process. It doesn't get any more personalized that that!

Therapists use this to help people get beyond situations and trauma that don't meet the standard definition of mental illness. Not everyone struggling has concerns with depression or anxiety. Some people have been through horrific scenarios due to bullying, neglect by their parents, racism, divorce, and domestic violence. The invisible restraints these issues put on them are hard to describe and even harder to break free from.

Through ACT, a person has the tools and methods they need to cope with what happened. Remember, this therapy focuses on accepting what has already happened and focusing on changing what you can. For example, how can you prevent that from happening again? ACT also focuses on releasing negative feelings and negative energy. Letting go of anger, sadness, thoughts of self-harm, and guilt makes room for positive feelings and thoughts.

The human mind is amazing, and scientists continue to be in awe of all it offers. Yet the mind can also be destructive and put someone on a path that isn't good for their mental health. The brain is also designed to protect us from things that can harm us. This is why experiential avoidance happens. Our mind doesn't want to deal with something that is upsetting to us.

Working through situations with the use of ACT changes the way your mind thinks. It helps you to let go of the past and focus on the present. It takes time to learn this. It takes patience and understanding as you take what you learn in therapy and apply it to your life. It takes time to coach your mind, so it responds the way you want it to, not the way it has before.

All these changes do carry over into areas of mental health. It is proven ACT can help with reducing stress and anxiety. It can stop that tape from being on repeat with thoughts and memories that aren't good for your thought process. This is also where the paradox comes in. Facing the situation can cause some anxiety and discomfort before you feel better.

However, you can decide to work through it and march forward or continue to go in circles with it. For those ready to give ACT a try and strive for their best life, the choice is easy. They what to work through it and focus on a happier life and better outcomes for the person they desire to be.

ACT challenges many of the rules at the foundation of Western psychology. Rather than feeling shaken up by this, many experts love that there is a new direction to consider. A unique treatment plan for a patient has always offered a better success rate than the one size fits all concept. There are too many variables and sometimes, ACT is the best fit for a patient. It works for them when nothing else did!

Common Misconceptions about ACT

Before we go any further, it is important to point out some of the common misconceptions about ACT. They can cloud the correct details about how valuable this type of therapy can be. Part of the reason there are misconceptions is due to different therapists using different techniques. This all comes down to creating the ideal treatment plan for that specific person.

Another misconception is that ACT doesn't give someone time to feel deeply or to grieve if the situation calls for it. These types of feelings are valid, and they should be explored. The problem develops though when trauma or negative thoughts take over the person all day long. They don't find joy in much else because they can't let go of what occurred.

ACT isn't trying to get anyone to go through life suffering but pretending they aren't. The goal is to promote healing and the ability to move forward. Learning to accept that is just how things are and that you can't change them doesn't mean your feelings and thoughts weren't valid. What it means is that you are no longer willing to let that define you now or in the future.

ACT methods aren't admitting you have failed, or you gave up the fight. Instead, it promotes inner peace and forgiveness. We tend to be harsh on ourselves and that punishment can be endless. The way we talk to ourselves and the way we perceive ourselves can be heartbreaking! Be gentle on your soul and while you should be accountable, you have to stop beating yourself up for mistakes. Make the commitment to move forward and to learn what you can from those mistakes.

There is a misconception that ACT causes people to be taken advantage of. This stems from the concept of tolerance that is introduced. Finding your inner peace means choosing your battles wisely. It doesn't make sense to fly off the handle due to a traffic jam or because the lady at the drive-up window got your order wrong.

ACT means setting boundaries and being true to yourself. Previously, we talked about determining your core values. Once you establish them, you will use that information to dictate what you allow and what you don't. It can mean some hard discussions with a boss, a partner, and loved ones. You can establish your boundaries without letting emotions or negative feelings take control of the situation.

Be clear about what you want and how you wish to accomplish it. Sure, it can be uncomfortable and difficult to have those discussions, but it must be done. If the other party isn't willing to make changes after you have shared with them you can't tolerate that behavior, you will have to re-evaluate their place in your life. What you tolerate sets the tone for how people will treat you.

Research and Data to Backup Claims ACT Works

We could write a book just on the research and data to back up claims ACT works! Here, we will touch on a few of those important points. First, ACT has proven time and again to work well, even when applied to a diverse range of clinical conditions. This includes:

- Addiction to drugs and/or alcohol
- Anxiety
- Chronic pain
- Eating disorders
- OCD
- PTSD
- Schizophrenia
- Stress

A study completed by Bach & Hayes showed after 4 hours of ACT, schizophrenic patients have fewer symptoms. Another study indicates after 12 hours of ACT, the return to a hospital admission for previous patients was reduced by 50% in the six-month period between when they were last hospitalized and started ACT.

Overview of the Therapeutic Process in ACT

In the beginning of ACT, the discussions with the therapist will focus on the challenges you face and anything you can't seem to let go of. You will talk about feelings and events. You will talk about mental health and any concerns that may arise.

It isn't uncommon for a mental health evaluation to be conducted in the first few sessions. This provides the therapist with information they can use to make the correct diagnosis and details for the treatment plan. It is important to be open and honest in therapy for the best outcome.

The therapist will ask about what you have tried that worked for you and what you have tried that didn't work. They will ask you about the emotions you feel and behaviors you engage in. All of this is reviewed and analyzed so they can create goals with you and develop a unique treatment plan using the six processes of ACT.

Building a relationship with your therapist is important. You must feel comfortable talking to them and answering questions. You must feel confident in their abilities and willing to try the methods they present to you. Showing up on time for each therapy session and giving 100% while you are there is going to help you get the most out of ACT.

Train your Mind
During these sessions, your therapist will help you train your mind to be aware of your present surroundings and scenarios. They will help you identify negative thoughts and ways to stop them from continuing. As soon as you recognize a negative thought emerging, you can use the tools and techniques taught with ACT to put a positive spin on things.

This is the process involved in changing the negative thoughts you have about an event and changing them to acceptance. Once you can accept them for what they are, you can focus on positive thoughts to move forward in your life. You won't continue to rehash that previous experience again and again.

Core Values
What are your core values? Don't worry if you aren't sure now! Many patients in ACT develop a deeper understanding of them when they are finished. To reach your core values, you must explore facts and perceptions. You must weed through what you once thought was valid and true and verify that is really the case. Letting go of anything that isn't fact-based and true will help you identify your core values. Your therapist will guide you through this process.

Some important questions to ask yourself when it comes to core values help you create a foundation for where you will be in the future. How do you want to identify as a person? What do you want your life to look like? How are you going to be the person you want to be and experience the life you want?

Actions and Commitment
Your therapist will help you identify recurring thought and behavior patterns. That must be done so you can focus on what you will change. If you have several areas that need work, you aren't alone. The therapist

will help you break it down into smaller pieces. As you make progress in certain areas, new goals can be added to the treatment plan.

Typically, the changes that will impact you the most are handled first. ACT requires commitment, discipline, and mindfulness. Many of us get through areas of life on autopilot. It is time to be aware of what is going on around you and not just go through the motions. At the core of this is the fact that you must accept what you can't change and focus only on what is within your control.

As you learn the various methods and techniques of ACT, your therapist can guide you with applying them. In time, the goal is for you to identify which options to apply to a given situation. As you continue to use those tools, it will help you create the life you want. You will continue to use what you learn. In time, it will become part of your subconscious thought patterns.

CHAPTER TWO

EXPLANATION OF THE SIX PROCESSES OF ACT

At the heart of ACT are the six processes of ACT. Each of them is very important in their own right. Collectively, they create the unique elements of this type of therapy. None of them holds more weight than the others, but how much emphasis is put on them for an individual's therapy does vary.

In this chapter, we will touch on each of them a bit as well as the process collectively. However, each of these six processes is significant to the success with ACT so we will be further breaking each of them down into their own chapter. This focus enhances the learning and ensures the value of what they bring to this form of therapy is fully embraced.

It is important to note that these six processes involved in ACT tend to have variations of the wording when they are used. Don't get hung up on the titles, focus on the meaning and what they offer for therapy. Focus on the techniques and methods because, in the end, the wording of the name of it isn't what the system is all about.

To this book, we will use the following titles for the six processes of ACT:
- Contacting the present moment (often referred to as awareness or mindfulness)
- Defusion
- Acceptance
- Self as Context (often referred to as observing self)
- Values (often referred to as core values or core beliefs)
- Committed Action (often referred to as an action plan or call to action)

Each of these processes has unique methods incorporated with them. This includes the types of exercises the therapist asks someone to take part in and the homework they are assigned. In the workbook chapter, we will cover some excellent exercises you can take part in to challenge yourself when working with ACT in each of these processes.

Interactions between the Six Processes of ACT

The overall benefits with these six processes of ACT involve flexibility at a psychological level. Life isn't always going to be black and white, there are so many shades of gray in the mix due to circumstances and perceptions. They were developed to help patients reach a level of acceptance and focus on present time rather than what has already happened to them.

Both acceptance and mindfulness are at the core of ACT but that is just part of it. Those are both elements that create the framework and foundation of it. When you add commitment and strategies specifically designed to change behaviors, you can see the walls and parameters put up and strongly attached to that foundation.

When we talk about psychological flexibility what does that include? This is the ability a person must stay in the present frame of mind even when there are unpleasant situations or thoughts taking place. It is the decision to stay in tune with the senses and the feelings experienced, even when they are uncomfortable. Next, it involves selecting appropriate behaviors that align when a person's values and the situation they are currently dealing with.

The six processes work as a unit to help an individual work through thoughts and feelings rather than trying to avoid them or acting impulsively to get away from them. When a person works through situations, they often feel guilty or second guess what they do. ACT processes encourage no judgment so you can look at the situation objectively and let go of the negative feelings associated with it.

The commitment to embracing challenges that come along rather than hiding from them or avoiding them can completely change relationships, a career, moods, and how you feel about yourself. It involves mindfulness and doing yourself to understand the six processes so you can use them when you need to.

Each of these techniques offers help in three substantial areas where change can benefit a patient:

- Experiential avoidance
- Letting go of judgment
- Living a life of value

These areas are important to look at closely because your quality of life isn't where it should be if you have negative thoughts and impulsive behaviors. When past experiences are avoided or they are repeated but with the wrong methods to handle them, it can increase symptoms of anxiety, depression, and other ailments. Feeling helpless and ashamed about what happened can diminish self-esteem.

As a person learns to work through challenging feelings or situations, even when they are uncomfortable, they stay in control. This reduces symptoms and improves both self-esteem and quality of life.

Therapists must share how each of these elements works together but also show how they are uniquely identified as separate units. A patient can feel overwhelmed when too much is shared with them at once. Information overload can make it difficult to stay focused.

Breaking it down and introducing one or two of the processes at a time is a good way to give them something to work with in a manageable chunk. They can work on those concepts and complete exercises relating to them. When the therapist feels they are ready, they can add more of the process to the treatment plan. This continues until all six of them are introduced and being worked on.

When a person starts to lack motivation in therapy, it is important to remind them that they can be happy and live the life they want. Inevitably, we will all experience pain and suffering as that is part of human nature and our emotions. We all experience loss or go through experiences that were out of our control and we wish they didn't happen.

The six processes work to help heal a person from the trauma or the pain they have experienced. It doesn't happen overnight, but it is a quest to be as happy as possible. Those with a positive attitude and a good mindset don't have a perfect life either. They use tools and techniques to help them get through the hard times. They focus on the present and they do what they can to bring joy and happiness into their life.

Initially, the ACT processes can seem complex, and a person can experience fear because these methods make them aware and vulnerable at the same time. However, they also help them move forward to a position where they can stop dwelling on the past and focus on what they must be grateful for today.

When someone puts this spin on it, ACT is something they enjoy using. They hold themselves accountable and they find practical ways to incorporate these methods. They report back in their next therapy session what happened when they applied these methods. When they have a positive outcome, it reinforces the value of these six processes.

If they didn't handle a situation as well as they could have, they get feedback from the therapist. As a team, they work through it and identify what could have been introduced for a better outcome. It is a teaching tool using real-life situations instead of just exercises, and that makes it personal.

One of the tools a patient can use with these methods is to remember ACT as steps for them to take:

A = Accept what is going on and accept your thoughts and feelings, be present
C = Choose a direction that aligns with your core values
T = Take action rather than avoiding

Assessing Psychological Inflexibility

One of the duties of a therapist is to assess psychological inflexibility and help the patient break it down. This is a barrier that must be to eliminate so they can continue to move forward. This barrier stands in the way of the six processes of ACT. When a person is controlled by the past, they limit their ability to grow as a person. They limit their ability to be in control of what they feel and how they think.

It is important to discuss in therapy how much time the patient is spending focusing on the past. How much time are they spending worrying about the future? To further break it down, what exactly are they relieving or worrying about? That is all negative energy that prevents them from the life they want.

All of this can consume time and thoughts, leaving them disconnected from where they want to be as a person too. Exploring the situations, thoughts, feelings, and behaviors associated with this can help someone open to ACT methods so they can move forward and be mindful of the present instead of looking back or worrying about the future.

A patient may come into therapy with unhealthy cognitive thoughts. They have strict rules or expectations deeply embedded into their thought process. This holds them back because of fear and because of self-judging. They may feel like they are worthless and there is no hope for them to have a great future. They often avoid dealing with situations because they don't have the right skills and methods to do so effectively. ACT processes can give them the tools and information they need.

When a person doesn't know their core values, they can't take action in a way that aligns with them. In therapy, those core values will come to light and the ACT helps with that too. Individuals that are merely trying to survive and get through their day process information differently than someone thriving. As the negative is removed from the thoughts and behaviors, the core values can be explored and discussed in therapy.

Many patients in therapy have mechanisms in place they use to avoid situations. They already know that doing so isn't effective, but they don't have the knowledge to break that cycle. They will learn that through ACT and effective coping skills as the therapy sessions progress. Practicing the methods and learning will give them the tools and techniques they need to handle their situations.

Techniques for Incorporating the Six Processes into Therapy

Each patient is treated with respect and as an individual with ACT methods. The assessment tools a therapist uses determine what will go into the treatment plan. They want to help someone succeed, not set them up to fail. The specific techniques in place to incorporate the six processes depend on where someone is.

If they lack coping skills and other essential skills, those must be introduced as part of the foundation. Otherwise, the six processes will be difficult for them to grasp and put into use. When they have good coping skills and communication skills, it is easier for them to build on top of that without everyone coming crumbling down around them.

The patient should be part of the decisions for the treatment plan. They are treated as an equal by the therapist. This creates a healthy bond between the two parties, and it encourages the patient to do their part outside of the sessions. A person is more likely to stay motivated when they are part of the decisions rather than being told to do this and that.

In therapy, the decisions often focus on thought processes and behaviors. What happened? How did you react? Why did you choose that behavior? What were you thinking and feeling during this time? All of this helps the patient go through the analysis of what they did well and where they can improve.

Exercises and homework are techniques incorporated into the six processes for ACT. The patient does this outside of the sessions and brings the information back to their next session for discussion. The exercises and homework are designed to help them think positively, be mindful, and not avoid situations.

The therapist will tune into what is working well for a patient and what isn't. The treatment plan can be modified and something new introduced if the outcome isn't what they had hoped for. As a person does well with ACT, they can move into new areas of treatment. That is when additional concepts and tools are introduced to them.

Acceptance without judgment is important for a patient to learn with ACT. That technique is introduced in sessions so it can carry over into the self-talk dialect. Exploring thoughts and feelings and accepting them is a new concept for many people. Letting go of shame, fear, and other negative feelings is a freeing experience.

Learning to establish boundaries and stick with them is another technique often introduced in therapy. As a person determines their core values, they must make sure others around them uphold them. If someone isn't, how do you communicate that to them? What do you do if they continue to overstep those boundaries? The right information to handle those challenging situations can help someone stay on track towards being who they wish to be and living the life they want!

Common Challenges in Working with the Six Processes

When a person is in a crisis or a situation they deem as difficult, it can prove to be a challenge to continue with psychological flexibility. A person may be overcome with fear, worry, anxiety, and uncertainty which causes them to fall back on old patterns of behavior. It can prevent them from acting in a way that coincides with their values.

Self-acceptance can be a challenge for someone to reach. We often toss around terms associated with this including self-esteem and self-worth. To truly live a life with self-acceptance, you let go of conditions and expectations that once influenced your decisions and how you saw yourself. It also means letting go of any qualifications that you once used to define your value.

Negative thoughts and judgments can prevent us from self-acceptance. Yet reaching that goal is an important step in ACT and the value it brings with it. It can feel uncomfortable to be vulnerable, but it is necessary to identify our worth in our eyes, not what we perceive it to be through the eyes of someone else.

One of the reasons that self-acceptance is hard to reach is we tend to compare ourselves with others. Social media plays a huge role in that. You may feel like others have a better financial situation, better relationships, better job, etc. than you do. All of this can cause you to feel like you fall short. Avoid comparing yourself to others, focus on what you can do to live the life you truly desire.

For many individuals, they don't know how to regulate their emotions. Their thoughts and behaviors have been emotionally charged for as long as they can remember. Through ACT and therapy sessions, they can learn how to regulate them, so they are in control. When they are no longer controlled by emotions it changes the dynamics of how they think and the choices they make.

A lack of coping skills can make it harder for someone to implement the six processes too. A therapist never wants this to hold someone back from using ACT. If a patient doesn't seem to have decent coping skills, that is something they can be taught in individual sessions or group therapy. Until that is part of their structure and the tools, they must live their best life, they may continue to struggle with different types of situations.

The fear of being vulnerable causes some people to put up walls that prevent anyone from getting in. They think they are protecting themselves, but they are being cut off from society. They struggle to make friends or find a partner. They often struggle at work too and feel isolated and alone. ACT can help with that, but a person must put themselves out there.

They must feel vulnerable to work through those feelings and emotions. In therapy, they can learn the difference between putting up walls and establishing boundaries. Putting up walls creates more problems while establishing boundaries can be a solution. Boundaries help promote healthy relationships and eliminate those with toxic characteristics.

A therapist will look for these challenges and barriers to the success of ACT and break them down with the patient. There can be other challenges someone has that is unique to their situation or perceptions. The questions asked in therapy give a person a chance to explore what is in the way so they can remove it. As they work to remove challenges and incorporate ACT methods, they can see positive changes shaping up and influencing their life!

ACT in Group Therapy to Encourage the Six Processes

While ACT is mainly conducted in individual therapy, it can also be applied in a group setting. This can help everyone in the group with exercises that help them learn to use the six processes in their daily lives. It can reinforce learning when they have support from peers. Groups should be small to ensure everyone has the chance to talk and interact.

The group sessions should be guided and directed by a trained therapist. Each session should have key points to share and exercises to explore or a skill to teach. It can help with time constraints to use group sessions too where everyone is learning the same thing instead of doing that with each person in an individual session. Group therapy should be used in ACT along with individual sessions though, not in place of them.

Group therapy with ACT seems to work well on adolescents because they may struggle to connect as much with an adult in therapy. When they are in sessions with other teens, they don't feel isolated and alone. They don't feel like they are the only person going through that situation. No matter what age a patient is, group ACT offers great opportunities to open, validate feelings, and practice being vulnerable in a new setting.

There should be rules in place for everyone in the group to follow. A commitment to show up to the sessions on time is important. It is disruptive if people show up late or leave early. Failing to show up for sessions is going to hold someone back from the value ACT offers.

Group interactions only take place within the group. Members aren't supposed to talk to each other outside of group sessions. They shouldn't form support groups on their own or friendships. They must refrain from any type of romantic interaction with another group member.

Everything that is shared in a group session is confidential and remains within that group. It doesn't get shared with anyone outside of it. The only time it can be discussed is in a future group session or a private session with the therapist. Everyone in the group is shown respect and compassion. There will be differences of opinion and they can be expressed in a healthy way.

When there is a disagreement, it can make some group members uncomfortable. This is the ideal time to put ACT methods into practice and work through the feelings and choose behaviors wisely. While it can be hard to watch someone struggle in therapy and not rescue them, they need to work through the scenario. Trust the process and the methods.

Mindfulness is encouraged in each group session. Being present and contributing to the discussion is essential for ACT to work. The therapist should include various exercises to promote mindfulness at the beginning of each session.

In the following chapters, we will break down each of the six processes and what they offer for ACT. As you learn about them and get a deeper understanding, it is easier to see how each of these concepts works together to help someone reach their goals.

CHAPTER THREE

CONTACTING THE PRESENT MOMENT

Living in the present moment, even when the circumstances aren't ideal, is part of ACT. Rather than the fight or flight response, it is time to face challenges and deal with them objectively. Handling emotions and working through this is a skill someone can use for every situation in their life.

Acting in a way that aligns with core values helps someone stay on track rather than creating more problems. Avoiding issues causes them to compound and control too much of your thought process. It isn't healthy for you to do so, but it is a learned behavior for many people. For others, it has been a survival response, but now they wish to have control over their life again. ACT can help make that happen.

One of the differences between other forms of therapy and ACT is you aren't going to overanalyze your thoughts or feelings. You will accept them and not judge yourself about them. The goal is to then refocus on what is taking place in the moment. This could be your job, your commute, spending time with your children, or taking part in some type of self-care.

Training the mind to be present in the moment takes awareness. Many of us juggle multiple things all day long, so our mind wonders. If you are in a meeting at work, how many times have you realized you were thinking about what you had to do that night or even what to make for dinner?

Our minds can take control if we aren't aware of our thoughts. As a parent, we can worry all the time about our children. Will they get sick? Is there a risk of a shooter when they go to school? Will they make good choices? Not only do we worry about ourselves and our past experiences, but now we have other people depending on us too. It is a huge weight to carry around.

When we focus on the past or worry about the future, we don't focus on the good things. We miss out on opportunities in front of us in the moment. We don't rely on our senses to enjoy experiences or make positive memories. Life flies by, and a positive outlook while focusing on today is a great way to enjoy it to the fullest. There are so many things outside of our control and it doesn't do any good to worry about them. Instead, we must focus our thoughts and behaviors on what we can control and our core values.

Building up Skills
Being present in the moment requires building up skills. They are designed to help a person stay focused on the present. These skills include coping concepts and communication methods that help them work through emotions and engage in behaviors that are positive. These skills help them to work toward the life they wish to live and to hold true to their core values.

Being present is important because the thoughts you have and the behaviors you engage in take place in the present. If you are thinking about past trauma or worrying about the future, you are still dealing with emotions and actions right then. It is better to focus on the present elements around you and handle anything uncomfortable. You can also focus your attention on the good things around you in that moment.

Studies indicate approximately 47% of adults are not in the present moment several times throughout their day. Based on this information, most of us can find value from building up these skills. You don't need a mental health concern or to be involved with ACT to find value in it.

Technology is often blamed for adults not staying in the moment. How many times do you see someone playing on their phone or another device instead of interacting with people around them? How often do you see someone on the phone with someone instead of enjoying what is going on around them? Sometimes, those tools can be useful, but they can often get in the way of being present. Limiting when and where you use them can be a wonderful gift you present yourself with.

Awareness
Your mind and body are designed to keep you safe, and that is why you must be aware. What are you feeling? Are there certain people or locations that trigger negative emotions and behaviors? Establishing boundaries can help you prevent that from continuing.

Such feelings can help you avoid dangerous situations too. You may be compromising your safety because you aren't paying attention to people or your surroundings. You don't want to live your life in fear, but don't put yourself into risky situations where you are likely to experience pain or harm either.

Stay in Contact with the Present Moment
When you stay in contact with the present moment, you are fully aware of what is going on right then. However, that is just part of it, you must do more than just show up somewhere! You must show you are

interested and be receptive to what is going on. Showing you are fully engaged in what you are doing and focused on the outcome is important. It opens your thoughts and behaviors in a positive way.

Such thoughts and behaviors often get noticed by others around you. Your friends and loved ones will see you enjoy spending time with them. Your boss will notice you pay attention during training or an important meeting. The benefits aren't just for them though.

When you are in the present moment, you create feel-good emotions and boost your mood. Even when you face a challenging situation, you can feel confident your choice of communication and behavior to handle it was the best you could do with that set of circumstances. You won't avoid the issue and you won't make it worse. That brings inner peace with it, even when you must set boundaries with someone else because of their behavior.

Mindfulness Exercises and Techniques
One of the best mindfulness exercises and techniques is to focus on your breathing. We do it all day long, but rarely focus on it! Closely inhale, count to 10, and then slowly exhale. Focus as you take each breath in and out. This will help you stay calm and give you time to process a situation.

Redirecting your attention to the present moment takes time and conscious awareness. Any time you notice your thoughts drifting elsewhere, firmly remind yourself that you need to focus on what is going on right now. It takes time to train your mind to do this, especially if you are constantly multi-tasking.

Self-care is a huge part of being mindful. Remove some of the clutter from your calendar. You don't have to attend everything you are invited to. You don't have to be busy every single day. Carve out time to relax and for activities you enjoy. Get enough sleep and put forth the effort to keep your relationships with people strong.

Meditation and journaling are wonderful ways to stay mindful. They help the mind relax and eliminate the clutter. They can help you work through thoughts and emotions and start the healing process. Complete all the exercises and homework your ACT therapist assigns. These concepts are created to help you become mindful with your daily life.

How to Integrate Mindfulness into your Daily Life
Being mindful isn't going to develop for you in a few days. The more you consistently focus on it, the easier it becomes. At first, you will have to consciously train your brain to do this. Several times each day you may have to tell yourself to get back to what is going on right then. You should have to remind yourself less and less though with self-talk as you practice mindfulness.

Get into a routine with some time to relax the mind and body. This will give you a chance to reflect so you don't have to do it when you should be paying attention to other things. In time, mindfulness will be part of your subconscious behaviors and thought processes. Be patient as you learn this new skill!

Tune into your senses to help you become mindful too. You can use them in just about any situation. What do you see? What do you hear? What do you feel? What do you smell? If you are enjoying a meal, what do you taste? Take it all in and find joy in it! This will boost your mood and as you positively reinforce positive elements in your life, mindfulness will become easier for you to engage in.

Stick with it, even when the situation is challenging. If you often avoid situations because they make you vulnerable or uncomfortable, you have to learn to accept those feelings. Working through discussions at work, with a partner, and even with your children can help you feel in control over your feelings and behaviors.

Accept what you can't change as you work on being mindful. It doesn't do any good to dwell on the past or worry about future things that you can't control. Do your best to enjoy today and feel good about the decisions you made because they are consistent with your core values. Appreciate the small things and pay attention to what brings you happiness.

Explanation of Mindfulness and its Role in ACT

One of the key concepts of ACT is mindfulness. This type of awareness keeps a person in the present. They aren't on autopilot or dwelling on the past. They aren't evoking negative thoughts. Instead, they use their senses to help them focus on the facts and change what is within their control if it isn't creating positive energy.

ACT doesn't mean a person never has a bad day or a difficult situation to face. It doesn't mean they never experience stress. Instead, it gives them the tools and techniques they need to cope and work through such events. They don't avoid them, and they aren't making them worse due to negative thoughts or impulsive behaviors. ACT gives them the skills and methods necessary to change that narrative!

Mindfulness will keep you grounded and focused. If your mind often jumps from one thing to the next, you will have to train it to stay focused. Too many of us are on autopilot with many things around us. For example, how many times have you driven to or from work and then not remembered much of what you saw along that route? Your mind was thinking about other things.

Being mindful isn't something you do and then go back to what you were thinking. It is the objective of being in the present moment and identifying:

- How do you feel?
- What external factors can you identify in that environment?
- What physical sensations are you exposed to?

Along with staying focused and present, there is another piece to mindfulness you must incorporate. This is the non-judgmental element.

You can't judge how you feel or what you think. You simply must learn to accept them for what they are.

Practice, practice, and practice some more when it comes to mindfulness. This is the only way it will become an ingrained part of your thought process. You can practice it when you go to work or when you hang out with friends. You can practice mindfulness when you spend time with your partner or your children. You will be amazed at how much more you enjoy your life when you learn to stay in the moment.

We are often taught that we must go at a fast pace and multi-task. While there are times those skills serve us well, it shouldn't be a lifestyle you are associated with. If you are doing that all the time, you miss out on so much around. It is a telling sign you need to slow down and cut down on some of the things you have on your schedule. You don't have to feel guilty for relaxing and enjoying the moment!

Breathing techniques are a wonderful way to focus on mindfulness. It will help you calm the mind and body so you can let go of what is distracting you. Use your senses too to feel, see, and smell what is going on around you. In theory, mindfulness sounds like such a small change, right?

The reality though is mindfulness is HUGE when it comes to the positive impact it has on your well-being. It can bring balance to your life and help you reduce both stress and anxiety. Mindfulness can help you enjoy people and experiences, creating positive memories.

For many, it helps bring them inner peace and boosts their mood. Individuals practicing mindfulness tend to be happier! The value spills into every single aspect of your life. It is a gift you bring to yourself that will be at the foundation of the person you wish to be and the life you wish to have.

There is a Time and Place to Visit the Past and Future
It is important to understand there is a time and place to visit the past and the future. It is comforting to look back at memories from days gone by and enjoy the positive feelings that come with them. Sometimes, we look back at hard times in the past to see how far we have come since then.

It makes sense to focus on the future too, deciding where you want to be a year from now or 5 years from now. For example, planning to go back to college and commit to furthering your education. With being present in the moment, there are times to look at each of these directions but do so with moderation. Don't let going back to the past or focusing on the future interrupt what you have right in front of you.

When it is mostly a problem is when you go to the past and you continue to replay painful or traumatic experiences again and again. You go through the emotions of anger, hurt, and shame with them. The same is true with the future, you can't worry about what is beyond your control. If you are filled with dread and worry about the unknown of the future, you destroy your opportunity to be happy in the present.

Self-love and self-acceptance help with finding the balance between being present and reflecting on the past. It helps with identifying where you wish to be in the future, but not losing sight of what is going on right now. You owe it to yourself to let go of the past and forgive mistakes. You deserve to be happy and part of that is accepting who you are and only focusing your energy on what is within your control. Anything else can let those negative emotions and feelings of avoidance take a toll on you. Do your part to prevent that from happening by applying ACT concepts, including being aware of what is taking place around you now.

Take some time each day to reflect on the positive experiences you felt that day. Think about how you felt and how you behaved. You can choose to do this internally or write it all down in a journal. It can be a relaxing experience to do so but also a way for you to stay aware and remain accountable for your actions and behaviors.

Look for the learning moments in life. None of us have all the answers and we make mistakes. When you have a purpose and you are mindful of your actions, you can also see ways to make positive changes. How you choose to handle a situation plays a role in how you feel about it and how you decide to continue in the future when a tough situation emerges.

Being present in the moment gives you more control over your emotions and behaviors. It helps reduce stress and anxiety because you aren't feeling emotions or acting impulsively over things that already occurred or what you fear could occur in the future.

Studies show being mindful and, in the moment, gives a person a mood boost. There is almost always something to be thankful for in the moment. Sometimes, you must look a bit harder than others. Train your mind to appreciate the little things, the time you get with others you love, small accomplishments, and even relish a great-tasting meal. When you appreciate the life you have, it all starts to fall into place.

It takes time to accept emotions that don't feel good, but we all go through them. It takes time to work through problems rather than letting them manifest because you are avoiding the underlying issues. Time is going to pass by, and you have the choice to use it wisely and to your benefit. When you do so, you make a commitment to accept yourself, accept what has happened, and find happiness in your life. It will improve your quality of life and the satisfaction you get from it.

Understanding the Process and making Peace with it

With proper coping skills and problem-solving skills, you can understand the process involved. You can make peace with it, even when the outcome isn't what you desired or none of the choices are appealing to you. We can easily get caught up in a dilemma if we give it too much control and power over how we feel and how we think.

Sometimes, a situation can be handled in the moment and then you move on. With other situations, there isn't a quick fix for it. You do have to give it more attention so you can evaluate options and have healthy discussions. Ending relationships or careers are two examples where you don't just give it up one day. It is a process you go through to decide what is best for you.

Analyzing the value involved with doing things one way or doing them another is important. This gives you the chance to slow down and not behave impulsively. Never make huge decisions when you are angry, upset, or to get back at someone. Have the courage to look at it objectively and see the situation for what it really is. When you make decisions based on emotions, you will likely regret them later.

Often, there is no perfect solution to a given situation. With ACT, you are given tools and techniques you can use to work through the process. Sometimes, you must decide because otherwise, you are avoiding the problem. Select the decision that offers the best outcome after you look at the pros and cons of the situation. Make your peace with it from that point forward.

Avoiding a dilemma is allowing your old habits to continue to win, to take control. It doesn't serve any purpose, and it only makes the outcome worse. Sometimes, the only decision you can make is that you will continue to investigate the matter for the next day before you decide anything. That is a commitment to action and a decision.

Reflecting before you make decisions and after is part of the natural process. When you aren't behaving impulsively, this is going to unfold. Be forgiving and compassionate toward yourself if you later realize you should have done something differently. If you did your best with the situation at that point, you need to be proud of the steps you took with it.

CHAPTER FOUR

DEFUSION

The process of defusion means we take a step back from what we feel and observe it objectively. We don't get wrapped up in those emotions and we don't allow them to have control over us. This reduces the risk of acting impulsively due to those emotions or avoiding dealing with a situation because you don't like the way it makes you feel.

The mind can become overwhelmed when it thinks too much and worries too much! Many of us went through this at the height of the COVID-19 pandemic. We worried that we would get sick. What if someone in our household became ill? When would it get back to normal? There was plenty of controversy about getting the vaccinations and boosters or not.

In 2009, Russ Harris made a comment about defusion and ACT that still stands strong today. He said that it allows us to look at thoughts rather than look through thoughts. A good way to visualize this is to think about thoughts in your mind being on a poster board. What do you see when you look at them that way? It is different because you are being objective, like someone looking at your thoughts instead of experiencing them.

Harris made a point of sharing that when we let thoughts and emotions come and go, they have less of an influence on us. If we try to hold onto them, that is all we can focus on. Think about grains of sand in your hand for a moment. If you clench your fist to hold them in place, you must focus on doing that and nothing else! Yet the grains are still going to slip through, there is no way to prevent that.

If you have a looser hold on the sand in your hands, you don't focus on just that. Sure, the grains still slide through, but you didn't cause yourself pain (a clenched fist will hurt after a bit) and you weren't locked into just that one thought or action. With defusion, you can still navigate rather than feeling frozen in your tracks.

Most of that was outside of our control. What each of us could control was doing our part to reduce germs in our home and environment.

Wearing a clean mask was a good idea, even when it wasn't mandated. Each adult had to weigh the pros and cons of the vaccines and boosters with their own core values, health, and other concerns. Some felt backed into a corner because their employer or their doctor mandated it. Otherwise, they had to find a new job or find a new healthcare provider.

In any such situation, take a step back to ask yourself what good is this worry going to do. What can I do to stop worrying about it? What is within my control? What is outside of my control? The answers to those questions can put the situation into perspective. It can stop the mind from running wild with the worst outcome scenario.

A common question people have is what is the difference between acceptance and defusion? They are similar and that is why people often think they are the same. Yet there are enough differences that they shouldn't be lumped together. Both acceptance and defusion though play a role in successfully using the processes of ACT.

Acceptance includes noticing when you have flashbacks to a previous experience, including trauma. It involves noticing when you have certain emotions or sensations due to triggers. You are accepting these things, but you aren't allowing them to control how you feel or how you act.

With defusion, you are aware of your private thinking and the emotions it brings with it. However, you aren't responding to it in a way that gives it power or control over your thoughts or your actions. You don't avoid the situation either, or you don't judge what you feel.

Defusion is more about changing the way you respond to what you think than changing what you think. This is a part of ACT that sets it apart from many other forms of therapy. With defusion, you can validate emotions that are sparked from confirmed truth, but they no longer have the same effect on you that they may have before when you thought about them.

When negative thoughts and emotions are allowed to manifest, they get the best of us. We only have so much energy to work with, and it can either be negative or positive. Your mind and body are going to struggle for peace when the negative is outweighing the positive. Being mindful prevents your thought process from distorting the truth or creating worry due to irrational beliefs.

With defusion and acceptance, a person can let go of irrational beliefs and replace them with the truth. This results in clearer thought processing and thinking. This can give a person a path to positive thinking instead of negative thoughts. This isn't always easy to do, you must cut off the automated part of thinking and be mindful for the changes to occur. It takes practice but it is worth the commitment!

Explanation of Cognitive Defusion and its role in ACT
The role of cognitive defusion with ACT is to make sure you are basing emotions and decisions upon facts. It is important to understand what we think and what we perceive aren't always associated with the truth. There can be pieces of the truth or what we thought was the truth.

Our mind can tell us we must obey those truths or rules and that can have an enormous influence over us. It can affect how we think, what we feel, and the actions we engage in. Traumatic experiences can create the wrong truth in our minds. For example, if we were told not to tell that something was going on or it would result in pain, we may find it hard to open up when we don't like what someone is doing.

Defusion involves dissecting the truth we think we know and verifying it as facts. This is often done with the help of a therapist in individual sessions. Your private events have shaped the way you think and what you hold as truth. Another example as many women says, "all men are the same". They think that is true and because of it, they either don't trust other people, or they make excuses for the bad behavior of others.

When they start to break it down, they learn some men engage in poor behaviors. They may have seen that growing up within their own family dynamics. Therefore, it wasn't out of the ordinary for them to select a partner that had many of those same toxic characteristics. They didn't know any better because, to them, that is the truth of their world.

Now that they are in counseling, they can see how they can set boundaries with people they are in a relationship with. They can see how they can use communication skills to talk about tough subjects without it destroying the relationship. They can also reach self-acceptance with ACT and not be ashamed that they allowed someone to treat them like that for so long.

Defusion is about questioning and learning. It involves an open mind and a willingness to let go of thoughts and perceptions that you learn aren't the truth. Such changes will help you hold true to core values and live a life you can be proud of. As your thought process changes, you will learn that your thoughts and how you process them can change – for the better.

Think of a stream of water you see out in nature. As you follow the trail, there will be times when it flows heavily, and it is full of currents. In other areas, it is calm and flowing slowly. The stream can branch out in many directions with curves, dips, and even barriers such as rocks and trees it must move around. The water flow is ever-changing and that is how it is with your thought process.

Defusing our thoughts reduces the impact they have on us. It reduces the influence they have over our behaviors too. We should rely on the power of controlling our thoughts instead of letting them happen automatically. We should rely on the power of language to help us communicate with others as well as the dialect we choose for self-talk.

Get out of the looping process! How many times have you played out the same scenario from an experience in your mind? If it is more times than you can count, it is time to focus on getting out of that looping process. You can use the ACT processes and the guidance of your therapist to help you do this.

Breaking that cycle doesn't mean the situation never happened, and we don't want to undermine experiences. Instead, it means you can move on from it and you can redirect how you think. Instead of replaying that experience again and again evoking negative emotions, what can you focus on here and now that brings you joy and positive feelings?

That is the goal of defusion, not giving certain emotions or situations the ability to dictate how we feel or act. Not giving them the power to prevent us from living a quality life we find value from! Essentially, this method is going to condition the mind to focus on the good and work through the bad when you must. It conditions the mind to stay present and not give up so much energy to the past or the future.

Defusion involves plenty of focus and flexibility. It takes time to identify the best method or technique to help you through a given situation. Use the tools you acquire in ACT and with the therapist so you can feel confident applying them to different scenarios. You can start to feel the loop coming on and immediately tell yourself that you aren't going to revisit that story again today! Engage in mindful meditation if you need to find peace of mind as you work through such scenarios. Some forms of trauma or negative events will be harder to accept and stop reliving than others.

Detangling yourself from your thoughts and feelings isn't an easy feat. We are all creatures of habit, and what we have done often continues. Even when we know it doesn't create the results we want, regression is common. Defusion requires being mindful and staying present in the moment. It won't always be comfortable, and the urge to avoid the situation or to behave impulsively may emerge.

Learn your triggers and pay attention to what is taking place. Use your skills to de-escalate the situation. Stay in control and don't back away from the challenging situation. As you see the value it brings to push yourself to deal with things, the more you will be drawn to continue those behaviors. You will have a release instead of feeling like pressure just keeps accumulating.

There are several goals your therapist will share with you when defusion is introduced with ACT. They include:

- Focus on being present in the moment
- Practice psychological flexibility
- Reduce the power previous situations and feelings have on us today
- Reducing attachment to previous thoughts and experiences
- Reinforce positive thoughts and actions
- Verifying information as truth instead of accepting what we think to be true

How to Overcome Cognitive Fusion

The opposite of cognitive defusion is cognitive fusion. Overcoming cognitive fusion is an important part of being in control of your emotions and accepting them. A therapist and ACT can help with this, especially when someone has strong beliefs that they once thought was true.

Many of us wonder how someone can be held captive in a cult-like living situation. Others wonder why so many stay in an abusive marriage. It is often due to the rules and truths they find to be true. For example, in a cult-like situation, the person may feel they are going against their religious beliefs if they leave. Many of them were born into that situation and they don't know any other way of life. To them, it is normal.

Perhaps you grew up in an abusive household, and you don't expect anything different from your marriage. For others, they hold tight to their marriage vows including for better or worse. They don't see divorce as an option, even though they aren't happy. Sometimes, all they can do to get through each day is stay in survival mode due to the actions of their partner.

It isn't always easy to move from fusion to defusion, and anyone trying should feel proud of themselves for putting in the effort. With the help of a therapist, it is easier because they can help you develop coping skills and communication skills to work through thoughts. They can teach methods to self-talk and turn those negative thoughts into positive ones.

Accepting what you thought was the truth isn't always true can be a hard pill to swallow. It can shake a person to their core. Often, a person goes through an array of emotions as they determine what is the truth and what isn't. Work through those emotions so they don't come back to haunt you later because you avoided them. Share information with your therapist and apply the ACT techniques to help you defuse.

When you are in a state of fusion, something you think about can seem like it is the truth and nothing but the truth. You may feel like it requires you to follow those same emotions and behaviors you once did. Pay attention to those triggers and use the tools and techniques you learn with ACT to help you accept those emotions and not judge yourself. Practice kindness toward yourself as you work on defusion.

The Concept of Workability

Defusion and the rest of the ACT process all include the concept of workability. It is a big part of self-acceptance and the intervention process when your thoughts or behaviors don't align with core values. Before you think a certain way or behave a certain way, ask yourself this one question:

Is what I am thinking or what I am doing going to bring me happiness and make my life meaningful? If you can answer yes, then the thought or the action is workable. If the answer is no, the thought or action is unworkable and must be modified. You always have options, even in the direst of situations, about how you will think and how you will behave.

You don't always have to respond emotionally or with action immediately. Take your time to work through the process and analyze information. Do you need time to seek out the truth and confirm the information you base your thoughts or actions upon are valid? Do you need time to evaluate the pros and cons of possible outcomes and consequences?

Sometimes, you will feel like there isn't a good solution, but you still must choose the one that is best for you. A good example is when you attempt to establish boundaries with someone. If you have communicated them clearly and given them a chance to respond, the ball is in their court. If they continue to overstep those boundaries you still have a choice.

Your first choice is to accept that and let it continue. If you already know that isn't in your best interest, there is no value to you, and it isn't workable by the definition above. The other choice may be to end your relationship with them because they don't respect those boundaries. It can be a hard choice, but you know doing so will help you be happier and live according to your core values. It is a workable decision even though it won't be a simple one to make.

Don't be afraid to ask yourself tough questions to help you with defusion. If something is causing you pain or distress, is it worth holding onto? This includes personal relationships as hard as it may be to let them go. Is something you think or experience holding you back from the life you want? Are you allowing your own thoughts to bully you and prevent you from making progress?

You must learn to get out of your own way! This often starts by getting away from your thoughts and looking at them rather than through them. This change isn't easy, but it brings new light to how you see things. It is a big part of successful ACT treatment. Talk to your therapist if you struggle with the concepts or if you need more exercises to help you get this process deeply rooted into your daily routine.

Defusion works well for those struggling with depression or anxiety. However, studies show anyone that deals with negative thoughts that recur should try ACT to help them reduce the impact they have. A person's mood and behavior can be negative due to not dealing effectively with negative thoughts. Defusion and ACT can help turn this around, offering someone a positive lifestyle that brings them happiness and fulfillment.

CHAPTER FIVE

ACCEPTANCE

The third process of ACT is acceptance. While most people are familiar with the meaning of it, applying it to your daily life can be a challenge. It requires you to think differently and to stop overanalyzing situations. Instead, you observe them like an outsider looking in, accept them, and move forward. You don't let that moment define you.

Accepting you can't change certain things is important too. Don't worry about the future or what other people are doing. You don't have any control over those things, but they can deplete your energy if you think about them too much. Focus on what you can change, and that is yourself. Focus on surrounding yourself with people and memories that make you happy.

Acceptance is one of the core concepts of ACT, and it must be there for all six of the processes to work as they were intended. This is why therapists often spend a great deal of time going over the techniques and tools to use for acceptance. They offer an abundance of exercises and homework assignments to make acceptance a part of how you think about situations that have taken place before and those taking place in the moment.

When a person accepts what has happened or what is happening, they don't get anxious about it or defensive. They act in alignment with their core values rather than avoiding situations or letting any negative emotions they feel with it cause them to behave impulsively.

Acceptance is a focus on private experiences, those that you have which most people don't know about. You can choose to share those experiences with people you trust and your therapist. You can choose to keep them private, but you must accept them and not feel shame or guilt that they took place.

Sometimes, private experiences create triggers when people say something or do something. There may be locations or smells that trigger you too. Setting boundaries is a big part of healthy relationships, but you must evaluate what to set as a boundary too. Is it really a concern to address or something you need to address on a personal level and move forward from? Those are tough questions you must ask with your self-talk dialect.

With ACT methods and techniques, you can change some elements around you when they are triggering you. Look at the situation and identify what you can control to make it a better outcome. Strive to have a good relationship with yourself and with identifying your emotions. Doing so will promote a life full of happiness and purpose.

With acceptance, a person can experience the following, without the urge to control them. If there is an urge to control them, they understand they are still working on acceptance, and they don't give in to those urges. *This includes experiencing:*

- Emotions
- Flashbacks
- Sensations
- Urges

Acceptance also means you aren't avoiding the situation any longer. With avoidance, the fear of a situation continues to escalate. That often creates anxiety and stress. Acceptance encourages understanding what you can't change and gives you the self-confidence to work on changing what you can.

When we avoid our emotions, it often triggers impulsive or negative behaviors. It can cause a person to be defensive too rather than effectively communicating. Acceptance makes it possible to learn about your feelings and what they mean without giving them control.

Sticking up for yourself and working toward core values is important. You can't just stick your head in the sand and hope for the best. Choose your battles wisely though because your core values are the same as those of other people. Be respectful of those differences. If they aren't overstepping the boundaries you have in place, give them the space and encouragement to work toward a life that embraces their core values too.

The Role of Acceptance in ACT
When you are working on acceptance, you experience and feel your emotions as they happen. You accept they are a part of your world, even those that don't evoke the positive emotions you strive for. Connect with your emotions and identify them, without any shame or guilt. Don't dwell on them but don't avoid them either. When you behave in ways that help you stay true to your core values, you can be proud of how you handled the situation.

Engaging in valued behaviors is the objective of acceptance. That is where you change your outlook and the result with the use of ACT. Purposeful actions have meaning behind them, you aren't just trying to survive. You aren't making the situation worse or putting it off for another day.

This takes you back to living in the moment, dealing with anything that comes along. Then you accept it, and you move on. Rely on psychological flexibility tools and techniques to help you feel in control and confident as you navigate your way through various situations in your daily life.

There are several pieces to the process of acceptance with ACT that a therapist and patient explore. They include:

- Accept feelings, including unwanted emotions
- Apply cognitive defusion methods
- Focus on values and goes when speaking and with behaviors
- Keep it simple, don't overanalyze
- Mindfulness
- Psychological flexibility

ACT acceptance is a type of validation, it means the feelings and emotions exist. The patient isn't trying to hide them or ignore them. They aren't trying to put a spin on them either. Instead, they identify them at face value, and they don't try to figure them out or continue to focus on them.

How you act and react to your thoughts and feelings will shift as you practice acceptance. It will help you to stay positive and stay in the moment. You may not have control over how you feel, but you can control how you react to those thoughts and feelings when they emerge.

Cognitive Shifting
In therapy sessions and exercises, the therapist works on cognitive shifting with a patient. This is to help them train their brain to use the right dialect in self-talk to accept what is going on. Removing words like BUT and CAN'T from the equation validates emotions but also works towards a solution. Here is an example:

- *I would love to go to the party but I am too anxious about it.*

With cognitive shifting this can become:

- *I would love to go to the party but I am anxious about it.*

In the second thought process, the person is acknowledging they are anxious, but they aren't going to let it get in the way. In the first one, being anxious is the reason why they aren't going to follow through with something they are interested in.

Taking action without eliminating the emotion or giving the emotion too much of your time and energy is a big part of acceptance. You can still

ACCEPTANCE AND COMMITMENT THERAPY

181

vocalize how you feel and what you experience, but you aren't going to let that stop you.

When a person can accept the negative aspects of thoughts and emotions, they find the freedom to move away from them. This movement gives them the opportunity to move towards positive thoughts and emotions.

All of this requires psychological flexibility as a person has to use the correct skills and techniques for a given situation. This is the only way they can accept the emotions associated with it and select behaviors that are healthy. Mindfulness exercises and various other strategies the therapist introduced can be used.

As the patient sees the value from these new methods and steps applied to how they feel, they make the connection. They understand with acceptance they have a chance to be the person they want to be and live the life they wish to have. They also accept there will be challenging situations and events that evoke negative thoughts and emotions, but they can work through them. Such thought patterns help someone stay in the present moment rather than have flashbacks to the past or worry about the future.

The 4 As of Acceptance with ACT

Therapists often break down acceptance with ACT into 4 distinct areas for their patients. This gives them details they can apply to use this concept in their lives. Acceptance can be a tough one of the six processes for someone to completely accept and put in place.

The 4 As include:

- Acknowledge
- Allow
- Accommodate
- Appreciate

This is a formula the therapist will instill in the patient to help them with acceptance. They can work through each piece of the A's as they assess, and address a given situation. Each of them can help a person with inner acceptance so their world is more in tune with what they wish for it to be.

This formula can be applied to just about any situation a person faces. It includes day to day interactions, conversations with loved ones, work-related concerns, and even a crisis. Exercises and role-playing with the use of the 4 A's can be useful for someone trying to get a firm grasp on how to use acceptance as part of ACT.

How to Overcome Resistance to Acceptance

While it isn't always easy to accept things, it is a big part of ACT and moving forward. It is a way for you to live the life you want and to feel good about your core values in place. When you feel the urge to fight or flight, that is when you need to take a step back. Focus on breathing and slowing down. Identify the true facts of the situation and reflect on how you feel. Don't allow emotions to have control over what you say or how you behave.

If avoidance is one of your survival skills, you have to override it with acceptance. You may feel that need to get away from the situation or to ignore it rather than facing it. That is what you have done before, but it doesn't make things better. It tends to make them worse. Focus on being in the moment and handling what comes up using coping skills, communication skills, and other tools your therapist offers.

Identify how good it feels when you handle a situation in a healthier way than you did before. This positive reinforcement will help you continue to build your future responses on. Evaluating the situation and the thoughts is a good way to overcome resistance. Asking yourself if the emotions serve you well and asking yourself if the actions will be parallel to your core values can help you decide on what to do next.

It is hard to embrace unpleasant feelings and sensations, especially when they relate to your private experiences. Practice techniques that help you experience them and then release them. Work on focusing your attention on positive things so the negative ones don't get all of your attention.

Talk to your therapist if this part of ACT is a challenge for you. They will understand and work with you in sessions to reach the goal of acceptance. They will ask you to apply it in situations and report back what took place. Talking to them about the situations and how you handled them can give you feedback on your strong areas and how to do better with weaker ones.

Everything you do with acceptance should be part of your path to feeling better about yourself and loving the life you live! When it comes to acceptance, consider each of these factors to help you avoid resistance to the necessary changes:

- How can I communicate this to others I want to share it with?
- How will this motivate me?
- Is this important to me?

There is wisdom that stems from learning and acceptance with ACT. You won't always feel or behave the way that the models of this type of therapy teach you to. How can you change that next time you face a situation where there are challenges or triggers?

Tune into those emotions and find out what they are sharing with you so you can learn from them. For example, some emotions are there to teach you avoidance doesn't do anything but make the situation worse. Others are there to warn you such as when you feel them around certain people. Your emotions can be telling you that the relationship isn't a healthy one for you to continue with.

Negative emotions can give you positive energy to do something you feel is right too. For example, negative emotions you felt due to a given situation can encourage you to take action in a way that helps you heal and promotes justice for others. This can include asking management to change something at the office. On a larger scale, it can include volunteering or advocating for a given cause. Those negative emotions can help you commit to taking action and that can have a positive outcome.

It is a misconception that acceptance means you give people free rein to behave how they desire toward you and around you. Another piece to that is ACT and acceptance is faking it. Neither of these two concepts is true to ACT and the practices it promotes.

With ACT, you are encouraged to set boundaries. You can tell someone when they say or do something that it makes you mad or upset. Next, you can tell them what needs to change and give details of the boundary you are putting in place. You aren't faking it when you feel your emotions, but you don't let them control you.

For example, you may be furious that your co-worker continually doesn't do their part of the projects, but they take the credit when it goes well. You can share with them your feelings of resentment and disappointment and let them know if it happens again, you will report it to the supervisor.

You can feel that way and share how you feel but also effectively communicate it. You may be furious, but you don't have to shout at them or throw papers off their desk in the office to get your point across. You are purposeful with your actions rather than impulsive. You are using the value that you can't change what is outside of your control.

In such a situation, all you can control is your emotions and how you behave due to them. You can set boundaries and then follow through with the consequences when that person doesn't do what you ask. If they do change, encourage them to continue. Let them know you are thrilled they are diving in and taking on their share of the project. That positive reinforcement can encourage them to continue doing better.

Acceptance vs. Control

One of the barriers to acceptance is many people like to be in control. It is important to feel in control of your emotions, your actions, and your behaviors. However, you can't have complete control over situations because there are too many variables. Acceptance should be part of your thought process when circumstances are outside of your control.

Use the control over yourself and your environment where you can. Apply the core values to how you are living your life. The methods you use should help to improve your quality of life. Talk to your therapist about additional options if you struggle with this part of acceptance or if you need other tools to help you reach that goal.

When you practice acceptance with ACT, you give yourself freedom from elements outside of your control. You can focus your thought process and energy on what you can control. You can feel good knowing you are living your life according to the values that matter to you. When you can do this while acknowledging your feelings, you are authentic, and you should be proud of yourself as an individual!

Find the Motivation

Sometimes, it can be a challenge to find the motivation to continue moving toward goals. It can seem overwhelming at times but take a breath and step back from it. Do your best to observe and look in rather than get caught up in those emotions. When your goals are linked to your values, it is easier to stay motivated.

Review your goals and values from time to time, you may notice they have shifted due to learning. Revise them to help you continue to stay focused. This is a journey of small steps, not a race. Sometimes, all you can do is get through the day, and that has to be enough. Tomorrow you can get back to the challenges. On the days that are the hardest, your self-talk dialect should be calm and encouraging. This is a prime time for some self-care techniques too.

While we want to look on the bright side, it is important to understand there will be obstacles that come along. If you fall apart each time something like that happens, it isn't healthy. It takes far too long to put yourself back together. We can't predict what will happen that is outside of our control or when. All we can do is commit to working through it in a healthy way.

Find support through therapy, friends and family, and support groups. Find people that uplift you when you find it hard to do it on your own. Spend time with people that have characteristics you admire. Use reminders when you need them to stay mindful and aware. Always look for something positive and to appreciate it every single day!

CHAPTER SIX

SELF-AS-CONTEXT

Self-as-context is a wonderful part of the six processes to explore with a therapist. This process involves understanding your value isn't defined by your thoughts or feelings. How a person feels and how they see themself is the result of experiencing and observing the feelings and thoughts they have. This shift in a person's mindset can be accomplished with ACT methods and exercises.

Self-as-context is where personal experiences unfold and perceptions of what took place develop. It is a place where observations are made, even though it is still in the person's brain, it is considered a separate entity. It is that voice that tells you something feels right, or something seems uncomfortable.

This is why it is often referred to as the observing self. It involves stepping back and evaluating the situation as you would if you were watching the events unfold with someone else rather than yourself. It is also referred to simply as awareness because it is the conscious knowledge of who you are.

Often, patients struggle with areas of their life that prevent the self-talk dialect from being healthy. The therapist works with the client to assess where they need to make positive changes. The elements in the treatment plan are customized to help them achieve goals and to have better self-as-context outcomes.

Through these methods, a person can start to explore emotions and feelings but not be under seize by them. They can act responsibly and communicate about how they feel or think. They aren't acting impulsively or avoiding the situation to a point where it continues to be a problem for them that they fear dealing with.

When a person struggles internally with self-as-context, they are feeling out of control. They hold on tightly to what they know, even when it isn't factual or when it isn't serving them well. They aren't flexible, and that causes both stress and anxiety to increase.

No matter what you call it, think of self-as-context as the core of who you are. When you observe what is going on rather than reacting to it, you can be aware of your situation in the moment. You can focus on your individual experiences and the emotions and feelings they create.

Keep in mind, self-in-context can be confusing due to the perceptions a person has. We mentioned it earlier, but someone in a supportive home can thrive whereas someone without that is merely trying to survive. Their perceptions of events and the world around them are very different.

This is why ACT treatment is formulated to take the individual into consideration. With the help of a therapist, someone can start to observe their situation and then accept it rather than feeling helpless or ashamed by what has taken shape in their life at certain points.

It takes practice to reach self-as-context on a conscious level, but being patient and working hard towards the established goals will help. Focusing on exercises and techniques given by the therapist will help make this part of the six processes achievable.

It is important to mention how self-as-context influences attachment to the conceptual self too. The two concepts are at opposite ends of each other. If you are focused on the conceptual self, your therapist will give you ways to move more and more towards self-as context.

Until you reach that point, you won't be able to use psychological flexibility. This makes it hard to handle situations well because you are too locked into rigid thought processes. You have to observe the situation, think about your options, and think about how to act and react in a way that is parallel with your identified core values.

It is almost impossible to live a valued life until you reach self-as-context because negative feelings including anger, fear, shame, and helplessness can continue to define how you feel and what you do. A therapist can help someone learn to let go of what isn't true and perceptions that aren't real so they can focus on the here and now.

What is the Role of Self-as Context in ACT?
There are several roles self-as context offers to a patient through ACT. Many of these concepts carry over to all aspects of a person's life. It influences how they view themselves, their mood, interpersonal relationships, and the quest to take actions taking them closer to the life they desire to live.

Individuals learn through ACT how to be flexible with the view they have of themselves. They learn to observe so they can find the truth and not take everything they thought they knew at face value. There is no judgment with this process, so a person can let go of negative emotions when they realize certain thoughts they once held as truth aren't valid.

When a person can reduce their attachment to a concrete definition of who they are, they have the freedom to embrace change. We all have different focuses and options at various points in our lives. This means that the ebb and flow of the life we wish to live will also change with time. Don't worry if you aren't sure of all your core values when you first start

ACT. As your therapy progresses, you will discuss this more and more with your therapist.

By the time your ACT ends, you will have a solid idea of your core values. You will also know the questions to ask with self-dialect to keep you on the right path to living a life that is aligned with those core values. Along the way, you will continue to grow and learn. This evolution process is something you should embrace and use to motivate yourself to be the best version of who you can be.

As you get in touch with your core self through therapy, you can observe your thoughts and feelings. You can feel in control of them rather than controlled by them. This is where acceptance can fall into place, so that process and this one go hand in hand with ACT models and techniques. That is why they are often introduced at the same time in therapy sessions.

The goal of this type of training in therapy is to guide a person through the thought process. The thoughts and feelings have a safe space where they can move about and be processed. We can then observe those experiences, but we don't get caught up in them. Instead, we stay focused and in the present.

All changes and all experiences go through this process in the mind with self-in-context correctly in motion. It is going to change the mindset of a person and allow them to let go of past trauma that has caused a variety of symptoms for them such as anxiety and fear. Remember, with ACT we don't treat the symptoms, but they often are reduced or eliminated as the six processes of ACT are successfully implemented into the lifestyle of someone.

How to Handle Other People with ACT

Effective communication skills are an essential part of creating and maintaining healthy relationships. It doesn't matter if you are referring to your partner, your loved ones, friends, people you work with, or introducing yourself to someone new. Most people agree their self-confidence gets a boost when they know their communication skills are effective.

In assessing skills someone has, the therapist may determine they lack effective coping skills and lack effective communication skills. They will introduce these concepts during ACT even though they aren't part of the six processes. They are important enough because they are part of a strong foundation to create the life you want.

A common question that emerges in therapy is how to handle other people with the use of ACT. I big part of that goes back to remembering to focus on what you can control and let go of what you can't. You can't control how someone else acts, but you can strive to hold them accountable.

Never assume someone knows how you feel about something, even if your mindset is they know you well enough that you shouldn't have to tell them. If you take the time to be vulnerable and share how you feel and what you think about a given topic with them, most will listen. Hopefully, they have a desire to continue to grow that relationship, so they ask questions and come to an agreement. If they don't respect the boundaries you put in place, their decisions are theirs to make.

You either must decide to accept that and allow it to continue, but that doesn't give you any value. It doesn't line up with your core values. You can still acknowledge your thoughts and feelings with someone and react in a way that is healthy.

For example, you may have a wonderful friend that is always on their phone when you hang out. They are texting, checking social media, and answering calls from others. It makes you upset at times and lately, it has you angry. You feel like they don't value your time with them. Talk with them and share with them you enjoy spending time with them but feel like they aren't present in the moment due to always doing things on their phone.

Ask them to please put it away while you are together so that you can enjoy that time. Hopefully, they tell you they didn't realize it was an issue and that you are important to them too. The issue is resolved, and you can move on. If they tell you, it isn't a big deal, stand firm with them and tell them it is a big deal to you. They have the choice of how they will act from that point forward. Their choice will share with you how they feel about your relationship.

Your therapist will encourage you to have such conversations and use ACT methods to do so. Such conversations aren't always pleasant, but you must remember that avoiding problems allows them to get worse and worse. When you start to handle situations in the moment and don't let them continue to occur repeatedly, you can move forward from it much sooner.

Such discussions will help you feel understood and valued most of the time. In situations where they don't, you must carefully look at that relationship. Is it offering you value? Do you feel good around that person, or do they evoke negative emotions often? Don't get trapped in relationships with people because they are related to you or because you have known them for a long time.

As you change and move toward the life you want, the reality is there won't be space for everyone you currently know. The dynamics of many of those relationships will change when you speak up and set boundaries. They will change as you learn effective skills to cope and communicate. Some of them will get stronger and others you will have to decide to reduce interactions with them or end those relationships completely.

ACT methods can be useful to help patients when they need to do any of the following. Often, they will discuss the situation with their therapist. The two may spend time in sessions discussing how to handle the situation correctly to ensure the person isn't overwhelmed by it or their anxiety doesn't take control of the emotions they feel as they express them.

Some of the situations that may arise like this that a therapist can guide someone through include:

- How to end a relationship with someone
- How to convey the desire to start a relationship with someone
- Working through emotions and thoughts when a relationship has a conflict, or it hits a rough patch
- Identifying a person's own behaviors that may contribute to problems within relationships (this is often brought up by the therapist if they see a pattern within their relationships)
- Teaching new skills or techniques to help a patient handle interpersonal relationships. This can include conflict resolution, positive reinforcement, and how to set boundaries.

The role of the therapist is to validate that there are difficulties within relationships. The complexity of them can vary depending on the patient, but it is an issue that they need help with so that they can learn better ways to have healthy relationships. This is also a prime time for the therapist to introduce elements of relationships and skills training into the goals for the patient along with ACT.

How to Overcome Attachment to the Conceptualized Self

For ACT to work properly, a person must learn to overcome their attachment to the conceptualized self. Otherwise, they will be held captive in their own mind due to the rigidness of our thought process and those negative feelings. Too many people identify who they are with their feelings and that is their reality. This often causes depression and troubled relationships.

They tend to struggle to be happy and they aren't living the life they really want. They are held back by things outside of their control. They haven't learned yet that they must let go of what is out of their control. They must identify who they are and how they are going to live a meaningful life.

When a person feels stuck, they don't have the tools and concepts to change their patterns of thoughts or behaviors. The problem with that is it all starts to become overwhelming. They withdraw further and further. They avoid more and more. They don't know how to change things, and their life isn't fulfilling for them. These ways of thinking often lead to impulsive conversations or behaviors that cause more harm than value.

If you get locked into believing the narrative of your conceptualized self, especially due to a traumatic experience, you don't think you can do better. You don't believe you are worthy of people loving you. Often, a person is unkind to themselves and engage in risky behaviors. They don't have any self-worth, so they fail to set boundaries with others to form healthy relationships.

Overcoming attachment to the conceptualized self often requires therapy. ACT can work with this when many other forms of therapy didn't because of this specific focus. It doesn't mean you ignore how you feel but it means that you observe and release those feelings and emotions. You don't hold them inside and you don't act or behave because of what you feel.

Actions are often the result of thoughts, so ACT works on changing the actions and changing how you think. You can still feel angry but instead of having a wild outburst like you used to, you calmly speak about why you are angry and what can be done to change that.

Overidentifying with the pain and trauma can be a trap if you aren't careful. This means that a person may continue to play that scenario repeatedly because they think feeling something is better than feeling nothing at all. With self-in-context, you can feel those emotions and accept them, but you also focus on being mindful and present in the moment.

When people give up on changing or living a better life, they are attached to that conceptualized self. They have to make the commitment to change through mindset modification and their actions to choose a different path. It isn't easy to do, but a skilled therapist will listen and guide someone.

They will make sure the patient has the correct tools, methods, and techniques to work with self-in-context. The more a person does this, the more they move from the end where they are stuck to where they see options and they feel like they have regained control.

They no longer feel hopeless or a victim of these recurring patterns that don't serve them well. Instead, they find motivation and inner peace with the use of tools and concepts ACT offer along with other forms of learning that take place in therapy. Giving up that deeply seeded idea of being rigid in thought and process is replaced with flexibility and observation.

With ACT, the therapist will teach the patient how to be observant of themselves while also experiencing some detachment. Internal experiences change often throughout the day. Accepting who you are is significantly much deeper than what you have experienced or what has happened to you is a powerful shift in thinking. As you make this shift, your internal experiences carry less weight than they once did. You can focus your energy and attention on living the life you want as each day comes along.

Self-as-context provides a person with the opportunity to see the options they have for thoughts and behavior. They should be consistent with the circumstances and align with core values. When a person is inflexible, they only see a black or white answer to something. That situation may warrant someone that is somewhere between that black and white. That is why I love to say there are many shades of gray when it comes to solutions!

Changing perceptions open the mind to learn and gain wisdom. Unlearning habits and perceptions that weren't true takes time, but as you let go of them, you gain so much on a deeper level. It gives you a clear thought pattern and calming behaviors. It provides you with a boost in self-esteem, and the chance to learn from mistakes rather than beating yourself up over them.

Keeping it simple may seem too easy, but it is a reminder many therapists give their patients. Overthinking and overanalyzing situations or emotions can give them the ability to take up too much of your time and energy. Don't give them more time or space in your head than you absolutely need to!

Positive affirmations are a wonderful concept, they bring so much appreciation and relaxation to a person. They can be useful for reaching self-in-context too. Make sure you tell yourself often that you are more than your thoughts and your feelings. You are also more than your memories or urges you may have.

Not every story or memory in your mind is correct either. It may seem hard to believe that, but it is true! Try to look at other narratives to help you with your story as you look at it from a new mindset and perspective. This can help you to finally release any limitations that have been holding you back.

You always have the freedom to choose and options. In some situations, the options you have may not be ideal by any stretch of the imagination. Do your best to process through them and choose the best one with the information you have at the time. If it isn't a crisis, back away and conduct research. Verify facts and information before you react. You will feel more comfortable making decisions and directly communicating with others when you give yourself that extra time.

When you focus on the core of yourself, it is steady, and it is strong. The world around you and the circumstances taking shape will change all the time. Yet that core is going to remain the same. Commit to reaching self-in-context and letting go of anything standing in the way. Openly share concerns with your therapist so they can help you navigate this very important part of ACT.

CHAPTER SEVEN

VALUES

We have touched on the topic of core values many times in this book. It is an independent process with ACT, but one that works very closely with all the others. Asking yourself if what you are doing and how you are reacting is coinciding with your core values is an important part of the self-talk dialect with ACT.

It is important to understand values aren't the same as goals. They do intertwine often though as your values can give you the motivation to take action toward your goals. A goal is something you will achieve in a certain amount of time. A value isn't something you accomplish; it gives you direction.

For example, the decision to be responsible with money is a value. The decision to buy a home in the next two years is a goal. That value is going to help you have a good credit score and prove creditworthiness so you can qualify for a home loan with an excellent interest rate.

Some experts refer to values as your compass of life, and that is a great way to view it. Your choices are based on the direction you wish to go at that point in your life. Since life is full of experiences, opportunities, and growth that direction will shift with time. Where you are headed today isn't going to be a straight path. It is going to be windy, move in new directions, and end up very different than what you had in mind initially.

This doesn't mean you failed at all! In fact, it means you are using the tools and techniques you learned to help you grow and become flexible. It means you have important skills for coping and communicating to assist you with enjoying life to the fullest. Isn't always going to be upbeat, there will be times of pain and intensity with struggles. How you learn to work through them is important, and your values help you learn to trust your decisions.

Each of us has different core values, and they make us unique. Often, people have similar values, and that helps them to bond in relationships. It is difficult to have a partner you trust and get along with if you are on two different pages with core values. Not everything will be the same, but how you treat each other, how you raise children, and other important concepts are worth discussing before you commit to spending the rest of your life with them.

Otherwise, you may in for a life of uneasiness and turmoil. Relationships are tough because you have two independent people coming together in certain areas. Yet they remain individuals on other levels. You should never compromise your values for the sake of a relationship. There are times when you must respect the values of others, even if they aren't the same as your own.

When you feel your boundaries are violated due to differences in values, that can turn it into a negative situation. Open and honest conversations must take place. This is where ACT methods and good communication skills can help you discuss your values in a way that keeps you in control of your emotions and behaviors.

Values also connect strongly with committed action, and we will discuss that process in the next chapter. When you can think about your core values, then you can see why taking certain actions is the logical step toward realizing those values. You can feel good about decisions because they are based on your values.

With ACT, you can start to see those values take shape. As we change and grow in life, our values can shift too. Growing up, certain values may be forced upon us like rules. We take them at face value because that is what is expected of us. That is what we see our families taking part in. It is natural for children to have a desire to please their parents.

As you get older, you may start to question certain values. They may not hold true for you anymore. One of the areas where there are strong differences in values for people is religion. This doesn't mean any one person is right and the others are wrong, it simply means they value different aspects of it in their own lives.

If you had a traumatic childhood, it may be filled with experiences where you didn't see any values being upheld. The messages you got from your upbringing can be confusing too. They may have said one thing, but their actions were another direction from that. It didn't provide you with a good foundation of values to build on as an adult.

ACT offers ways to review your values and undo the learning you may have that isn't accurate. As you explore the truth and look for facts, you can decide what values you will incorporate into your life for them to have meaning to you. Observing your emotions instead of putting them in the driver's seat gives you a chance to stand back and ask if what you are thinking, feeling, and thinking of doing is in alignment with those values or not.

Values can be lost, forgotten, and even neglected when our needs aren't met. If you are in survival mode or you are going through life on autopilot, you won't be focused on your values. It is never too late to identify them or even change them, and ACT can help with that.

Your therapist will remind you that ACT involves not judging and it involves accepting. You must accept some of your values no longer serve you well so you can let them go and focus on those that do. You must forgive yourself for any values you once held that weren't true or that turned out to be self-destructive.

Clarifying values helps a person move forward in life. It also holds them accountable, ensuring their actions and thoughts are lining up with what they say they hold dear to them. It triggers the desire to take committed action and that is where changes occur, and you can see progress. These values lead to behavior changes, and that is why they are such a big part of therapy and ACT.

Defining Values

The definition of value is what you find important in your heart and your soul. It has nothing to do with where you live or how much money you make. Your values influence what type of person you wish to be and what type of life you want to live. It isn't enough to just identify your values though, you must commit to working towards them and staying true to them.

When you have values, your self-worth improves, and your decision-making can be easier. Keep in mind, you should be flexible with what you believe and look for truth and facts. If your values are based on something that isn't real, it can be taking you in the wrong direction.

With values in place, you must work through difficult emotions and challenging situations. You will face new dilemmas too. For example, you may love your job but feel activities the company engages in aren't ethical even though they are deemed legal. Do you continue to work for them, or do you find a job that is more in tune with your values?

Certain relationships may hit a point where they have to evolve, or they have to end because of the values and boundaries you have now. Not everyone is going to continue that journey of growth with you. Don't let others hold you back from the peace of mind and happiness you long for.

Standing up for your values is something you can do without conflict most of the time. Use your communication skills to convey the message you want to share with someone. For example, let someone know you don't find it acceptable for them to call you names when you disagree and that you won't tolerate that behavior to continue from them.

This conversation sets boundaries, and it shares with them a value you hold as truth in your life. You are sending a clear message you aren't going to engage in a relationship with someone that is adversely affecting your mental health or your self-esteem due to their own choice of behaviors.

When you have values that matter to you, the decision to stand up for yourself and even to commit to action for others isn't wavered. For example, you may feel that there is an injustice to children of color in your community when it comes to education. You can stand up for that by talking to the school board, volunteering in the classrooms, tutoring, and being a mentor to these students.

What is the Role of Values in ACT?

With ACT techniques and methods, values help a person stay focused on what they wish to achieve and why they are striving for positive changes. Values help them determine the life they want and what it will take to live it. Values help them see the person they desire to be, and what actions they must take to love the person they are.

One of the complexities of value with ACT is that it doesn't always work well with acceptance. On one hand, we are taught to accept what is going on around us and that is outside of our control. On the other, we are taught that we must identify and follow our core values to reach our true potential and have a life we find meaning with.

From a therapist's point of view, that can be confusing at times. Many patients reach out to their therapist when they are in such a situation. They may really enjoy their friendship with someone, but when they discover that person is stealing or cheating on their spouse, it doesn't hold up well with their own values.

Accepting you can't change what the other person is doing is important. You can have a discussion with them though and share you don't agree with certain behaviors they engage in and that you have concerns about the path they are on. Let them know you care, but beyond that, it is up to them to decide the type of life they wish to live. You can't rescue them and if you try, you may end up drowning yourself!

It isn't selfish to put your values and needs ahead of those of others in your life. You may have to limit your contact with them or end relationships. When you have solid values in place, ACT can help you learn better coping skills and communication skills. You will find when you surround yourself with positive people that also have great values, you find support in those relationships.

They help you reach your goals and give you the motivation to live the best life possible. You enjoy spending time with them because doing so creates happy memories and positive emotions. It can boost your mood and help you accept the person you are because they aren't judging you. Instead, they are supportive, and they help you work on ways to reduce barriers in the way of what you want.

Your values can be categorized into four distinct areas. A common experience with ACT is to write down all your values that come to mind. They are uniquely yours, not what your therapist wishes for you to value. They may point out some great values you have though that you haven't identified, and that can be useful to you.

These four categories include:
- Leisure
- Personal growth and health
- Relationships
- Work and education

Without values, we are driven to avoid uncomfortable thoughts and emotions. Without values, we are more likely to engage in impulsive behaviors that only make problems worse. ACT focuses on changing what is within your control, and that includes these important areas. Staying motivated during therapy can be a challenge at times.

Values identify what you are reaching for and why your goals will make a positive impact in your life. They can prevent you from giving up when you aren't sure the hard work is something you want to continue with. Values can help you make decisions too, especially when you are at a crossroads or when you don't really like any of the options, but you must make a decision.

When your values align with your behavior you will reap the following benefits with ACT:

• Confident in decisions made, following the decision-making process is easier
• Less likely to struggle with psychological issues
• Less like to experience symptoms of depression or anxiety
• Mood improves
• Motivated
• Self-esteem increases

How to Identify and Pursue Meaningful Values
It is a personal journey of growth and development to identify and pursue meaningful values. It gives life purpose and direction, and you will feel much better about yourself and your decisions. In ACT, you will work with your therapist to remove underlying elements preventing you from enjoying a life that brings you joy and satisfaction.

There are a variety of exercises and assignments they can offer to you as you work with them to pinpoint your values. As you feel in control of your emotions and thoughts, you can focus your attention on your values. You can ask yourself questions to help you stay on track with both actions and thoughts due to those values.

What is important to you? That is the key question to ask when you assess your core values. It helps if you take steps back and think about what brings you joy and happiness. For many people, it is spending time with certain individuals. What characteristics do they have which you appreciate the most?

Your values are often identified by your personal characteristics too. Sadly, many of us focus on our flaws rather than what we bring to relationships that are positive. If you are creative and compassionate, you have plenty of values in place. You don't judge others and you encourage them. You don't know all they have been through, but you treat them with kindness and respect.

Being open-minded is part of your values too. It means you have your opinions and thoughts, but you are ready to learn more about topics. You will listen to other people as they share why they feel a certain way about something. You may not agree with them, but you can respect their position on it.

Psychological flexibility plays a role in success with values too. If they are too rigid, they become rules and they can get in the way of the future you truly want. As your focus in life and your mindset shift, you will notice your values do along the way. There is nothing wrong with your values being different than what they are right now.

Many of us make this shift as we get older. For example, when we are younger our values don't always include time for friends and family. We don't always focus on good choices because don't have life experiences yet to help shape that. As we get older, we appreciate the small things in life more than we used to. This helps us form values that bring us peace and happiness at that point in our life.

Values should give you the information you need to make workable choices. We covered that in a previous chapter. It is a good way to check yourself in observation mode before you think and before you act a certain way. If the options are workable, they can help you promote growth and your values. If they aren't workable, look for other options so you are working toward your goals and not making decisions that conflict with them.

It is impossible to list all your values, but you should have a good idea of them. Your therapist may ask you to create a list so you can work as a team with ACT and apply them to your goals and decision-making process. The values on your list serve many purposes both in life and therapy sessions. They include:

- Assist with establishing clear boundaries
- Enhances relationships that are important to you
- Guidance when you need to make decisions
- Identifies areas where you want to feel different and behave differently
- Improved confidence and feelings of self-worth
- Motivation when the struggles are difficult
- Reduce stress and anxiety
- Reminders of what is important to you

Values provide us with purpose, direction, and motivation. They encourage us to feel good about ourselves and the choices we make. They encourage us to act in a way that provides purpose in our life. Quality values can translate to a quality life, but we must remember to focus on them. We must appreciate our efforts and see where we can still make positive changes to move forward.

Don't get too comfortable where you are, or you miss opportunities for growth, learning, and development. Don't take your values for granted and don't overlook them when you make decisions, or you go through

CBT + DBT + ACT Workbook

experiences. Let them create a well-lit path to guide you through the dark and back into the light when you face a challenge.

Identifying your values is a wonderful gift to offer to yourself. It creates personal awareness. It can help you be present in the moment, so you enjoy what is taking place rather than worrying or having flashbacks to unpleasant circumstances out of your control. Values are a way to link to your inner self, and they are an essential part of our mental health.

You will never get to the end of the line with values, and that is a concept to overcome as there is no finish line. The clarification of your values will continue to develop and evolve. If they don't, you aren't taking any risks and you aren't living your life to the fullest. What you value and how you choose to think and act according to those values will define the life you have! The question to ask yourself is are you doing what you can right now to reach that life of fulfillment you desire?

CHAPTER EIGHT

COMMITTED ACTION

The discussion of values leads us into the last of the six processes, committed action! When your values are guiding you, thoughts and actions are based upon them. These behaviors are motivated by your values. A person makes a commitment to them, even if they will face obstacles along the way. Sometimes, those obstacles are internal and other times they are external.

What is Committed Action?

The process of committed action involves setting goals and using your values to guide them. You take planned action to reach those goals and stay in step with your values with the strategy you create. It involves a decision to follow those values, even if it is uncomfortable at times.

It may create situations where you must talk to people about your values and why you are committed to something. Rather than avoiding this or being full of anxiety, think of it as a teaching opportunity. You can share with them how you feel and why you feel that way. If they value the relationship, they will respect your point of view on it.

This also opens the chance for them to share why they see it differently. There is no right or wrong when it comes to values and committed action though. Each of us has a different view of who we wish to be and the life we wish to have. For healthy relationships, you will find many of the values are similar.

We can learn a great deal about compassion and acceptance in our differences. They don't always have to be negative. It is when someone isn't respectful of your values and the boundaries that you set when you must decide if this is important to you. If it is, you may have to make a decision that is painful because of it. Keep in mind, a decision can be the right one, even if you don't always experience positive emotions because of it.

For example, if you are in a toxic relationship with someone who puts you down and brings you anxiety, it can be heartbreaking to end it. You have tried to set boundaries and they don't respect them. You have accepted you can't change their behaviors, so your choice is to end that relationship and no longer have contact with them. This can make you sad and hurt, but in time you will work through those emotions.

When you walk away from such toxic relationships, you have room for healthy ones. Sometimes, a person you have known for a short period of time has better intentions toward you than someone you have known for years. Pay attention to people and what they say and how they act. Also, understand when people don't act the way you think they should, it rarely has anything to do with you.

Everyone has their own battles internally to handle. Everyone has triggers in their external environment they haven't yet worked through. For those that can't effectively communicate or identify emotions, it can be hard to read them. Their behaviors can be impulsive and unpredictable, causing negative emotions in yourself when you are around them.

Commitment is a key part of accepting yourself and accepting emotions. You make the commitment to face the situation and not avoid it. You embrace the challenge before you and use the tools learned to identify emotions, process thoughts, and decide how to behave. All of this is going to shape the experience you have with that situation and the outcome.

Being mindful throughout the process is important. If you aren't in the moment, you can lose sight of what you are trying to accomplish. If you base your thoughts, emotions, and behaviors on past experiences that were upsetting, you aren't going to get beyond that. If you worry about the future, you may be frozen and fearful to make any decision. You don't want it to be the wrong one.

With committed action, you hold yourself accountable to see things through. It isn't always easy, especially when you are in a crisis or one that makes you uncomfortable. The commitment takes you on a defined course with detailed objectives and a plan to complete them. If barriers get in your way, you work to reduce and eliminate them.

Sometimes, psychological flexibility comes into the picture with committed action. This is because something you perceived as true has now been determined not to be. This can change the action plan you initially came up with. You always have the choice to select a different option for a solution if you believe it is going to co-exist with your core values. As we discussed previously, even core values can change with time. Don't be afraid to evolve!

What is the Role of Committed Action in ACT?

Using ACT and working with a therapist, many patients find their symptoms of mental health conditions and other concerns are reduced or eliminated. Planned actions help someone stay on task with their thinking, accepting their emotions, and with their behaviors. Committed to action also helps a person remain focused on the present and being mindful.

It isn't enough to say you want to change, that you want to be a better person and live a better life. You must commit to action for those changes to manifest. ACT shows the process and then gives this final process to help the patient make it all happen. You can daydream all you want, but it doesn't change reality! The commitment to action is where it all comes together.

Committed action is the part of therapy with ACT where a therapist can reiterate traditional therapy and mix it into the treatment plan. The type of exposure the therapist offers depends on what the patient is being seen for and where they are at with treatment. New concepts are only introduced if they are going to offer value to the patient and their action steps to reach goals.

For therapists, when they see patients engaged in the ACT processes, it is encouraging. It confirms that this can be the right treatment for them to be successful and reach their goals. When they see them commit to action, it confirms they have learned from the sessions and put the skills to use.

When a patient is committed to actions, it shows they may be ready to end therapy soon. They have a solid understanding of the six processes and how to apply them to situations in their life. They can continue to do this and will soon be able to do it without the therapy sessions in the mix.

Before someone is at the end of therapy, there are discussions about the next steps. There are discussions about talking openly with trusted individuals or in a support group. A person shouldn't feel that without the help of their therapist, they can't use ACT to continue to see positive results.

They should feel confident they can do this, and they should feel motivated to continue because it is working for them. At the same time, they know they can reach out to the therapist if they have questions, or they feel overwhelmed by a situation. They have a safety net in place, but most of the movement forward from that point will be handled by the patient on their own.

Committed action and ACT help someone fully commit to their values and long-term goals. It isn't something they do today and forget about tomorrow. Instead, it is something they continue to build upon because of how it enriches their life. Such individuals tend to do more for themselves through self-care too. This is because they know it keeps them happy and helps them continue to develop into the person they wish to be.

Valued-based actions reinforce what you learn in ACT and all the skills taught by the therapist. They can put all the tools out there, but each of us must decide when and how we will use them. The more aware you are of your values, the easier it is for you to commit to completing your intended steps for that situation.

To do this successfully, you must learn when to rely on:

- Awareness
- Connection
- Flexibility
- Optimism
- Regulation

How to Overcome Barriers to Committed Action

There are four powerful steps you can put in motion for committed action. If you feel like you have barriers in place, go through each of them and see where you can make some movement in the right direction.

- Choose an area of your life where you feel change is needed
- Choose the values that apply to this part of your life
- Identify goals that can be guided with those values
- Be mindful in your actions, thoughts, and emotions

Conscious awareness of what is important to you and warrants a meaningful life can help you get things back into perspective. When you feel like you don't have direction or balance, it is time to take a step back and observe what is going on. Get back to the core of your being and take steps toward values and commitment to action again.

For committed action to work as it was designed with ACT, you must have your core values identified. Don't worry if you don't have all of them memorized, but as you become aware of them, use them to your benefit! You can then translate those values into committed action.

You must work hard to make behavioral choices and thought choices that align with who you want to be and the life that brings you meaning. You must select your actions and work through your emotions so you can focus on what you wish to accomplish.

Some committed actions are very simple for you to follow. Others take more observation and problem-solving to come to a decision. If your commitment is there and you are true to yourself, you are making progress. Never allow the intimidation of someone else to make you compromise your values!

Avoidance tends to be a trap people fall into when it comes to barriers and committed action. Putting it off because you don't want to deal with it as a fight or flight response. It can be part of your core, even though there isn't any value with it. You must be aware of it and commit to working through it. If you continue to avoid situations, ACT isn't offering you the benefits it could!

Talk to your therapist if you struggle with avoidance, even though you have gone through it previously in therapy. They need to know that you are still working through that barrier. They will have you practice mindfulness, acceptance, and developing values so you can see why you should work through a given situation instead of avoiding it.

The goal is to show you the positive reinforcement that stems from dealing with situations rather than avoiding them. It reduces stress and anxiety. It improves mood and it can help you sleep better. It can help you feel in control over what you can and help you let go of what you can't control.

While therapists assign exercises and homework as close to real situations as they can, there will be variables within the circumstances of a given situation. Trust the six processes of ACT to guide you and help you so that your committed action is something you feel confident pursuing. Situations change so verify the facts and make sure you are practicing being flexible when necessary.

When you are flexible, the inevitable changes in your life aren't going to feel like major hits from all directions. Instead, you can rely on your core values that are always there under the surface of what is taking place. There will still be times you feel your thoughts and behaviors fell short of what you would have liked them to be.

That means you are learning, you are analyzing, and you are also accepting things for what they are. Learn from shortcomings when they happen and identify what you will do better next time. Then move on from it and don't dwell on what could have been or should have been. You have the power and ability to get your actions and thoughts back on track with your values.

When you have those values in place, you can commit to action to reach specific goals. Those goals should be detailed and defined along with an estimated timeframe assigned to them. Your goals will also change as you reach them because will then have something new in place.

For example, a concrete goal can be to complete your master's degree within 3 years and commit to studying at least an hour each night. Once you graduate with that degree, what is your plan? Your next goal may be to complete a powerful resume and secure a job you love in this field within the next 3 months.

Remember, goals are going to change often as you reach them. However, core values tend to be a constant motivator. They are a driving force behind the actions you take and the behaviors you choose. These values can change with time, but not at the same rate or to the same degree as your goals will.

CHAPTER NINE

ACT IN PRACTICE

Understanding ACT in practice is exciting and interesting. As you can gather from all the previous chapters, there are many elements to this form of therapy. They are all intertwined, and a person will often take part in several of them at the same time with their treatment plan.

It is the purpose of the therapist to touch on all six of the processes involved with ACT so the patient can see the whole concept. However, what they focus on the most in sessions and with exercises and homework depends on the patient. Through assessments and discussions, they will identify with the patient the areas where they wish to improve the most.

The techniques and methods to assist them with such changes are then put in motion to help them achieve those goals. No matter where someone is with ACT, acceptance and learning to control emotions is part of a healthier well-being and that is promoted in these sessions. Identifying goals and committed action are key elements to decision-making and living the life you wish for. All of it works together, and the patient finds a balance with the use of these ACT options.

It wouldn't be fair for a therapist to toss all of this out there to a patient in their first session. They would feel defeated, overwhelmed, and not know where to start. This is why the therapist introduces one or two concepts at a time and works through them. Once the patient is doing well with them, more can be added to the mix for the treatment plan.

ACT doesn't treat symptoms, and that makes it clearly different from other forms of therapy. Yet time and time again, research and data verify ACT methods will help reduce or eliminate symptoms because of how someone changes their behaviors and regains control over emotions. Letting go of judgment, shame, and other negative feelings makes room for happier ones.

The use of ACT processes doesn't end when the therapy sessions stop. Instead, the therapist is confident the patient has the tools and guidance they need to successfully continue to use it all in their lives. They feel confident they can do so without the assistance of the therapist. They have come to the point in the road where they are ready to continue the journey on their own!

Role-Playing

ACT information alone isn't enough, the patient must feel comfortable using it. A great therapist creates a bridge between the theory and the application of ACT processes. This is what makes the difference for patients, and why they are successful with this form of treatment.

There are several steps involved from intake through the completion of treatment with ACT. A therapist will always encourage someone to make progress, but not force it. They encourage the patient to take part in the treatment plan development and strive to motivate them to continue reaching for those goals and objectives.

There is only so much that can be done in each therapy session. Most patients see their therapist for an hour a week. That isn't realistically enough time to put this all together. What happens in those sessions though is discussions and a framework for what they can work on between sessions.

They may have a particular situation where it can work well, but they need assistance from their therapist with the dialect. Role-playing exercises in sessions are a great way to work on these skills. For example, someone may wish to talk with their partner about boundaries.

They aren't sure how to approach it or the right way to go about it. They aren't sure how their partner will react either. The therapist can role-play with them so they get comfortable with the format this type of conversation will take. They can work with them on the key elements they need to share and the best way for them to handle various scenarios that may emerge from that discussion.

This can give the patient confidence to try the techniques in that real-life situation. It can boost their self-confidence once they see the value this brings versus avoidance or impulsive behaviors. They can see the value handling emotions and thoughts effectively brings to their life that was lacking before.

All of this further reinforces their decision to continue with ACT methods. They know they are on a path to align how they think and how they feel with their goals and values. They know their behaviors are influenced by their thoughts and emotions, so they strive to keep it balanced in all these areas for the best outcome.

Exercises and Homework

Specific forms of exercises and homework are assigned by the therapist at the end of each session. It is important for the patient to commit to completing them and bringing that information with them to the next session. Resistance to these exercises and homework prevents ACT from working as it was intended.

You can't just dip your toes into the water so to speak with these processes. You must get yourself wet and you must focus on swimming to the other side. There will be barriers and challenges along the way, but if you know your end goal you can see it and you can focus on reaching it.

Adapting ACT for Different Populations

It is unrealistic to expect a therapist to know all the details of different populations. However, they should do their best to learn about that culture and understand it. Many therapists offering ACT work with a specific type of population due to the area where they reside. Understanding it and respecting it help create a strong bond between them and their patients.

It is vital that the patient determines their goals and values. Often, they are based on their background. They may not be the same goals and values the therapist would select for them, but they must be careful not to cross that line. Remember, ACT is individualized to help each patient have the life they desire and be the person they wish to be. Each of us is unique and the therapist must remember that as they design a therapy strategy for a particular patient.

Cultural diversity is often a target area of testing and data collection relating to ACT. The good news is research confirms this method of therapy works well with both genders and across different cultures and populations. It works for people from all walks of life, all mental health concern areas, and even different economic groups. This is why it is such a powerful resource for helping people enjoy life and find purpose with it.

Some of the in-depth studies conducted on this took place in Canada and Japan. It is widely known that Canada has one of the most diverse populations. This is due to the different ancestry and history links people have to the region. Another substantial part of this is Canada welcomes refugees and displaced individuals from around the world.

Such individuals can take part in educational programs at the various universities. Most of them come to Canada for a new life, one that offers plenty of opportunities for them and their family. The demand for more people in the workforce to fill jobs has opened several programs for qualified refugees to welcome them into Canada to fill those jobs.

The study in Japan was in-depth and this location was selected due to the value individuals put on their culture. This can create conflicts for them internally because their values don't always align with what the culture says they should follow. Those steadfast rules they grew up with may be hard to break down and accept they are perception and not fact-based.

It is important to look at ACT diversity from the perspective of the age groups of individuals too. When we think about mental health concerns or letting go of trauma, we often think about adults. However, many therapists focus their attention on ACT for adolescents. The methods are found to work well for a variety of situations that youth may be exposed to at a young age.

The goal of ACT for adolescents is to help them learn about processes they can use to heal. This gives them the information they need to do so as they continue to grow and shape their lives. They can live the life they want at a younger age; those negative experiences don't have to be a weight on their shoulders for the next 20 years!

None of us can change what has already happened, but we can change what will happen next. We can work on what we can control and learn to let go of the rest. Sadly, too many adults are still haunted by negative emotions tied to events that happened when they were younger, when they couldn't control anything about it.

ACT is becoming a larger part of therapy options for adolescents due to the value it offers. When children grow up in a cycle of abuse or neglect, it can cause them to engage in risky behaviors and act impulsively. They can repeat that cycle with their own children. Through ACT and other skills training, they can break that cycle, not only to improve their life but that of any offspring they have.

Other studies indicate that Latino and African American children are more likely to struggle with depression. ACT can be a method to help them reduce those symptoms. It can help them enjoy their childhood and be happier. It can help them experience growth because of the tools and techniques they learn so they don't struggle to process feelings or emotions as an adult.

Ethical Considerations in ACT

A therapist has plenty of leeway when it comes to creating the treatment plan with ACT. They can introduce ideas and concepts that aren't part of these six processes if they feel the patient needs them. The therapist always has an ethical responsibility to do no harm. They must create these treatment plans with the objective of helping the patient be successful.

It isn't ethical for a therapist to project their own views, values, or goals on the patient. They have to help them go in the direction that feels right to them. They can provide guidance, examples, and give them assessments to help information come to light in therapy.

ACT focuses on self-care, and there are plenty of moral dilemmas tangled up with core values and goals. What a person believes to be true has a hold on them. Is it ethical for them to be taught in therapy what they have always known and believed may not be true? From a scientific point of view, it is ethical because it gives them the chance to see for themselves how to differentiate facts from perceptions.

From a medical point of view, ACT is ethical because it promotes healing and taking good care of your needs. It focuses on accepting what is outside of your control and it reduces the risk of self-harm. The moral dilemma with it though is not everyone sees the same values and that can influence their thought process and decisions.

A good point to make about this ethical situation though is everyone has choices, and everyone can establish boundaries. Not everyone has the skills and methods to do this and that makes them feel helpless and evokes negative emotions. ACT can help people to be who they want to be and live a meaningful life; most will see that as a wonderful gift and concept that should be promoted.

Overcoming Challenges in Implementing ACT

Not all patients are ready to dive into the concepts of ACT, they have other challenges that get in the way. The two biggest ones are they lack coping skills, and they lack communication skills. Another big one is they don't have adequate problem-solving skills.

The role of a therapist is to identify if these elements are strong, weak, or simply not there at all. They can offer skills training individually or in group sessions to teach these techniques and help a person gain from the use of them in their daily life. These concepts help set the foundation for ACT processes to be added in on top of them.

Fear of failure is common for someone without self-esteem. They must understand ACT is a learning process and they will still make some mistakes with it. The goal is to stay in alignment with core values and learn from any mistakes. Finding a solution that could work better next time can be the outcome of something that didn't work out as you would have liked it to.

Avoidance is another factor that often gets in the way of implementing ACT. Avoiding situations because they make someone uncomfortable is a survival technique. However, it doesn't serve them well at all, it only manifests negative emotions. It often makes the outcome worse than it should have been and it increases anxiety and stress.

A good way to overcome this challenge with avoidance is to ask the patient what did they gain by putting off doing something or discussing something that was causing negative emotions? They won't be able to pinpoint anything positive from doing so. Next, ask them what they gained by finally dealing with that situation. When they can see that avoidance isn't helping them reach their goals, they can implement ways to change that.

Without these concepts, a person may continue in a cycle that doesn't work for them. They aren't equipped to accept emotions or start the healing process. They don't have the skills they need to set boundaries with others or control urges to avoid situations rather than deal with them. A therapist must help the patient identify these challenges so ACT methods and techniques can work as they were designed to.

Such therapy can't be forced upon someone, they must find value in it and decide they will take action to work on their behaviors and thought processes. One of the ethical dilemmas though is introducing ACT for those that engage in self-harm or those that are in treatment centers for mental health concerns.

Many experts feel ACT could be a turning point for those patients if they were exposed to it. These methods could lower the risk of them being hospitalized for mental health in the future. It can give them tools to use to live a healthy lifestyle rather than struggling in relationships, jobs, and not being happy with their life.

There is a difference with introducing treatment and forcing it on someone. In some facilities, there are professionals opposed to just using medication to help with mental health. They believe the treatment should include therapy, so the person is less likely to need medications ongoing. The debate on this ethical issue continues and takes on many challenges.

In the mid-1990s, some of the discussions about ethical concepts and ACT were introduced to patients that had been exposed to it. The goal was to gather their input about if they were forced into treatment or engaged in it voluntarily. The goal was to gain insight about how useful ACT has been for them based on where they are at in life at that time.

Many of the individuals that took this survey shared they were happier, and they felt that they had better relationships with others due to ACT. A common report is that people felt they has a voice, and they could change the future even though they couldn't change their past.

Not all the feedback from previous patients of ACT was positive though in this research. Some of them felt that the program they were involved with confined them too much. Others complained they didn't want to take medication but were forced to do so along with the therapy in an in-house facility.

The rights a patient has about treatment today for any type of therapy and medication is much different than it was in the 1990s. The one exception is parents and legal guardians have the final say about ACT and other forms of therapy for those under the age of 18.

Future Directions for ACT Research and Practice

The future direction for ACT research and practice is encouraging. Time and time again, studies show that ACT has been the solution for patients that didn't respond well to other forms of therapy or didn't get the level of results they were interested in from it.

This is important as those individuals may have given up. When they learn about ACT though, it can be a new option for them to consider. Most agree they have nothing to lose but plenty to gain by trying this process to see how it improves life for them.

Another topic that often comes to light is moving away from starting with other forms of therapy from the beginning. If ACT can work when other types of therapy failed for someone, why not introduce it first? At the very least, a therapist can consider talking to the patient about shifting from the current therapy plan to try ACT if it doesn't seem to be working well for them.

As more people learn about ACT and the value it offers, it is something patients are asking about. They want to learn more about the concept and see if it is a good fit for them or a loved one. As more therapists learn about the value of ACT, they can promote it as a viable treatment option.

Additional training and certification are required to use ACT techniques, but many therapists are signing up to get that training. They want to be involved in this wonderful method to help people live their best life possible. They believe in the six processes of ACT and they are willing to help someone tackle their personal challenges and use these methods successfully.

This will offer more resources for those that can benefit from ACT and all it entails. A significant focus is on underserved populations. This includes those living in poverty, the homeless, children, and people from certain cultures. The goal is to identify who would benefit the most from programs and ACT methods so they can work on behavior changes that serve them well.

CHAPTER TEN

WORKBOOK

Mental health is extremely important, and concerns about it shouldn't be hidden or ignored. Therapy can help treat a variety of mild, moderate, and severe forms of mental illness. However, concerns including anxiety and insomnia all fall into the category of your mental well-being.

This is why we owe it to ourselves to find solutions to improve our moods, thoughts, emotions, and behaviors. There are scenarios in our lives that we wish didn't happen. They were outside of our control and not our fault. However, healing from them is our responsibility.

You don't have to do it alone; a trained therapist can help you select ways to change behaviors. They can help you address what holds you back. Even if you have tried therapy before, ACT offers something new with the direction it takes. Each of us can benefit from effective coping skills and communication skills.

The treatment plan will be created with you specifically in mind. Work closely with your therapist and be part of that plan. It is your future and your mental health you have the chance to improve. Don't be afraid to try something new and explore the outcome. You may find this is something that changes your entire future. It can be your learning opportunity to move forward and take part in healing.

In simplest terms, ACT can help a person get unstuck from where they are and where they can't move in any direction. They feel that they can't let go of the past and they worry so much about the future. They aren't in a position where they enjoy or appreciate today. That isn't a place that offers much value to anyone, and ACT can help a person get out of that mindset and start to see some refreshing changes.

With the various ACT processes, you must know what you can gain from all of them. Here are some thoughts to help you stay motivated with it:

- Better self-care actions and activities
- Be the person you want to be

- Communicate thoughts and boundaries
- Get your needs met
- Experience feeling vulnerable without feeling out of control
- Experiencing life with fulfillment and purpose
- Feel better emotionally
- Identify triggers
- Let go of what you can't control
- Live in the moment
- Live the life you wish to have
- Practice forgiveness and compassion
- Problem-solve with a purpose
- Reduce impulsive behaviors
- Regain control over emotions
- Self-acceptance
- Stop avoiding
- Understanding your core values
- Use your senses to enjoy life

When you feel like there is a payoff and you are solving problems with integrity, it all starts to make sense. You feel better about decisions and you aren't afraid that life is just passing you by. It is difficult to take an open and honest look at your life, your behaviors, and your patterns. ACT gives you a chance to do that with support and structure.

Many of us struggle and we wish we had done things differently. We didn't realize we had other options, so forgive what has taken place and do what you can to have a happier future. Apologize to others where you may have created conflict due to your previous behaviors. Show compassion and forgive when others don't act in a way that you find pleasing. They may have some huge burdens they haven't addressed yet that you don't know anything about.

One of the strong motivators of the six processes with ACT is when you see those positive changes within yourself. When you can realize the growth, you have made and the inner peace that comes from letting go of negative emotions and thoughts. It encourages you to continue practicing what you have learned. Enjoyment stems from living in the moment and being mindful is one of the best ways to create that improved mood!

In this chapter, we will look at exercises and worksheets for each of the six processes. We will look at techniques you can use in your daily life. This is just a small sample of the various exercises and techniques for ACT and each of the six processes. Your therapist will determine which of them you need to work on first. They may assign more exercises and homework with some of the concepts than others because they are aware of your needs.

Create your own workbook to journal how you feel, for reflection, and to complete the various exercises offered here. Each of them can be applied to your own situations and thought patterns. Don't focus on being right all the time, focus on being mindful and doing what you can to have a meaningful life. We all have days that are better than others. The following day is a chance to start over again and make it better!

Learn from your mistakes but don't stop trying to reach your goals. Don't push your values aside because they can cause challenges for you. Be compassionate about the beliefs and values of others, but also use the workbook to help you strive to become the person you want to be. It brings great happiness when you accept who you are and what you feel. A workbook where you collectively work through emotions and thoughts can help you see the transformation you long for!

Contacting the Present Moment

Exercise

Pick out a piece of fruit you enjoy eating. Focus on being mindful with it. What does it taste like? What does it smell like? How does it feel when you hold it? What is the texture as you chew it? Focus on the sounds and sensations that take place in your mouth as you consume it.

As you are doing this, there will be distractions. Your phone may ring, something is on TV, or someone may be talking to you. The challenge with this exercise is to continually focus on NOTHING else but consuming that piece of fruit. Your thoughts should only be on that taking place in the moment. If your mind wanders to anything else, immediately redirect it back to the fruit and the process involved in eating it. You may be surprised how many distractions popped up including thoughts in your mind when you were trying to be mindful in these few minutes on one certain topic.

Worksheet

Write down a thought or scenario that continues to replay in your mind. Think about the emotions associated with it and why it has so much control over it. Think about why you wish to change this behavior and make a commitment to be mindful to do so.

....

....

....

....

Over the next week, do your best to not think about that scenario or to think about it less. When you do think about it, try to detach from those emotions and work through them so that you aren't giving them control over your thoughts or actions. Evaluate how often you thought of that scenario during that week and what you have gained from being mindful.

Mark this page with a bookmark and remember to return to it in two weeks. If you are using ACT and being mindful, you should think about it less and less. When you do think about it, you should be able to accept the emotions and move on. As you do this, you give that replay in your mind less and less power over your mood and behaviors. If the scenario is still playing out frequently, try it again in two more weeks. This is a great way to see the value of ACT and how it is applied to your thoughts and processing. It gives a person insight to see that they really do have more control than they thought, and that is empowering. It motivates them to continue to work on additional behavior changes.

Techniques
There are several wonderful techniques that help someone stay in tune with the present moment and being mindful. They include:
- Adequate sleep each night
- Awareness
- Breathing techniques
- Healthy lifestyle habits including diet and exercise
- Identify triggers
- Find solutions instead of succumbing to avoidance
- Focus on listening to others instead of jumping in to respond
- Lighten your schedule
- Reduce distractions
- Tune into the 5 senses

Defusion

Exercise

Think about a negative self-judgment you have about yourself right now. For example, you may be thinking "I am a horrible parent". Focus on that thought for at least one minute. How did it make you feel? What negative emotions and thoughts were flowing through you as you focused on that negative element?

Next, try it with something positive inserted in the mix. For example, say "I am a good parent, doing the best I can with everything going on". Focus on that thought for one minute. What positive thoughts and emotions were going through your mind that time? What great memories did you have of moments with your children?

What many people notice with this defusion exercise though is the second thought process has LESS of an impact on them than the first one! The goal is to make the positive thoughts and emotions have MORE of an impact on you than negative ones. Sadly, we can hear 10 good things and 1 bad one, and we may focus all day long on that 1 bad thing! Awareness can help you change that around and modify your mood and your thought process.

Worksheet

Defusing the power your emotions and thoughts have on you can be done by writing them down. This worksheet process is much more than just journaling though. There are three main areas where people get caught up:

- Only seeing one side of things
- Perceptions
- Triggers

They are often interlinked, but that isn't always the case. Make a list of a particular trigger you can't get out of your head in column 1. Underneath it, list all the feelings and emotions that come along with that trigger.

In the second column, what is your perception of it? What do you think about it? Next, dig around and find information to validate those perceptions. What is true? What isn't? What is based on your own internal processes or previous experiences? When you can see it for what it is, you can then accept it.

Sometimes, it is hard to see more than one side of things. That limits our options relating to it. Write down your side of it. Ask your therapist or people you trust to give you input on how they see that same thought. Use the internet and search to see what others must share about it. As you see another side to that narrative, it can help you generate options you didn't know existed.

....

....

....

....

....

....

....

....

....

Techniques

Here are some wonderful defusion techniques to try!

- I notice statements – Tell yourself a narrative such as I notice I am thinking about (**XXX**) and I know it isn't true.
- Talk to your mind – Thank your mind for information and feedback, just like you would if the information came from a trusted friend.
- Mindful watching – This involves being open to your thoughts and letting them come and go. You don't try to change them or control them, you just let them flow.
- Use a silly voice for irrational thoughts
- X button – visualize an X button in your mind where you can close out a thought like you do a tab on your computer.

Acceptance

Exercise

Observing and exploring emotions is a big part of acceptance. Remember, you can't judge what you feel. This is an exercise for any emotion that makes you uncomfortable. First, identify that emotion for what it is. For example, you may feel angry, but the underlying emotion is actually hurt or fear not anger. Use your senses to help you identify it and then write it down.

Sit in a quiet area and close your eyes. Imagine the word on that paper right in front of you. Visualize moving that emotion a foot away from you. Now visualize it five feet away from you. Focus on removing yourself from a connection to that emotion so you can observe it. Taking a step back takes some practice but stay focused on that task.

Ask yourself some questions. If the emotion had a size, would it be small, medium, or large? What shape would it be? What color? You may feel silly doing this at first, but it helps you put the emotion in perspective. It helps you isolate it and take away the power you were giving it before.

As you reflect on the emotion, you should notice that how you feel about it changes when you distance yourself from it. When you accept it for what it is, your emotions and behaviors aren't controlled by that uncomfortable feeling. Try to complete this task daily with one of your emotions and reflect back on it over a one-month timeframe. This will help you train your thought process to accept emotions, even those you aren't fond of.

Worksheet

Draw a circle in the middle. Write your observation point or emotion in that circle in large letters. Next, start at the top and go around it and write key information relating to that thought. Ask yourself these questions as you write out the details. Doing so will help you accept the thought or emotion if you are struggling to do so.

- What do I see, hear, smell, and feel (both emotionally and with touch)?
- What can I do to express gratitude toward myself with this subject?
- Is this thought or emotion important to my goals and values?
- Did I have control to do so something different? If not, can I accept that?
- How strong were the thoughts or emotions at that moment? How strong are they now?
- Did how I handle that moment help me achieve where I want to be?
- What can I learn from the thoughts and emotions I am experiencing?
- What is true about these thoughts or feelings?

Techniques

There are plenty of techniques to apply with acceptance and it often depends on the situation. With ACT, a person can learn about many of them and role-play in therapy sessions. This will help them decide what technique to apply in a given situation. Such techniques include:

- Accept unwanted feelings and emotions
- Balance perspective and truth
- Defusion
- Focus on goals and values
- Mindfulness

Self-as-Context

Exercise

One of the great benefits with self-as-context as it teaches compassion. Too often, we get stuck on something someone said or did and we allow it to define us. Usually, when someone is negative toward you it has to do with things going on in their world and nothing to do with you specifically.

When you have a challenging moment with someone, ask yourself is there something more you need to ask them about the situation. If not, let it go. This doesn't mean you give people a free pass to be unkind to you. It simply means you don't define who you are or how your day goes because of the actions or words from others. If you let everyone else ruin your day or your mood, you will struggle to be happy.

Worksheet

With self-as-context, you must see the picture clearly of what you are doing and why you are doing it. You must see the value in it and that it correlates with your goals and core values. Writing down information and answering questions can help you see if it fits or not. If it doesn't, you must change your thoughts and behaviors relating to that concept.

Write down the topic you have a situation with at the top of the paper. Be honest with your answers and dig deep into your thoughts if you need to so you can get answers.

- **Ask yourself what is the purpose of this?**

- **How is it relevant to your goals and values?**

- **What will you get out of it that is going to help you live a life you love?**

- **Is it necessary?**

The goal of this worksheet is to get you in the habit of thinking like this with concepts relating to self-as-context. Focus your time and energy on things you need to work on and let the rest go. Focus on what you can change and not on what you can't. Don't waste your energy on things that don't offer you value or they aren't really an influence in the quest for the better life you seek.

....

....

....

....

....

....

....

....

....

Techniques

Get to know yourself but also observe yourself. There are techniques to help you do this:

- Be forgiving
- Focus on being the person you want to be
- Let go of what you can't change
- Identify goals and values to help guide your thoughts and behaviors
- Practice acceptance

Values Clarification

Exercise

Ask yourself the following questions to help you identify core values that matter to you today.

- Who do you care about the most and why?
- What matters to you and why is it important?
- What tends to trigger negative emotions in you and why?
- What are you inspired by?
- Think about your emotions and what makes you happy? Sad? Scared? Excited?
- What do you enjoy doing in your free time?
- When do you feel the most grateful? What are you appreciative of and why?
- What brings you personal satisfaction in your life?

Worksheet

For each section, write down the values you feel in your heart that fall into each of these categories.

Leisure	Personal growth and health	Relationships	Work and education

Techniques

A wide range of techniques will help you with values and staying true to yourself. Such examples are:

- Effective communication skills
- Establish boundaries
- Focus on facts and not perceptions
- Forgive the mistakes you make
- Identify emotions but don't be controlled by them
- Identify your values that presently apply to the life you wish to live
- Stop giving time to replaying scenarios in your head of things you couldn't change
- Use coping skills

Committed Action

Exercise

Find at least one way in your life each day where you can show committed action. This is easier than you think! For example, it can be the commitment to show up to your therapy appointments as scheduled and follow through will all the assignments. It can be sitting down and talking with your partner about boundaries you want to put in place. Focus on one committed action at a time. Once you have it in place, add another!

Worksheet

Write down an area of your life you want to change, one that is a priority. Part way down the page, write down the core values that pertain to that area of your life which you will follow. Create goals to achieve the change you want while holding true to those values.

The goals should be detailed including what you want and when you want it. Some goals are long-term, and others are short-term. For those that are long-term, break them down into smaller segments and timeframes so you can celebrate those victories along the way. It will help you see the progress and remain motivated.

What action steps can you take physically and mentally to help you achieve those goals? Make sure you list being mindful as one of them!

Techniques

Keeping it realistic and staying motivated are important parts of committed action. What you work on has to be achievable and you have to find ways to keep going, even when it gets hard. Some techniques to help you include:

- Detailed goals and how you will achieve them
- Focus only on what you can change
- Journaling
- Incorporate values
- Reflection
- Solutions rather than avoidance

CONCLUSION

The research involved with ACT and how well it works is astounding! This has encouraged more therapists to pursue the training it requires to teach these methods and techniques. It is exciting to see this area of therapy growing and helping so many people transform their lives! It can work when other types of therapy weren't enough for someone to reach the level of success they desired.

With ACT, a person can find the dialect and self-talk methods they need to break away from cycles that don't promote the life they want. Any time we try to make positive changes, we encounter barriers. They can evoke negative feelings and thoughts. Instead of giving up, we have to work through them and use the tools and techniques to help us do so in a healthy manner.

It can be difficult to open up in therapy and share your private experiences. Talking about the thoughts you have, images you see, feelings you experience, and even any urges you may have can help your therapist give you the right tools and techniques for you to get value from. Create a bond with your therapist and share the memories with them – both the good and the bad.

With ACT, you will learn mindfulness skills to assist you with dealing with those difficult and challenging situations. The barriers can get smaller and smaller so you can continue to forge a path toward your goals. Don't get discouraged at times when the steps are small, progress is still progress.

Should you get into a situation where you move backward, don't give up. That is the ideal time to dig deep and apply the tools and coping skills you learned with ACT. Don't hesitate to reach out to your therapist when you need some extra support through a challenging event either. As you apply what you learn more and more to your daily life, you will find you can handle what comes along on your own.

Intervene in Harmful Cycles with Therapy
This type of therapeutic intervention should only be introduced by a licensed professional. They have the extra training and credentials to

successfully use ACT as part of an individualized treatment plan. The goal of this is to help them face what has been causing the negative thoughts and feelings instead of avoiding them.

Accepting them at face value takes away their power. Each patient still has their private experiences. The change through ACT though is the impact on them no longer triggers unwanted feelings and harmful thoughts that prevent someone from being happy. This all relates back to the concept of mindfulness, being present in the moment.

When you get into a fight with someone, you always have the option to walk away if they are treating you badly. There is no way to do that when the negative thoughts and feelings are coming from your own head. You can't run away from that, so the best thing you can do is treat yourself with kindness.

Open up to your private experiences and make room for them in your heart. When those feelings come along you can change them into something positive. When you accept what the situation is, you can end that internal struggle. It is unfair that trauma and circumstances beyond our control can have such an effect on us and make us feel guilt or shame. ACT gives you tools to stop feeling like that so you can heal and focus your energy on inner peace.

Don't waste your thoughts on how much energy, time, or even money you have wasted rehashing those experiences time and time again. All of that is something you can't change. What you can change though with ACT is how you will respond NOW and how you will respond from this day forward! It is a freeing experience and it will help you focus on the life you want.

Guided values take shape when you remove the negative, these are your core values. Living a life you are satisfied with isn't determined by how much money you make or how many people you know. The quality of life is determined by how happy you are with the person you see in the mirror. It is determined by how you find happiness in everything around you because you are mindful of your surroundings and senses.

Interventions involved with Act are focused on helping a patient accept their private experiences without judgment or fear. It focuses on accepting those circumstances aren't anything you can control or change.

The second part of this is making a commitment to think and behave in a manner that promotes a life of value.

The role of the therapist with ACT is to offer compassion and empathy while giving the patient direction. The bond develops because the patient feels valued and respected in the sessions. It is important for the therapist to help someone embrace methods to be positive with thoughts and feelings. Such changes also influence their behaviors. It will reduce the risk of acting impulsively or the risk of self-harm. None of us get a straight line in life from where we start to where we wish to be. The path can wind, have dead-end streets, and the mountain may seem so tall we don't think we will get over it.

ACT offers a different type of therapy than the norm, and many patients do extremely well with it. We have to appreciate the fact that we are all different. Being kind to ourselves and others is important. We are aware of our own internal struggles, but we also have to remember others have had their own personal moments to work through too.

Applying the six processes of ACT to your life can be a game-changer. It can give you control over yourself and your thoughts. It can give you control over your feelings and behaviors. You will never have control over other people or certain situations, but you must embrace what you can change to experience the life you wish to have.

The six processes of ACT include:

- **Contacting the present moment**
- **Defusion**
- **Acceptance**
- **Self as Context**
- **Values**
- **Committed Action**

Each of these six processes of ACT has been explained and explored in detail in previous chapters. It is important to have a firm understanding of each of them and how you can incorporate these processes into your thought process and actions. In the end, only you can hold yourself accountable. Only you can find the motivation to create the changes you wish to see in your life.

Learning to live with your demons as some will say, is important. When you take away that control they have over you, the sun shines brighter and your mood is lifted. You don't have to continue feeling like you live in darkness due to what happened to you. Choose a direction and see where it takes you. If you find that road isn't the path to the full life you desire, change it up!

Your life can be what you want from it, and that gives you a full cup to also help others from. You will find you are a better employee, spouse, parent, and friend when you take care of your own needs. It isn't realistic to think we will always be happy or there will never be painful experiences we have to go through.

Life is full of events that bring with it stress, worry, and sometimes even physical pain. Rather than giving in to the fear of that situation, take positive action and do what you can to have the best outcome despite the situation that occurred. Fear is often the manifestation of avoidance. The longer we put off doing something, the more fear we develop about it.

Sometimes, you have to dive in and face that fear. That fear isn't any less real in your eyes, but you can be proud of the effort you put forth to combat it. ACT gives you the skills and techniques you can reach into yourself for when you need them the most. You won't feel isolated and you will have the self-confidence to see how you can put a better outcome on this scenario.

Put an end to that voice in your head that is always doubting, always looking at the worst-case scenario. Let go of regrets too about what you could have done or should have done. If you can honestly say you did the best you could with what you had or what you knew in that moment, then you should be proud of that! If you made a mistake, learn from it. That mistake only defines you if you allow it to hold you in place rather than trying something different to keep moving forward.

Living a life that is meaningful to you and of value to you, there will be times when you have to take risks. There will be situations where you have to step outside of your comfort zone. This can cause some anxiety due to the uncertainty, but trust your instincts. Trust the tools and techniques you learned with ACT to guide you and assist you.

The coping elements of ACT give you ways to take action but you don't have to worry about a certain outcome. Instead, you select a valued direction, knowing the results are going to be outside of your control. This is going to curb that natural instinct of fight or flight. That response is often tied to impulsive behavior and anxiety.

When you embrace the concepts of ACT, you can focus on taking action to help accept a situation as it is. As you learn more of the concepts involved in this type of therapy, you have flexibility with regard to the tools you use. Being present in the moment will help you experience what is taking place right then! This will help you stop avoiding situations and emotions, even when they may make you uncomfortable.

You can expect the following with ACT methods and techniques:

- **Ability to accept problems and challenges as a part of life**
- **Action steps to be the person you desire and live the life you want**
- **Overcome negative feelings and thoughts**
- **Select the path you wish to build your life upon with core values at the center**

It is possible to have a life of value with plenty of wonderful memories once you learn to accept your life. Your therapist will help you identify any triggers in your life that could cause anxiety or stress. When that happens, it can promote negative thoughts and feelings. Recognizing such triggers gives you the opportunity to change the scenarios where you can. When you can't control or change it, use your tools to help you accept it and move on from it.

You have to learn to accept what goes on around you. At the same time, you can't ignore what is going on inside of you. The two are intertwined and often overlap. Being mindful gives you self-control and it is empowering. When you live in the present you can focus on what is best for you. There will be times when that means you stop doing what is best for other people.

Mindfulness isn't selfish and it isn't about getting your own way. Instead, these ACT techniques teach boundaries and better ways to communicate. Often, you can release negative thoughts and emotions by having an honest conversation with the person that is creating them in your life. If you don't speak up, you give them a free pass to continue creating those negative feelings and emotions in you.

ACT releases the grip that toxic feelings and emotions relating to past events have had on you. It is time to redefine your values and the direction you wish to take in this life. It is never too late to turn around and move in a new direction if the road you are on doesn't bring you happiness and a feeling of self-worth. It is all worth it when you experience inner peace and a calmness that was missing before.

Mental health is a huge concern in our society, and too many people don't get a proper diagnosis or the treatment they need. For others, treatment failed them, and that caused them to sink further and further down into a hole. ACT may be the ladder down that hole to pull them back out, one step on the ladder at a time!

ACT is proven to help reduce symptoms of mental health, even though it is not designed to target symptoms. The reduced or eliminated symptoms are a byproduct of the methods and techniques of ACT. Studies show people using these methods are less likely to relapse to old behaviors and they are less likely to require hospitalization for a mental health concern.

The length of time a patient is in ACT depends on their needs and the speed of their progress. The therapist will give you exercises and techniques to apply to your life outside of the sessions. The goal is for you to implement them as much as you can and then report the outcome of doing so at your sessions.

Take all of the techniques and exercises you use in therapy and use them daily. Take the information found here and the exercises in the workbook chapter and apply them to your day to day activities. You will find this gives you a built-in support and processing foundation to help you through the good days as well as the hard days.

ACT is personalized and continues to evolve. Data indicates it can be used for many mental health ailments. It is also recognized to help those that have struggled with bullying and other concerns that don't fall into a mental health category. Incorporating ACT into your life can help you each day to live the life you really want. I encourage you to continue to seek new information and resources on the topic as they become available.

I hope you have found this book on ACT to be informative and thought provoking. It is a wonderful therapy and of great value to those that haven't had the success they wanted with other forms of therapy. It focuses on some different elements from DBT and that can be the difference for someone interested in living a life that is happy and calm.

I encourage you to share your review about this book as your feedback is important. It helps me shape my writing and influences the motivation and passion I have to share information. It is an amazing feeling to know the information I share has had a positive impact on someone. Perhaps it will encourage you to seek a therapist offering ACT. Your feedback may help someone else decide to read this book and gain value from all of the information too.

BOOK 4

THE

PTSD

Embark on a Journey of Recovery and Discover
Strategies to Reclaim Your Life from the Clutches of
Post-Traumatic Stress Disorder

Reflection Page: Your Personal Journey with PTSD

Dear Reader,

This section is dedicated to you and your personal journey with PTSD. It's a space for reflection, a canvas where you can paint your thoughts and emotions. Here, you are invited to write openly and honestly about your experiences. It's a place of understanding and acceptance, where every word you inscribe is a step toward healing.

Current Feelings: (Describe your general emotional state.). (Are you feeling hopeful, frustrated, or something else entirely?)

Recurring Thoughts: What thoughts keep circling in your mind? (This space is for you to acknowledge and express those persistent notions or questions.)

....

....

....

....

Emotional Waves: How have your emotions fluctuated with your experience of PTSD? (Document the highs and lows, the calm and the storms.)

....

....

....

....

....

Lessons Along the Way: Reflect on the insights and understandings you've gained about yourself and your journey with PTSD. (Big or small, every realization counts.)

....

....

....

....

....

Gratitude Reflections: Despite the challenges, there might be moments or people that bring light into your life. (Note down anything or anyone you feel thankful for.)

....

....

....

....

....

Instances of Resilience: (Identify times when you've felt particularly resilient or strong.). (Remember, bravery is found in facing your fears, not in their absence.)

....

....

....

....

....

Confronting Challenges: What hurdles have you encountered? (Write about these challenges and ponder your approach to overcoming them.)

....

....

....

....

....

A Note to Self: (Pen a message to yourself.). (It might be words of encouragement, a gentle reminder, or an affirmation of your journey and growth.)

....

....

....

....

....

Additional Thoughts: Feel free to add any other thoughts, feelings, or reflections that come to your mind. (This is your personal reflective space.)

....

....

....

....

Your reflections are valuable footsteps on the path to understanding and healing. As you navigate this journey, remember that your story is unique and your resilience is remarkable.

INTRODUCTION

I magine we're sitting down over a cup of coffee, and you've just asked me about this thing called PTSD. Well, let me tell you, it's a tough topic, but it's something a lot of folks might encounter. PTSD, or Post-Traumatic Stress Disorder, is what can happen to someone after they've been through a bad scare—like a major accident, a natural disaster, or something else that's just too much to handle.

What's tricky about PTSD is that it doesn't just pack up and leave when the event is over. No, it lingers like a shadow, affecting thoughts, feelings, and even how a person reacts to everyday things. People might keep reliving the event in their heads, start avoiding places or people that remind them of it, feel all sorts of negative changes in their thoughts or mood, or even feel jumpy or easily angered.

It's super important for everyone to understand a bit about PTSD, not just the doctors and therapists who treat it. Knowing about it can help friends and families be there for each other. It's like knowing the signs of a storm—if you can see it coming, you can find shelter sooner.

Talking about PTSD openly is a big deal. It helps break the ice and gets rid of that unnecessary shame or secrecy. It's about making sure no one goes through it feeling alone or misunderstood. Plus, chatting about it can lead to better support, smarter community understanding, and even smarter decisions by the folks who make the big calls in healthcare and policy.

Also, when people talk about their own experiences with PTSD, it gives them a voice. It's about sharing not just the tough times but also the victories, big or small. Each story told is a step towards a world that gets it—a world that's ready to support and heal together.

So, this book is all about getting the full picture of PTSD. We want to educate, stir up some empathy, point out how to spot it early on, offer help and hope, share real-life stories, and keep the conversation going. It's about seeing the person, not just the PTSD, and recognizing the incredible strength and resilience in each story. Let's aim for a world that understands a bit more and judges a bit less.

CHAPTER ONE

WHAT IS PTSD?

Alright, let's dive into Chapter 1, "What is PTSD?", like we're unraveling a mystery together. Talking about the tough stuff in life, especially the scary experiences, isn't exactly a light topic. But, you know, understanding these darker moments is kind of like night fishing—it's challenging, but it's also where some of the most insightful discoveries are made. So, let's gear up and wade into the world of Post-Traumatic Stress Disorder, or PTSD for short.

PTSD isn't just some medical term to toss around; it's a heavy reality for a whole lot of people out there. Imagine it as this persistent shadow or an unwelcome echo from a past event that just sticks around, messing with someone's head and how they interact with the world.

In this part of the book, we're going to sail through some rough seas. We'll investigate what PTSD really is, why chatting about it isn't just important but necessary, and how getting a grip on it can be a beacon of hope and healing. This isn't just about the nitty-gritty medical side of things; it's about the human stories, the uphill battles, and the kind of strength and resilience that deserves its own standing ovation.

As we move through the pages, keep in mind that this might tug at some sensitive strings in your own heart or strike a chord with hidden battles you've faced or are facing. But amid all that, remember there's a promise here—a promise of deeper understanding, empathy, and a pathway to healing. So, let's dive into "What is PTSD?" peeling back the layers to really grasp its essence.

Now, let's break down PTSD and its symptoms a bit more. After a traumatic event has turned someone's world upside down, they might develop PTSD. It's normal to have a whole mix of reactions afterward—fear, horror, even guilt. But when these intense feelings don't fade and you feel like you're stuck in a constant state of alertness or horror, that's when it might be PTSD. It's like the mind is trapped in an ongoing state of shock.

The symptoms of PTSD can wiggle their way into various aspects of life, and they're generally grouped into four types:

Intrusive thoughts: These are the relentless, unwanted memories, the nightmares, or the flashbacks that are so vivid it's as if the traumatic event is happening all over again right in front of you.

Avoidance: This means steering clear of places, activities, or even thoughts that remind you of the trauma. It's like the mind's attempt to avoid reliving the pain.

Negative changes in thinking and mood: This might manifest as ongoing negative thoughts about oneself or the world, a sense of doom, or feeling detached and just unable to feel much joy.

Changes in physical and emotional reactions: This includes being jumpy, easily startled, having trouble sleeping, or feeling irritable. It's the body's way of being in a constant state of guard.

Understanding these symptoms is like having a map to recognize PTSD in oneself or others. It's vital to remember that experiencing these symptoms right after a traumatic event doesn't necessarily mean one will develop PTSD—it's more about the long-term persistence and intensity of these symptoms.

As we delve deeper into understanding PTSD, it's important to remember that having PTSD isn't about personal weakness. It's complex, with various factors, from genetics to personal history, playing a role in who experiences it and why. What matters most is recognizing the signs, seeking out help, and supporting those around us who are on this tough journey. That's the start of the healing process.

In the following sections, we'll also explore the historical context and how our comprehension of PTSD has evolved over time. From its early mentions in ancient texts to the more sophisticated understanding we have today, the journey of understanding PTSD is a testament to human resilience and our ever-growing knowledge of mental health. Stay tuned as we unpack the layers and reveal the many facets of this deeply human condition.

Continuing our journey through the historical context and evolution of understanding PTSD, we begin to see how deeply rooted this condition is in human history. The understanding of PTSD stretches back centuries, evolving alongside humanity's understanding of psychology and medicine.

From Ancient Understandings to Modern Times

Ancient warriors returning from battles exhibited symptoms we might now recognize as PTSD, although it was understood through a very different lens. Terms and interpretations have shifted dramatically over time. From "soldier's heart" in the American Civil War to "shell shock" during World War I, each era brought its own understanding and terminology, reflecting the societal and medical knowledge of the times.

The 20th Century and the Birth of PTSD

It was the aftermath of the Vietnam War and the advocacy of veterans that really brought PTSD into public consciousness. Their experiences and the vocalization of their struggles were pivotal in shaping the modern understanding of PTSD. In 1980, the condition was formally recognized in the Diagnostic and Statistical Manual of Mental Disorders (DSM-III), marking a significant turning point in its official medical recognition and treatment.

This recognition was a huge step. It meant that PTSD was not just a "soldier's ailment" but a serious condition that could affect anyone who had experienced a traumatic event. This broader understanding helped shift the stigma and opened avenues for more research, better treatment, and a deeper societal understanding of the condition.

Today's Understanding: A More Nuanced View

Today, our understanding of PTSD is far more nuanced. We recognize that it can affect anyone, from soldiers to survivors of natural disasters, serious accidents, or personal assaults. The condition is seen as a spectrum, with symptoms and severity varying widely from person to person.

Advancements in neuroscience have given us a clearer picture of how trauma affects the brain and body. This has led to more effective treatments and therapies tailored to individual needs. We now understand that treatment must be holistic, considering not just the psychological aspects of PTSD but the social, biological, and individual factors as well.

The Current Landscape of PTSD Treatment and Advocacy

As our journey through understanding PTSD continues, the landscape of treatment and advocacy keeps evolving. There's a growing emphasis on early intervention, reducing stigma, and providing support networks for those affected. Advocacy and awareness campaigns have brought PTSD into public dialogue, fostering a more informed and empathetic society.

Moreover, the treatment of PTSD has become more patient-centric, integrating various approaches including cognitive-behavioral therapy, EMDR (Eye Movement Desensitization and Reprocessing), and mindfulness techniques, among others. There's a recognition that healing from trauma is a personal journey and that support needs to be compassionate, informed, and responsive to individual experiences.

Looking Ahead: The Future of PTSD Understanding

As we look forward, the journey to understand and treat PTSD continues. Future generations will receive the knowledge and care they require because of ongoing research, developing therapies, and expanding public discourse. The goal is not just to treat PTSD but to foster a society that's informed, empathetic, and supportive, creating an environment where healing and resilience can flourish.

So, as we continue to turn the pages of understanding PTSD, let's remember that this is more than just a medical condition; it's a human experience. It's about the stories of resilience, the challenges faced, and the collective effort to understand, support, and heal together. As we move forward, let's carry with us the lessons learned, the stories shared, and the commitment to a more compassionate and informed world.

Types of PTSD

Let's think of PTSD not as a one-size-fits-all kind of deal but more like a tree with different branches. Each branch represents a type of PTSD, and understanding these differences is super important for getting the right kind of help. So, let's walk through the garden of the mind and look at these various branches.

Uncomplicated PTSD

Imagine Uncomplicated PTSD as a tree struck by lightning once. It's the kind of PTSD that comes from a single traumatic event. Though it's called "uncomplicated," don't be fooled—it's not simple for those going through it. Folks might have flashbacks, feel emotionally numb, or try to avoid anything that reminds them of that one bolt of lightning. Even if it's from a single event, it's tough and needs care tailored to heal those specific wounds.

Complex PTSD

Imagine a tree weathering a relentless storm, season after season. That's Complex PTSD. It comes from facing ongoing, repeated trauma—like long-term abuse or living in a war zone. This storm leaves deep, complex scars, including difficulty managing emotions and feeling hopeless. The roots of C-PTSD are deep and tangled, making healing a journey that requires patience and specialized care.

Comorbid PTSD

Think of Comorbid PTSD as a tree with several different types of vines growing around it. This is when PTSD coexists with other conditions like anxiety, depression, or substance abuse. It's a complicated mix because the symptoms of PTSD are intertwined with those of other disorders, like vines twisting together. Treating Comorbid PTSD means carefully addressing each vine to help the tree thrive again.

Dissociative PTSD

Imagine a tree that's started to split into two—part of it here and part of it elsewhere. Dissociative PTSD includes feeling detached from reality or forgetting parts of the trauma. It's like a natural defense, where the mind tries to protect itself by stepping away from the pain. Those with dissociative PTSD might feel disconnected or as if they're living in a dream. Healing involves gently guiding the tree back to a whole, feeling present and grounded.

PTSD with Prominent Anxiety or Depressive Symptoms
This is like a tree in a constant state of wilting, overshadowed by dark clouds of anxiety or depression. In these cases, the anxiety or depression is just as prominent as the PTSD symptoms. It's a heavy blend that can really weigh on a person, making everyday life feel extra challenging. Treatment focuses on clearing the clouds and nurturing the tree back to health, addressing both the trauma and the intense anxiety or depression.

Understanding these types doesn't just help doctors or therapists; it's good for everyone to know. It's like understanding that different trees need different care. By recognizing the variety of PTSD experiences, we can offer more personalized, effective support and walk together towards a more understanding and healing world. Each journey is unique, but with the right knowledge and care, there's hope for every tree in the garden, no matter how storm-tossed it's been.

PTSD vs. Other Anxiety Disorders

As we continue down the path of understanding mental health, let's further clarify how PTSD distinguishes itself from other anxiety disorders. It's like differentiating between various types of storms; each has its own unique patterns and impacts, requiring specific strategies for navigation and safety.

Delineating PTSD in the Anxiety Disorder Spectrum:

Anxiety disorders form a broad category, like a forest with various types of trees. Each tree, whether it's Generalized Anxiety Disorder, Panic Disorder, or Social Anxiety, has its own characteristics. PTSD, while rooted in the same soil of fear and worry, grows differently due to its direct link to traumatic events. It stands out in this forest as a unique tree that has undergone traumatizing storms.

Fine-Tuning the Differences:

Origin Story: PTSD starts at a specific moment of trauma, setting its narrative apart from other anxiety stories. It's like a play that begins with a dramatic scene, defining everything that follows. Other anxiety disorders might have a more gradual or varied onset, lacking a single, defining traumatic event.

Symptom Set: PTSD's symptoms are a unique constellation in the sky of anxiety disorders. The vivid reliving of trauma, avoidance of reminders, and alterations in mood and perception are stars that shine specifically in the PTSD universe. Other anxiety disorders might share some common stars, but they don't form the same patterns in the sky.

Timeline and Triggers: The narrative of PTSD follows a particular timeline, typically emerging after the traumatic event and persisting in a way that deeply impacts life. Other anxiety disorders weave their stories over different timelines, often independent of a single traumatic event, and can be more chronic in nature.

Anxiety's Focus: In PTSD, the anxiety and fear are tethered to the trauma, like a boat anchored to a particular spot in a vast ocean. In other anxiety disorders, the anxiety might drift more broadly, touching many aspects of life without a single anchor point.

Unique Features: The flashbacks, nightmares, and dissociative experiences are distinctive chapters in the PTSD story. These aren't generally found in the narratives of other anxiety disorders, making them critical in understanding and identifying PTSD.

The journey to healing is tailored to the type of anxiety disorder one faces. For PTSD, the path might involve trauma-focused therapies that directly address the traumatic memories and their ongoing impact. Other anxiety disorders may journey down different therapeutic paths, addressing the broader, more generalized nature of anxiety.

Myths and Misconceptions

Let's sit down and have a real chat about some of the tall tales and misunderstandings that swirl around Post-Traumatic Stress Disorder. Clearing up these myths is like cleaning a smudged window; it helps everyone see the situation more clearly and offer the right kind of support.

Myth 1: PTSD is Just a Soldier's Issue

Imagine thinking that lightning only strikes in one place. Just like storms can hit anywhere, PTSD isn't picky about who it affects. Sure, soldiers and veterans are often in the spotlight because of their high-risk roles, but trauma doesn't have an exclusive guest list. It can show up in anyone's life who's experienced or witnessed a traumatic event, be it through accidents, disasters, or personal violence.

Myth 2: PTSD Means You're Not Tough Enough

Now, this one's as untrue as saying people who get colds are weak. PTSD is about how your brain responds to trauma, not about muscle or moral strength. It's a complex interplay of factors like the type of trauma, personal history, and even genetics. Developing PTSD is not a failing; it's a sign that you've been through something incredibly tough and need a specific kind of support.

Myth 3: PTSD Shows Up Right After the Trauma

This is like expecting all flowers to bloom at the same time. Just as different plants have their own timelines, so do people's reactions to trauma. For some, PTSD symptoms might indeed spring up soon after the event. For others, they might take months or even years to surface, often because the mind has its own ways of coping and might delay the full impact until it feels "safer" to emerge.

Myth 4: Trauma Equals PTSD for Everyone

If that were true, we'd all be in the same boat. But just as people react differently to life's ups and downs, not everyone who experiences trauma will develop PTSD. It's a particular response that depends on a whole bunch of factors, including personal resilience, the nature of the trauma, and the support available at the time.

Myth 5: Once You Have PTSD, That's It

Thinking PTSD is an unchangeable, permanent condition is like saying a broken leg will never heal. Sure, PTSD is serious and can be complex to treat, but it's not untreatable. With the right combination of therapies, support, and sometimes medication, many people with PTSD can and do find their way back to a place of more peace and less pain.

By busting these myths, we're not just setting the record straight; we're paving the way for more understanding, better support, and hope. It's about replacing old wives' tales with real, solid support and ensuring that anyone grappling with the shadows of trauma knows they're not alone and that healing paths are out there.

. . .

End of Chapter One

It's time to draw the curtain on our first chapter, a chapter that has taken us on a journey to understand the essence of Post-Traumatic Stress Disorder, or PTSD. We've tried to give it a definition, outline its main symptoms, and delve into how it creeps into the lives of those affected. We've touched on its profound impact on individuals, attempting to unravel its complexity and the various ways it can rear its head.

As we wrap up this chapter, let's eagerly anticipate our next meeting in the second chapter. In our upcoming discussion, we'll delve into the causes of PTSD, aiming to uncover the roots of this intricate condition and how various factors contribute to its development. So, stay tuned, and we'll see you in the second chapter as we continue our journey into the world of PTSD.

Reflection Section

After engaging with "What is PTSD?" and contemplating the statements above, take a moment for introspection. How has your perception of PTSD evolved? Are there certain insights or aspects that you found particularly impactful? How might this enhanced understanding influence your interactions, your support for others, or your own self-care strategies?

Write your personal reflections here.

CHAPTER TWO

CAUSES OF PTSD

In this second chapter, titled "Causes of PTSD," we are dedicated to delving into what lies beneath this complex condition. We understand that PTSD doesn't just appear out of nowhere; it is the result of profoundly impactful experiences and an array of contributing factors.

Here, we're going to dig deep into the origins and causes, aiming to shed light on how PTSD can take hold in someone's life. This journey will lead us through the intricacies of individual experiences, the influence of biological factors, and the broader social context in which PTSD finds its place. Understanding these causes is a significant step towards fostering empathy and providing effective support to those grappling with PTSD.

Traumatic Events

Trauma is when bad stuff happens that shakes you up. Not even a minor scare or injury can leave you feeling all sorts of jumbled; it is the large, weighty objects that do the trick. Whether it's from a serious accident, a scary personal attack, or the horrors of war, it's about those moments that really stick with you and change things inside.

So, what kind of things are we talking about? There are personal attacks, like getting mugged or beaten up, that can scare you. Soldiers in war see and go through some scary stuff. Big natural disasters like earthquakes or floods can wreck everything around you. Even seeing a bad accident or someone else getting hurt can leave a mark.

The thing is everyone deals with this stuff differently. Some people get over it quickly, while others might have a harder time and keep reliving the fear and pain repeatedly. Some might even develop something called PTSD, which is like a long-lasting panic that's tough to shake.

But the key to overcoming trauma is realizing that it's normal to feel extremely shaken up by these significant, terrifying events. It's normal. The important part is finding ways to feel better, whether that's talking to someone like a therapist, hanging out with friends or family who make you feel safe, or sometimes getting some help from medicine.

Knowing all about trauma helps everyone. It's not just for people who've gone through it, but for everyone else too, so we can all be there for each other. It's a tough thing to deal with, but with the right support and understanding, people can start to feel better and move past it.

Unveiling the Complex Factors Behind PTSD Vulnerability

Let's get real about PTSD: not everyone who goes through something tough ends up with it. It's like a complicated recipe where different things mix to make some people more likely to get PTSD after a scary event. Let's examine the factors that can increase someone's vulnerability to severe trauma.

First off, your family's mental health history matters. If your family has a history of feeling anxious or depressed, it might mean you're more likely to feel that way too after something scary happens. And just the way you are, like if you're someone who worries a lot or gets nervous easily, can make a difference.

Your own past plays a big part too. If you've been through rough times before, like bad stuff in childhood or other scary moments, it can make new scary things hit harder. And if you're already dealing with things like anxiety or depression, a traumatic event might make those feelings even stronger.

Your surroundings matter as well. Having people around to support you after something bad happens can make a huge difference. If you're feeling alone or you've got other stresses like money worries or problems at home, it can make it harder to bounce back from trauma.

Even who you are, like your age or whether you're a man or woman, can change how you deal with trauma. And, of course, the actual scary event itself—the longer and more intense it is and the closer you are to it, the bigger the impact might be.

But remember, everyone's got their own way of dealing with tough stuff. Some people have strong ways of coping with stress, which can help them avoid PTSD. And the way you react right after something traumatic can clue you in on whether you might have trouble later.

It's key to remember that just because you have some of these risk factors doesn't mean you'll get PTSD. And even if you have a lot of things stacked against you, that doesn't mean you can't get through them. Knowing all about these factors helps us figure out better ways to help and support people who've been through trauma, making sure they get what they need to heal and move forward.

Understanding all these different bits and pieces helps us see why some people get PTSD and others don't. It's all about being there for each other, with the right kind of help and a whole lot of understanding.

Understanding Resilience Factors

Understanding resilience in the context of post-traumatic stress disorder (PTSD) is critical to grasping the full spectrum of its impact and the varied responses individuals have to traumatic events. While PTSD can profoundly affect an individual's life, leading to significant distress and dysfunction, not everyone exposed to trauma develops the disorder. This variance is largely due to resilience factors—aspects of a person's background, personality, social environment, and physiology—that can help buffer against the development of PTSD after a traumatic event.

The concept of resilience

Resilience is often described as the ability to "bounce back" or adapt in the face of adversity. In the context of PTSD, it refers to the capacity to maintain or regain psychological well-being in the aftermath of confrontation with traumatic stress. It's important to note that resilience doesn't mean being unaffected by stress or trauma; rather, it refers to the ability to effectively navigate and recover from challenges.

Personal Resilience Factors

Positive Outlook: Individuals with a generally positive outlook on life tend to be more resilient. They're more likely to view challenges as temporary and believe they have the resources and ability to overcome them.

Self-Efficacy: Self-efficacy is the belief in one's ability to influence events that affect one's life. Higher levels of self-efficacy are linked with greater resilience, as individuals feel more capable of handling stressful situations.

Adaptability: The ability to adapt to changing circumstances and flexibility in thinking and behavior can significantly contribute to resilience. People who are adaptable can modify their coping strategies to suit the situation.

Problem-Solving Skills: Effective problem-solving skills allow individuals to identify solutions during stressful events, reducing feelings of helplessness and the impact of stress.

Sense of Purpose: Having goals, aspirations, and a sense of purpose can provide individuals with a guiding focus and motivation, contributing to resilience.

Social Resilience Factors

Supportive Relationships: Strong, supportive relationships with friends, family, and community members can provide emotional support, practical assistance, and a sense of belonging, all which bolster resilience.

Feeling Connected: Feeling part of a community or larger social network provides individuals with a sense of identity and support. Community involvement and social engagement are linked with higher resilience.

Access to Resources: Having access to physical, emotional, and financial resources can help individuals cope with and recover from trauma. This includes healthcare, education, and community services.

Physiological and genetic factors

Genetic Predisposition: Some individuals may have a genetic predisposition that influences their physiological response to stress and trauma, impacting their resilience.

Neurobiological Factors: Differences in brain structure and function, particularly in areas related to fear and stress regulation, such as the amygdala and prefrontal cortex, may influence resilience.

Physical Health: Good physical health and regular physical activity can enhance an individual's resilience by improving mood, reducing stress, and strengthening the body's response to adversity.

Building Resilience

Understanding resilience factors is not only about recognizing why some people might not develop PTSD after trauma; it's also about identifying ways to enhance these factors in individuals and communities to prevent and mitigate the impact of traumatic events. Strategies for building resilience may include:

Promoting Positive Relationships: Encouraging strong social connections and community support can provide individuals with resources and emotional support to cope with stress.

Developing Coping Strategies: Teaching effective coping strategies, including stress management, relaxation techniques, and adaptive problem-solving, can empower individuals to handle challenges more effectively.

Enhancing Self-Efficacy: Helping individuals recognize and build upon their strengths and successes can boost their confidence and ability to cope with stress.

Encouraging Adaptability: Promoting flexibility in thinking and behavior can help individuals adjust to changing situations and find alternative solutions to problems.

Supporting Physical Health: Encouraging regular physical activity, good nutrition, and adequate sleep can improve physical and psychological well-being, contributing to resilience.

A variety of psychological, social, and physiological factors all have an impact on resilience, which is a multifaceted concept. While it does not make individuals immune to the effects of trauma, understanding and enhancing resilience can significantly reduce the risk of developing PTSD and facilitate recovery for those who have experienced traumatic events.

The Impact of Childhood Trauma

Imagine growing up under a long, dark shadow that follows you into adulthood. That's what it's like for people who've experienced childhood trauma, especially when it leads to something as serious as Post-Traumatic Stress Disorder (PTSD). This isn't just something that happens to adults who've been through war or major disasters; it can also deeply affect kids who've felt unsafe or scared.

When you're a kid, your brain is still figuring things out—learning how to deal with emotions and the world around you. Trauma can mess with this big time, changing the way a child's brain works. This can lead to big-time fear, messed-up memories, and trouble handling feelings.

Right after something bad happens, kids might start acting out or pulling away. They might get super angry, scared, or not want to feel anything at all. You might see them being clingier or even going back to behaviors they had outgrown, like wetting the bed. Trauma can also make it hard for them to focus, remember things, or do well in school. Sometimes, their bodies react too, with aches or trouble eating or sleeping.

But it doesn't stop when they grow up. Those early scars can make it harder for them to deal with their feelings or trust other people, even leading to unhealthy relationships. They might be more likely to feel depressed, anxious, or turn to drugs or alcohol. And believe it or not, all that stress and heartache can lead to real physical health problems later, like heart disease or diabetes.

So, when we talk about childhood trauma, we're talking about something that can really change a person's whole life—how they think, feel, and even how healthy they are. It's like carrying a heavy load that makes everything more difficult.

That's why understanding and helping people with these experiences is so important. It's all about helping lift that shadow so they can have a brighter, healthier future.

The Story of Luis: A Child's Battle with PTSD

I want to tell you the story of Luis, a seven-year-old boy with a bright smile and laughter that could light up the darkest room. He lived in a small, crowded house in a lively city, but his home life was anything but cheerful. His dad struggled with his own troubles and often became violent, while his mom, caught up in her own struggles, couldn't be there emotionally. Luis, being the oldest, felt it was his duty to look after his younger siblings, trying to be their shield and comfort.

Imagine living every day on edge, never knowing when the next shout or worse would come. That was Luis's life. He was always alert, always scared. It wasn't long before the stress started showing. He fell behind in school, became quiet and jumpy, and sometimes he'd suddenly get angry over little things. His teachers noticed something was off, but they didn't know the half of it. Things came to a head one night when a fight at home got bad, leaving his mom hurt and the authorities stepping in. Luis and his siblings were taken into foster care. It was supposed to be safer, but for Luis, it just piled on more trauma. He started having nightmares and would relive the scary moments over and over. He was always tense, got scared easily, and would lash out. He felt so guilty about being away from his mom and siblings, even though none of it was his choice or his fault. That's when he was diagnosed with PTSD, a term that seemed too small for all he was feeling.

Moving through the foster system was tough. Each new place meant losing whatever little stability he had started to build. But then, in his third foster home, he met Mrs. Alvarez. She was kind and patient and committed to helping Luis heal. She educated herself on caring for kids with trauma and worked with therapists to make her home a place where Luis could feel safe and start to heal.

It took, lots of time, with therapy, patience, and plenty of love, but slowly, Luis began to get better. He used play therapy to express his feelings, something that felt much easier than talking. He met other kids in group therapy who had been through similar things, which made him feel less alone and more understood.

Luis's story doesn't have a fairy-tale ending. The scars from his trauma stayed with him, affecting how he saw himself and the world. But he didn't let that be the end of his story. With the help and support he got, he learned to manage his feelings, make friends, and find a positive path forward. He turned his pain into purpose, advocating for kids in the foster care system to make sure they got the help and care they needed.

The story of Luis is a reminder of how childhood trauma can leave deep marks but also how care, intervention, and support can make a world of difference. It's about recognizing the signs of trauma and doing everything we can to help heal those wounds. It's about giving kids like Luis a fighting chance to define their future not by their past traumas but by their resilience, courage, and incredible spirit.

As we close

We've talked about how some people are more likely to get PTSD because of their past, their genes, or just not having enough support when they need it most. It's like some folks are walking into the storm with a sturdier umbrella, while others have none. One of the heaviest parts of our journey was looking at how bad stuff from childhood can really stick with you. We have recounted a brief PTSD story where it affected young Luis and how his early traumas didn't simply vanish; they shaped his life, illustrating how profound childhood experiences can be. But it wasn't all doom and gloom. We also talked about resilience—that awesome ability to bounce back. It's not something you're just born with; it's like a muscle you can build up with a good outlook, solid problem-solving skills, and people around you who care. As we zip up this chapter, let's remember that PTSD is complicated. It's a mix of what happened, who you are, and what you've got in your corner. Knowing all this helps us spot PTSD in ourselves or others and get the right kind of help. Next up, we're going to keep unraveling the mystery of PTSD, looking at how it twists lives and what we can do to untangle the mess. Stick with us as we continue exploring this tough but important topic.

YES / NO
CHECKLIST
Applying Insights from "
Causes of **PTSD** *"*

This checklist includes personalized questions inspired by the chapter "Causes of PTSD." Reflect on each statement and select "Yes" or "No" based on your personal experiences, feelings, or understanding. This exercise aims to encourage introspection and a deeper personal connection with the content of the chapter.

Questions:

1   Have you ever experienced a traumatic event that left a significant impact on you, changing how you view yourself or the world?   YES ☐   NO ☐

2   Do you believe that your past experiences or family history have an impact on how you react to traumatic or stressful situations?   YES ☐   NO ☐

3   Are you aware of any personal tendencies, like a general sense of worry or anxiety, that might affect how you cope with traumatic events?   YES ☐   NO ☐

4   Do you believe that having a strong support network (friends, family, and community) has helped or could help you cope with stressful life events?   YES ☐   NO ☐

5   Have you noticed that your immediate reactions to stress or trauma might be indicative of your long-term coping capacity?   YES ☐   NO ☐

6   Do you think that societal and environmental factors, such as your social network or access to healthcare, play a significant role in your ability to overcome traumatic experiences?   YES ☐   NO ☐

7   Are you conscious of any resilience factors **YES** **NO** within yourself, such as a positive outlook or □ □ adaptability, that help you navigate through adversity?

8   Do you actively work on building resilience, **YES** **NO** such as by fostering positive relationships or □ □ developing effective coping strategies, to better handle life's challenges?

9   Have you ever sought professional help or **YES** **NO** resources (therapy, support groups, etc.) to □ □ assist in coping with or recovering from a traumatic event?

10   Do you feel equipped or motivated to support **YES** **NO** others who might be dealing with PTSD or □ □ trauma, based on your understanding and personal experiences?

After contemplating these questions, take a moment to reflect on any new insights or affirmations you've gained about yourself and your approach to trauma and resilience. How might the understanding from this chapter shape your future actions or perspectives, either for personal growth or in supporting others?

CHAPTER THREE

THE SCIENCE OF PTSD

In our exploration of Post-Traumatic Stress Disorder, we delve deeper into its scientific underpinnings. Our journey takes us into the complex labyrinth where the mind, body, and environment intertwine, shaping the trajectory of PTSD. In this chapter, we will dissect the intricate interplay of elements that construct the trauma response mosaic.

PTSD transcends the mere shadows of a traumatic event. It embodies a sophisticated nexus of neurons, genes, and life experiences. We will explore how the brain, an organ of remarkable complexity and subtlety, processes these profound experiences, giving rise to the hallmark symptoms of PTSD. Our focus will also turn to the subtle hints of genetic inheritance that may predispose individuals to heightened vulnerability, alongside the stark reality of environmental factors that can either intensify or mitigate the disorder.

This inquiry is more than a scholarly pursuit; it is a mission to equip ourselves with the knowledge necessary for a more effective battle against PTSD. By delving into the scientific intricacies, we aim to pave the way for advanced treatments, more compassionate support networks, and solid preventative strategies. We come to understand PTSD as a quantifiable, understandable, and treatable response to the extreme stress some people experience rather than as a symbol of defeat.

As we venture further into the science of PTSD, it's crucial to remember that behind every statistic and study are real people with their own narratives. These stories are not mere scientific data; they are accounts of resilience, struggles for recovery, and testaments to the human spirit's ability to adapt and surmount challenges. Thus, with a dedication to empathy and a yearning for understanding, we continue our exploration of the science behind PTSD.

Neurological Impact of Trauma

Venturing into the human mind's depths, we must recognize the critical importance of understanding the neurological aftermath of trauma. PTSD, a condition affecting countless individuals, is not just a psychological construct. It exerts a profound impact on the brain's structure and function. In this section, we embark on a quest to untangle the complex consequences of trauma, diving into a knowledge abyss where traumatic experiences have the power to reshape the brain's intricate wiring. This reshaping leaves an enduring imprint on an individual's behavior, emotions, and thoughts, revealing the profound and lasting impact of trauma.

The Brain's Response to Trauma: A Tale of Vigilance

When confronted with the harrowing specter of trauma, the human brain springs into action, thrusting itself into a heightened state of alertness. At the center of this emotional maelstrom stands the amygdala, a small, almond-shaped sentinel entrusted with the solemn duty of processing our most visceral emotions. It morphs into a hyperactive guardian, akin to an ever-vigilant watchman patrolling the boundaries of our consciousness, tirelessly scanning for impending threats.

This heightened state of awareness is nothing short of a marvel during the throes of the traumatic event itself, as it prepares the body for the primal dance of fight-or-flight. Stress hormones such as cortisol and adrenaline surge forth, and the body's ancient defense mechanisms engage in a desperate bid for survival.

Yet, the conundrum manifests when the amygdala stubbornly clings to this state of hyperactivity, long after the traumatic tempest has subsided. Those who suffer from the unrelenting PTSD specter find themselves trapped in an unending cycle of constant threat perception. Anxiety, hypervigilance, and a ceaseless inability to find solace become the haunting companions of their existence. The relentless grip of this protracted stress, like a malevolent specter, extends its reach to wreak havoc upon other delicate regions of the brain, leaving a trail of tumultuous turmoil in its wake.

Hippocampus and Memory

Within the intricate tapestry of the human brain, the hippocampus stands as a sacred chamber, revered for its role in the grand symphony of learning and memory. Picture it as the brain's diligent librarian, meticulously cataloging and shelving the memories of life's vivid tapestry, both the ordinary and the heart-wrenching.

But alas, when confronted with the relentless siege of chronic stress, this venerable librarian finds itself under siege. In individuals grappling with the unrelenting specter of PTSD, the hippocampus is not immune to the ravages of trauma's relentless storm. It can, with unforgiving cruelty, begin to diminish in size, a phenomenon known as atrophy. This tragic shrinking of this vital brain region unfurls a cascade of consequences. It sets the stage for a tragic drama where forming new memories becomes a Herculean endeavor, akin to sifting through the ashes of a burned library, searching for fragments of the past. Retrieving cherished recollections from the labyrinthine depths of memory turns into an arduous quest, often culminating in the tormenting spectacle of individuals forced to relive the traumatic event as if it were a relentless echo of the present. It's a cruel and vicious loop where the brain, in its valiant attempt to process and catalog the traumatic memory, unwittingly re-traumatizes the very soul it seeks to protect.

Prefrontal Cortex and Impulse Control

Now, cast your gaze upon the prefrontal cortex, the eminent executive center nestled within the cerebral realm. It reigns supreme, orchestrating the intricate dance of decision-making, strategic planning, and the formidable discipline of impulse control. Yet, it too bears the scars of chronic stress.

Under the relentless siege of prolonged adversity, the prefrontal cortex, that noble sentinel of rationality, finds its once-firm grip faltering. Its regulatory influence diminishes, akin to a fading beacon in the darkest of nights. The consequences of this reduction ripple through the individual's existence.

Impulsivity, that unruly and impetuous force, begins to exert its sway. The once-stalwart fortress of sound decision-making crumbles, leaving in its wake a barren wasteland of poor choices. Emotion regulation, once a sanctuary of serenity, becomes a turbulent sea of discord.

The consequences are evident for those who are under the PTSD's relentless grip. Minor triggers become the catalyst for overwhelming overreactions, like thunderbolts in a summer storm. The once-simple act of planning and decision-making transforms into an arduous odyssey, a labyrinth of confusion where even the most trivial choices seem insurmountable. In this battle for control, the prefrontal cortex becomes a battlefield where reason and impulsivity wage an unceasing war.

Neurotransmitter Systems and Mood Regulation

Let us journey into the intricate orchestra of neurotransmitters that orchestrate the very essence of our being. These chemical messengers, akin to the poets of the brain, traverse the intricate pathways, communicating vital information that shapes both mind and body. Within this melodious ensemble, two distinguished soloists' step into the spotlight: serotonin and dopamine, the virtuosos of mood regulation and well-being.

Picture, if you will, a grand symphony. Trauma, like a tempestuous conductor, wields its baton with an unforgiving hand, casting discord into the harmonious balance of neurotransmitters. Serotonin, the maestro of tranquility, and dopamine, the herald of pleasure, both fall under the spell of trauma's malevolent sway.

Disruptions in this delicate balance reverberate through the individual's psyche, casting shadows on the soul. The once-clear skies of emotional equilibrium become shrouded in the darkness of depression, anxiety, and tempestuous mood swings, much like a turbulent sea in the throes of a relentless storm. The symphony of neurotransmitters, once a serenade of well-being, transforms into a cacophony of disarray. In the shadowy world of PTSD, these neurotransmitter systems bear witness to the toll of trauma's cruel hand, and they sing a somber lament.

The Body's Symphony of Stress

The hypothalamic-pituitary-adrenal (HPA) axis' intricate baton, which orchestrates the body's response to stress, emerges as a mesmerizing crescendo in the grand composition of our existence. It is a symphony of survival, a ballet of balance, choreographed to perfection. Ordinarily, this masterful system orchestrates a return to tranquility once the storm of threats has passed. But in the haunting shadow of PTSD, the graceful return to serenity falters, leaving the individual ensnared in a perpetual tempest of physiological arousal.

The very rhythm of life itself goes awry. A heightened state of alertness becomes the norm, like an unceasing drumbeat resonating throughout one's existence. The consequences reverberate through every fiber of the being, and the symptoms of PTSD come to life. Insomnia, that restless specter of the night, casts its long shadow. Irritability, like a discordant note in an otherwise harmonious symphony, emerges. An exaggerated startle response, like a thunderclap in a quiet room, becomes a constant companion.

In this symphony of stress, the once-elegant dance of the HPA axis takes on a haunting quality. The body, in its valiant attempt to protect, inadvertently becomes a prisoner of its creation, trapped in a cycle of turmoil and tension.

Neural Plasticity and PTSD

Amidst the seemingly desolate landscape of the brain's response to trauma, there exists a beacon of hope—a concept known as neural plasticity. It's a testament to the remarkable malleability of our most complex organ and a reminder that the brain is capable of transformation and adaptation.

In the hands of skilled practitioners and with the aid of appropriate treatments, such as trauma-focused therapy and, at times, medication, individuals afflicted by the relentless grip of PTSD embark on a journey of profound change. This journey involves nothing less than the rewiring of the brain's response to trauma, a remarkable endeavor where new, healthier neural pathways emerge while the old, maladaptive ones gradually fade into obscurity.

Imagine it as a grand symphony, where the discordant notes of trauma find themselves replaced by harmonious melodies of healing. The very essence of neural plasticity lies at the heart of hope in the realm of PTSD treatment. It's a declaration that recovery isn't a distant dream; it's a tangible reality, waiting to be embraced.

In this symphony of transformation, the human spirit shines as a resilient force, rewriting the story of PTSD with each deliberate step toward healing and renewal.

The Role of Genetics in Neurological Response
In the intricate tapestry of human experience, we find that not every soul grappling with the tempest of trauma succumbs to the haunting specter of PTSD. Amidst this enigmatic variability lies a profound truth—our genetic heritage plays a pivotal role in shaping how our brain navigates the tumultuous waters of stress.

For some, the threads of their genetic inheritance weave a robust shield, rendering their brains remarkably resilient to the ravages of trauma's storm. Others, however, bear a tapestry that is more delicate, were sensitivity reigns supreme.

Imagine it as a symphony of genes, each note of DNA encoding a unique response to the trials of life. Some melodies, passed down through generations, fortify the mind against the onslaught of trauma, acting as guardians of resilience. Others resonate with vulnerability, amplifying the impact of adversity.

Inflammation and the Brain
As we peer into the ever-evolving landscape of PTSD research, a compelling revelation emerges—a spotlight on the intricate interplay between inflammation and the traumatized brain. The tempest of traumatic stress, it seems, can ignite an inflammatory response deep within the recesses of our minds, casting a dark shadow on the path to recovery.

In this unfolding narrative, the very battlefield lies within, where inflammation fuels the flames of adversity, intensifying the already formidable symptoms that accompany PTSD. The pursuit of healing takes on a new dimension as we explore uncharted territories in search of solutions.

Anti-inflammatory medications and the art of lifestyle adjustments emerge as beacons of hope. They offer a lifeline, promising to calm the storm within and soothe the raging fires of inflammation that threaten the fragile balance of the mind.

Future Directions in Neurological Research on PTSD
Our dedicated researchers, armed with cutting-edge imaging techniques and information gleaned from genetic testing, tirelessly unravel the intricate tapestry of this condition.

But this effort is not limited to the ivory towers of academia; it resonates with meaning in the real world. With each discovery, we come closer to the promise of more effective treatments, a beacon of hope for those who bear the weight of the scars of trauma. Perhaps, in the not-so-distant future, we may even glimpse the dawn of prevention strategies where the specter of PTSD is kept at bay before it can inflict its relentless torment.

In this ongoing odyssey, the human spirit shines brightly, a testament to our unwavering dedication to understanding, healing, and ultimately easing the burdens that PTSD brings.

Empowering Individuals through Neurological Understanding
Finally, those who suffer from PTSD can become more empowered by understanding the neurological effects of trauma. It shifts the narrative from one of personal failure or weakness to a narrative of biological and psychological processes that can be addressed and healed. This understanding can reduce stigma, encourage individuals to seek help, and provide a solid foundation for recovery.

The neurological impact of trauma is profound, affecting not just the brain but the entire person. However, with continued research, effective treatments, and a supportive environment, recovery is not just a possibility; it's a probability.

Long-Term Effects on Health

The influence of Post-Traumatic Stress Disorder extends well beyond the immediate repercussions of a traumatic incident, infiltrating every aspect of an individual's life over time. PTSD is not confined to mere flashbacks or anxiety; it is a condition that can fundamentally transform mental and physical health, relationships, and daily functioning.

Beginning with the mental aspect, the unceasing stress and hyper-vigilance associated with PTSD are not transient states; they gradually erode a person's mental equilibrium. It's commonplace for those affected to grapple with depression or anxiety or to turn to substance use as a means of coping with their symptoms. This relentless struggle can trap individuals in a vortex of despair, sometimes leading to suicidal ideation or attempts.

Physically, the implications are equally profound. Imagine a body perpetually primed for danger; such unrelenting tension is both exhausting and detrimental. This chronic stress can have severe consequences for cardiac health, elevating the risk of cardiovascular diseases. It may also weaken the immune system, rendering the body more susceptible to infections and illnesses. The digestive system can become disrupted, and muscles, often in a state of tension, can result in various painful conditions. In essence, PTSD can cause the body to start deteriorating.

Sleep, which is essential for healing and restoration, often becomes an unattainable luxury for many with PTSD. Nightmares, insomnia, and restless sleep become the norm, leading to an exhaustive state where even basic tasks appear monumental. This sleep deprivation does more than induce fatigue; it can contribute to severe health problems, impair cognitive functions, and even lead to weight issues.

Socially and relationally, PTSD can foster feelings of isolation, misunderstanding, and burdensomeness, distancing individuals from much-needed support networks. This isolation can lead to further emotional turmoil and a decline in life quality as connections with loved ones weaken.

Cognitively, the chronic nature of PTSD is alarming. The disorder can cloud one's thinking, impair memory, and hinder decision-making. This isn't just about minor forgetfulness; it's about struggling with the complexities of daily life, which can feel overwhelmingly intricate for those affected.

Behaviorally, those with longstanding PTSD may find themselves in a perpetual state of alertness or resorting to unhealthy coping mechanisms. A life limited by fear results from a series of evasion tactics for potential threats, both real and imagined. Additionally, the persistent state of stress and inflammation can predispose individuals to other serious health conditions like chronic fatigue syndrome or autoimmune disorders. It's as though the body, in a constant state of alarm, begins to turn against itself, further deteriorating health and well-being.

Understanding the full spectrum of PTSD's long-term effects highlights the necessity of early and effective intervention, along with sustained support. Treatment must be holistic, addressing the emotional, physical, and social dimensions of the disorder. By comprehending the extensive impact of PTSD, we can better advocate for and implement comprehensive care strategies, aiding individuals not just in surviving but in thriving after experiencing trauma.

PTSD in Children vs. Adults

When talking about trauma, or rather, PTSD, it is essential to understand that both children and adults can be affected by this condition, but the way it manifests itself and affects their lives can differ significantly. Recognizing these differences is very important to providing the right care and support. Let's explore how PTSD presents in children compared to adults, considering symptomatology, response to trauma, and approach to treatment.

Differences in Symptom Manifestation:

When we delve into the realm of Post-Traumatic Stress Disorder, we must ask ourselves: how does this condition, so profound in its impact, manifest differently in children compared to adults? And what implications do these differences have for providing effective care and support? In exploring these questions, we unveil the unique facets of PTSD in children versus adults, examining variations in symptoms, responses to trauma, and treatment approaches.

Children often show regressive behaviors, reverting to earlier developmental stages like bedwetting or excessive clinging. They may express their trauma through play, reenacting aspects of their experience in games, drawings, or stories. Their inability to articulate feelings verbally might result in irritability, mood swings, or aggression. Trauma can disrupt their education, affecting their concentration and interest in learning. Moreover, children may report physical symptoms like stomach aches and headaches that lack a medical explanation.

In contrast, adults with PTSD frequently experience intrusive memories or flashbacks, vividly reliving the trauma. They might avoid reminders of the trauma, withdraw from social activities, and experience negative shifts in thinking and mood, such as hopelessness or negative self-perception. Hyperarousal is also common, manifesting as heightened startle responses, tension, or sleep disturbances.

Response to Trauma:
Children, in their limited understanding of trauma, may respond with confusion and fear. The responses of the adults around them frequently influence their immediate and unfiltered reactions. The presence or absence of support from caregivers can significantly influence their ability to cope and recover. Their developmental stage means they possess fewer strategies for managing stress and trauma.

Adults, with a more developed cognitive capacity, often recognize the effects of trauma on their lives. They have more freedom to control their environment and ask for help and established coping mechanisms—which can be either healthy or unhealthy—influence their responses.

Approach to Treatment:
In treating children with PTSD, involving the family is crucial. Therapeutic approaches often include play therapy, tailored to the child's developmental level, and collaboration with schools to provide a supportive educational environment.

For adults, treatment may focus more on individual therapy, such as cognitive-behavioral therapy, and group therapy, offering a platform to connect with others who share similar experiences. Medication is also more commonly used in adult treatment plans to manage symptoms.

In our quest to understand PTSD, we must not only recognize the shared burden of this condition across ages but also the distinct ways it manifests and impacts lives. How can we tailor our approach to meet the unique needs of each age group? And how can this knowledge empower us to offer more effective, compassionate care and support? These questions guide our exploration as we seek to understand and address the multifaceted nature of PTSD in both children and adults.

Chapter's End

As we draw this chapter to a close, we have immersed ourselves in the intricate realm of PTSD and its extensive ramifications. But have we truly grasped the depths of its impact? We began by scrutinizing the "Neurological Impact of Trauma," delving into how traumatic experiences fundamentally alter the brain's architecture and functionality. This journey into the brain's labyrinth has illuminated the reasons behind the enduring and disquieting symptoms of PTSD, which infiltrate memory, emotions, and self-regulation.

Moving forward, we ventured into the "long-term health effects" of PTSD, confronting the sobering truth that its repercussions ripple far beyond the immediate wake of trauma. Individuals battling PTSD are ensnared in a web of increased susceptibility to chronic ailments, ranging from cardiac disorders to autoimmune diseases, heralding a decline in overall health and well-being. Doesn't this revelation accentuate the dire need for prompt, sustained, and empathetic care?

Subsequently, our focus shifted to the contrast in PTSD's manifestation in "Children versus Adults," recognizing the unique expressions and coping strategies across the age spectrum. We discovered that while children may express their trauma through altered behaviors or play, adults often resort to avoidance or experience severe mood fluctuations. Isn't this insight a clarion call for customized, age-specific interventions and a robust support system to foster healing?

In summing up this chapter, the message resonates with clarity: an in-depth understanding of the scientific foundations of PTSD is imperative for delivering effective and compassionate care. Acknowledging the varied ways individuals encounter and navigate through PTSD, coupled with the profound alterations it inflicts on brain function and overall health, equips us with the knowledge to devise more humane and effective support methods. This wisdom enables us to stand in solidarity with those confronting this daunting yet conquerable adversity, shepherding them toward a path of recovery and resilience.

The Emotional Journal

In this journal, you will find a series of prompts that will guide you through reflecting on the content of the chapter. Feel free to express your thoughts, feelings, and personal experiences related to the topic of PTSD. This space is for you to explore and understand your own journey, as well as the scientific aspects of PTSD discussed in the chapter.

Neurological Impact of Trauma
Reflect on a time when you felt extremely vigilant or on edge. How did this feel manifest in your body and mind?...

The hippocampus plays a significant role in memory. Have you experienced any difficulties with memory or concentration that you relate to past trauma? If so, describe these challenges....

Consider the role of the prefrontal cortex in impulse control. Can you identify any moments when your decision-making or emotional regulation felt compromised due to stress or anxiety?...

Serotonin and dopamine greatly influence our mood. Reflect on any patterns or changes in your mood that you have noticed. How do you think these might relate to your neurotransmitter activity?...

....

....

....

The HPA axis responds to stress. Describe any physical reactions you've had to stressful or traumatic events (e.g., increased heart rate, muscle tension) ....

....

....

....

Neural plasticity signifies the brain's ability to change and adapt. Can you think of any positive changes or growth you have experienced in your journey of healing from trauma?...

....

....

....

Genetics can influence our susceptibility to PTSD. Reflect on any family history of trauma or stress-related disorders and how this might relate to your experiences....

....

....

....

Inflammation in the brain can impact mood and behavior. Have you noticed any physical symptoms that coincide with periods of high stress or emotional distress?...

....

....

....

As we look toward the future of PTSD research, what are your hopes for new discoveries or treatments?...

....

....

....

Understanding the neurological effects of trauma can be empowering. How has learning about the brain's response to trauma changed your perspective on your experiences?...

....

....

Long-Term Effects on Health

Reflect on how PTSD might have influenced your mental health over the long term. Are there particular thoughts, emotions, or behaviors you associate with this impact?...

....

....

....

Have you noticed any long-term physical health changes that you might relate to past trauma or ongoing stress?...

....

....

....

Sleep disturbances are common in PTSD. Describe your sleep patterns and any difficulties you've faced....

....

....

....

PTSD can have an impact on social relationships. Reflect on your connections with friends, family, or partners. Have these relationships been impacted, and if so, how?...

....

....

Cognitive effects, such as difficulty concentrating or making decisions, can be a part of PTSD. Share any experiences you've had with these challenges....

....

....

....

Behavioral responses, like avoidance or hypervigilance, are common in PTSD. Reflect on any behaviors you have developed in response to trauma....

....

....

....

PTSD in Children vs. Adults

If you experienced trauma as a child, reflect on how your responses then might differ from how you respond to stress now as an adult....

....

....

....

Consider the treatments or support you received (or wish you had received) as a child vs. the treatments or support available to you now. How do these compare?...

....

....

Reflect on the role of caregivers or significant adults during times of trauma in your childhood. How did their responses affect your coping mechanisms?...

....

....

....

As an adult, how do you approach seeking help or support for trauma-related issues? Has this approach changed over time?

....

....

....

CHAPTER FOUR

DIAGNOSING PTSD

Diagnosing PTSD presents a landscape replete with challenges that necessitate a nuanced, patient approach from healthcare providers. How do clinicians navigate the maze of PTSD co-occurring with mental health issues like depression and anxiety without losing sight of the primary source of distress? Skillful navigation through these overlapping conditions is essential to ensuring an accurate diagnosis.

The reluctance of individuals to discuss their traumatic experiences, often stemming from stigma or the pain of reliving memories, poses another substantial barrier. Isn't creating a trusting, empathetic environment crucial for encouraging disclosure and a comprehensive understanding of their condition?

Furthermore, the dynamic nature of PTSD symptoms, which may fluctuate in intensity and presentation over time, demands continual observation and adaptation from clinicians. This fluidity calls for a comprehensive, patient, and multifaceted approach, focusing on the whole person and their journey through and beyond trauma.

Despite these challenges, the goal remains unwavering: to provide a diagnosis that mirrors the true experience of the individual, facilitating a path to effective and personalized treatment.

Signs and Symptoms of PTSD: Deciphering the Silent Echoes

In the deeper exploration of PTSD, we observe signs and symptoms that often whisper silently or hide in plain sight, manifesting through behavior and emotional responses. This journey resembles assembling a complex puzzle of distress and disruption, where symptoms vary in appearance and intensity but are bound by common threads of suffering.

Invading memories may haunt people, reliving trauma through vivid flashbacks or upsetting dreams where sleep becomes a battleground. Beyond psychological turmoil, their bodies may remain perpetually on alert, reacting intensely to unexpected sounds or touches. Profound mood changes paint their worldview in stark hues of hopelessness and detachment. Early detection is pivotal, turning these lingering symptoms from a shadowy burden into a call to action.

Recognizing these signs is not just observant—it's a critical, compassionate step towards initiating recovery. As we read on, let's remember the importance of extending understanding and support to those affected, recognizing the courage it takes to acknowledge and confront the haunting echoes of PTSD.

Professional Diagnosis Criteria: Navigating the Terrain of PTSD
In professional diagnosis, mental health experts rely on standardized criteria from the DSM-5 to navigate the complex terrain of PTSD. Central to these criteria is exposure to a traumatic event, characterized not just by its intensity but by the profound impact it leaves on the individual's psyche.

The DSM-5 outlines specific symptom clusters that must persist for at least a month, significantly disrupting daily life. These include persistent, distressing recollections, avoidance of reminders, negative alterations in cognition and mood, and marked changes in arousal and reactivity. Clinicians must ensure these symptoms cause significant impairment in personal, social, or occupational domains and rule out other factors like substance abuse or medication. Understanding these criteria is vital, providing a structured lens through which both clinicians and individuals can view PTSD, clarifying the diagnostic pathway, and offering hope and understanding in times of distress and confusion.

Tools and Tests Used in Diagnosing PTSD: The Instruments of Understanding
In diagnosing PTSD, mental health professionals utilize various tools and tests to uncover its multifaceted nature. The Clinician-Administered PTSD Scale (CAPS) is a prominent tool, offering a structured interview format for deep symptom understanding.

Supplementing CAPS, self-reported questionnaires like the PTSD Checklist (PCL) allow individuals to articulate their experiences, enriching the clinician's understanding with personal narratives. These instruments capture symptom frequency and severity, aiding in differentiating normal stress reactions from the more debilitating conditions of PTSD. Their use represents a comprehensive, sensitive approach to diagnosis, respecting the complexity of PTSD and each person's individual journey. They are pivotal in the collaborative effort between clinician and patient, guiding towards a clear, accurate understanding of the condition and effective treatment pathways.

Challenges in Diagnosing PTSD: Navigating the Complex Path
Diagnosing PTSD presents a landscape filled with challenges that require a nuanced and patient approach from healthcare providers. One significant hurdle is the co-occurrence of PTSD with other mental health

issues, such as depression and anxiety, complicating the task of distinguishing the primary source of distress. Clinicians must skillfully navigate through these overlapping conditions to ensure an accurate diagnosis.

The reluctance of individuals to discuss their traumatic experiences, often due to stigma or the pain of reliving memories, poses another substantial barrier. Creating a trusting and empathetic environment is essential for encouraging disclosure and a comprehensive understanding of their condition.

Furthermore, the dynamic nature of PTSD symptoms, which may change over time in intensity and presentation, demands continual observation and adaptation from clinicians. This fluidity necessitates a comprehensive, patient, and multifaceted approach, focusing on the whole person and their journey through and beyond trauma.

Despite these challenges, the goal remains steadfast: to provide a diagnosis that reflects the true experience of the individual, facilitating a path to effective and personalized treatment.

Differential Diagnosis: Distinguishing PTSD from Other Disorders

Differential diagnosis plays a critical role in accurately identifying PTSD and ensuring individuals receive tailored and effective care. PTSD's unique symptomatology can often overlap with or resemble other mental disorders, such as acute stress disorder, anxiety disorders, and depressive disorders, each with its own nuances and treatment implications.

Clinicians are tasked with the careful examination of an individual's history, symptoms, and their impacts, considering the timing and evolution of symptoms. This thorough assessment allows for a nuanced understanding of the root cause and nature of the distress, ensuring that the diagnosis reflects the true condition of the individual.

Precision in differential diagnosis is more than academic rigor; it's a vital step in guiding appropriate treatment and avoiding the pitfalls of misdiagnosis, which can exacerbate suffering or delay recovery. This process, undertaken with care and expertise, is fundamental in providing clarity and hope in a time of distress, setting the stage for a journey toward healing and recovery.

Conclusion

As this chapter on diagnosing PTSD concludes, we recognize the complexity and commitment required to understand and treat this condition. It's a challenging yet crucial endeavor, marking the beginning of an informed path to recovery. With a correct diagnosis, individuals and clinicians can collaborate on a treatment plan tailored to the unique needs and experiences of each person, fostering a hopeful, and understanding approach to overcoming the challenges of PTSD.

CHAPTER FIVE

TREATMENT OPTIONS FOR PTSD

Navigating the landscape of PTSD treatment is akin to exploring a map filled with diverse paths. Each route offers unique perspectives and tools designed to help individuals regain control of their lives. Why does healing not conform to a one-size-fits-all model? What makes each journey towards wellness so deeply personal? As we embark on this exploration, we aim to illuminate the multifarious nature of PTSD treatments, highlighting their benefits while appreciating the necessity of a tailored, personal approach to recovery.

Overview of Treatment Modalities

The treatment landscape of PTSD is rich and diverse, offering various paths tailored to the intricate nature of trauma. These modalities are not standalone solutions but are often woven together to create a comprehensive treatment plan that addresses the multifaceted symptoms and personal experiences of the individual. From the established efficacy of traditional talk therapies to the innovative strides in neuromodulation techniques, each approach is designed to alleviate symptoms, bolster coping mechanisms, and facilitate a journey of recovery and empowerment.

Traditional psychotherapies like Cognitive Behavioral Therapy (CBT) and Eye Movement Desensitization and Reprocessing (EMDR) stand as pillars in the treatment of PTSD, offering structured methods to unravel and reframe the traumatic memories. These therapies are complemented by pharmacological interventions, aimed at alleviating the acute symptoms of PTSD, thus paving the way for therapeutic work. Alongside these, a surge in complementary and alternative therapies reflects a growing understanding of the mind-body connection and the need for holistic healing.

As we explore these modalities, it's crucial to recognize that the journey of healing from PTSD is as personal as the trauma itself. The efficacy of each treatment varies among individuals, necessitating a personalized approach that considers the individual's history, symptoms, strengths, and preferences.

Cognitive Behavioral Therapy (CBT) for PTSD

Cognitive Behavioral Therapy (CBT) stands at the forefront of psychological interventions for PTSD, offering a beacon of hope to those entangled in the aftermath of trauma. This therapy is grounded in the understanding that thoughts, feelings, and behaviors are interconnected, and that altering one can led to significant changes in the others. CBT for PTSD involves a variety of structured techniques aimed at confronting and altering the distressing thoughts and behaviors that perpetuate the cycle of trauma.

The journey through CBT begins with education about trauma and its effects, fostering an understanding of the common symptoms and reactions that individuals may experience. This foundational knowledge sets the stage for the more active phases of therapy, where individuals learn to identify and challenge the negative thought patterns that have taken root after their traumatic experience. Techniques such as cognitive restructuring empower individuals to reshape these thought patterns, replacing them with more balanced and less distressing perspectives.

A critical component of CBT for PTSD is exposure therapy, where individuals are gradually and systematically exposed to the thoughts, feelings, and situations that they have been avoiding since the trauma. This controlled exposure aims to reduce the fear and distress associated with these memories, diminishing their power, and allowing individuals to regain control over their emotional responses. Throughout the therapy, individuals are also equipped with coping and problem-solving skills to handle future stressors and triggers. The therapist works collaboratively with the individual, often assigning tasks or practice exercises between sessions to reinforce the skills learned and encourage real-world application.

CBT is typically a time-limited, goal-oriented therapy, making it a practical choice for many. Its effectiveness has been supported by numerous studies, showing significant reductions in PTSD symptoms, as well as improvements in related areas such as anxiety and depression. As with all treatments, the success of CBT depends on a variety of factors, including the individual's specific circumstances, their commitment to the therapy process, and the quality of the therapeutic relationship.

Cognitive Behavioral Therapy represents a structured, evidence-based approach to overcoming the debilitating effects of PTSD. Through education, cognitive restructuring, exposure techniques, and skill development, CBT offers individuals a path out of the shadow of trauma and into a life defined not by fear and avoidance, but by resilience and empowerment.

Eye Movement Desensitization and Reprocessing (EMDR)

Eye Movement Desensitization and Reprocessing (EMDR) is a distinct, phased psychotherapeutic approach that has gained recognition for its effectiveness in treating PTSD. Unlike traditional forms of talk therapy, EMDR focuses directly on the memory of the traumatic event and the disturbing emotions and beliefs associated with it. The goal is to process these traumatic memories thoroughly, reducing their lingering effects and allowing individuals to develop more adaptive coping mechanisms.

The core of EMDR therapy involves the patient recalling a traumatic event while simultaneously undergoing bilateral stimulation, typically in the form of guided eye movements. This bilateral stimulation is believed to mimic the psychological state of REM sleep, which is involved in processing daily emotional experiences. The eye movements are thought to facilitate the reprocessing of the trauma, helping the brain to integrate the traumatic memory into a more adaptive and resolved mental framework.

EMDR is conducted in eight distinct phases, starting with history taking and ending with evaluation of treatment results. Key phases include preparation, where the therapist ensures the patient is well-informed about the process and techniques of EMDR; assessment, identifying the traumatic memory and associated components; desensitization, where the memory is processed alongside bilateral stimulation; and installation, aiming to strengthen positive beliefs. One of the most compelling aspects of EMDR is its ability to produce quick and lasting relief for many individuals. Some patients report significant reductions in PTSD symptoms after just a few sessions. This efficiency makes it an attractive option for those looking for rapid results. Moreover, EMDR is not just about diminishing symptoms; it's about changing how traumatic memories are stored and reducing the distress they cause, potentially leading to more profound and enduring healing. It's important to note that EMDR should only be conducted by a trained and qualified therapist, as the process can evoke strong emotional reactions. The safety and comfort of the patient are paramount, with therapists providing guidance and support throughout each session.

EMDR represents a unique contribution to the field of trauma therapy, offering a structured, evidence-based approach to reprocessing and resolving traumatic memories. For many suffering from PTSD, it provides a path to recovery that is both effective and efficient, helping them to move past their trauma and reclaim a sense of psychological freedom.

Medications and Their Role in PTSD Treatment

Medication often plays a significant role in the treatment of PTSD, particularly in managing its most acute and debilitating symptoms. While no single medication eliminates PTSD, various types can help individuals manage specific symptoms such as anxiety, depression, insomnia, and hyperarousal. The goal is to improve overall functioning and provide a level of symptom relief that allows individuals to engage more effectively in other forms of treatment, such as psychotherapy.

Antidepressants

The most prescribed medications for PTSD are antidepressants, particularly selective serotonin reuptake inhibitors (SSRIs) and serotonin-norepinephrine reuptake inhibitors (SNRIs). These medications can help alleviate feelings of sadness, anger, worry, and numbness. They work by affecting neurotransmitters in the brain that are involved in mood regulation. Examples include sertraline (Zoloft), paroxetine (Paxil), and venlafaxine (Effexor).

Anti-Anxiety Medications

Anti-anxiety medications can also be used, particularly for short-term relief of severe anxiety and panic. However, due to their potential for dependency and withdrawal issues, they are generally not recommended for long-term use. Instead, they might be used during particularly intense periods of anxiety or while waiting for antidepressants to take effect.

Prazosin

For nightmares and sleep disturbances, which are common in PTSD, prazosin, a medication typically used to treat high blood pressure, has shown effectiveness in reducing or eliminating nightmares related to PTSD.

Mood Stabilizers and Atypical Antipsychotics

In some cases, particularly when symptoms are severe or co-occurring conditions are present, other medications such as mood stabilizers or atypical antipsychotics may be prescribed. These can help control symptoms like severe agitation, impulsivity, or dissociation.

Important Considerations

It's crucial for individuals to work closely with their healthcare provider to find the right medication and dosage. What works for one person might not work for another, and it often takes time to find the most effective medication with manageable side effects. Open communication about how the medication is affecting symptoms, as well as any side effects, is key to finding the right treatment.

Medications are often most effective when combined with other treatments, such as psychotherapy. For many individuals, medication can reduce symptoms to a manageable level, making it easier to engage in therapy and other activities that promote recovery. While medications are an important tool in the treatment of PTSD, they are typically part of a broader, comprehensive treatment plan.

Alternative and Complementary Therapies for PTSD

Alternative and complementary therapies have gained popularity as adjunctive treatments for PTSD, offering a holistic approach that addresses not only the mind but also the body and spirit. These therapies often focus on the mind-body connection, providing individuals with additional tools to manage symptoms, reduce stress, and improve overall well-being.

Mindfulness and Meditation

Mindfulness and meditation practices have shown promise in reducing symptoms of PTSD by helping individuals focus on the present moment and develop a nonjudgmental awareness of their thoughts, feelings, and bodily sensations. These practices can reduce rumination and hyperarousal, increase emotional regulation, and improve overall mental health.

Yoga

Yoga, with its combination of physical postures, breathing exercises, and meditation, can be particularly beneficial for individuals with PTSD. It promotes relaxation, physical strength, and flexibility while also reducing stress and anxiety. The emphasis on connecting with one's body can be especially therapeutic for those who feel disconnected or numb because of their trauma.

Acupuncture

Acupuncture is an ancient practice that involves inserting thin needles into specific points on the body. It's thought to stimulate the body's natural healing processes and balance energy flow. Some individuals with PTSD have found acupuncture helpful in alleviating symptoms, particularly anxiety, depression, and sleep disturbances.

Art Therapy

Art therapy allows individuals to express their thoughts and feelings through creative activities such as drawing, painting, or sculpting. It can be particularly helpful for those who find it difficult to articulate their experiences verbally. Art therapy provides a safe outlet for expression and can facilitate the processing of traumatic memories in a non-threatening way.

Integrating Alternative Therapies into PTSD Treatment

While alternative and complementary therapies can provide significant benefits, they are generally considered adjuncts to, rather than replacements for, more traditional treatments like psychotherapy and medication. It's important for individuals to discuss any alternative therapies they are considering with their healthcare provider to ensure they are safe and appropriate.

The effectiveness of these therapies can vary greatly among individuals, and personal preference plays a significant role in their success. What works well for one person might not work for another. Therefore, a trial-and-error approach, guided by professional advice, is often necessary to find the most effective combination of treatments.

CHAPTER SIX

LIVING WITH PTSD

L iving with PTSD is indeed a continuous journey, not a destination. Isn't it about navigating everyday life with resilience, understanding, and strategies to manage the multifaceted symptoms and challenges that accompany this condition? This chapter seeks to provide insights and guidance for individuals and their loved ones on creating a supportive environment and leading a fulfilling life, despite the hurdles posed by PTSD.

Daily Life and Challenges

In this section, we aim to illuminate the day-to-day realities and challenges faced by those living with PTSD. Isn't one of the most significant daily challenges the persistent sense of danger and hypervigilance? Individuals with PTSD often feel compelled to be constantly vigilant against potential threats. This unending state of alertness can be draining, turning ordinary situations into overwhelming experiences and leading to fatigue, irritability, and difficulty concentrating. The world can seem like a minefield, where any misstep might trigger a flashback or a surge of anxiety.

Nightmares and insomnia are common sleep disturbances, transforming the night from a time of rest and rejuvenation into a period of increased anxiety and fear. A lack of restful sleep not only worsens PTSD symptoms but also impacts overall health, mood, and stress-coping abilities. Establishing a calm bedtime routine and environment is essential, yet often challenging to achieve.

Social interactions can become complex and fraught. PTSD can lead to withdrawal and isolation, as individuals might avoid social settings to escape triggers or misunderstandings. Relationships can suffer as loved ones struggle to comprehend and cope with the unpredictable and sometimes explosive behavior that PTSD can evoke. The person with PTSD might feel an intense sense of loneliness and disconnection, even amidst family and friends.

Employment poses another significant challenge. The symptoms of PTSD can hinder concentration, effective communication, or handling a typical workday's stress. Individuals might find themselves unable to maintain a job or may frequently switch jobs due to conflicts or dissatisfaction. This instability can lead to financial stress and feelings of failure or inadequacy, further worsening the condition. Even routine activities like grocery shopping, driving, or attending appointments can become daunting, with the world seemingly full of potential triggers.

Relationships and PTSD
Navigating interpersonal connections can be one of the most daunting aspects of dealing with PTSD, impacting both the person with PTSD and their loved ones. For individuals with PTSD, fear and anxiety might compel them to remain constantly guarded, even with those closest to them. This state of hypervigilance can cause misunderstandings and feelings of alienation. They might inadvertently push loved ones away, fearing that closeness will lead to hurt or disappointment. Intense emotions, flashbacks, or outbursts can create an atmosphere of walking on eggshells, where family members or partners feel uncertain about how to act or what to say, fearing triggering a negative response.

Communication often becomes a significant challenge. Those with PTSD might find it difficult to articulate their experiences and emotions, leading to frustration and isolation. They may withdraw into themselves to avoid the pain of reliving traumatic memories or out of a belief that they're shielding their loved ones from their pain. Conversely, partners, friends, and family may feel excluded and helpless, uncertain about how to offer support or bridge the growing emotional divide.

Trust issues are another common challenge in relationships affected by PTSD. The trauma that led to PTSD might involve betrayal or harm from others, making it challenging for the individual to fully trust anyone. This lack of trust can strain relationships, as partners and family members might feel that their support and love are constantly being questioned or rejected.

The unpredictability of PTSD symptoms can also create a tense and sometimes volatile home environment. Loved ones might feel they're constantly on alert for mood changes or other signs of distress, disrupting the normalcy and comfort that relationships typically provide. This heightened tension can lead to conflicts, misunderstandings, and a cycle of guilt and recrimination that further strains the relationship. Despite these challenges, many relationships not only survive but also grow stronger. Open communication is key. Both parties must learn as much as possible about PTSD, and understand its symptoms, triggers, and effects. Professional therapy, including couples or family counseling, can provide a safe space to express feelings, fears, and frustrations and to learn strategies for supporting each other.

Building a strong support network is also essential. Friends, family members, and support groups can offer understanding and assistance, helping to reduce the sense of isolation often accompanying PTSD. Loved ones should also take care of their mental and emotional health, seeking support when need and ensuring they can be a stable source of strength and comfort. Patience and empathy are perhaps the most critical elements in maintaining and strengthening relationships affected by PTSD. Understanding that recovery is a journey, not a destination, and that setbacks are part of the process, can help maintain a perspective of hope and progress.

Strategies for Managing Symptoms

How can those afflicted with PTSD regain control over their lives? What changes can they make to reduce the impact of symptoms on their daily activities? Strategies for managing PTSD symptoms are indispensable in enhancing life quality for those affected. Implementing diverse techniques and lifestyle adjustments can aid in regaining control and mitigating symptom interference in daily life.

One of the most efficacious strategies lies in establishing a routine. Regularity offers a sense of control and predictability, often absent in the lives of those with PTSD. Structuring the day with fixed times for meals, work, relaxation, and sleep can alleviate anxiety and uplift the mood. It's crucial to integrate healthy activities that foster well-being, like exercise, which is known for diminishing symptoms of anxiety and depression.

Mindfulness and relaxation techniques also prove highly beneficial. Methods such as meditation, deep breathing, and progressive muscle relaxation can soothe the mind and lessen stress responses. Learning to focus on the present and regulate breathing can reduce anxiety and stress intensity, facilitating trigger and symptom management.

Another key strategy is enhancing sleep hygiene, as sleep disturbances frequently afflict those with PTSD. Establishing a consistent sleep schedule, creating a comfortable sleeping environment, and avoiding stimulants before bedtime can significantly elevate sleep quality. Practices like unwinding before bed or using white-noise machines can also be effective.

Journaling serves as a therapeutic tool, providing a private space for expressing thoughts and feelings. Writing about experiences, emotions, and daily occurrences can offer insights into patterns and triggers, aiding in the development of more effective coping strategies. It also tracks progress, offering a sense of achievement and growth.

Social support stands as a cornerstone in PTSD management. Connecting with understanding individuals who offer encouragement is invaluable. This might involve participating in support groups, maintaining contact with friends and family, or engaging in community activities. Sharing experiences with trusted people can alleviate isolation and offer fresh perspectives on challenges.

Lastly, educating oneself about PTSD is empowering. Understanding the disorder, its symptoms, and its underlying reasons can demystify the experience, reducing fear and confusion. This knowledge enables individuals to better advocate for themselves and make informed decisions regarding treatment and lifestyle choices.

Incorporating these strategies demands patience and perseverance. Recognizing small victories and understanding that progress may be slow and non-linear is essential.

PTSD in the Workplace

PTSD in the workplace requires attention and understanding from both employees and employers. For those with PTSD, navigating work environments presents various challenges, but with appropriate strategies and support, they can maintain productivity and enjoy fulfilling careers.

Firstly, understanding one's rights is vital. Many regions have laws protecting individuals with disabilities, including PTSD, from discrimination. Knowing one's rights regarding reasonable workplace accommodations is crucial. These might include flexible schedules, quiet workspaces, or the ability to take breaks as needed.

Open communication with employers or human resources about one's condition can lead to enhanced support and understanding. Discussing specific needs and challenges related to PTSD while maintaining privacy is essential. Conversations about potential workplace triggers and management strategies can create a more supportive work environment.

Self-care is paramount to managing PTSD symptoms at work. This includes taking regular breaks to manage stress, practicing relaxation techniques, and seeking professional help when necessary. Employees should be encouraged to use vacation time for rest and recovery and engage in well-being activities outside of work.

Time management skills can greatly reduce work-related stress. Breaking tasks into smaller parts and setting realistic deadlines can prevent feeling overwhelmed. Prioritizing tasks and focusing on one thing at a time can help maintain focus and reduce anxiety. Building a workplace support network, including trusted colleagues or a support group, can offer understanding and encouragement during challenging times.

Employers play a crucial role in supporting employees with PTSD. Providing training on PTSD and its workplace impact can cultivate a more inclusive and supportive environment. Implementing mental health-promoting policies, like counseling services or mental health days, benefits all employees.

Workplace accommodations might also involve telecommuting options or workload adjustments during challenging periods. Employers should be flexible and understanding, recognizing that employees with PTSD may experience fluctuating days.

Having a clear, accessible process for reporting issues or requesting accommodations is beneficial. A well-defined procedure enables employees with PTSD to seek support without fear of stigma or repercussions.

Managing PTSD in the workplace is a collective responsibility. By understanding the challenges, rights, and support strategies, individuals with PTSD can excel professionally. Employers fostering a supportive environment not only assist their employees with PTSD but also create a healthier, more productive workplace. As awareness and understanding of PTSD increase, it's hoped that more workplaces will adopt practices supporting the well-being and success of every team member.

Long-Term Outlook and Coping Mechanisms

Understanding the long-term outlook and coping mechanisms for PTSD is crucial in managing and living with the condition over time. As individuals' journey through their healing process, embracing a long-term perspective aid in setting realistic expectations and cultivating patience and resilience.

Here are insights into maintaining a balanced outlook and effective coping strategies:

1. Embracing a Holistic Approach: Long-term coping with PTSD involves a holistic approach that encompasses physical, emotional, and mental well-being. Regular exercise, a nutritious diet, adequate sleep, and mindfulness practices like meditation can significantly contribute to overall health and resilience. Integrating these aspects into daily life can provide a strong foundation for coping with PTSD symptoms.

2. Continuous Therapy and Support: Continuous engagement in therapy, whether individual or group, provides ongoing support and adaptation of coping strategies. As life changes, so might the triggers and responses to stress. Ongoing therapy helps in addressing these changes promptly and effectively. Additionally, support groups provide a sense of community and understanding, which can be incredibly reassuring.

3. Education and Awareness: Staying informed about PTSD and its developments in treatment options can empower individuals to make informed decisions about their care. Understanding the condition reduces stigma and promotes a more compassionate self-view. Education also involves recognizing early signs of worsening symptoms, which is crucial in preventing relapses.

4. Developing and Refining Coping Skills:
Over time, individuals learn what coping mechanisms work best for them. This might include relaxation techniques, structured routines, creative outlets like art or writing, or spending time in nature. Regularly practicing and refining these skills ensures they are readily available and effective when stress levels rise.

5. Setting Boundaries and Self-Care:
Learning to set healthy boundaries with others and oneself is vital in managing everyday stressors and preventing burnout. This includes saying no to excessive demands, taking breaks when needed, and engaging in regular self-care activities. Self-care is not a luxury but a critical component of long-term coping.

6. Fostering Positive Relationships:

Surrounding oneself with understanding and supportive people can make a significant difference in managing PTSD. Positive relationships provide comfort, advice, and a sense of belonging. They act as a buffer against stress and can offer practical help during tough times.

7. Adapting to Change:

Life is dynamic, and change is inevitable. Developing flexibility and adaptability helps in adjusting to new situations and challenges. This might mean revising expectations, changing routines, or seeking different forms of support as circumstances change.

8. Celebrating Progress:

Acknowledging and celebrating progress, no matter how small, is important. It reinforces the value of effort and the possibility of change. Celebrating milestones helps in building confidence and a positive outlook towards the future.

9. Maintaining Hope:

Perhaps most importantly, maintaining a sense of hope is crucial. PTSD is challenging, but with the right support and strategies, individuals can lead fulfilling lives. Hope is not just a feeling but a strategy for resilience; it involves setting goals, imagining a better future, and taking proactive steps towards it.

In the realm of treating Post-Traumatic Stress Disorder, understanding, and implementing enduring coping strategies demands patience, dedication, and a robust support network. This process involves sculpting a life that not only acknowledges the constraints of PTSD but also propels individuals toward their goals and personal development. Over time, with appropriate strategies and unwavering support, individuals can transcend mere symptom management; they can flourish despite the challenges posed by their condition.

Conclusion

As we conclude Chapter 6, focusing on the experience of living with PTSD, we have delved into the intricacies of daily life, interpersonal relationships, workplace dynamics, and the long-term management of PTSD. We have recognized the profound impact and pervasive nature of PTSD while simultaneously acknowledging the potent strategies and support systems that foster coping and resilience.

This chapter has underscored the importance of custom-tailored strategies in managing PTSD symptoms, the vital role of support in personal relationships and professional environments, and the necessity of embracing a hopeful future equipped with realistic and supportive long-term coping mechanisms. While the path is undeniably fraught with challenges, it is also replete with opportunities for growth and betterment. As we progress, it is vital to bear in mind that with persistent effort, deep understanding, and unwavering support, individuals grappling with PTSD can lead rewarding lives. The journey is continuous, and the learning is unending. Let us persevere in our quest to explore, support, and empower those navigating this path.

Emotional Journal:
Living with PTSD

This journal gives you a place to think about what you read in the chapter and how it applies to your own life. Feel free to write down what you think, how you feel, and any personal stories that have something to do with living with PTSD.

Reflect on moments when you felt a persistent sense of danger or were hypervigilant. How did this affect your day-to-day activities?

....

....

....

....

Describe how nightmares or insomnia have impacted your life. How do you cope with these sleep disturbances?

....

....

....

....

Reflect on trust issues in your relationships. How has PTSD influenced your ability to trust others?

....

....

....

....

Reflect on the importance of social support in your life. How do friends, family, or support groups help you manage PTSD?

....

....

....

....

Reflect on your rights and accommodations in the workplace. How have you navigated employment while managing PTSD?

....

....

....

....

CHAPTER SEVEN

PREVENTING PTSD AND PROMOTING RESILIENCE

In this concluding chapter, we strive to endow you, the reader, with insights not just to comprehend post-traumatic stress disorder but to actively participate in its prevention and in fortifying the resilience of individuals and communities. As we wrap up our extensive journey through the intricacies of post-traumatic stress disorder, we gaze optimistically towards a future where trauma's toll is lessened, and recovery becomes a universally accessible path. Join us as we navigate these crucial strategies for fostering a healthier, more resilient society. Our exploration will encompass a variety of early intervention tactics, including critical incident stress debriefing, prompt psychological first aid, and the use of screening tools for identifying those at heightened risk. Central to our discussion is the pivotal role of timely, sensitive, and efficacious intervention in preventing the transformation of trauma into full-blown post-traumatic stress disorder.

The Power of Early Recognition

In the realm of PTSD, the Power of Early Recognition emerges as a crucial, proactive stance, shining as a beacon of hope. It signifies a decisive moment for interrupting the trauma cycle and directing individuals towards recovery and resilience. Early recognition is about discerning the nuanced ways trauma impacts an individual's psyche and behavior and responding with both empathy and accuracy. Isn't it more than just spotting early signs of trauma? Isn't it equally about enacting strategies to foresee and avert its intensifying effects?

Anticipating trauma demands a multifaceted approach. Education and awareness form the bedrock, enabling communities to debunk mental health myths and replace them with knowledgeable, compassionate perspectives. It's about detecting early distress indicators, like social withdrawal, mood or behavioral shifts, or diminished performance in professional or educational settings. By grasping PTSD's nature, its diverse manifestations, and its repercussions, individuals and communities can proactively recognize signs of struggle.

Beyond mere detection, anticipation entails equipping people with the capabilities and resources for an effective response. This might include training in psychological first aid, fostering open communication, and advocating for methods like mindfulness and stress management that can alleviate initial trauma symptoms. Healthcare professionals, educators, and community leaders can contribute by organizing workshops and supplying resources to nurture a supportive atmosphere.

Moreover, constructing a supportive network is paramount. Motivating friends, family, and community members to actively offer support and understanding cultivates a caring culture. This involves not only identifying distress but also understanding how to approach someone in difficulty, lending a sympathetic ear, and directing them towards professional assistance when needed.

Acknowledging the diversity of trauma and its effects is equally critical. Given that PTSD can manifest differently in different people depending on their background, culture, and prior experiences, each individual case calls for a tailored approach. This sensitivity honors individual paths and guarantees that interventions are suitable and effective.

Early recognition also plays a vital role in diminishing mental health stigma. By initiating open dialogues about trauma and its impacts, communities start to perceive mental health issues as a common human experience. This transparency encourages individuals to acknowledge symptoms within themselves and seek aid without fear of judgment, fostering a network of support and empathy. Ultimately, the power of early recognition alters the narrative from isolation and despair to hope and community. It illustrates a society that cherishes mental health as a communal responsibility, ensuring everyone is seen, heard, and supported. Early recognition isn't just about intervening early; it's about conveying a clear message: "You are not alone; we see you, and we are here for you." This mindset doesn't just transform individual lives; it has the potential to revolutionize entire communities by promoting a proactive attitude towards mental health and well-being.

Critical Incident Stress Debriefing (CISD)

Critical Incident Stress Debriefing (CISD) unfolds as a pivotal intervention in trauma's immediate aftermath, addressing the needs of those immersed in harrowing events, like first responders. This approach transcends mere conversation; it's a strategic intervention aimed at providing psychological relief and a trajectory toward long-term recovery. In the early, malleable post-trauma days, how crucial is CISD in shaping the mind and emotions? What role does it play in influencing long-term outcomes?

In trauma's wake, CISD offers a structured haven for communal healing. The facilitator, adept in trauma response, guides participants through shared narratives, acknowledging and validating the spectrum of emotions that emerge post-trauma. This process isn't just cathartic; it normalizes reactions, fostering a sense of community in the often-isolating aftermath of trauma. Additionally, CISD facilitates the exchange of coping strategies, serving as a pool of collective wisdom.

CISD's end goal is twofold: reducing immediate distress and preventing chronic conditions like PTSD, while also acting as an early screening tool for those needing further support. It's a recognition that trauma affects the mind and soul, necessitating immediate, structured care. As our trauma understanding evolves, so will CISD methods, maintaining its core aim of fostering resilience and paving the way for recovery. CISD is not merely a debriefing; it's the first step in a healing journey, offering hope and understanding in darkness.

Immediate Psychological First Aid

Immediate Psychological First Aid, akin to its medical counterpart, is vital post-trauma, designed to mitigate distress and prevent severe psychological issues. It's about offering immediate support, acknowledging trauma, and providing stability in the storm of post-traumatic stress. The core of this aid lies in respecting and upholding the dignity of survivors, restoring their sense of empowerment and autonomy. Practitioners approach with empathy and sensitivity, ensuring physical and psychological safety as a foundation for healing.

Emotional stabilization is crucial, as trauma leaves individuals disoriented and overwhelmed. Practitioners employ non-intrusive techniques, focusing on active listening, reassurance, and grounding intense emotions. They balance gathering information about immediate needs with not overwhelming the survivor, tailoring support to be as effective as possible.

Finally, connecting individuals to social support and services is essential. Psychological first aid is an immediate response that bridges the gap to long-term recovery methods. Practitioners guide survivors towards the next steps, ensuring a clear and accessible path to recovery. This aid isn't a standalone solution but a vital link in the chain of healing and resilience.

Screening Tools and Early Assessment

In the context of PTSD management, the role of screening tools and early assessment is foundational. Recognizing individuals at risk is a vital step to curb symptom escalation and facilitate timely intervention. A variety of instruments, including questionnaires and structured interviews, are utilized to discern the presence and intensity of post-traumatic stress symptoms. These tools, crafted with sensitivity and specificity, identify those who may benefit from further evaluation and care. But how do we measure the true impact of early screening on averting the deepening of PTSD? And what is the role of these tools in guiding individuals towards healing?

The significance of early detection lies in its potential to transform outcomes. Untreated PTSD can spiral into a debilitating condition, pervading every aspect of life. Early detection offers a crucial window for intervention, with treatments that can mitigate symptoms or thwart the full onset of the disorder. By pinpointing those at risk, clinicians can provide immediate support, education, and resources, initiating the journey to recovery.

Screening tools come in diverse formats, each tailored with specific questions or prompts to glean insights into the individual's experiences, symptoms, and functional status. Some tools are self-reported, empowering individuals to articulate their symptoms in their own words. Others, administered by trained clinicians, delve deeper into the psychological state, reflecting the criteria for PTSD as outlined in diagnostic manuals.

Structured interviews form another critical pillar of early assessment. Unlike broader screening tools, these interviews facilitate an in-depth exploration of individual experiences and symptoms. Clinicians conducting these interviews, trained to discern the subtleties of PTSD, make informed judgments about the nature and extent of an individual's trauma and stress-related symptoms. Through these interviews, clinicians gather detailed information about the traumatic event, symptom onset and duration, and the impact on daily functioning.

Guiding the use of these tools is a profound understanding of PTSD and its various manifestations. Clinicians must be attuned to PTSD's diverse presentations and adept in interpreting tool results, considering the individual's cultural background, personal history, and current circumstances, which can influence symptom expression and help-seeking behavior. Following identification, targeted interventions are implemented, including psychoeducation, stress management techniques, and referrals, equipping individuals with the necessary resources and skills to manage symptoms and prevent chronic PTSD.

Importance of Timely and Sensitive Intervention
The criticality of timely and sensitive intervention post-trauma is paramount. Intense emotional experiences ranging from fear to despair are frequently present in the immediate aftermath of trauma, along with shock and disorientation. This is when the right support can significantly influence the recovery trajectory. Timely intervention involves providing support as soon as possible after the event, aiming to stabilize, mitigate distress, and prevent more severe symptoms. This might include practical assistance, psychological first aid, or specialized service referrals.

However, the timing is just one facet. The sensitivity of delivery is equally vital. Trauma can profoundly affect a person's sense of safety and trust. Interventions must be respectful, compassionate, and attuned to the individual's needs and circumstances. Sensitivity encompasses being attuned to cultural, social, and personal factors influencing the trauma experience. People from diverse cultural backgrounds may express distress differently and hold varying beliefs about recovery. A culturally sensitive approach adapts interventions to these differences, working collaboratively with the individual to identify the most effective path forward.

Interventions must also be flexible and responsive to changing needs. The journey post-trauma is often long and complex, with evolving needs. Early interventions should establish a foundation for ongoing support, fostering resilience and coping strategies for long-term well-being. Recognizing and responding to signs of distress or deterioration is crucial, as reactions to trauma vary widely. Caregivers and service providers must be alert to these signs and ready to offer additional support or specialized referrals as necessary.

Resilience Journal:
Navigating the Path to Preventing
PTSD

This resilience journal is designed to guide you through the journey of understanding and preventing PTSD, helping you to cultivate resilience within yourself and your community.

How do you personally understand the importance of early recognition of PTSD symptoms? What steps can you take to enhance your awareness?

....

....

....

....

Reflect on a situation where early signs of distress were evident. How did you or those around you respond? What could be done differently?

....

....

....

....

What specific actions can you take to promote education and awareness about trauma and PTSD in your community?

....

....

....

....

How can you actively contribute to supporting those experiencing trauma?

....

....

....

....

How do you perceive the role of immediate psychological first aid following a traumatic event? What specific actions can you take to be prepared to offer or seek such aid?

....

....

....

....

Think about a situation where early intervention could have made a difference. What lessons can you learn from this, and how can you apply them in the future?

....

....

....

....

Identify one strategy that you can implement to enhance your resilience against PTSD. How will you integrate this strategy into your daily routine?

....

....

....

Reflect on the importance of community support in preventing PTSD. How can you contribute to building a supportive and resilient community?

....

....

....

Remember, your insights and reflections are valuable steps toward understanding and action. There's no right or wrong way to express them. Keep this journal as a companion on your journey towards a more resilient self and community.

CONCLUSION

As we conclude the fourth book in our series, we take a moment to reflect on our journey through the intricate and profoundly human world of Post-Traumatic Stress Disorder (PTSD). Our exploration has led us to unravel the complexities of PTSD, shedding light on its many layers and implications.

Our journey began with defining PTSD, recognizing it not merely as a collection of symptoms but as a severe, enduring response to traumatic events that surpass the realm of ordinary human experiences. We acknowledged how PTSD manifests in diverse ways, impacting not only the mind but also infiltrating every facet of an individual's life, altering their sense of self, relationships, and worldview.

Discussing the causes of PTSD, we understood that it doesn't arise in isolation. Rather, it often springs from a confluence of traumatic experiences, individual vulnerabilities, and environmental factors. We learned about the wide range of traumatic events, from combat and sexual assault to natural disasters and serious accidents, and how these experiences shatter individuals' assumptions about their world and themselves, creating a lasting impact that can spiral into PTSD.

In our quest to understand the science behind PTSD, we delved into how trauma affects the brain, influencing memory, emotions, and behavior. The critical role of memory in PTSD, particularly the intrusive, involuntary recollections known as flashbacks, was a focus. We also discussed the long-term health effects of living with PTSD, which extend far beyond mental health, impacting physical well-being and increasing the risk of various medical conditions.

Recognizing PTSD is crucial. We outlined the signs and symptoms, the professional criteria for diagnosis, and the tools and tests used in diagnosing this complex disorder. We addressed the challenges in diagnosing PTSD, emphasizing the need for a careful, comprehensive approach to distinguishing PTSD from other mental health conditions.

We explored treatment options for PTSD, highlighting the effectiveness of therapies such as Cognitive Behavioral Therapy (CBT), Eye Movement Desensitization and Reprocessing (EMDR), medications, and alternative approaches. The importance of personalized treatment plans was stressed, acknowledging that each journey to recovery is unique.

Living with PTSD was a significant focus, examining the day-to-day challenges, the impact on relationships, strategies for managing symptoms, workplace considerations, and long-term coping mechanisms. We aimed to offer insights into the struggles and the strategies and resources available for managing and overcoming them.

We delved into special topics in PTSD, focusing on unique challenges faced by certain populations and circumstances, requiring tailored understanding and approaches. This included discussions on PTSD in military personnel and veterans, individuals who have experienced sexual assault, the concept of complex PTSD, and cultural considerations in understanding and treating PTSD.

In our final chapter, we turned our attention to preventing PTSD and promoting resilience. We emphasized the power of early intervention, community-based prevention programs, education, and awareness campaigns. We explored strategies to bolster resilience in at-risk populations, recognizing that while traumas cannot always be avoided, their impacts can be mitigated through informed, compassionate, and proactive measures.

As we conclude, we remember that though PTSD is a profound and often debilitating condition, there is hope. Recovery is not just possible; it occurs daily. Through ongoing research, improved treatments, and increased awareness, we can alter the course of PTSD for many, offering a path back to a fulfilling life. As we conclude this book, we carry forward our comprehension, empathy, and dedication to helping those who are suffering from PTSD and illuminating the way to recovery.

The journey to overcome PTSD is not linear; it is fraught with challenges and setbacks. Yet, every step towards healing, no matter how small, is significant. You are not alone in this fight. Hold on to hope, even in the darkest moments. Your journey is a narrative of resilience and survival. Each obstacle you overcome not only brings you closer to healing but also paves the way for others who struggle. You demonstrate that PTSD can be confronted and that life, in all its beauty and complexity, can be embraced again.

Remember, your experiences, pain, and progress hold immense value. You are more than your trauma. You are a warrior, a survivor, and an inspiration to those also battling PTSD. Continue to push forward, seek joy, and never underestimate the power of your resilience.

So, fight bravely, love fiercely, and never give up. Your journey is a testament to your strength, and in your fight, you are never alone.

. . .

Thank you for engaging with this comprehensive guide on PTSD. Your willingness to learn more about this complex condition is admirable. If this book has offered you insights, understanding, or support, please consider sharing your thoughts in a review on Amazon or your preferred platform. Your feedback is invaluable, helping us as authors and aiding others who may find solace and guidance in these pages. Your contributions shape the conversation around PTSD and foster a more informed and compassionate community. Thank you again, and may your path be one of healing and growth.

Emily

BOOK 5

VAGUS
NERVE

Your Reflection Space

INTRODUCTION

Welcome to the fascinating and mysterious world of the vagus nerve, an unsung hero of the human body that plays a crucial role in maintaining our physical and mental well-being. This book stems from my passion for accessible science and a desire to share with you, dear reader, the wonders of the human body in understandable and applicable ways. The vagus nerve, with its extensive pathway that traverses and influences various vital organs, has captured my attention, and I imagine it will capture yours too.

I'll speak to you as I would to a friend. I'll tell you how this remarkable nerve influences everything from your ability to digest food to your response to stress. I'll show you how, through simple daily practices, you can optimize its function to enhance your health and well-being.

As we progress, I invite you to think of this book not only as a guide but as a dialogue. I'm here to explore with you, to marvel with you, and, above all, to learn with you. The science of the vagus nerve is vast and still partly mysterious, but together, we can uncover how to harness its power to live a healthier and happier life.

I'll show you how the vagus nerve can be your ally in managing stress, fighting inflammation, and even improving your social relationships. From physical exercise to meditation, diet to breathing exercises, I'll share evidence-based strategies with you that you can implement into your daily routine.

This journey we're about to embark on together is not just a path of learning; it's an adventure toward a deeper understanding of how body and mind are intrinsically connected and how we can harmonize them for our betterment.

So take a moment, breathe deeply, and get ready to uncover the secrets of your vagus nerve. I'm thrilled to share these pages, my knowledge, and my experiences with you, in the hope that they may illuminate your path to a fuller and healthier life.

Welcome to this extraordinary adventure.

CHAPTER ONE

EXPLORING THE VAGUS NERVE

Imagine having within your body a secret key capable of unlocking doors to better health, a sense of calm, and enhanced emotional resilience. This key is none other than the vagus nerve, an unsung hero of the nervous system that holds the power to profoundly influence our well-being. Throughout this chapter, I'll lead you to discover this remarkable nerve, exploring its unique anatomy, its myriad vital functions, and how we can, through knowledge and simple practices, optimize its power to significantly improve our lives.

From here, we'll embark on our journey into the heart of the human body, unveiling the central role played by the vagus nerve in maintaining not only our physical health but also our emotional and psychological balance. Prepare to be amazed by the complexity and beauty of your body as we guide you through the various functions and potentials of your vagus nerve, your internal superpower waiting to be discovered and empowered.

The vagus nerve, an essential part of the parasympathetic nervous system, acts as a conductor in the body, directing a symphony of vital functions without us even being aware. Its ability to communicate between the brain and the heart, lungs, digestive system, and beyond is crucial for our daily functioning. This unique nerve has the extraordinary ability to decrease heart rate, control saliva production, manage digestive processes, and modulate inflammation, demonstrating its extensive influence on our physical health.

One of the most fascinating functions of the vagus nerve is its ability to directly influence our response to stress and our emotions. Through the vagal reflex, it can calm the body after periods of high stress, reducing heart rate and lowering blood pressure, promoting a sense of calm and relaxation. It's this ability to bring the body into a state of balance and tranquility that underscores the critical role of the vagus nerve in stress management and mental health.

Furthermore, research has highlighted how high vagal tone, indicating a healthy and well-functioning vagus nerve, is associated with better emotional regulation, reduced susceptibility to stress, and even greater psychological resilience. This connection between vagal tone and mental health opens new perspectives on how we can influence our emotional well-being through the body.

Vagus nerve stimulation, whether through natural methods like deep breathing, meditation, and physical exercise, or through clinical interventions for specific conditions, has shown promising results in treating a variety of disorders. From mental conditions like anxiety and depression to physical ailments like epilepsy and chronic inflammation, vagus nerve stimulation offers an innovative approach to improving health.

This chapter not only sheds light on the vital importance of the vagus nerve in our bodies but also invites reflection on how we can actively participate in improving our health and well-being. Through understanding how the vagus nerve works and implementing daily practices to support it, we can harness its power to live a more balanced and fulfilling life. The vagus nerve, also known as the tenth cranial nerve, is one of the longest nerves of the parasympathetic system and plays a crucial role in managing the body's involuntary functions, such as digestion, heart rate, and respiration. Originating from the medulla oblongata at the base of the brain, it branches into two trunks that descend on both sides of the neck, traverse the chest, and extend into the abdomen, innervating various vital organs along its pathway.

The unique structure of the vagus nerve allows it to influence a wide range of bodily functions. In the chest, it sends fibers to the lungs and heart, regulating breathing and heart rate. Continuing into the abdomen, the vagus nerve innervates most of the digestive organs, including the stomach, liver, pancreas, and intestines, playing a fundamental role in digestion and nutrient absorption.

This extensive network of connections is essential for the so-called "rest and digest reflex," which activates the body into a state of calm, promoting digestion and regeneration. The vagus nerve's ability to transmit information bidirectionally between the brain and internal organs is crucial for maintaining homeostasis and effectively responding to environmental and internal stresses.

Unveiling the Hidden Superpower: Understanding the Role of Well-Being

The human body is a marvel of complexity, with its intricate systems working in harmony to sustain life. Yet, amidst the vast array of bodily functions, there exists a hidden superpower that often goes unnoticed: the vagus nerve. This unassuming nerve, also known as the "wandering nerve," plays a profound role in our overall well-being, influencing everything from our physical health to our emotional resilience.

At the core of this hidden superpower lies its ability to regulate the body's autonomic functions, those involuntary processes that keep us alive and functioning without conscious effort. From controlling heart rate and digestion to modulating inflammation and stress responses, the vagus nerve acts as a silent guardian, ensuring our body remains in a state of balance and equilibrium.

But what exactly is the vagus nerve, and why is it so crucial to our well-being? To understand its significance, we must first delve into its anatomy and functions. Originating in the brainstem and extending down through the neck, chest, and abdomen, the vagus nerve branches out like an intricate network of pathways, reaching nearly every major organ in the body.

This extensive reach allows the vagus nerve to exert its influence far beyond its anatomical confines. Through its intricate connections with the brain, heart, lungs, and digestive system, the vagus nerve serves as a communication highway, transmitting signals that regulate bodily functions and maintain homeostasis.

One of the most remarkable aspects of the vagus nerve is its role in stress management and emotional resilience. Through a process known as the vagal reflex, this nerve can initiate a cascade of physiological responses that promote relaxation and calmness in the face of stress. By slowing heart rate, lowering blood pressure, and reducing inflammation, the vagus nerve helps to counteract the body's stress response, allowing us to navigate challenging situations with greater ease.

But the influence of the vagus nerve extends beyond the physical realm into the domain of mental health. Research has shown that individuals with a higher vagal tone, indicating a healthy and responsive vagus nerve, are better equipped to regulate their emotions, cope with stress, and bounce back from adversity. This link between vagal tone and psychological resilience highlights the importance of nurturing this hidden superpower for overall well-being.

Fortunately, there are ways to enhance vagal tone and optimize the functioning of this remarkable nerve. Practices such as deep breathing, meditation, and physical exercise have been shown to stimulate the vagus nerve and promote relaxation and stress reduction. By incorporating these simple techniques into our daily routine, we can harness the power of the vagus nerve to enhance our physical and emotional well-being.

In addition to natural methods, there are also clinical interventions that target the vagus nerve for therapeutic purposes. Vagus nerve stimulation (VNS), for example, involves the use of electrical impulses to activate the nerve, with promising results in the treatment of conditions such as depression, epilepsy, and chronic inflammation. These innovative approaches offer new avenues for improving health and quality of life.

The Orchestra Conductor: Anatomy of the Vagus Nerve

VAGUS NERVE

To truly grasp the significance of the vagus nerve, we must delve into its intricate anatomy, akin to the conductor of a grand orchestra guiding each instrument to play in harmony. Emerging from the medulla oblongata, the vagus nerve extends its branches like delicate tendrils, weaving through the body's intricate pathways with precision and purpose.

As it descends through the neck, the vagus nerve branches out into various regions, forming connections with crucial structures such as the heart, lungs, and digestive system. These connections allow the vagus nerve to orchestrate a symphony of vital functions, seamlessly coordinating the body's activities to maintain optimal health and balance.

Within the chest, the vagus nerve sends fibers to the heart, regulating its rhythm and ensuring proper functioning. Through its intricate network of connections, the vagus nerve influences heart rate variability, a key indicator of cardiovascular health. By modulating the balance between sympathetic and parasympathetic activity, the vagus nerve helps to regulate blood pressure and maintain cardiovascular homeostasis.

Continuing its journey into the abdomen, the vagus nerve innervates most of the digestive organs, including the stomach, liver, pancreas, and intestines. Here, it plays a fundamental role in the process of digestion, stimulating the release of digestive enzymes and promoting nutrient absorption. Additionally, the vagus nerve helps to coordinate the movements of the gastrointestinal tract, ensuring the smooth passage of food through the digestive system.

But the influence of the vagus nerve extends far beyond the realms of cardiovascular and digestive health. With its extensive connections to the brain, the vagus nerve plays a crucial role in regulating mood, cognition, and emotional well-being. Through its intricate network of pathways, the vagus nerve serves as a bidirectional communication channel, transmitting signals between the brain and body that influence our mental state and emotional resilience.

Symphony of Vital Functions: The Vagus Nerve's Influence

In orchestrating this symphony of vital functions, the vagus nerve acts as a silent conductor, guiding the body's activities with precision and grace. From regulating heart rate and digestion to modulating stress responses and emotional resilience, the vagus nerve plays a multifaceted role in maintaining overall health and well-being.

One of the most remarkable aspects of the vagus nerve's influence is its ability to modulate the body's stress response. Through its intricate connections with the brain's limbic system, the vagus nerve can dampen the activity of the sympathetic nervous system, which is responsible for triggering the body's fight-or-flight response. By promoting relaxation and calmness, the vagus nerve helps to counteract the detrimental effects of chronic stress, reducing the risk of stress-related disorders such as anxiety and depression.

Furthermore, the vagus nerve's influence extends into the realm of inflammation, a key player in numerous chronic health conditions. Through its connections with the immune system, the vagus nerve can modulate the body's inflammatory response, helping to prevent excessive inflammation and promote tissue healing. By maintaining a healthy balance between pro-inflammatory and anti-inflammatory pathways, the vagus nerve plays a crucial role in safeguarding overall health and resilience.

In addition to its role in stress management and inflammation, the vagus nerve also plays a vital role in regulating mood and emotional well-being. Research has shown that individuals with higher vagal tone, indicative of a healthy and responsive vagus nerve, are better equipped to cope with stress, regulate their emotions, and maintain a positive outlook on life. By nurturing the vagus nerve through practices such as meditation, deep breathing, and physical exercise, we can enhance our emotional resilience and cultivate a greater sense of well-being.

Direct Influence on Stress Response

One of the most remarkable aspects of the vagus nerve's influence is its direct impact on the body's stress response. In moments of perceived threat or danger, the sympathetic nervous system initiates the well-known fight-or-flight response, preparing the body to react quickly and decisively. However, this response can be detrimental if activated excessively or chronically, leading to a cascade of physiological and psychological consequences.

Here enters the vagus nerve as a crucial regulator of the stress response. Through its intricate connections with the brainstem and limbic system, the vagus nerve acts as a counterbalance to the sympathetic nervous system, promoting a state of calmness and relaxation. This regulatory mechanism, known as the vagal brake, helps to dampen the body's stress response, preventing it from spiraling out of control.

By stimulating the vagus nerve through practices such as deep breathing, meditation, and relaxation techniques, we can activate this vagal brake and promote a sense of calmness and tranquility. These simple yet powerful interventions allow us to modulate our stress response, enabling us to navigate life's challenges with greater ease and resilience.

Promoting Emotional Balance and Resilience

Beyond its role in regulating the body's physiological stress response, the vagus nerve also plays a pivotal role in promoting emotional balance and resilience. Through its intricate connections with the limbic system, the vagus nerve influences mood regulation, cognition, and emotional processing.

Research has shown that individuals with higher vagal tone, indicative of a healthy and responsive vagus nerve, are better equipped to cope with stress, regulate their emotions, and maintain a positive outlook on life. By enhancing vagal tone through practices such as mindfulness meditation, yoga, and aerobic exercise, we can cultivate greater emotional resilience and well-being.

Moreover, the vagus nerve's influence extends beyond individual emotional regulation to interpersonal dynamics and social connectedness. Studies have found that individuals with higher vagal tone tend to have more satisfying relationships, greater empathy, and better social skills. By nurturing our vagus nerve and fostering strong social connections, we can enhance our emotional well-being and build a supportive network of relationships that buffer against stress and adversity.

Natural and Clinical Vagus Nerve Stimulation
The power of the vagus nerve can be harnessed not only through mindfulness practices and social support but also through more direct interventions known as vagus nerve stimulation (VNS). VNS involves the use of electrical impulses to stimulate the vagus nerve, with the goal of modulating its activity and promoting health and well-being.

One of the most well-known methods of natural vagus nerve stimulation is through deep breathing exercises. By engaging in slow, diaphragmatic breathing, individuals can activate the parasympathetic nervous system and stimulate the vagus nerve, promoting relaxation and reducing stress. Similarly, practices such as yoga, tai chi, and meditation have been shown to enhance vagal tone and improve emotional regulation.

In addition to natural methods, there are also clinical interventions that utilize VNS for therapeutic purposes. VNS therapy has been approved by the FDA for the treatment of certain neurological and psychiatric conditions, including epilepsy, depression, and migraine headaches. During VNS therapy, a small device is implanted in the body, typically in the chest, and delivers electrical impulses to the vagus nerve at regular intervals.

From Anxiety to Inflammation: Treating Disorders with Vagus Nerve Stimulation
Anxiety disorders are among the most common mental health conditions worldwide, affecting millions of individuals and impairing their ability to function in daily life. Fortunately, VNS has emerged as a promising treatment option for anxiety disorders, offering relief for those who struggle with persistent worry, fear, and panic attacks.

By modulating the activity of the vagus nerve, VNS can help to regulate the body's stress response and promote relaxation, thereby reducing

VAGUS NERVE

symptoms of anxiety and improving overall quality of life. Research has shown that VNS therapy is effective in reducing anxiety symptoms in individuals with generalized anxiety disorder, panic disorder, and post-traumatic stress disorder (PTSD).

In addition to its role in treating anxiety disorders, VNS therapy has also shown promise in the management of inflammatory conditions such as rheumatoid arthritis and inflammatory bowel disease. By modulating the activity of the vagus nerve, VNS can help to regulate the body's immune response and reduce inflammation, thereby alleviating symptoms and improving quality of life for individuals with these chronic conditions.

Overall, VNS represents a promising avenue for the treatment of a wide range of disorders, from anxiety to inflammation. By harnessing the power of the vagus nerve, VNS therapy offers hope for individuals struggling with these debilitating conditions, providing relief, and restoring health and well-being. As research into the therapeutic potential of VNS continues to advance, the future looks bright for this innovative approach to improving health and quality of life.

Active Participation in Health Improvement

Understanding the vital role of the vagus nerve in our physical and emotional well-being empowers us to take an active role in improving our health. By implementing daily practices that support vagal tone and function, we can harness the power of this hidden superpower to enhance our overall quality of life.

Implementing Daily Practices for Vagal Support

There are numerous simple yet effective practices that we can incorporate into our daily routine to support vagal tone and function:

- **Deep Breathing:** Engaging in slow, diaphragmatic breathing exercises can stimulate the vagus nerve and promote relaxation. Take a few minutes each day to focus on your breath, inhaling deeply through your nose and exhaling slowly through your mouth.

- **Mindfulness Meditation:** Practicing mindfulness meditation can help to quiet the mind, reduce stress, and enhance emotional resilience. Spend a few minutes each day in quiet reflection, focusing on the present moment, and cultivating a sense of inner peace.

- **Physical Exercise:** Regular physical exercise has been shown to stimulate the vagus nerve and promote overall health and well-being. Incorporate activities such as walking, jogging, swimming, or yoga into your daily routine to support vagal tone and function.

- **Social Connection:** Building strong social connections and fostering supportive relationships can help to enhance vagal tone and promote emotional well-being. Spend time with friends and loved ones, engage in meaningful conversations, and participate in group activities that bring you joy and fulfillment.

- **Healthy Lifestyle Choices:** Making healthy lifestyle choices, such as eating a balanced diet, getting enough sleep, and managing stress, can support vagal tone and function. Prioritize self-care and make time for activities that nourish your body, mind, and spirit.

In Conclusion

As we conclude this chapter, it's clear that the vagus nerve is far more than just a simple conduit for nerve impulses—it's a hidden superpower with the potential to transform our health and well-being. By understanding its anatomy, functions, and influence on our physical and emotional health, we can unlock its transformative power and embark on a journey towards greater vitality, resilience, and flourishing.

In the chapters to come, we'll delve deeper into the science of the vagus nerve, exploring its role in various aspects of health and wellness, and learning practical strategies for harnessing its power to optimize our lives. So let us embrace the profound influence of the vagus nerve and embark on this journey together, towards a brighter, healthier future.

CHAPTER TWO

THE VAGUS NERVE'S
ROLE IN ANXIETY

A nxiety disorders have often been misconstrued, leading to misunderstandings about their origins and management. It's important to recognize that anxiety is not solely a product of the mind; rather, it often originates from imbalances within the body. These imbalances can predispose individuals to anxiety disorders, making it challenging for the mind to regain equilibrium.

While a trained mind can certainly help in coping with anxiety, it's crucial to address the underlying bodily imbalances that contribute to its onset and persistence. The body's inability to find a balance between relaxation and stress modes can perpetuate feelings of anxiety, leading to prolonged periods of distress.

It's worth noting that anxiety caused by psychological factors can persist for extended periods as the body and mind adapt to new fears. However, a healthy and well-functioning body is better equipped to naturally shift into relaxation mode, mitigating the effects of anxiety. Conversely, when anxiety stems from bodily imbalances, it may persist for years without proper intervention.

Treating anxiety disorders often requires addressing both the mind and body. While psychological stressors can trigger physiological symptoms, it's essential to recognize that imbalances within the body can also contribute to anxiety. For example, conditions like a hiatal hernia, which irritates the vagus nerve, can lead to anxiety symptoms originating from the body rather than the mind.

Understanding the complex interplay between the mind and body is crucial to managing anxiety effectively. The nervous system, including the vagus nerve and spinal cord, plays a central role in regulating the body's response to stress and relaxation. Disruptions in this system can manifest as anxiety disorders, highlighting the need for a holistic approach to treatment.

By addressing both psychological and physiological factors, individuals can work towards restoring balance and finding relief from anxiety. Recognizing that anxiety can stem from both mental and bodily imbalances allows for a more comprehensive and empathetic approach to treatment. With proper care and support, individuals can navigate their journey towards better mental and emotional well-being.

There are two main areas where mechanical pressure can affect the vagus nerve:

1. The atlas-axis joint, also known as C1, which is the upper cervical vertebrae. Misalignment of the atlas can exert pressure on the vagus nerve in that region. Stiff or tense suboccipital muscles can hinder proper functioning of the atlas-axis joint. A well-qualified osteopath or chiropractor can address atlas misalignments.

2. The hiatus in the diaphragm, often associated with a hiatal hernia. In this case, the stomach exerts pressure on the vagus nerve as it passes through the hiatus. Again, a qualified osteopath or chiropractor can address this issue.

Symptoms of a compressed or pinched vagus nerve can vary widely among individuals. Common symptoms include anxiety, nausea, heartburn, tachycardia, vertigo, headache, a sensation of a lump in the throat, cold hands and feet, diarrhea, constipation, sweating, and more.

Compression or irritation of the vagus nerve can occur at the diaphragm, where tension or tenderness may develop. Abnormal breathing patterns or poor posture can contribute to the formation of trigger points in the diaphragm. Trigger point therapy or osteopathic diaphragm release may help alleviate tension and eliminate trigger points.

It's essential to observe how your anxiety responds to changes in body posture. Note whether adjusting your neck position affects your anxiety levels. In many cases, anxiety disorders stem from mechanical causes that may compress or pinch nerves. Nerves play a crucial role in regulating blood supply by dilating blood capillaries.

It's important to note that many individuals experience bodily symptoms without anxiety involvement. However, when anxiety follows physical symptoms, it's likely that the vagus nerve is directly involved.

Continuous anxiety following bodily symptoms indicates body-induced anxiety, where the vagus nerve plays a role.

Gentle exercises are crucial for aiding the body's recovery. Starting with the Ping Shuai gong three times a day for the first three months, then transitioning to or combining it with the Zhan Zhuang exercise, can be beneficial. Biking, accompanied by internal qigong exercises, is also helpful. Internal exercises leave us refreshed and energized compared to external exercises, which can leave us feeling exhausted.

When the cause of symptoms is unknown, focusing on Zhan Zhuang exercise is recommended. Symptoms of anxiety disorders can often manifest in different areas of the body than the actual cause, making diagnosis challenging.

Zhan Zhuang exercises help the body build new neural pathways, facilitating communication through the electromagnetic medium. Start with as little as 15 seconds and gradually increase to at least 15 minutes, up to a maximum of 40 minutes. It's crucial to keep the upper body relaxed and not exert too much strain

New symptoms and setbacks during the healing process are indications of the body experimenting with new neural pathways to achieve equilibrium. Healing is not linear and may involve periods of progress and regression. However, the cumulative effect of healing becomes apparent over time, even if results are not immediately noticeable.

Vagus Nerve and Anxiety: Exercises to Tone and Reduce Stress

The vagus nerve plays a crucial role in relaxing the body, contributing to reduced heart rate, relaxed breathing, improved digestion, and more. The good news is that you have the power to promote the health and strength of your vagus nerve, enabling it to effectively relax your body whenever needed.

Activating Your Parasympathetic System

Understanding and recognizing the vagus nerve is essential, as it empowers you to help reactivate the functions of the parasympathetic system, which is responsible for relaxation and restoration, thus maintaining balance within your body.

As I've mentioned before, your nervous system regulates various sensations associated with stress and anxiety. Originating from your brain, the nervous system sends signals to different parts of your body to perform automatic functions like heartbeat, breathing, digestion, and more. Additionally, it activates your body during stressful situations and facilitates relaxation once the danger has passed.

To induce relaxation, activating the parasympathetic system is essential, and much of this activation is governed by the vagus nerve.

The Longest Cranial Nerve

The vagus nerve, the tenth of the twelve pairs of cranial nerves originating from the brain, plays a significant role in relaxation, with both the right and left branches collectively responsible for 75% of parasympathetic functions. It is the longest of all cranial nerves, traversing virtually the entire body from the brain to the anus, making it particularly relevant in understanding stress and anxiety.

Functions of the Vagus Nerve

The vagus nerve regulates motor functions of the larynx, diaphragm, stomach, and heart, while also generating sensory functions of the tongue, ears, and visceral organs such as the stomach, intestines, kidneys, and liver. Its functions include reducing heart rate, calming breathing, regulating digestion, conveying sensations from the throat, tongue, and ears, and optimizing immune system function.

Additionally, the vagus nerve facilitates movement in certain body parts and enhances awareness of bodily sensations. Interestingly, humming or cooing activates the vagus nerve in mothers, promoting relaxation in both them and their children.

Signs You Need to Tone Your Vagus Nerve

Recognizing sensations such as tingling or strange feelings in the tongue, difficulty swallowing, throat discomfort, irregular digestion, heart rate fluctuations, altered taste perception, facial muscle tension, speech difficulty under stress, sudden nausea, social disconnection, heightened empathy for negative news, difficulty socializing, or ear sensations can indicate the need to tone your vagus nerve.

By toning your vagus nerve, you may also alleviate symptoms like tinnitus. Paying attention to these signs and implementing exercises to strengthen your vagus nerve can significantly enhance your overall well-being and resilience to stress and anxiety.

Vagus Nerve, Empathy, and Socialization

One fascinating aspect of the vagus nerve is its connection to socialization. Many of its functions involve regulating facial expressions and vocal tone. This means that how you feel can be reflected in your speech and facial expressions, conveying messages about your current state to others.

The vagus nerve also plays a role in generating oxytocin, known as the attachment hormone, which we release during activities such as breastfeeding and sexual intercourse. Positive social interactions and strong connections with others can help reduce stress levels and even prevent degenerative neurological diseases.

Furthermore, the vagus nerve is activated when we interact with others and need to regulate our facial expressions. Thus, one way to stimulate our vagus nerve is through specific facial movements in addition to healthy social interactions.

Do you find it difficult to communicate or open to others when you're feeling down?

VAGUS NERVE

Individuals with a history of post-traumatic stress may also need to work on their vagus nerve, as experiencing trauma often leads to difficulty in communicating or connecting with others during times of emotional stress. Additionally, you may experience heightened empathy toward others' problems. Stimulating your vagus nerve can help address these challenges.

Sometimes, we disconnect from others as a protective mechanism, avoiding socialization to avoid feeling threatened. However, learning to positively stimulate our vagus nerve can help us establish healthy and positive connections with others. Some scientists also suggest a link between the vagus nerve and feelings such as gratitude and compassion for oneself and others.

How to Tone Your Vagus Nerve

Understanding that a healthy vagus nerve facilitates relaxation, it's important to explore ways to tone it without overdoing it or forcing relaxation. Here are some methods you can try:

1. Wash your face with cold water or take baths with fresh water. The sensation of fresh water on your face, forehead, and neck can help tone your vagus nerve.

2. Singing is another way to stimulate your vagus nerve. Put on your favorite songs and sing along.

3. Gargling can stimulate the vagus nerve, but remember not to overdo it. A daily gargling session is sufficient.

4. Practice deep breathing exercises, focusing on breathing from your diaphragm. Proper oxygenation is essential for reducing stress in the body.

5. Treat yourself to therapeutic massages to relax facial and back muscles, promoting vagus nerve health.

6. Improve your posture, as proper alignment can help optimize vagus nerve function. Practices like yoga can be particularly beneficial.

7. Consume probiotics to support gut health, as the vagus nerve controls many stomach functions.

8. Engage in positive social interactions with trusted individuals. Spending time with supportive people can positively impact vagus nerve function.

9. Respect your body's natural rhythms, including sleep, hunger, and thirst cues. Listen to your body's needs and adjust your daily routine accordingly.

10. Balance between alertness and relaxation is crucial. Strive to maintain a balance between tense, apprehensive attitudes and relaxed, present-focused states.

11. Ensure regular, healthy meals containing essential nutrients to support your body's functions.

12. Stay hydrated by drinking water throughout the day, aiming for at least 2 liters daily.

13. Aim for restful sleep of 6 to 8 hours per night to promote overall well-being.

14. Incorporate aerobic exercises like walking, swimming, or yoga into your routine to reduce stress and promote toxin release through sweating.

15. Practice muscle relaxation techniques, such as stretching or massages, to release tension and promote muscular relaxation.

16. Focus on effective breathing techniques to bring oxygen to your diaphragm and promote relaxation.

17. Listen to your body's needs and respond promptly to cues for hydration, nutrition, rest, and movement.

18. Alternate periods of work or concentration with moments of healthy recreation to prevent mental and physical exhaustion.

19. Practice meditation or mindfulness to allow your brain to rest and recharge, even if only for a few minutes each day.

20. Focus on emotional balance to maintain overall well-being and harmony within your body.

Remember, it's essential not to try to change everything at once. Start by incorporating activities that resonate with you and gradually build upon them. By prioritizing your body's needs and allowing it to restore its balance naturally, you can cultivate a healthier and more resilient lifestyle.

VAGUS NERVE

In conclusion, understanding the role of the vagus nerve in promoting relaxation and reducing stress is essential for our overall well-being. By recognizing its significance in regulating facial expressions, vocal tone, and social interactions, we gain insight into how to enhance our emotional resilience and foster positive connections with others.

Through various techniques such as cold-water therapy, singing, and deep breathing exercises, we can effectively tone and stimulate the vagus nerve, promoting relaxation and reducing stress levels. Additionally, prioritizing activities that support gut health, posture improvement, and regular socialization can further optimize vagus nerve function.

By respecting our body's natural rhythms, maintaining a balance between alertness and relaxation, and incorporating healthy lifestyle habits, we can support the health of our vagus nerve and cultivate a greater sense of well-being. It is through these efforts that we can empower ourselves to navigate life's challenges with resilience and embrace a state of inner balance and harmony.

CHAPTER THREE

POLYVAGAL THEORY:
IMPROVING EMOTIONAL REGULATION

Welcome to the third chapter. Stimulating the social nervous system and activating these features takes a while for some people. Thankfully, there are a few things you can do to properly do this, and we'll discuss a few how-to aspects that'll help you with stimulating this and using the Polyvagal Theory to better your life.

Trust and the Polyvagal Theory

The first thing to understand is that you need to have a trust-based relationship. Find someone you can trust. Whether it be a partner, a therapist, or someone else, when tackling this issue, you need to first and foremost learn to trust others again. The problem with tackling trauma, stimulating the social engagement system, and learning to come out of shutdown when facing these traumatic moments is that if you aren't working with someone you fully trust, it'll cause you to re-traumatize, which is definitely not a good thing. When seeking a therapist to tackle these traumatic instances, you want someone you can trust. Otherwise, you'll get traumatized once again, which isn't fun whatsoever. It will make even the hardest traumatic moments ten times harder. You want to express your feelings to this person, but you can't with other people. Shameful feelings, anger, issues with sexual response—in essence, you want to be able to say what you need to say. If you can't do that, the sad thing is that you'll never heal, and you need a trusting relationship. This is very hard for some people, especially those with PTSD or even C-PTSD, but by learning to find someone you can say this to, you'll feel secure. By having this safe person, you'll be able to activate your social regulation system. After all, it works when you're safe and sound, right? By having that safe person to go to, you'll be so much happier, and you won't feel bogged down by the stressful situations.

VAGUS NERVE

Your Calm Center

This is another personal thing you can do. A lot of people who are in distress struggle with calming down and finding their center. Often, staying in the moment when talking with someone and trying to understand and handle your distress will help you improve your social engagement. When you start to dissociate, try fighting this. I know it's hard. Fighting this urge feels like an impossible task, but the thing is, no matter how hard the subject matter is, you need to fight this, and you need to ensure you don't try to dissociate. The reason you do this is because you want to run away. But when working with a therapist who handles heavy trauma, you need to work to re-engage with it and get that support to help you face it and overcome it. The easy solution is to run away. That's what our bodies naturally do. We either fight or flight, and when we can't do that, we freeze in the moment. Every time we freeze, though, it keeps us in that moment, never letting us escape it, which means that we're not fully running away from this moment, and instead, we are frozen in time. We'll always bounce back to that moment, frozen in time, if we can't come out of it. But when you safely re-engage with that trauma with someone who has the experience to take care of it, it'll change you. You'll be able to face the moment and rewrite everything that's in your brain, which will help you build better support within your mind. Remember when we touched on the neuroplasticity of the brain? That the brain will rewrite and change over time, that it's never just one specific instance? Well, that applies here, and you need to work to rewrite this so you can change your response to it. Stay calm, and when facing the moment, learn to understand and fully grip the emotions and work to make it so your body's response is fine and not overdone.

Be more assertive

When you're facing these moments and stimulating your vagus nerve, you're properly able to face the trauma. You need to understand that an emotional shutdown occurs when you aren't fully communicating and discussing this. You need to practice assertiveness and work on trying to be more in control. This takes time. Not every person will be able to face this right away. Sometimes, they'll feel angry at the moment since they're facing this on purpose, and they need to stay in control. But, by working out the anger and learning how to properly understand and attain what you need from this, you'll be happier. Assertiveness isn't necessarily a bad thing. A lot of people think that when you're assertive, that's bad. But for those who don't have proper social regulation, they immediately succumb to the freezing aspects of this. But, by learning the power of asserting yourself, you'll be happier, and you'll be able to move towards a healthier relationship pattern over time. You'll be much better off as well. For most people, there are a lot of fears that come from being assertive. They might never have done this. Being assertive, being able to face your emotions, and getting through this will help you feel better and let you stay in the moment. It will change your life, and understand that you'll be happy to truly make a change if you take some time to truly be yourself.

Attentional Control: A Valid Mechanism

This is a mechanism some PTSD survivors will use. Essentially, it's the ability to choose what to pay attention to and what to ignore. It's also called executive attention control. This can essentially be a voluntary means to concentrate. The frontal regions of the brain mediate this most of the time. It is closely related to working memory and other executive functions. Our attention works on three different networks. The first is alertness, orientation, and executive control, which is where you resolve conflict. These are usually all working in different ways. When we perceive threats, at first, we'll be on the alert, and we'll look at information, and then we'll use executive control. The research from this shows some MRIs depict attention and, of course, different interactions between alertness, other orienting, and, of course, executive controls. When our attention isn't controlled properly, one of these is usually overstimulated. For example, the conflicts are never resolved, but instead, they just hang there, and our attention is always on them. We are focused too much on one thing or another. If there is something that reminds us of traumatic experiences, we tend to immediately focus on it. This can actually relate to the vagus nerve. The vagus nerve and the polyvagal theory say that each of these different parts, when not in balance, will cause various issues. Often, our attention immediately focuses on the other parts of this, which means that we're not fully resolving the conflicts and determining which ones don't get our full attention. Those who have autism, anxiety, or ADHD tend to have issues with attentional control—either too much power in one part of their lives or not enough control over something else. Many times, this can develop early on in childhood, but sometimes it may show up later. Disrupted attentional control can also cause disruption in executive functions, including working memory, across many different disorder groups. How does this all show itself, though? Well, there is still some research being done about it. Learning to better control your attention can help offset the effects of disruptions in your polyvagal system. If you have low attentional control, you may experience other attentional conditions, especially ADHD, hyperactivity, and then impulsivity, which can cause impairment in activities in life. It can also happen in those with schizophrenia and in other problems too. If you have social anxiety, anxiety that's generalized, or depression, it can cause issues with attentional control too. Those who respond better and have better control over their executive functions will have lower levels of depression and anxiety. There is also a chance you may develop psychopathology because the ability to shift your focus from the threat information is very important in processing these emotions. Many researchers are also accounting for attentional control and might not always focus on attention and how attention shifts from the different stimuli to the threat. Improving your attentional control and working to improve it is a good way to improve your life. This does play a part in your polyvagal system, and we'll discuss how you can improve it here.

Attentional Control and Polyvagal Theory

When we experience trauma, our brains immediately focus on that trauma and how it stimulates us instead of learning to overcome it. This can cause us to have trouble processing the emotions of the moment and the situation at hand. When this happens and our other vagal systems take over, we suddenly will think it's a bad thing to do anything or see everything as a threat. That's what we'll perceive, and from there, we won't be able to improve or overcome the trauma. But by learning to physically control our attention in a voluntary state and not hyper-focus on the things we can't do anything about, we'll be much better off. Our polyvagal system works in a balanced manner. Homeostasis is achieved through balance. When one of these is imbalanced, trouble occurs there, whether in a sympathetic or a parasympathetic system. It can cause issues with how we process emotions. This is why trauma sticks around. It's because our minds start to focus only on this instead of moving forward and overcoming the struggles. Those with PTDS, in particular, have a lot of trouble with attention control. That's because when they give this a bias, they'll immediately process only negative information over positive information. It can hurt our own personal attentional control, which means we don't have good control over our thoughts. Instead, we feel anxiety over the whole mess. How can we overcome this? The best way to do it is through mindfulness and learning how to shift our control and work to process these emotions. Therapy to tackle the trauma and face it is ideal. Still, there are a few things you can do on your own to help improve your ability to keep a better, more balanced life so you're not disrupted by these negative thoughts. When we know how to use this, we'll better approach these cognitive processes and, from there, understand how the control occurs. But the biggest thing you can do is practice mindfulness. Even just four days of mindfulness will change your working memory, along with your executive functions as well. However, you won't be able to act involuntarily. This will just help you control the problems manually so that you're not hurt either. If you try to manually inhibit, switch, or detect different objects and practice mindfulness, it can help reduce the stress. It doesn't directly affect your natural, intentional control. Still, it influences your general emotional well-being, which is why more and more people see mindfulness as one of the best things for you to do. Finally, another way to tackle this is, of course, to learn about it. You should become versed in the different cognitive faculties you use to better yourself and understand how this works for you.

CHAPTER FOUR

EXERCISES TO ACTIVATE THE VAGUS NERVE

Incorporating the Vagus Nerve: Techniques for Activation and Healing

In the pursuit of well-being, there are three powerful techniques to activate the vagus nerve, each rooted in ancient practices that have stood the test of time. These methods offer not only simplicity but also profound benefits for our physical and mental health. Let's explore them together.

Twisting the Trapezius

From infancy, we engage the trapezius muscle extensively. Babies utilize this muscle to crawl, supporting their weight and propelling them forward. However, as we grow and adopt sedentary lifestyles, this muscle can become imbalanced, leading to poor posture and reduced blood flow to the brain.

Counteracting this imbalance is crucial for our overall well-being. One effective way to do so is by performing trapezius-twisting exercises throughout the day. These exercises not only revitalize our bodies but also realign our posture, promoting better blood circulation and mental clarity.

The technique involves three variations:

- **Crossed Arms Twist:** Begin by sitting or standing comfortably. Cross your arms in front of you and place your palms on your elbows. Without moving your hips, briskly twist your torso from side to side, feeling the activation of the trapezius muscles.
- **High-Arm Twist:** Similarly, cross your arms, but this time hold them higher than your chest. Maintain a forward-facing position

as you twist your torso from side to side, focusing on engaging the trapezius muscles.

- **Overhead Twist:** Raise your crossed arms above your head and twist your torso vigorously from side to side. Feel the tension release as you engage the trapezius muscles.

These exercises may seem simple, but their impact on posture and energy levels is profound. Consistent practice can lead to immediate revitalization and improved vitality.

Acupuncture Techniques

Acupuncture, a time-honored practice, offers another avenue for stimulating the vagus nerve. By targeting specific points on the body, particularly in the facial region, acupuncture promotes relaxation, enhances circulation, and rejuvenates facial muscles.

Key points to stimulate include the LI 20 point, also known as the "beauty triangle," located above the fold between the cheek and upper lip. Applying gentle pressure and circular motions to this area can induce muscle relaxation and promote a brighter, more vibrant complexion.

By incorporating acupuncture into our self-care routines, we not only enhance our physical appearance but also cultivate a sense of inner calmness and well-being, improving our social interactions and overall quality of life.

Meditation and the Vagus Nerve

Meditation serves as a powerful tool for activating the parasympathetic nervous system, including the vagus nerve. By cultivating mindfulness and deep relaxation, meditation techniques can alleviate stress, enhance self-awareness, and promote emotional balance.

Mindfulness Meditation

In mindful meditation, we focus our attention on the present moment, observing our thoughts and sensations without judgment. By anchoring our awareness to the breath, we can cultivate a state of inner calmness and clarity, activating the vagus nerve and promoting overall well-being.

Breath Awareness Meditation

Like mindfulness meditation, breath awareness meditation centers on the breath as a focal point for relaxation and self-awareness. By consciously regulating our breathing patterns, we can induce a state of deep relaxation, soothing the body and mind.

Transcendental Meditation

Transcendental meditation offers a spiritual approach to meditation, aiming to transcend thought and experience a state of pure awareness. By repeating mantras and adopting specific postures, practitioners can access higher states of consciousness, fostering profound inner peace and clarity.

Body Scan Meditation
Body scan meditation involves systematically scanning the body for tension and releasing muscular tightness. By directing our attention inward and acknowledging physical sensations, we can promote relaxation and alleviate stress, activating the vagus nerve and promoting holistic healing.

Kundalini Meditation
Kundalini meditation harnesses the power of energy located at the base of the spine, known as kundalini energy. By awakening this energy and channeling it throughout the body, practitioners can purify their systems and achieve heightened states of consciousness.

The Wim Hof Method
The Wim Hof method incorporates cold exposure, breathing techniques, and commitment to promote holistic well-being. By exposing the body to cold therapy, practicing controlled breathing, and maintaining consistency in practice, individuals can activate the vagus nerve, balance the autonomic nervous system, and enhance physical and mental resilience.

Cold Therapy
Cold therapy, also known as cryotherapy, is a cornerstone of the Wim Hof Method, which utilizes three main principles: cold exposure, breathing techniques, and commitment. Cold exposure has been shown to have numerous health benefits, including weight loss, reduced inflammation, and the release of endorphins. By gradually exposing the body to cold temperatures, whether through cold showers or ice baths, individuals can strengthen their resilience, boost their immune system, and activate the vagus nerve.

Breathing Techniques
Controlled breathing is another essential component of the Wim Hof Method. Through specific breathing exercises, individuals can regulate their autonomic nervous system, increase oxygen levels, and induce a state of deep relaxation. By practicing techniques such as power breathing and breath holds, individuals can optimize their respiratory function, enhance mental clarity, and activate the vagus nerve, leading to profound physiological and psychological benefits.

Commitment
Consistency and dedication are paramount to realizing the full potential of these techniques. Just as physical exercise requires regular practice to

VAGUS NERVE

see results, meditation, and cold exposure demand commitment to yield long-term benefits. By incorporating these practices into their daily routines and embracing them as integral components of holistic wellness, individuals can unlock the transformative power of the vagus nerve and cultivate a profound sense of vitality, resilience, and inner harmony.

In summary, the activation of the vagus nerve through physical exercises, acupuncture, meditation, and the Wim Hof Method offers a holistic approach to healing and well-being. By harnessing the body's innate capacity for self-regulation and resilience, individuals can embark on a journey of self-discovery, empowerment, and holistic transformation. Through consistent practice and unwavering commitment, we can tap into the boundless potential of the vagus nerve and cultivate a life of vitality, balance, and inner peace.

CHAPTER FIVE

ACTIVATE AND ACCESS THE POWER OF VAGUS NERVE

A ctivate and gain access to the power of the vagus nerve. After gaining an understanding of the functions of the vagus nerve, you will become aware of the possibility of exerting influence over it to alter the functioning and efficiency of the body. As an additional benefit, the mechanism makes it simple to work with the nerve, rather than allowing it to become trapped when it is malfunctioning.

Since it improves communication throughout the body, the vagus nerve is an essential component of your body. Your heart, brain, and digestive system, along with other major organs and muscles, are all coordinated by it. However, conditions such as physical trauma, stress, and inflammation can hurt the nerve's ability to function properly.

You are in luck because there are a variety of ways in which you can exercise and activate the vagus nerve to restore good health and strengthen the vagal function at the same time. To recover from sleep disorders and trauma, as well as initiate deep relaxation, you will learn in this chapter the straightforward methods that you can use to regulate social functioning and the vagus nerve. You will find that it is possible to eliminate most chronic conditions if you can establish a connection between social functioning and the health of the vagus nerve.

In addition to being helpful for medical professionals, caregivers, bodyworkers, and psychotherapists, the information is also beneficial for individuals who suffer from chronic health conditions such as anxiety, depression, and stress. In this chapter, you will find a clear demonstration of how you can optimize the functioning of the vagus nerve to keep the body safe and activate its healing power.

Establish regular routines

You need to establish a daily routine to make sure that your body is accustomed to these types of activities, which will assist it in adjusting to the changes that you bring about. You should make it a habit to engage in activities daily that not only contribute to the various aspects of your life but also stimulate the vagus nerve. Physical, mental, spiritual, and emotional well-being are some of the most important aspects that should be incorporated into these practices.

There are profound connections between the practices you engage in daily and the enhancement of the functionality of your vagus nerve. By activating your vagus nerve, you intend to improve the functionality of your body as well as the chronic healing conditions that are present in your body. It is important that you keep the goal in mind because it is the primary factor that drives you to engage in the daily practices that you accomplish.

Additionally, you should understand how the daily practices work for you, which is why it is necessary to schedule a specific amount of time for the practice routine. You will be more likely to be punctual for the preparation if you have a diary, and it will also keep you engaged until the time has passed. As a result of the schedule, any other plans that may come up during the practice will not be able to take precedence.

To getting the most out of the routines you engage in daily, you should choose activities that are not only interesting to you but also comfortable and convenient for you. In addition, the practices ought to have significance to guarantee that you will achieve favorable outcomes in the long run. Taking part in activities that require a significant amount of your time but produce little to no results is something you would prefer to avoid. Both the functionality of the vagus nerve and the success of your endeavors are significantly influenced by the practices that you find most comfortable following.

Consistency is something that is required for daily practices because missing them on a regular basis can be counterproductive and could easily lead to losing interest. Inviting a friend who has goals that are comparable to yours is one of the things you could do to establish and maintain consistency. To ensuring that you are not missing anything for best practices, a checklist is also essential for ensuring that your supplies are always available.

You can keep a record of the practices that you engage in daily, which allows you to avoid duplicating exercises or skipping out on important workouts. In a similar vein, you could use the same checklist as a progress record to provide feedback on how you are doing, which would make it simple to develop motivation and adjust.

It is certain that you will experience benefits in the reduction of tension, stress, anxiety, and chronic pain if you engage in effective daily practices. Increasing the functionality of the vagus nerve, which in turn increases the body's response to injuries and infections, can be accomplished by stimulating the nerve. Because the nerve is connected to the gastrointestinal tract, it is essential to engage in daily practices because these practices improve digestion, metabolism, and weight loss. Because of this, they lessen the likelihood of opportunistic conditions like obesity and heart attacks. Participating in daily activities stimulates your vagus nerve and maintains its alertness. This helps to ensure that your heart rate and lungs are under control, which in turn enables you to respond effectively to the circumstances that are present in your environment. When the vagus nerve is functioning properly, it strengthens the immune system, which in turn makes your body more protectable and defensive against both minor and major attacks. To stimulate the vagus nerve, do some basic exercises.

Stimulating the Vagus Nerve with Basic Exercises:

It is possible to develop medical conditions that are characterized by stress, poor digestion, food sensitivities, brain fog, and fatigue if one lives a life that is both mentally stimulating and physically stressful. Typically, these symptoms are the result of a lower vagal tone, which indicates that the vagal nerve is not activated or is not functioning properly in the concerned individual. Because it is the brain's medium for controlling the vital body system, the vagus nerve is extremely important due to the far-reaching effects it has. The activation and stimulation of the nerve play a significant role in the fight against a variety of health conditions, including autoimmune conditions, poor circulation, and heart diseases.

To stimulate the nerve, you might need to perform some simple exercises that you might not consider essential. Participating in social interactions is a great way to stimulate your vagus nerve, and it has the potential to offer positive results if you do it frequently and on a consistent basis. When you express these feelings more frequently to your loved ones and friends, you bring about psychological and emotional shifts that, when combined with a strong sense of connection to other people, allow you to feel more connected to them. It is possible to give the impression of being happier and more socially connected by expressing feelings of joy, serenity, interest, amusement, and hope.

Similarly, altering the sensations that your skin is experiencing will result in vagal stimulation because your skin will communicate these changes to the rest of your body. As a result of the decrease in the fight-or-flight response of the sympathetic system, acute cold exposures cause the body to initiate the parasympathetic system through vagal mediation. This leads to an increase in the rate at which digestion occurs. To be effective, these fundamental exercises do not require any specialized knowledge or equipment. To make it a routine that ultimately results in nerve stimulation, all you need to do is continue acting in the same manner as you normally would.

An example of something that can increase your heart rate variability (HRV) is chanting or singing out loud. In the process of singing out loud, you are putting your throat through a task, which stimulates the vagal nerve. Although this may appear abnormal and disturbing to others, you are aware of the positive effects that singing and chanting have on your health. In addition, you might choose to watch comedies and fun times, listen to them, or imagine yourself doing so. If the imagination you create causes you to laugh several times, one of the most effective methods for increasing your heart rate variability (HRV) has been demonstrated to be laughter. Additionally, it works by improving your cognitive functions, which are essential in preventing heart disease from occurring in the first place.

Being in a humorous state has been shown to reduce levels of the stress hormone cortisol and to have positive effects on the cardiovascular system by increasing levels of nitric oxide and beta-endorphins. Since you have seen that stimulation of the throat makes it simple to activate the vagus nerve, it is necessary to look for fundamental exercises that involve your throat to have the best results. Gargling with a glass of water on a regular basis is one of these activities that can be done to engage the muscles that are located around the throat. Since it stimulates both the vagus nerve and the digestive tract, you should make a note to remind yourself to perform this fundamental exercise.

Relaxing while reading or listening to music is another practice that can be used to stimulate the vagal nerve. The most significant effect of the relaxed mode is that it maintains the tone of your vagus nerve. Because you can also activate your vagus nerve while you are in a calm state, you do not need to engage in activities that are physically demanding to do so. It is therefore recommended that you do not consume your lunch while you are in a hurry or while you are using your computer, because doing so will prevent you from concentrating and relaxing. In some of the most fundamental situations, failing to pay attention can have long-lasting and detrimental effects on your body in various ways.

In a state and environment that are conducive to relaxation, you select the appropriate food and chew it thoroughly. By stimulating the vagal nerve and tasting the food, the exercise makes digestion easier, and the act of feeling stimulates the vagal nerve. In addition to the following specific practices, a well-detailed routine consisting of these fundamental exercises may be significant in activating your vagus nerve.

Massages are provided

The stimulation of your vagus nerves can be achieved by massaging different parts of your body. Because of the sensitivity of the hands and the movements, this exercise stimulates the tissues of the body. Because of this, you will feel the effects on the nervous system, the vascular system, and the muscular system of your body. Depending on the combination of movements and techniques that you select, the massage may have the purpose of either stimulating the system or bringing about relaxation when it is performed.

An example of this would be the application of the effleurage technique, which involves applying pressure to the area that is being targeted using the palm. This method involves applying pressure to the lymphatic and venous flow to achieve the desired effect. Because of the flow, the massage therapist can perform a return stroke that is light and gentle while simultaneously making the hands flexible and allowing them to have complete control over the palmar surface.

The vagal nerve is stimulated by superficial movements, which in turn cause a response in the circulatory networks of the skin. This is a significant feature of superficial movements. Additionally, it enhances the flow of lymphatic and venous blood. It is well known that superficial movements include the reflex response of stroking, which is known to enhance both the contraction and relaxation of facial muscles. Through a mechanical response to the pressure, the deep stroking movement influences the venous circulation, while at the same time, it removes congestion in the veins through the arterial circulation.

There is an improvement in circulation and lymphatic flow, both of which are necessary for the removal of waste products from the body, when the effleurage technique is performed with deep movements. During the petrissage technique, the body tissues are compressed and lifted away from the bone beneath them to apply pressure in a firm manner while simultaneously encouraging relaxation. This technique is also referred to as kneading because it involves applying less pressure to areas of the body that are less strongly muscled.

This method could be carried out with either one hand or both hands combined. When kneading, the hands of the person doing the kneading should be fluid and unassuming. The method is carried out in a manner that is determined by the dimensions, contours, and volume of the receiving area. While the hands glide slowly along with the muscles of the receiving partner, the giver has the primary responsibility of applying force and directing it to the heart. When working on large muscles like the back, the flat-handed kneading technique is typically used. This technique is distinguished by greater depth and less squeezing than other techniques. Kneading in a circular motion is most effective when performed with both hands on either side of the body while simultaneously applying pressure to the muscle shaft in a circular motion. Kneading with the fingers is an effective technique for the area around the shoulders, where the person performing the technique presses the muscle against the bone in a circular motion using their thumb and fingers.

A technique called friction is applied in which pressure is applied to the area that is being targeted to stimulate the sensory receptors, causing them to respond. Because of the lack of movement in this method, friction is best performed using the tip of the finger or thumb, which are the most sensitive parts of the body. In addition to the use of fingers and thumbs, the forearms, elbows, knees, and feet can also be used in the application of friction. The technique is effective in relieving pain, increasing range of motion, reducing tension, improving muscle flexibility, and promoting relaxation. It is also possible to incorporate other techniques into this technique, such as compression, which involves applying pressure to the area that is being targeted using the fingers, thumb, or palm.

You can also stretch your muscles

The stimulation of the vagus nerve can also be achieved through stretching the muscles. As a result of this activity, it is possible to stimulate the parasympathetic nervous system and reduce the level of cortisol in the body. When done regularly, this technique can lead to an increase in blood flow, a decrease in muscle tension, and an improvement in posture. Since the stretching movement stimulates the muscles and ligaments, it is also an effective way to improve the functioning of the internal organs and maintain the health of the nervous system.

It is important to warm up your muscles before you stretch them to prevent injury. In addition to increasing your heart rate, warming up increases the blood flow to your muscles, making them more pliable and less prone to injury. Because the warm-up increases your body temperature and stimulates the production of synovial fluid, which lubricates the joints, it is important to do it before you stretch. The muscles that you are going to stretch should be targeted during the warm-up, and you should perform gentle movements that gradually increase in intensity to prepare your body for the stretch.

It is important to breathe deeply and slowly as you stretch to increase the flow of oxygen to your muscles and decrease the level of cortisol in your body. Since the stretching movement can be painful, it is important to breathe deeply and slowly to relax your muscles and reduce the tension in them. By holding your breath, you increase the level of cortisol in your body, which can cause your muscles to contract and become more tense. In addition, holding your breath can increase your heart rate and make it difficult for you to relax.

When you stretch, it is important to focus on the muscles that you are stretching to increase the effectiveness of the stretch. By focusing on the muscles that you are stretching, you can increase the flow of blood to them and decrease the tension in them. In addition, by focusing on the muscles that you are stretching, you can increase their flexibility and decrease their risk of injury. By focusing on the muscles that you are stretching, you can also increase their range of motion and improve your posture.

There are many different types of stretches that you can do to stimulate the vagus nerve, and it is important to choose the ones that are right for you. Some of the most effective stretches for stimulating the vagus nerve include the following:

1. Neck stretches: These stretches can help to relieve tension in the neck and shoulders and improve blood flow to the brain. Some of the most effective neck stretches include the following:

- *Neck rotation stretch:* Sit or stand up straight and slowly turn your head to the left as far as you can without causing pain. Hold the stretch for 10 to 30 seconds, and then slowly return to the starting position. Repeat the stretch on the other side.

- *Neck side bend stretch:* Sit or stand up straight and slowly tilt your head to the left as far as you can without causing pain. Hold the stretch for 10 to 30 seconds, and then slowly return to the starting position. Repeat the stretch on the other side.

2. Shoulder stretches: These stretches can help to relieve tension in the shoulders and upper back and improve blood flow to the arms and hands. Some of the most effective shoulder stretches include the following:

- *Shoulder roll stretch:* Sit or stand up straight and roll your shoulders backwards in a circular motion. Repeat the motion 10 to 20 times, and then reverse the direction of the roll.

- *Shoulder stretch:* Sit or stand up straight and clasp your hands behind your back. Straighten your arms and lift them up towards the ceiling as far as you can without causing pain. Hold the stretch for 10 to 30 seconds, and then slowly return to the starting position.

3. Chest stretches: These stretches can help to relieve tension in the chest and improve breathing and circulation. Some of the most effective chest stretches include the following:

- *Chest opener stretch:* Stand up straight and clasp your hands behind your back. Straighten your arms and lift them up towards the ceiling as far as you can without causing pain. Hold the stretch for 10 to 30 seconds, and then slowly return to the starting position.

- *Doorway stretch:* Stand in a doorway with your arms outstretched and your hands resting on the doorframe. Lean forward slightly until you feel a stretch in your chest. Hold the stretch for 10 to 30 seconds, and then slowly return to the starting position.

4. Spinal twists: These stretches can help to relieve tension in the spine and improve flexibility and circulation. Some of the most effective spinal twists include the following:

- *Seated spinal twist:* Sit on the floor with your legs extended in front of you. Bend your right knee and place your right foot on the outside of your left knee. Place your left elbow on the outside of your right knee and twist your torso to the right as far as you can without causing pain. Hold the stretch for 10 to 30 seconds, and then slowly return to the starting position. Repeat the stretch on the other side.

- *Supine spinal twist:* Lie on your back with your arms outstretched to the sides and your palms facing down. Bend your knees and lift your feet off the floor. Lower your knees to the right side of your body until they are resting on the floor. Turn your head to the left and hold the stretch for 10 to 30 seconds. Return to the starting position and repeat the stretch on the other side.

5. Hip stretches: These stretches can help to relieve tension in the hips and improve flexibility and mobility. Some of the most effective hip stretches include the following:

- *Figure 4: Stretch:* Lie on your back with your knees bent and your feet flat on the floor. Cross your right ankle over your left knee and flex your right foot. Reach through the space between your legs and clasp your hands behind your left thigh. Pull your left thigh towards your chest until you feel a stretch in your right hip. Hold the stretch for 10 to 30 seconds, and then slowly return to the starting position. Repeat the stretch on the other side.

- *Hip flexor stretch:* Kneel on the floor with your right knee bent and your left foot flat on the floor in front of you. Place your hands on your left thigh and shift your weight forward until you feel a stretch in the front of your right hip. Hold the stretch for 10 to 30 seconds, and then slowly return to the starting position. Repeat the stretch on the other side.

In conclusion, stimulating the vagus nerve through basic exercises such as chanting or singing out loud, laughing, gargling with water, reading, or listening to music, and massaging and stretching the muscles can have numerous health benefits, including reducing stress, improving digestion, increasing heart rate variability, and promoting relaxation. By incorporating these exercises into your daily routine, you can improve your overall health and well-being.

BOOK 6

EMDR

THERAPY

INTRODUCTION

UNDERSTANDING EMDR

EMDR, or Eye Movement Desensitization and Reprocessing, stands as a transformative therapeutic modality that has revolutionized the treatment landscape for trauma and related mental health conditions. Developed by Dr. Francine Shapiro, EMDR emerged from a serendipitous observation regarding the potential of specific eye movements to attenuate the emotional charge associated with distressing memories. This observation spurred an extensive journey of exploration and research, resulting in the refinement of EMDR therapy into a structured and evidence-based approach that transcends traditional talk therapy.

At its core, EMDR operates on the foundational premise that the mind possesses an innate capacity for healing, akin to the body's ability to recover from physical injuries. When individuals experience traumatic events, particularly those that overwhelm their normal coping mechanisms, the brain may struggle to process and integrate these memories effectively. As a result, traumatic memories may remain stored in a fragmented and unprocessed state, replete with intense emotions, cognitive distortions, and physiological sensations.

The hallmark of EMDR therapy lies in its distinctive approach to trauma resolution. Unlike conventional therapeutic modalities that rely heavily on verbal processing and cognitive restructuring, EMDR prioritizes the reprocessing of traumatic memories at a neurological level. Through a structured protocol, clients are guided to access distressing memories while simultaneously receiving bilateral sensory stimulation, such as eye movements, auditory tones, or tactile tapping. This bilateral stimulation is thought to facilitate the activation of the brain's natural information processing mechanisms, akin to those observed during REM sleep, thereby fostering the adaptive reprocessing of traumatic memories.

Over the years, the scope of EMDR therapy has expanded significantly beyond its initial application in treating PTSD. Empirical research and clinical experience have demonstrated its efficacy in addressing a broad spectrum of psychological conditions, including anxiety disorders, depression, phobias, grief, and complex trauma. Moreover, EMDR has been successfully adapted to cater to diverse populations, including children, adolescents, adults, veterans, and survivors of natural disasters or mass trauma.

One of the key strengths of EMDR lies in its integrative and holistic approach to healing. By addressing the interconnectedness of mind, body, and spirit, EMDR acknowledges that trauma is not solely a psychological phenomenon but also manifests in the physiological, emotional, and interpersonal realms. Through the systematic desensitization and reprocessing of traumatic memories, EMDR aims to alleviate distressing symptoms, promote emotional regulation, and facilitate the development of adaptive coping strategies.

Furthermore, EMDR embodies a collaborative and empowering therapeutic model. While the therapist serves as a guide and facilitator throughout the treatment process, the client remains the agent of change, actively engaging in their own healing journey. This client-centered approach fosters a sense of empowerment, self-efficacy, and autonomy, empowering individuals to reclaim control over their lives and narratives.

In essence, EMDR represents a paradigm shift in trauma treatment, offering a potent blend of neuroscience, psychology, and somatic approaches to facilitate profound and enduring healing. As research continues to elucidate its underlying mechanisms and efficacy across diverse populations and contexts, EMDR remains at the forefront of innovative and evidence-based interventions for trauma-related disorders.

Now, let's integrate the additional details and elaborations on EMDR therapy:

EMDR therapy, with its eight-phased approach, encapsulates a comprehensive strategy for trauma resolution. Each phase serves a distinct purpose, from history-taking and treatment planning to reevaluation, ensuring a systematic and structured approach to healing. Moreover, the therapy's reliance on bilateral stimulation, coupled with its emphasis on targeting negative cognitions and installing positive beliefs, underscores its nuanced understanding of trauma processing and integration.

Central to EMDR theory is the Adaptive Information Processing (AIP) model, which provides a conceptual framework for understanding the underlying mechanisms of trauma and its resolution. This model posits that psychological disorders arise from maladaptive memory networks, which can be reprocessed and integrated through bilateral stimulation and cognitive restructuring. By addressing the root cause of distressing symptoms, EMDR facilitates lasting and transformative healing.

The therapeutic applications of EMDR extend far beyond PTSD, encompassing a wide range of psychological conditions and populations.

From anxiety and depression to phobias and grief, EMDR offers a versatile and evidence-based approach to addressing trauma-related disorders. Moreover, its adaptability to diverse cultural contexts and age groups underscores its universal relevance and efficacy.

At its essence, EMDR embodies a collaborative and empowering approach to healing, wherein clients are active participants in their own recovery journey. By harnessing the brain's innate capacity for adaptation and growth, EMDR empowers individuals to overcome the debilitating effects of trauma and cultivate resilience and well-being. As a pioneer in trauma treatment, EMDR continues to inspire hope and transformation in countless lives, heralding a new era of trauma-informed care and holistic healing.

CHAPTER ONE

THE EVOLUTION OF EMDR
Origins of EMDR therapy

Following the introduction to the origins of EMDR therapy, we delve into the Methodological Evolution and Clinical Acceptance of EMDR, tracing its journey from a controversial new therapy to a widely recognized and respected treatment modality.

Methodological Evolution and Clinical Acceptance

When Francine Shapiro discovered the potential of Eye Movement Desensitization and Reprocessing (EMDR) in 1987, it was met with skepticism. The initial premise—that lateral eye movements could reduce the intensity of disturbing thoughts—challenged established psychotherapeutic techniques. However, the methodological evolution of EMDR is a testament to its efficacy and the scientific community's willingness to explore and validate innovative approaches.

Refinement of Protocols

The early years of EMDR saw rapid development and refinement of therapeutic protocols. Shapiro's foundational research laid the groundwork, but it was the subsequent studies that expanded the understanding of EMDR's mechanisms and its potential applications. Key to this evolution was the standardization of the eight-phase treatment approach, which provided a structured framework for therapists. This structure includes client history-taking, preparation, assessment, desensitization, installation, body scan, closure, and reevaluation, ensuring a comprehensive process that addresses traumatic memories thoroughly.

Empirical Validation and Expansion

The journey towards clinical acceptance gained momentum as empirical evidence mounted. Numerous studies demonstrated EMDR's effectiveness, particularly for Post-Traumatic Stress Disorder (PTSD), leading to its endorsement by prominent health organizations worldwide. The American Psychological Association, the World Health Organization, and the Department of Defense are among the entities that recognize EMDR as an effective treatment for trauma. This acceptance was bolstered by research that not only showed EMDR's efficacy in treating PTSD but also its adaptability to various other psychological conditions, including anxiety, depression, and specific phobias.

Integration and Innovation

As EMDR's methodological framework became more sophisticated, its integration into broader psychotherapeutic practice saw significant advancements. The Adaptive Information Processing (AIP) model, which posits that EMDR facilitates the accessing and processing of traumatic memories to bring them to an adaptive resolution, offered a theoretical basis that complemented existing therapeutic models. Moreover, the flexibility of EMDR allowed for its adaptation to different cultural contexts and patient needs, further enhancing its global acceptance and application.

Professional Training and Dissemination

The clinical acceptance of EMDR was also driven by the development of rigorous training programs and certification processes, ensuring that therapists are adequately prepared to deliver EMDR therapy effectively. Organizations such as the EMDR International Association (EMDRIA) in the United States and similar bodies worldwide have played a crucial role in maintaining high standards of practice. These organizations offer comprehensive training, support research, and facilitate professional networking, thereby contributing to the methodological sophistication and clinical efficacy of EMDR therapy.

The methodological evolution and clinical acceptance of EMDR therapy are reflective of the dynamic nature of the psychotherapeutic field. From its inception as a controversial technique to its status as a globally recognized treatment for trauma and other psychological disorders, EMDR has undergone significant development. Its journey is marked by rigorous scientific scrutiny, empirical validation, and a commitment to improving therapeutic outcomes for patients. As EMDR continues to evolve, its integration into clinical practice and its potential for further innovation remain pivotal aspects of its legacy in mental health treatment.

Fundamental Principles of EMDR

Transitioning to the second part of the first chapter on Fundamental Principles of EMDR, we delve into the Theoretical Basis: Information Processing and the Adaptive Information Model. This core aspect of EMDR therapy explains not only how the therapy works but also why it is effective for treating trauma and other distressing memories.

Theoretical Basis: Information Processing and the Adaptive Information Model

Information Processing System

At the heart of EMDR's theoretical foundation is the belief in an innate information processing system in the human mind, which is designed to handle and integrate experiences into an accessible and useful format. Under normal circumstances, this system processes experiences, assimilating them into existing memory networks in a way that makes sense of the present and guides future actions. However, when a person experiences trauma, this natural processing can become overwhelmed, leading to the disturbing experiences being stored in an isolated memory network, unprocessed and disconnected from adaptive coping mechanisms.

Adaptive Information Model

Francine Shapiro further developed this understanding into what is known as the Adaptive Information Processing (AIP) model. The AIP model posits that psychological health is based on the adaptive resolution of memories; when memories are adequately processed, they do not cause distress. However, traumas are stored in an unprocessed form, containing the emotions, thoughts, and physical sensations experienced at the time of the event. These unprocessed memories are easily triggered, leading to PTSD symptoms, anxiety, depression, and other disorders.

EMDR therapy, through its structured approach involving targeted recall and bilateral stimulation (typically through eye movements), facilitates the activation of the natural healing process. The therapy helps to forge new connections between the unprocessed memory and more adaptive information stored in the brain. This reprocessing allows the disturbing memory to be integrated into the larger memory network, thus reducing its emotional charge, and allowing the individual to develop new understandings and coping mechanisms.

The Role of Bilateral Stimulation

A distinctive element of EMDR is the use of bilateral stimulation, often in the form of eye movements, which is believed to mimic the psychological state associated with Rapid Eye Movement (REM) sleep. This state is thought to be conducive to the processing of emotional experiences. The bilateral stimulation in EMDR facilitates the communication between the two hemispheres of the brain, helping to move the traumatic memory from an isolated state to one where it can be integrated with adaptive information. This process is what allows the individual to reprocess the trauma, leading to a decrease in the trauma's power over their current psychological state.

The theoretical basis of EMDR, grounded in the information processing system and the Adaptive Information Processing model, provides a framework for understanding how EMDR facilitates the healing of trauma. By leveraging the brain's natural processing capabilities, EMDR therapy helps individuals reprocess traumatic memories, leading to significant reductions in the distress they cause. This foundation underpins the efficacy of EMDR in treating a wide range of psychological issues, making it a valuable tool in the field of psychotherapy.

Continuing with the Fundamental Principles of EMDR, let's explore the Neurophysiological Mechanisms that underlie the therapy's effectiveness. This section delves into the biological and neurological processes that are engaged during EMDR therapy, offering insights into how the therapy impacts the brain and contributes to the treatment of trauma and other psychological disorders.

Neurophysiological Mechanisms

The Brain's Response to Trauma
When an individual experiences trauma, the brain's normal processing mechanisms can be overwhelmed. The amygdala, responsible for processing emotions and fear responses, becomes hyperactive, while the hippocampus, which is involved in forming memories, may function less effectively. This imbalance can lead to the traumatic memory being stored in a raw, unprocessed form, with the emotional intensity and physiological responses preserved.

Bilateral Stimulation and Neural Integration
EMDR therapy employs bilateral stimulation, typically through eye movements, to facilitate neural integration and processing of traumatic memories. The exact neurophysiological mechanisms by which this occurs are still being researched, but several theories have been proposed. One theory suggests that bilateral stimulation activates the same neural mechanisms involved in Rapid Eye Movement (REM) sleep, a phase of sleep associated with processing emotions and memories. This activation may help to facilitate the communication between the amygdala, hippocampus, and prefrontal cortex, enhancing the brain's ability to process and integrate the traumatic memory.

Another perspective focuses on the dual attention component of EMDR, where the patient focuses on the traumatic memory while simultaneously experiencing bilateral stimulation. This dual focus may help decrease the emotional intensity of the memory, enabling the prefrontal cortex to process the experience more adaptively. The repeated back-and-forth movement of the eyes or other forms of bilateral stimulation might also encourage a more balanced engagement of the brain's hemispheres, promoting emotional regulation and cognitive processing of the trauma.

Changes in Brain Activation

Research using functional magnetic resonance imaging (fMRI) and other neuroimaging techniques has shown that EMDR therapy can lead to changes in the activation patterns of the brain. Studies have documented reduced activation in the amygdala, indicating a decrease in emotional distress, and increased activation in the prefrontal cortex, reflecting enhanced cognitive processing of traumatic memories. These changes suggest that EMDR helps to normalize the brain's response to traumatic memories, moving them from emotionally charged and disruptive to integrated and less distressing.

The Role of the Adaptive Information Processing Model

The neurophysiological changes observed with EMDR therapy align with the Adaptive Information Processing (AIP) model's premise. By reactivating the traumatic memory within a controlled, therapeutic context and facilitating its processing through bilateral stimulation, EMDR therapy helps to unlock the brain's natural healing mechanisms. This process allows for the adaptive integration of traumatic memories, reducing their pathological impact and promoting psychological resilience.

The neurophysiological mechanisms underlying EMDR therapy are complex and multifaceted, involving changes in brain activation and the enhancement of neural integration. Through the strategic use of bilateral stimulation, EMDR therapy engages the brain's innate processing capabilities, facilitating the reprocessing and integration of traumatic memories. This understanding of EMDR's impact on the brain provides a compelling explanation for its effectiveness in treating trauma and underscores the therapy's significance in the field of mental health.

Following the exploration of EMDR's theoretical basis, we move on to understand the Structure of Therapy: Phases and Components. This structured approach is what makes EMDR therapy distinct and effective, consisting of eight specific phases designed to ensure comprehensive treatment and resolution of traumatic memories.

Structure of Therapy: Phases and Components

Phase 1: History Taking and Treatment Planning

The initial phase involves a thorough assessment of the client's history and the identification of specific target memories for EMDR processing. This phase sets the foundation for treatment, allowing the therapist to understand the client's background, identify potential targets for EMDR (including memories, current triggers, and future aspirations), and develop a comprehensive treatment plan.

Phase 2: Preparation

During the preparation phase, the therapist introduces the client to EMDR, explaining the process and its potential effects. This phase is crucial for establishing trust and ensuring the client feels comfortable and safe. Techniques for emotional regulation and coping strategies are also taught, preparing the client for the reprocessing phases to come.

Phase 3: Assessment

In the assessment phase, the therapist and client select a specific target memory to work on. Components of this memory, including the most disturbing image, negative beliefs about oneself, emotions, and body sensations, are identified. The client also selects a positive belief to replace the negative belief once the memory is reprocessed.

Phase 4: Desensitization

This phase focuses on the processing of the targeted memory, with the therapist leading the client through sets of bilateral stimulation (usually eye movements). The client is asked to focus on the memory and the associated sensations while simultaneously engaging in the bilateral stimulation, which helps to reduce the emotional impact of the memory.

Phase 5: Installation

Once the distress associated with the target memory is reduced, the installation phase aims to strengthen the positive belief that the client has chosen to replace the original negative belief. Bilateral stimulation is again used to reinforce this positive belief within the context of the targeted memory.

Phase 6: Body Scan

After the positive belief has been installed, the client is asked to think about the original target memory and notice any residual physical tension or discomfort in their body. The therapist uses bilateral stimulation to process these physical sensations until the client no longer feels distress when recalling the memory.

Phase 7: Closure
The closure phase ensures that the client leaves each session feeling better than at the beginning. If the targeted memory has not been fully processed within the session, the therapist will use stabilization techniques learned in the preparation phase to help the client return to equilibrium.

Phase 8: Reevaluation
At the beginning of subsequent sessions, the therapist and client review the work done to ensure that the positive effects have been maintained. They then determine if further reprocessing is needed, either on the same memory or on new target memories and plan the next steps accordingly.

The structured approach of EMDR therapy, through its eight phases, ensures that the therapeutic process is thorough, systematic, and tailored to each client's needs. This structure facilitates the processing of traumatic memories in a safe and controlled manner, promoting healing and resolution. By working through these phases, clients are able to reprocess traumatic memories, significantly reducing their psychological distress and enhancing their overall well-being.

EMDR and Research
Continuing with the third part of the first chapter on EMDR, we delve into Studies and Evidence on the Effectiveness of EMDR. This section highlights the empirical support for EMDR therapy, showcasing its efficacy across various conditions and populations.

Studies and Evidence on the Effectiveness of EMDR

Efficacy in Treating PTSD
One of the most robust areas of research on EMDR focuses on its effectiveness in treating Post-Traumatic Stress Disorder (PTSD). Numerous studies have demonstrated that EMDR can significantly reduce the symptoms of PTSD, often in fewer sessions than traditional forms of therapy. A landmark meta-analysis published in the Journal of Clinical Psychiatry found that EMDR was as effective as, or even more effective than, cognitive behavioral therapy (CBT) for treating PTSD, highlighting its efficiency and potential for rapid results.

Broad Applications Beyond PTSD
While EMDR's efficacy in treating PTSD is well-documented, research has also explored its application to other psychological disorders. Studies have shown positive outcomes when using EMDR to treat anxiety

disorders, depression, and specific phobias. For instance, research published in the Journal of Anxiety Disorders demonstrated that EMDR could effectively reduce symptoms of anxiety and panic disorders, providing a viable alternative to traditional exposure therapies.

Effectiveness with Children and Adolescents

EMDR's adaptability extends to treating children and adolescents who have experienced trauma. A review in the Journal of Child Psychology and Psychiatry concluded that EMDR is effective for youth with PTSD, with results showing a significant reduction in trauma symptoms. This is particularly important given the unique challenges of engaging young people in therapy and the need for age-appropriate treatment methods.

Long-Term Outcomes and Stability of Treatment Gains

An important aspect of evaluating any therapeutic intervention is the longevity of its benefits. Studies tracking the long-term outcomes of EMDR therapy have found that the positive effects are stable over time. Research in the Journal of EMDR Practice and Research reported that individuals treated with EMDR maintained their treatment gains at follow-up periods ranging from 3 to 12 months post-treatment, indicating the enduring impact of EMDR on reducing trauma symptoms.

Comparative Studies and Meta-Analyses

The body of research on EMDR includes numerous comparative studies and meta-analyses, which have consistently ranked EMDR as a highly effective treatment for trauma and PTSD. These studies often compare EMDR to other evidence-based treatments, such as CBT, finding that EMDR not only holds up in comparison but also offers certain advantages, such as the potential for quicker symptom relief and the ability to treat individuals who might not respond well to other therapies.

The research on EMDR therapy provides compelling evidence of its effectiveness across a range of conditions, notably PTSD, but also extending to anxiety, depression, and issues affecting children and adolescents. The empirical support for EMDR underscores its value as a powerful tool in the psychotherapeutic arsenal, capable of facilitating healing and recovery for those affected by trauma and other psychological distress. This body of evidence not only validates the clinical use of EMDR but also encourages continued exploration and application of the therapy to meet the diverse needs of patients.

Continuing with the exploration of EMDR and Research, the next focus is on Comparisons with Other Forms of Therapy. This section examines how EMDR stands in relation to other therapeutic approaches, especially in treating conditions like PTSD, anxiety, and depression, based on research findings and clinical observations.

Comparisons with Other Forms of Therapy

EMDR vs. Cognitive Behavioral Therapy (CBT)

One of the most frequent comparisons in psychotherapy research is between EMDR and Cognitive Behavioral Therapy (CBT), particularly for treating PTSD. Both therapies are endorsed by various health organizations as effective treatments for PTSD. However, studies have highlighted differences in the mechanisms of action, with EMDR focusing on desensitization and reprocessing of traumatic memories through bilateral stimulation, and CBT employing cognitive restructuring and exposure techniques.

Research indicates that both EMDR and CBT are highly effective, but EMDR may achieve significant therapeutic outcomes in fewer sessions. This efficiency of EMDR is particularly notable in cases where clients are resistant to the confrontational nature of exposure therapies commonly used in CBT.

EMDR in the Treatment of Complex Trauma

When comparing EMDR to other therapies for complex trauma, such as Dialectical Behavior Therapy (DBT) or psychodynamic therapy, EMDR's structured approach and focus on memory processing offer distinct advantages. Its ability to rapidly process traumatic memories without extensive verbal discussion can be beneficial for individuals who struggle with traditional talk therapies. The Adaptive Information Processing model underlying EMDR provides a theoretical framework that complements the experiential focus of these therapies.

Advantages Over Exposure Therapies

While exposure-based treatments are a cornerstone in trauma therapy, some individuals find these approaches challenging due to the intense emotional distress they can provoke. EMDR offers an alternative by allowing for the processing of traumatic memories without requiring detailed verbal recounting or prolonged exposure to the traumatic stimuli. This can reduce the likelihood of dropout and make therapy more accessible to those who are hesitant about exposure techniques.

EMDR and Pharmacotherapy

Comparisons between EMDR and pharmacotherapy, particularly SSRIs (Selective Serotonin Reuptake Inhibitors), have also been explored. While medication can be effective in managing symptoms of PTSD and anxiety, EMDR addresses the root cause of distress—the unprocessed traumatic memories. This can lead to longer-lasting relief without the need for ongoing medication, highlighting EMDR's potential for enduring therapeutic benefits.

Meta-Analyses and Systematic Reviews

Meta-analyses and systematic reviews that compare EMDR to other forms of therapy consistently affirm its effectiveness and efficiency. These studies not only support EMDR's efficacy in reducing symptoms of PTSD and other disorders but also emphasize its applicability to a broad range of clients, including those with complex trauma histories and those who may not have benefited from other therapeutic approaches.

The comparative research on EMDR and other forms of therapy underscores EMDR's unique position in the therapeutic landscape. Its effectiveness, efficiency, and the ability to be tolerated by a wide array of clients make it a valuable treatment modality. While no single therapy is universally superior, EMDR offers distinct advantages that make it an essential option for individuals seeking relief from psychological distress, particularly trauma and PTSD. The ongoing research and clinical observations continue to refine our understanding of EMDR's place in psychotherapy, encouraging its integration into comprehensive treatment plans.

Continuing our discussion on EMDR and Research, we now address the Limitations and Critiques of Current Research on EMDR therapy. While EMDR has been extensively studied and applied, it's important to critically examine the research to understand its scope, efficacy, and areas for future investigation.

Limitations and Critiques of Current Research

Methodological Concerns

A significant portion of the critique centers around methodological issues in EMDR research. Some studies have been criticized for small sample sizes, which can limit the generalizability of the findings. Additionally, there's a variability in the application of EMDR protocols across studies, making it challenging to compare results directly. The lack of blinding in many EMDR studies is another concern, as it can introduce bias into the results.

Comparison with Placebo and Control Groups

Critics also point out that not all studies include active control groups, making it difficult to ascertain whether the effects of EMDR are due to the specific mechanisms of the therapy or to general therapeutic elements, such as therapist attention or the therapeutic alliance. Studies that do include control groups sometimes use waitlist controls, which may not adequately account for the placebo effect or the natural course of psychological conditions over time.

Scope of Research

While EMDR has been primarily validated for PTSD, critics argue that more research is needed to fully understand its effectiveness across a broader spectrum of psychological disorders. The research on EMDR's application to conditions such as complex trauma, personality disorders, and somatic symptoms is growing but remains less conclusive than the evidence for PTSD.

Long-Term Efficacy

Although there is evidence supporting the long-term efficacy of EMDR, critics call for more longitudinal studies to better understand how its benefits hold up over time. Particularly, there is a need for research that follows individuals for years, rather than months, after treatment to assess the stability of therapeutic gains and the need for additional interventions.

Theoretical Underpinnings

Some of the skepticism towards EMDR has been directed at its theoretical basis, particularly the role of eye movements in the processing of trauma. Critics have questioned whether the eye movements in EMDR provide a unique benefit or if they are an unnecessary component of the therapy. While some studies suggest that the bilateral stimulation is a crucial element of EMDR's effectiveness, others argue that similar outcomes can be achieved through other means of distraction or dual attention.

Diversity and Cultural Considerations

Critiques also highlight the need for more research on EMDR's effectiveness and applicability across diverse populations and cultures. Understanding how cultural, ethnic, and socio-economic factors influence the efficacy of EMDR is crucial for tailoring the therapy to meet the needs of a wider range of individuals.

While EMDR therapy is a powerful tool for treating trauma and other psychological conditions, the existing research is not without its limitations and critiques. Addressing these methodological concerns, expanding the scope of research, and investigating the long-term efficacy and theoretical underpinnings of EMDR will be vital for its continued development and application. Additionally, exploring EMDR's effectiveness in diverse populations will ensure that the therapy can be adapted and utilized in a culturally sensitive and inclusive manner. These areas for future research offer opportunities to deepen our understanding of EMDR and enhance its utility in psychotherapy.

As we conclude Chapter 1, we have traversed the foundational aspects of Eye Movement Desensitization and Reprocessing (EMDR) therapy, from its origins and theoretical underpinnings to its structure, applications, and the research supporting its efficacy. This comprehensive overview lays the groundwork for understanding EMDR not just as a therapeutic tool but as a significant advancement in the treatment of trauma and other psychological disorders.

Key Takeaways

- Origins and Development: The journey of EMDR from its serendipitous discovery by Francine Shapiro to a globally recognized and researched therapy underscores the evolution of psychotherapeutic methods and the openness of the mental health field to innovative approaches.

- Theoretical Basis: The Adaptive Information Processing (AIP) model provides a robust framework for understanding how EMDR facilitates the processing of traumatic memories, promoting healing and integration within the individual's broader psychological framework.

- Structure of Therapy: The eight-phase approach of EMDR ensures a comprehensive and systematic treatment process, allowing for the careful identification, processing, and resolution of traumatic memories, with an emphasis on the client's safety and stability.

- Research and Efficacy: The body of research supporting EMDR's effectiveness, particularly in treating PTSD but also extending to other conditions, reflects its significant impact on individuals' lives. Comparative studies further highlight EMDR's advantages in certain contexts, offering an alternative for those who may not benefit from traditional therapy models.

- Limitations and Future Directions: Acknowledging the critiques and limitations of current research is crucial for the ongoing development of EMDR. Future investigations are needed to address methodological concerns, explore long-term outcomes, expand its applicability to diverse populations, and deepen understanding of its mechanisms.

EMDR therapy represents a confluence of innovation, empirical research, and clinical practice, offering profound possibilities for healing and recovery. As we continue to explore and understand EMDR, its role in addressing the complex landscape of psychological disorders will likely expand, providing hope and healing to those affected by trauma. The journey of EMDR is a testament to the dynamic nature of psychotherapy and the continuous quest for effective treatments that honor the complexity of the human mind and experience.

As we move forward into subsequent chapters, the insights gained from this foundational chapter will inform our exploration of EMDR's practical applications, challenges, and the personal experiences of both therapists and clients. The evolution of EMDR is not just a story of a therapeutic technique but a narrative about the resilience of the human spirit and the transformative power of therapy.

CHAPTER TWO

PRACTICING EMDR

The practice of Eye Movement Desensitization and Reprocessing (EMDR) therapy is both an art and a science, requiring therapists to integrate the method's structured protocols with their clinical acumen to meet the unique needs of each client. This chapter delves into the intricacies of practicing EMDR, covering the preparatory steps, the execution of the therapy's phases, and strategies for managing the challenges that arise during treatment. Through an understanding of these components, therapists can more effectively facilitate the healing process for those suffering from trauma and other distressing experiences.

Preparing for Therapy

Assessing Patient Suitability and Criteria
Determining a patient's suitability for Eye Movement Desensitization and Reprocessing (EMDR) therapy is a crucial first step in the therapeutic process. This assessment phase ensures that EMDR is the appropriate treatment modality for the client's specific needs, considering the nature of their trauma, psychological readiness, and any potential risk factors. This section outlines the key criteria and considerations involved in assessing patient suitability for EMDR therapy.

Nature and Complexity of Trauma
Type of Trauma: EMDR is most well-known for its effectiveness in treating Post-Traumatic Stress Disorder (PTSD) resulting from acute trauma events. However, its applicability extends to complex trauma, anxiety disorders, depression, and other conditions. Assessing the nature of the trauma helps in tailoring the EMDR approach.

Trauma History: A comprehensive trauma history is essential, including the number of traumatic events, their duration, and the age of onset. This information aids in understanding the potential complexity of the case and planning the treatment.

Psychological Stability

Current Psychological State: The client's current psychological stability is a critical factor. While EMDR can be highly effective, it is also emotionally demanding. Clients need a certain level of stability to manage the emotional responses that can arise during processing.

Comorbid Conditions: The presence of comorbid psychiatric conditions (e.g., severe depression, substance use disorders, psychosis) may require additional stabilization or alternative treatment approaches before proceeding with EMDR.

Coping Mechanisms

Existing Coping Strategies: The assessment should include an evaluation of the client's current coping mechanisms. Understanding how a client manages stress and emotional distress is vital for determining their readiness for EMDR therapy.

Ability to Tolerate Emotional Distress: Clients must be able to tolerate the emotional distress that can accompany the recalling of traumatic memories. Assessing this tolerance helps in deciding whether preparatory sessions to build coping strategies are needed.

Motivation and Expectations

Client's Motivation: The client's motivation and commitment to the therapy process play a significant role in the outcome of EMDR therapy. It is important to discuss and align on the therapy goals.

Therapeutic Expectations: Clear communication about the therapy process, potential challenges, and realistic outcomes is crucial for setting appropriate expectations and building a therapeutic alliance.

Potential Risk Factors

Dissociative Tendencies: Clients with significant dissociative tendencies may require a modified approach to EMDR or additional preparatory work to ensure their safety during processing.

Suicidality and Self-Harm: A thorough risk assessment for suicidality or self-harm behaviors is essential. Clients at high risk may need more intensive support or stabilization before engaging in EMDR therapy.

Assessing a patient's suitability for EMDR therapy involves a careful consideration of various factors, including the nature of their trauma, psychological stability, coping mechanisms, motivation for treatment, and any potential risk factors. This comprehensive assessment is fundamental to creating a tailored and effective treatment plan that addresses the client's unique needs. By thoroughly evaluating each of these criteria, therapists can ensure that EMDR therapy is conducted safely, ethically, and effectively, maximizing the potential for healing and recovery.

Following the discussion on assessing patient suitability and criteria for EMDR therapy, we move to the crucial aspects of Establishing Safety and Building a Therapeutic Alliance. This stage is foundational to the EMDR process, as it sets the tone for the therapeutic relationship and ensures that clients feel secure and supported throughout their treatment journey.

Establishing safety and building a therapeutic alliance

Establishing Safety

Safety, both emotional and psychological, is paramount in EMDR therapy, especially given that clients will be confronting and processing deeply distressing memories. Establishing safety involves several key components:

1. **Creating a Safe Space:** The therapeutic environment should be a haven where clients feel physically comfortable and assured of their privacy and confidentiality. This sense of safety is crucial for them to open about their trauma.

2. **Stabilization Techniques:** Before proceeding with trauma processing, therapists introduce clients to various stabilization techniques. These may include grounding exercises, mindfulness practices, and other strategies that clients can use to manage emotional distress. These tools are not only preparatory but also serve as resources clients can draw upon between sessions or when facing triggers in their daily lives.

3. **Safety Within the Self:** Part of establishing safety involves helping clients find a sense of security within themselves. This may involve identifying internal resources, strengths, or positive memories that can serve as anchors during challenging moments in therapy.

Building a Therapeutic Alliance

The therapeutic alliance, or the relationship between therapist and client, is a critical determinant of therapy success. In the context of EMDR, building this alliance takes on added significance due to the intense nature of the work involved.

1. **Trust and Rapport:** The therapist actively works to build trust and rapport from the first interaction. This involves demonstrating empathy, listening actively, and validating the client's experiences and feelings. Trust is the cornerstone of the

therapeutic alliance and is essential for clients to feel comfortable engaging in the deep work of EMDR.

2. **Collaboration and Empowerment:** EMDR therapy is a collaborative process. Therapists empower clients by involving them in decision-making, from identifying target memories for processing to setting goals for therapy. This collaborative approach fosters a sense of agency and control in clients, which is particularly important for those who have experienced trauma.

3. **Consistent Support and Reassurance:** Throughout the therapy process, the therapist provides consistent support and reassurance. This includes preparing clients for what to expect during and after sessions, debriefing after processing work, and being available to address concerns or questions that arise.

4. **Adapting to Client Needs:** Building a therapeutic alliance also means being responsive to the client's changing needs. The therapist must be attuned to the client's emotional state and readiness to proceed with therapy, adjusting as needed to ensure the client feels heard, respected, and supported.

Establishing safety and building a therapeutic alliance are critical first steps in the EMDR therapy process. These elements lay the foundation for a successful therapeutic journey, creating the conditions necessary for clients to engage in the challenging work of processing and healing from trauma. By prioritizing safety and the therapeutic relationship, therapists can better support their clients through the transformative process of EMDR therapy.

Stabilization Techniques and Stress Management

In the journey of EMDR therapy, stabilization techniques and stress management play a critical role, especially during the preparation phase and as ongoing support throughout the therapy process. These strategies are essential for ensuring clients have the tools to manage emotional distress that might arise from recalling traumatic memories. This section delves into various techniques aimed at enhancing emotional stability and providing clients with practical methods for coping with stress and emotional upheaval.

Grounding Techniques

Grounding techniques are designed to help clients detach from emotional pain and return to the present moment. These strategies are particularly useful for clients who experience dissociation or overwhelming emotions during therapy. Techniques include:

Sensory Awareness: Encouraging clients to engage their five senses to ground themselves in the present. This could involve identifying things they can see, hear, touch, taste, and smell.

Physical Grounding: Using physical movements or touches, such as holding a cold object, pressing feet firmly against the floor, or gently tapping the arms, to help clients feel more anchored to the present.

Breathing Exercises

Controlled breathing exercises are a cornerstone of stress management, helping to regulate the body's response to stress. Techniques such as deep diaphragmatic breathing, paced respiration, and the 4-7-8 breathing method can significantly reduce physiological arousal associated with anxiety and stress.

Safe Place Visualization

Safe place visualization involves guiding clients to imagine a place where they feel completely safe, calm, and comfortable. This mental imagery technique is used to create a psychological refuge that clients can "visit" mentally when they feel stressed or overwhelmed. The therapist helps the client to detail their safe place using all senses, making the experience as vivid as possible.

Self-Soothing Strategies

Teaching clients self-soothing strategies is essential for helping them manage emotional distress independently. These strategies might include listening to calming music, engaging in hobbies or activities they enjoy, practicing mindfulness or meditation, or using comforting self-talk.

The Container Technique

The container technique is a specific EMDR tool used to help clients manage overwhelming emotions or memories. Clients are guided to imagine a container where they can safely "store" distressing memories or feelings until they are ready to process them in therapy. This technique helps in managing emotional overwhelm and ensuring that the therapy does not retraumatize the client.

Positive Imagery and Affirmations

Using positive imagery and affirmations can bolster a client's sense of safety and self-worth. Encouraging clients to develop personal affirmations that reinforce their strength and resilience can be empowering and provide comfort during challenging moments in therapy.

Stabilization techniques and stress management are integral to the EMDR therapy process, providing clients with essential tools to navigate the emotional challenges that can arise. These strategies not only facilitate a sense of safety and readiness for processing traumatic memories but also empower clients to maintain emotional equilibrium outside of therapy sessions. By incorporating these techniques, therapists can help clients build a foundation of resilience and coping skills that supports their journey towards healing and recovery.

Managing Complications and Challenges

In the practice of EMDR therapy, therapists often encounter various complications and challenges that require careful navigation to ensure the efficacy of the treatment and the safety of the client. Among these, unexpected responses during sessions and resistance to treatment are common hurdles that therapists must be prepared to address.

Unexpected Responses and Resistance to Treatment

Unexpected Responses

During EMDR therapy, clients may experience unexpected emotional, cognitive, or physiological responses. These can range from intense emotional upheaval to physical manifestations of distress, such as shaking or crying, or even to unexpected memories surfacing. Such responses, while potentially alarming, are indicative of the processing and integration of traumatic memories.

Strategies for Managing Unexpected Responses:

Staying Present and Supportive: Therapists should remain calm and present, offering reassurance and reminding the client of their current safety. This presence can help anchor the client, guiding them through the intensity of the moment.

Utilizing Grounding Techniques: Employing grounding techniques discussed earlier can help clients manage dissociation or overwhelming emotions, bringing them back to the present moment.

Adjusting the Pace: Slowing down the therapy process or returning to stabilization techniques can help manage unexpected responses. It's crucial to ensure the client does not become retraumatized by the therapy itself.

Debriefing: After an intense session, spend time debriefing with the client. This can help them process their experience, integrate the memories more adaptively, and prepare them for future sessions.

Resistance to Treatment

Resistance in EMDR can manifest as reluctance to engage in the process, skepticism about the therapy, or difficulty accessing or discussing traumatic memories. Resistance is a natural part of the therapeutic process and often reflects underlying fear, shame, or a lack of safety felt by the client.

Strategies for Managing Resistance:

Building Trust: Continue to strengthen the therapeutic alliance. Trust and safety are paramount for clients to feel comfortable engaging in the deep work required by EMDR.

Exploring the Resistance: Gently explore the resistance without judgment. Understanding the client's fears or concerns can provide valuable insights and help tailor the approach to meet their needs.

Empowering the Client: Involve the client in decision-making processes and reassure them of their control over the therapy pace. Empowerment can reduce feelings of vulnerability associated with trauma processing.

Adjusting Expectations: Revisiting and adjusting expectations about the therapy process can help. Clarify that it's normal and okay to have mixed feelings about revisiting traumatic events.

Managing unexpected responses and resistance to treatment is an integral part of the EMDR therapy process. These challenges, while potentially daunting, offer opportunities for deepening the therapeutic work and facilitating significant breakthroughs in healing. By employing strategies to navigate these hurdles, therapists can support their clients in moving through their trauma processing journey with resilience and safety, ultimately leading to more effective and lasting outcomes.

Working with Complex Traumas and Dissociative Disorders

Treating clients with complex traumas and dissociative disorders presents unique challenges within the EMDR framework. These conditions often involve layers of psychological distress and coping mechanisms that have developed over years, making the therapeutic process more intricate. Successfully navigating these complexities requires a nuanced understanding of trauma, dissociation, and specialized adaptations of EMDR therapy.

Understanding Complex Trauma and Dissociation

Complex Trauma typically refers to exposure to multiple traumatic events, often of an invasive, interpersonal nature, resulting in a wide range of long-term effects. Individuals with complex trauma may experience pervasive emotional dysregulation, an impaired sense of self, and difficulties in forming healthy relationships.

Dissociative Disorders involve a disconnection and lack of continuity between thoughts, memories, surroundings, actions, and identity. These disorders often arise in response to trauma and serve as a coping mechanism, allowing individuals to distance themselves from experiences of severe psychological distress.

Adaptations in EMDR for Complex Traumas and Dissociative Disorders

1. **Extended Preparation Phase:** Clients with complex trauma or dissociative disorders may require a longer preparation phase. This includes building a strong therapeutic alliance, educating the client about dissociation and its functions, and teaching extensive stabilization and grounding techniques. Establishing a "safe place" and mastering the "container" technique are crucial before proceeding with trauma processing.

2. **Modified Approach to Phases:** Therapists may need to modify the standard EMDR phases when working with this population. This could involve slower pacing, shorter sets of bilateral stimulation, and more frequent check-ins to ensure the client remains grounded and present.

3. **Integration of Dissociative Parts:** Particularly in dissociative identity disorder, therapy may involve working with different dissociative parts or alters. Recognizing and respecting these parts, and sometimes engaging them directly in the therapy process, can facilitate a more cohesive sense of self and improve overall functioning.

4. **Use of Interweaves:** Creative and client-specific cognitive interweaves may be necessary to help clients who become stuck or overwhelmed during processing. These interweaves can provide additional support, perspective, and encouragement to move through difficult memories.

5. **Collaboration with Other Professionals:** Given the complexity of these conditions, collaboration with other healthcare professionals providing care to the client (such as psychiatrists or other therapists specializing in trauma and dissociation) can ensure a comprehensive and cohesive treatment approach.

6. **Managing Reactions Post-Session:** Clients with complex trauma and dissociative disorders may experience intense reactions after EMDR sessions. Developing a clear plan for self-care and coping strategies post-session is essential. Therapists should be available for support or consultation between sessions if needed.

Ethical Considerations and Therapist Self-Care

Working with complex traumas and dissociative disorders requires therapists to be mindful of their boundaries and limitations. Ethical considerations, such as ensuring competence through specialized training and supervision, are paramount. Additionally, the emotional toll of this work necessitates that therapists engage in regular self-care and seek peer support to maintain their well-being and effectiveness.

EMDR therapy for individuals with complex traumas and dissociative disorders demands a specialized, careful, and compassionate approach. By adapting EMDR protocols, employing advanced strategies, and maintaining a focus on safety and stabilization, therapists can effectively support clients through their healing journeys. Understanding the depth of these challenges and continuously striving for therapeutic excellence are key to facilitating recovery and resilience in this vulnerable population.

Supervision and Professional Consultation

In the realm of EMDR therapy, especially when addressing the intricacies of complex traumas and dissociative disorders, the role of supervision and professional consultation cannot be overstated. These elements are crucial for therapists seeking to enhance their skills, navigate challenging cases, and ensure the highest standards of care for their clients.

The Importance of Supervision in EMDR Therapy

Supervision provides a structured framework where therapists can discuss client cases, explore their own responses and feelings, and gain insights into the application of EMDR therapy. It serves multiple purposes:

1. **Skill Enhancement:** Supervisors help therapists refine their techniques, offering guidance on the nuanced application of EMDR's eight phases, particularly for complex cases that deviate from standard presentations.

2. **Case Consultation:** Discussing specific client cases allows for collaborative problem-solving, helping therapists address challenges and identify strategies for clients who are stuck, resistant, or experiencing intense reactions.

3. **Professional Growth:** Supervision encourages therapists to reflect on their professional practice, fostering ongoing learning and development. It helps therapists to remain current with EMDR research and methodology, enhancing their efficacy and confidence.

Professional Consultation for Complex Cases

Professional consultation goes beyond supervision by providing specialized expertise for particularly challenging cases. Consulting with colleagues or specialists in areas such as trauma, dissociation, or specific client populations can offer fresh perspectives and innovative approaches. This collaboration is especially valuable when therapists encounter clients with complex trauma histories or significant dissociative symptoms, where standard EMDR protocols may need to be adapted.

Building a Supportive Professional Network

Creating a network of professionals who understand and practice EMDR therapy enriches a therapist's resources, offering emotional support, clinical insight, and mutual learning opportunities. Networking can occur through professional associations, EMDR training programs, or online forums and groups dedicated to EMDR practitioners.

Ethical Considerations and Competency

Engaging in regular supervision and consultation is also an ethical imperative. It ensures that therapists maintain competency and adhere to best practices, particularly when working with vulnerable populations. Ethical practice in EMDR therapy requires a commitment to ongoing education, self-reflection, and openness to feedback.

Self-Care and Resilience

Finally, supervision and consultation play a critical role in therapist self-care and resilience. Discussing the emotional impact of trauma work with supervisors or consultants can mitigate the risk of vicarious traumatization and burnout. This support system enables therapists to process their own reactions and maintain emotional and professional well-being.

Supervision and professional consultation are indispensable components of practicing EMDR therapy effectively, particularly when working with complex traumas and dissociative disorders. These professional supports not only enhance therapeutic skills and ensure adherence to ethical standards but also contribute to the therapist's personal growth and resilience. By embracing these resources, therapists can navigate the challenges of their work more effectively, ensuring they provide the best possible care to those they serve.

Conclusion of Chapter 2

In exploring the intricate practice of Eye Movement Desensitization and Reprocessing (EMDR) therapy, this chapter has navigated through the foundational steps of preparing for therapy, the structured execution of its phases, and the adept handling of complications and challenges. The journey through these elements underscores the multifaceted nature of EMDR, highlighting both its profound potential for healing and the complexities inherent in its application.

The preparation phase, with its emphasis on assessing patient suitability, establishing safety, and building a robust therapeutic alliance, sets the stage for a therapeutic process that is as compassionate as it is effective. The introduction of stabilization techniques and stress management strategies early in the therapy ensures that clients are equipped to face the emotional rigors of revisiting traumatic memories. This preparatory work is crucial, laying the groundwork for a therapeutic environment where healing can occur.

As therapists navigate through the eight phases of EMDR, they engage in a delicate balance of structure and flexibility, adhering to the therapy's established protocols while also adapting to the unique needs of each client. This balance is particularly evident in the management of unexpected responses and resistance to treatment, where the therapist's skill in maintaining the therapeutic alliance and adjusting the approach as needed becomes paramount.

The challenges of working with complex traumas and dissociative disorders further illustrate the need for specialized adaptations of EMDR therapy. These conditions, with their layers of psychological impact, require therapists to employ a deepened understanding and an expanded repertoire of strategies to facilitate effective treatment. The incorporation of supervision and professional consultation is essential in these cases, providing therapists with the support and guidance needed to navigate the complexities of such profound trauma.

In conclusion, the practice of EMDR therapy is characterized by its depth, requiring a blend of scientific understanding, clinical skill, and compassionate presence. The journey from preparation through to the handling of complex traumas underscores the therapy's potential to facilitate significant psychological healing. As therapists engage with this powerful therapeutic tool, they contribute to the ongoing evolution of EMDR, expanding its reach and efficacy. This chapter has laid out the path for practicing EMDR with fidelity to its principles while adapting to the realities of diverse human experiences, marking a critical step in the broader journey of understanding, and applying EMDR therapy in the quest for healing and recovery.

CHAPTER THREE

EMDR IN VARIOUS CLINICAL CONTEXTS

ye Movement Desensitization and Reprocessing (EMDR) therapy has been primarily recognized for its effectiveness in treating Post-Traumatic Stress Disorder (PTSD), but its application extends far beyond PTSD to encompass a wide range of psychological disorders and clinical contexts. EMDR's fundamental principles facilitate the processing of distressing memories and maladaptive beliefs, promoting healing and adaptive functioning. As the understanding of EMDR has evolved, so too has its integration into various therapeutic landscapes. This chapter explores the application of EMDR across different clinical contexts, beginning with its well-established efficacy in treating PTSD, extending to its use in addressing anxiety, depression, and other disorders, and concluding with its adaptation for complex trauma and special populations.

The efficacy of EMDR in treating PTSD is one of the most extensively researched and clinically validated aspects of the therapy. Numerous studies have demonstrated its effectiveness in reducing the symptoms of PTSD, often achieving significant improvements in a shorter timeframe compared to traditional therapeutic approaches. Research consistently shows that EMDR can effectively decrease or eliminate the symptoms of PTSD, including intrusive thoughts, flashbacks, and emotional numbness. Meta-analyses comparing EMDR to other evidence-based treatments for PTSD, such as Cognitive Behavioral Therapy (CBT), have found EMDR to be equally effective, with some studies suggesting that EMDR may lead to quicker symptom reduction.

EMDR facilitates the processing of traumatic memories, allowing them to be integrated into the individual's adaptive memory networks. This process reduces the distress associated with the memory and alters the previously held negative beliefs related to the trauma. The bilateral stimulation component of EMDR, thought to mimic the psychological state associated with Rapid Eye Movement (REM) sleep, is believed to play a crucial role in this processing.

When treating PTSD with EMDR, therapists must be adept at assessing the client's readiness for trauma processing, ensuring that appropriate stabilization techniques are in place. The therapy's structured approach, tailored to everyone's needs, allows for the safe and effective processing of traumatic memories, leading to symptom relief and enhanced psychological resilience.

EMDR stands out not only for its efficacy but also for its ability to provide relief in a way that is often perceived as less distressing than traditional exposure therapies. As we delve deeper into this chapter, we will explore further the application of EMDR across different disorders, highlighting its versatility and capacity to facilitate healing in varied clinical contexts.

The case studies and testimonials presented in this text provide a glimpse into the profound impact of Eye Movement Desensitization and Reprocessing (EMDR) therapy on individuals suffering from PTSD and other trauma-related conditions. These narratives highlight the therapeutic efficacy of EMDR and the personal journeys of recovery, resilience, and empowerment that can be achieved with it.

Veterans and first responders occupy unique positions in society, frequently exposed to traumatic events that can lead to Post-Traumatic Stress Disorder (PTSD) and other stress-related conditions. The nature of their experiences—often characterized by high intensity, life-threatening situations, and moral dilemmas—requires specialized considerations when using Eye Movement Desensitization and Reprocessing (EMDR) therapy. Understanding the specific needs and challenges faced by these groups is crucial to tailoring EMDR therapy to be as effective as possible.

Veterans may carry trauma from combat exposure, including witnessing death, injury, and experiencing life-threatening situations. These experiences can lead to complex PTSD, where symptoms are intertwined with issues of guilt, moral injury, and identity crises. First responders, including police officers, firefighters, and emergency medical personnel, face cumulative stress and trauma from repeated exposure to violent incidents, accidents, and natural disasters. The need to remain calm during times of crisis frequently makes their trauma worse by delaying emotional responses until much later, which can result in dissociation and emotional numbing.

Tailoring EMDR for effectiveness involves building trust and safety, addressing complex PTSD and dissociation, integrating trauma, demonstrating cultural competence, addressing moral injury, and offering ongoing support. By adapting the therapeutic approach to address the complexities of their trauma, therapists can significantly improve the efficacy of treatment for these populations. Building trust and safety, addressing complex PTSD and moral injury, and ensuring cultural competence are all critical factors in delivering effective EMDR therapy. Through such tailored interventions, veterans and first responders can find meaningful recovery and healing, moving beyond the traumas of their service to lead fulfilling lives.

EMDR therapy, best known for its effectiveness in treating Post-Traumatic Stress Disorder (PTSD), has been applied to treat various psychological conditions beyond PTSD. The adaptive information processing model underlying EMDR suggests that many psychological disorders are rooted in unprocessed memories that continue to influence current emotions, sensations, and thoughts. This perspective has led to the exploration and application of EMDR in treating a broad range of conditions beyond PTSD.

Anxiety disorders include panic disorder, phobias, and generalized anxiety disorder (GAD). The therapy targets the distressing memories and present triggers contributing to the anxiety response, aiming to desensitize the individual to these triggers and adaptively reprocess the memories. Research suggests that EMDR can be a valuable tool in treating depression, particularly when depressive episodes are linked to specific traumatic or distressing life events. By processing these underlying memories, EMDR can help alleviate depressive symptoms, offering a new pathway for individuals who may not fully respond to traditional therapies or medication.

Other disorders include eating disorders, addiction, chronic pain and somatic symptoms, and chronic pain and somatic symptoms. EMDR facilitates healing by allowing the brain to resume its natural healing process. For individuals with anxiety, depression, or other disorders, EMDR helps by desensitizing distress, reprocessing memories, and improving emotional regulation.

When applying EMDR to conditions beyond PTSD, therapists must consider several factors: comprehensive assessment, client readiness, and adaptation of protocols. A growing body of research supporting EMDR's application beyond PTSD is promising, with studies indicating positive outcomes across a range of disorders.

The extension of Eye Movement Desensitization and Reprocessing (EMDR) therapy to the treatment of anxiety and depression has opened new avenues for therapeutic intervention, presenting both promising outcomes and unique challenges. The efficacy of EMDR in treating anxiety and depression has shown significant potential in reducing symptoms, such as decreased physiological arousal associated with anxiety triggers and improved emotional regulation.

The use of EMDR provides hope and healing to people suffering from anxiety, depression, and other psychological disorders. Its versatility and adaptability make it an essential tool in the psychotherapeutic arsenal, able to address the complex web of memories and emotions that underpins many psychological conditions.

Although EMDR therapy has been shown to be effective in treating anxiety and depression, it does present challenges such as symptom complexity, emotional tolerance, therapeutic resistance, and treatment expectations. To address these issues, therapists can use strategies such as integrating therapeutic techniques, adjusting the pace of therapy, developing emotional resilience, and conducting continuous assessments and flexibility.

Treatment with EMDR has proven adaptable and effective beyond its origins in PTSD treatment, with many clients reporting positive outcomes. The use of EMDR in the treatment of anxiety and depression has expanded into the pediatric population, providing a valuable approach for treating trauma and distressing experiences in children and adolescents. This demographic presents unique challenges and opportunities for EMDR practitioners, necessitating changes to the standard protocol to meet the developmental needs of younger clients.

Tailoring EMDR for younger clients involves using age-appropriate language, engaging activities, shorter sessions, and involving caregivers in the therapeutic process. Simplified language is used to explain the therapy process, engaging activities involve play and creative activities, shorter sessions are adjusted to match the child's attention span and emotional tolerance, and caregivers are involved to provide additional support and ensure understanding of therapy goals.

Research and clinical experience have demonstrated EMDR's effectiveness in treating trauma and related conditions in children and adolescents. Outcomes include significant reductions in PTSD symptoms, enhanced coping skills, and improved self-esteem. However, working with children and adolescents in EMDR therapy also presents specific challenges, including varied responses to trauma, family dynamics, and ethical considerations.

EMDR therapy has proven effective for treating anxiety and depression, but it also presents challenges such as the complexity of symptoms, emotional tolerance, therapeutic resistance, and expectations for treatment. Therapists must be attuned to these variations to tailor the therapy effectively and navigate the family environment carefully. By incorporating therapeutic techniques, adjusting the pace of therapy, building emotional resilience, and being flexible in adjusting treatment plans, EMDR continues to evolve as a powerful tool for alleviating the burdens of anxiety and depression.

Treatment with EMDR is a versatile technique that can be used to treat a variety of psychological issues, including attachment and relational traumas. Because of their complexities and profound impact on people's lives, these deeply ingrained traumas frequently necessitate lengthy therapy. The success of EMDR in this demographic demonstrates the therapy's versatility and ability to promote healing and resilience across the lifespan. As research advances, so will the strategies and approaches to optimizing EMDR therapy for children and adolescents, increasing its impact on young lives.

Attachment and relational traumas refer to the psychological distress that arises from significant disruptions or negative experiences in important relationships, often originating in childhood. These traumas can stem from neglect, abuse, loss, or inconsistency in caregiving, leading to long-term effects on trust, self-esteem, and the ability to form healthy relationships.

Challenges in treating attachment and relational traumas include the complex emotional landscape, dissociation and avoidance, and the impact on the therapeutic relationship. EMDR strategies for attachment and relational traumas involve establishing a sense of safety within the therapeutic relationship, creating an environment where clients feel seen, heard, and validated, and laying the groundwork for processing traumatic memories. A phased approach is often necessary, involving extended preparation and stabilization phases, with a gradual move towards processing traumatic memories.

EMDR therapy for attachment and relational traumas often focuses on early memories that serve as the foundation for dysfunctional patterns in relationships. By reprocessing these early experiences, clients can begin to develop a more adaptive understanding of themselves and their capacity for healthy relationships. Enhancing clients' internal resources is crucial in EMDR therapy for relational traumas, such as developing coping strategies, nurturing a positive sense of self, and building capacities for emotional regulation and interpersonal skills.

Addressing present and future concerns is essential for EMDR therapy, as it also focuses on present-day triggers and future anxieties related to attachment and relationships. This holistic approach ensures that clients are equipped to handle current challenges and move towards healthier relational patterns.

In treating personality disorders, EMDR presents a unique set of challenges and opportunities. Many individuals with personality disorders have histories of complex trauma, which can complicate the therapy process. Ensuring emotional stability and safety is crucial before proceeding with trauma processing with clients with personality disorders. Building a strong therapeutic alliance is particularly challenging but essential for successful EMDR therapy.

EMDR may need to be integrated with other therapeutic modalities, such as Dialectical Behavior Therapy (DBT) for borderline personality disorder, to address the full spectrum of symptoms and behaviors effectively. Strategies for personality disorders include an extended preparation phase that focuses on developing coping mechanisms, emotional regulation skills, and a sense of safety. Targeting the core beliefs and memories that underlie the dysfunctional patterns characteristic of personality disorders involves identifying and processing early traumatic experiences that have contributed to these pervasive patterns of thinking and behaving. Utilizing the Adaptive Information Processing (AIP) Model can help reprocess maladaptive memories and beliefs, facilitating more adaptive and healthier ways of relating to oneself and others.

EMDR therapy offers a promising avenue for addressing trauma and other psychological disturbances in children and adolescents, but it also presents challenges and opportunities.

Research on Eye Movement Desensitization and Reprocessing (EMDR) therapy's efficacy in treating personality disorders is still emerging, but clinical experiences suggest positive outcomes, particularly in reducing trauma-related symptoms and improving emotional regulation. Therapists should be mindful of the potential for intense emotional responses and the need for ongoing assessment of the client's stability and readiness for trauma processing.

Particularly when traumatic experiences and unhelpful beliefs are the root of or make personality disorders worse, EMDR therapy offers a promising treatment option. By focusing on the core issues that contribute to the development and maintenance of personality disorders, EMDR can facilitate profound changes in clients' self-perception, emotional regulation, and interpersonal relationships. However, given the complexity of personality disorders, a careful, integrated, and client-centered approach is essential to ensure safety and promote healing. As the field continues to evolve, further research will likely illuminate the most effective strategies for integrating EMDR into the treatment of personality disorders, expanding the potential for positive therapeutic outcomes.

In the context of EMDR therapy, certain cases—particularly those involving complex trauma, severe personality disorders, and deeply ingrained patterns of dysfunctional behavior—need extended interventions and a comprehensive approach to long-term treatment management. These cases often require a nuanced, phased, and integrative strategy that not only addresses immediate traumatic memories but also supports the individual's broader psychological needs over time.

The necessity of extended interventions becomes necessary when:

Multiple Traumatic Memories: There are numerous traumatic memories or a history of complex trauma that cannot be adequately processed in a short-term therapy framework. Severe Psychological Conditions: Clients present with severe psychological conditions, including certain personality disorders, that affect their ability to process trauma. Chronology of Issues: The issues have been present for an extended period, leading to deeply ingrained beliefs and behaviors that require time to address and modify.

Strategies for long-term treatment management in EMDR therapy include adopting a phased approach, integrating therapeutic modalities, periodic reevaluation, client empowerment, and building resilience and adaptive capacities. Challenges in extended interventions and long-term management include maintaining engagement, recognizing, and addressing therapeutic plateaus, and ensuring ongoing access to necessary therapeutic resources.

Extended interventions and long-term treatment management in EMDR therapy require a commitment to a holistic and adaptive therapeutic process. By recognizing the complexities of certain psychological conditions and the necessity for prolonged engagement, therapists can provide comprehensive care that addresses both the root causes and the broader psychological landscape of their clients' issues. This approach not only facilitates deeper healing but also supports sustained recovery and improved quality of life, underscoring the value of patience, perseverance, and flexibility in the therapeutic journey.

In conclusion, the journey of EMDR therapy is one of continuous discovery and adaptation, with its dynamic nature and evidence-based success in diverse clinical settings positioning it as an asset in the field of psychotherapy. The ongoing evolution of EMDR practice and research promises to further enhance its efficacy and applicability, expanding the horizons of healing for individuals grappling with a wide spectrum of psychological distress.

CHAPTER FOUR

TRAINING AND
SUPERVISION IN EMDR

The successful implementation of Eye Movement Desensitization and Reprocessing (EMDR) therapy is a result of the comprehensive training and ongoing supervision of therapists. As EMDR has evolved into a widely recognized and empirically supported therapeutic modality, it is crucial to ensure practitioners are well-equipped with both the theoretical knowledge and practical skills necessary to deliver this therapy effectively. This chapter delves into the critical aspects of EMDR training and supervision, outlining the pathways to becoming a proficient EMDR therapist, the role of continuous professional development, and the significance of supervision in refining and enhancing therapeutic practice.

The journey to becoming an EMDR therapist involves a structured training program that encompasses both foundational learning and advanced practice. This journey is designed to prepare therapists to apply EMDR therapy confidently and competently across a range of clinical situations and client populations. Foundational training introduces therapists to the core principles of EMDR, including the Adaptive Information Processing (AIP) model, the eight-phase treatment protocol, and the specific techniques of bilateral stimulation. This stage is crucial for building a solid understanding of the theoretical underpinnings of EMDR and developing the basic skills required to begin practicing.

Advanced training: Following foundational training, therapists are encouraged to pursue advanced training opportunities. These may focus on specific applications of EMDR, such as working with complex trauma, children and adolescents, or special populations like veterans and first responders. Advanced training also covers the integration of EMDR with other therapeutic modalities, enhancing the therapist's ability to provide comprehensive and tailored treatment.

Supervision is an integral component of the EMDR training process, offering therapists a platform for professional growth and development. Through supervision, therapists receive guidance on case conceptualization, treatment planning, and the application of EMDR in challenging clinical scenarios. Supervision also serves as a valuable space for addressing ethical considerations, managing countertransference, and fostering reflective practice.

Peer supervision and consultation groups can be immensely beneficial for EMDR therapists, providing a supportive environment for sharing experiences, discussing complex cases, and receiving feedback from fellow practitioners. Peer supervision encourages a collaborative approach to learning and problem-solving, further enriching the therapist's professional development.

Continuous professional development is essential for therapists to stay abreast of the latest developments and to refine their practice accordingly. This may involve participating in workshops, conferences, and advanced training courses, as well as engaging with the broader EMDR community through professional associations and networks.

The journey to becoming an effective EMDR therapist is one of continuous learning and growth, with a commitment to comprehensive training coupled with the support of supervision and the pursuit of professional development, ensuring that therapists are well-prepared to harness the full potential of EMDR therapy.

EMDR training is a comprehensive process designed to deepen therapists' understanding, refine their skills, and validate their expertise in the therapy. It incorporates various learning models to accommodate different styles of learning and ensure a comprehensive understanding and mastery of the therapy. These models include didactic instruction, experiential learning, supervised clinical practice, consultation groups, and certification.

Certification in EMDR therapy is a process that goes beyond initial training, representing a commitment to excellence and a deepening of expertise in EMDR. The specific requirements for certification can vary by country and accrediting organization, but typically include advanced training hours, documented clinical practice, supervision, demonstration of competency, and commitment to ongoing professional development.

The journey toward becoming a certified EMDR therapist is both rigorous and rewarding, offering mental health professionals a structured pathway for mastering a powerful therapeutic tool. Through a combination of didactic instruction, experiential learning, supervised practice, and ongoing professional development, therapists deepen their understanding and skills in EMDR therapy. Certification in EMDR not only signifies a therapist's commitment to providing high-quality care but also enhances their ability to facilitate healing and change in the lives of those affected by trauma and other psychological challenges.

Continuing education in Eye Movement Desensitization and Reprocessing (EMDR) therapy is crucial for therapists who wish to maintain their expertise, stay updated with the latest developments in the field, and refine their practice over time. Various resources and organizations offer opportunities for continuing education in EMDR, providing platforms for learning, professional development, and community engagement. Key organizations for EMDR Continuing Education include the EMDR International Association (EMDRIA), EMDR Europe Association, EMDR Institute, Inc., and EMDR Humanitarian Assistance Programs (HAP).

Online resources and publications such as the Journal of EMDR Practice and Research, the EMDR Research Foundation, and online learning platforms offer courses and webinars on a range of topics, from basic principles to advanced clinical applications. Attending workshops and conferences specifically designed for EMDR practitioners is another excellent way for therapists to engage in continuing education. Participating in peer consultation groups is an invaluable form of continuing education, offering a space for therapists to discuss cases, explore new ideas, and receive feedback in a collaborative environment, fostering ongoing learning and professional growth.

Supervision and professional support are essential components of a dedicated therapist's commitment to continuing education in EMDR therapy. By engaging with the resources and organizations available, therapists can ensure that their practice remains effective, evidence-based, and responsive to the evolving needs of their clients.

Supervision is a crucial aspect of the practice of Eye Movement Desensitization and Reprocessing (EMDR) therapy, providing a structured framework for professional growth, quality assurance, and ethical practice. It helps therapists refine their clinical skills, deepen their understanding of the therapy's principles and applications, and integrate EMDR more effectively into their broader therapeutic practice. Supervision also offers professional guidance and support, particularly for clients who have experienced significant trauma. This support helps therapists maintain their mental health and well-being while carrying out this demanding work.

Reflective practice is a key component of professional development in EMDR therapy, and supervision encourages therapists to critically reflect on their work. Supervisors assist therapists in examining their therapeutic approach, decision-making processes, and the dynamics of the therapist-client relationship, promoting continuous learning and adaptation.

Supervision plays a critical role in navigating the ethical considerations inherent in EMDR therapy. Supervisors ensure that therapists adhere to ethical guidelines and standards of practice, providing guidance on issues such as informed consent, confidentiality, and managing dual relationships. This ethical oversight helps to safeguard the well-being of clients and uphold the integrity of the therapeutic process.

The structure of EMDR supervision typically involves regular, scheduled sessions between the therapist and an experienced supervisor, which can be conducted individually or in group settings. Many therapists also engage in peer supervision groups as a complementary form of professional support.

Building a professional support network is an essential component of EMDR therapy practice. A broader network of peers, mentors, and colleagues provides a rich resource for collaboration, learning, and emotional support. This network not only enhances the therapist's professional development but also contributes to the resilience and sustainability of their practice.

Strategies for building a professional support network include engaging with professional associations, participating in continuing education, using online forums and social media, and forming or joining local peer consultation groups. These strategies help therapists stay connected with the latest developments in the field, develop a sense of community, and advocate for the recognition and application of EMDR therapy within the wider mental health field.

Eye Movement Desensitization and Reprocessing (EMDR) therapy is a therapeutic practice that prioritizes the welfare of clients while maintaining their dignity and respect. Ethical principles in EMDR therapy include client welfare, confidentiality, professional competence, integrity, and responsibility to society. These principles guide therapeutic decisions and actions, ensuring informed consent, respecting client autonomy, and practicing within one's scope of competence.

Clinical advancements, scientific discoveries, and the incorporation of EMDR into broader therapeutic practices are all driving the landscape of EMDR therapy to constantly change. This environment offers opportunities for professional growth and challenges practitioners to continuously adapt and expand their knowledge and skills.

Innovations in EMDR practice are multifaceted, encompassing technological advancements, new protocols, and exploring EMDR's application to a wider range of psychological issues. Recent years have seen the advent of virtual reality (VR) as a tool to enhance the immersive experience of recalling traumatic events, potentially increasing the efficacy of the therapy for certain individuals. EMDR protocols are also being improved for conditions like acute stress, complex PTSD, and attachment disorders. This shows that the therapy is flexible, and that people are always working to make it fit different patient needs.

Research into the mechanisms underlying EMDR's effectiveness continues to deepen our understanding of how the therapy facilitates psychological healing. More research into the effects of EMDR on neurobiological processes, memory consolidation, and the role of bilateral stimulation gives us a fuller picture of the therapy and its possible uses.

The integration of EMDR with other therapeutic modalities represents a significant area of development and exploration. This approach acknowledges the complexity of psychological disorders and the need for comprehensive treatment strategies that address the multifaceted nature of individual clients' experiences. For instance, combining EMDR with cognitive-behavioral therapy (CBT) can offer a powerful blend of trauma processing and cognitive restructuring, enhancing outcomes for clients with trauma and comorbid conditions like anxiety or depression.

Future challenges and research directions in EMDR therapy include ensuring accessibility and efficacy across diverse populations and cultural contexts, exploring EMDR's effectiveness in treating emerging psychological concerns, and pursuing a deeper understanding of the neurobiological mechanisms underpinning EMDR's effectiveness. The journey of professional growth in EMDR therapy is a dynamic and ongoing process marked by continuous learning, adaptation, and a commitment to exploring new frontiers in treatment.

CHAPTER FIVE

ETHICAL AND CULTURAL CONSIDERATIONS

In the ever-changing landscape of Eye Movement Desensitization and Reprocessing (EMDR) therapy, ethical and cultural considerations are critical to ensuring that treatment is effective while also respecting clients' diverse backgrounds. This chapter delves into the critical aspects of ethical practice and cultural sensitivity in EMDR therapy, emphasizing the importance of understanding and addressing the nuanced needs of clients from diverse cultural backgrounds. The goal is to create an inclusive and equitable therapeutic environment that values each client's unique experiences and identities.

Cultural sensitivity in EMDR therapy refers to the therapist's awareness, comprehension, and respect for the cultural differences and similarities that exist between themselves and their clients. This sensitivity is essential in creating a therapeutic environment that feels safe and welcoming to clients from all backgrounds. Understanding the impact of culture on trauma is critical for adapting EMDR therapy to various cultural contexts. Cultural beliefs and values can influence what constitutes trauma, how people cope with distress, and their willingness to seek and participate in therapy.

Incorporating cultural competence into therapy, making language and communication adjustments, modifying EMDR protocols, addressing cultural concepts of distress, engaging with the community, and being sensitive to socioeconomic and political contexts are all effective strategies for adapting EMDR to diverse cultural contexts. Embracing these adaptations allows therapists to ensure that EMDR is a culturally appropriate, effective, and respectful therapeutic option for people from all backgrounds.

Linguistic and communicative considerations are critical in the practice of EMDR therapy, especially when dealing with clients from various cultural backgrounds. Effective communication is the foundation of any therapeutic process, and in EMDR, which guides clients through emotionally charged memories, clear understanding and expression are essential. Adapting linguistic and communicative strategies to each client's needs makes EMDR therapy both accessible and effective.

To be effective and relevant for clients from various cultural contexts, EMDR therapy requires a strong commitment to cultural competence, sensitivity, and flexibility. By accepting these adaptations, therapists can ensure that EMDR remains a versatile tool for healing across cultures.

EMDR therapy is an effective method for treating clients who speak a different language than the therapist. Competent interpretation services are required, including fluent interpreters who are familiar with EMDR therapy terminology and concepts. Cultural nuances in communication can have a significant impact on how emotions are expressed or discussed, and understanding these nuances allows EMDR therapists to tailor their communication approach to ensure clients feel understood and respected.

Nonverbal cues play an important role in communication, and they vary greatly between cultures. Therapists should be aware of these differences and adapt their therapeutic approach accordingly. This could include finding more comfortable methods of bilateral stimulation for the client or explaining the purpose of eye movements in a way that is consistent with the client's cultural understanding.

Regularly checking for understanding is critical in EMDR therapy, especially when linguistic and cultural differences exist. Therapists should use straightforward language and avoid jargon, periodically asking clients to express their understanding of the process or instructions. This practice helps to identify miscommunications early on and ensures that the client fully understands and participates in the therapy process.

Training and self-education in linguistic diversity, cultural communication styles, and the use of interpreters in therapy are critical for gaining and maintaining competency in this area. Engaging in cultural competence training, seeking supervision from culturally informed practitioners, and learning from clients' diverse experiences are all effective strategies for improving communicative effectiveness in EMDR.

Eye Movement Desensitization and Reprocessing (EMDR) therapy is increasingly used in a variety of cultural settings. More and more research and clinical perspectives demonstrate how effective and adaptable it is. These studies and insights are critical for understanding how EMDR can be effectively tailored to meet the diverse needs of people from various cultural backgrounds, ensuring that the therapy is inclusive and accessible to everyone.

The effectiveness of EMDR in various cultural contexts is frequently dependent on the therapist's ability to tailor the therapy to the client's cultural, linguistic, and communicative norms. Studies have documented a variety of adaptations, including incorporating cultural rituals into the therapy process, changing the language used to describe and engage with the therapy, and adjusting the pace and structure of sessions to better match the client's cultural expectations of healing practices.

The use of EMDR is an effective treatment for clients who speak multiple languages, but it necessitates a thorough understanding of cultural nuances as well as sensitivity and awareness.

EMDR treatment has been shown to have a significant impact on clients' healing processes, especially when therapists consciously incorporate their cultural background into the therapy. This integration can increase the therapy's relevance and resonance for the client, creating a sense of validation and understanding that aids in the healing process. Studies and perspectives on EMDR therapy's cultural efficacy highlight the importance of cultural sensitivity and adaptation in its practice. EMDR therapists can ensure true inclusivity in their practice by embracing the diversity of the human experience and tailoring therapy to respect and incorporate cultural nuances.

Ethical practice is the foundation of any therapeutic intervention, and it plays an especially important role in Eye Movement Desensitization and Reprocessing (EMDR) therapy. Adhering to a strong ethical framework ensures that this potent therapeutic tool is used with the utmost responsibility, integrity, and regard for the client's welfare. Specific ethical principles in EMDR practice are intended to protect the client and improve the therapeutic process. These principles include beneficence and nonmaleficence, informed consent, confidentiality, competence, integrity, respect for autonomy, and the management of power dynamics and therapeutic boundaries.

Beneficence and nonmaleficence are central to EMDR therapy, as practitioners must ensure that the benefits of the therapy outweigh any potential risks to their clients. Informed consent entails providing a thorough explanation of the EMDR process, including potential risks and benefits, as well as any treatment alternatives. Confidentiality is essential in creating a safe therapeutic environment, and practitioners must safeguard sensitive client information. Therapists must maintain a high level of competence through continued education, training, and supervision. Integrity entails being honest, transparent, and truthful about their qualifications, potential EMDR therapy outcomes, and any limitations to their practice. Respect for autonomy highlights the significance of a collaborative therapeutic relationship in which the client's voice is central to the process.

Managing power dynamics and therapeutic boundaries is essential for creating a safe and respectful environment in EMDR therapy. Power dynamics are defined as an imbalance of authority and influence between the therapist and the client. In EMDR therapy, where clients frequently explore deeply vulnerable aspects of their experiences, sensitivity to power dynamics is even more important. Therapists must consciously adopt practices that minimize the potential for abuse of power, including:

Empowering the Client: encouraging clients to participate actively in their therapy, make treatment decisions, and express their needs and preferences. Transparent Decision-Making: Therapists should collaborate with clients to make therapeutic decisions, including the selection of specific EMDR protocols, explaining the rationale for these decisions, and considering the clients' feedback. Recognizing clients' vulnerability, particularly when processing traumatic memories, and approaching these moments with the utmost sensitivity and respect is critical to maintaining a therapeutic balance of power.

EMDR therapy is a therapeutic approach that prioritizes the client's needs and well-being while keeping the therapy professional and goal oriented. Maintaining therapeutic boundaries requires professionalism in interaction, physical and emotional boundaries, and boundary awareness. Confidentiality, informed consent, and patient rights are fundamental ethical principles in EMDR therapy that protect the client and create a trustworthy therapeutic environment.

Confidentiality refers to the therapist's obligation to keep all client information private, only sharing it with the client's explicit consent or when legally required. Informed consent informs clients about the nature of EMDR therapy, including its benefits, risks, and potential alternatives to treatment. Respecting patient rights includes the client's right to privacy, dignity, and respectful care. Therapists must respect their clients' autonomy, provide therapy free of discrimination or prejudice, and ensure access to care.

EMDR therapy is particularly effective when working with vulnerable populations, such as refugees and torture survivors. These populations frequently experience high levels of trauma and face unique challenges that can complicate traditional therapeutic approaches. The structured but flexible framework of EMDR can be especially effective in dealing with the complex trauma profiles that are common in these populations.

Working with refugees and torture survivors necessitates cultural sensitivity, an understanding of their cultural background and current context, as well as the establishment of safety and stability. This entails creating a safe therapeutic environment and employing EMDR stabilization techniques to manage acute distress and dissociation. The phased approach of EMDR is especially useful when working with this population, allowing for gradual exposure to traumatic memories after adequate stabilization has been achieved. Early phases are centered on developing trust, teaching coping mechanisms, and ensuring the individual has enough resources to confront their traumatic memories without becoming overwhelmed.

Integrated support is frequently required, and EMDR therapy should be part of a comprehensive care plan that addresses the diverse challenges that these individuals face.

EMDR therapy has shown promise in reducing PTSD symptoms and improving overall well-being for refugees and torture survivors. Success stories include significant reductions in flashbacks, nightmares, and anxiety, as well as increased feelings of hope and empowerment. These findings highlight EMDR's ability to promote profound healing, even in the face of extreme and complex trauma.

Eye Movement Desensitization and Reprocessing (EMDR) therapy is an effective method for addressing deep-seated traumas in vulnerable populations, such as refugees and torture survivors. Therapists can provide effective, compassionate care that promotes recovery and resilience by tailoring EMDR to their patients' specific needs and context.

Children and adolescents in vulnerable situations can benefit from EMDR therapy, which provides a trauma-informed approach that considers the developmental needs of younger clients. This group may include people who have been subjected to abuse, neglect, loss, or other traumatic events that have had a negative impact on their emotional and psychological health. Adapting EMDR interventions to be age-appropriate is critical, such as using simpler language, incorporating play therapy techniques, or employing creative methods like drawing or storytelling. Involving caregivers in the therapeutic process can provide additional support and strengthen the healing environment outside of therapy sessions.

Building trust and safety is critical because children and adolescents may feel especially vulnerable when discussing traumatic experiences. Establishing a safe and trusting therapeutic relationship encourages participation in the therapy process. Addressing complex trauma necessitates a phased approach that prioritizes stabilization and coping skills prior to trauma processing.

EMDR therapy has shown promising results in treating trauma in children and adolescents, with reductions in PTSD symptoms, anxiety, and depression. Furthermore, EMDR can help foster resilience, boost self-esteem, and improve overall functioning in school and social settings.

Because of its adaptability, EMDR therapy can be tailored to the elderly and people with disabilities, both of whom may have unique vulnerabilities and therapeutic needs. Adapting EMDR for the elderly may necessitate taking a life-span approach, accommodating cognitive and physical limitations, and making the therapy environment, bilateral stimulation, or assistive technologies accessible.

Ethical considerations in EMDR practice, such as managing power dynamics, maintaining therapeutic boundaries, and ensuring confidentiality and informed consent, are the foundation of trust and safety required for effective therapy. These principles guide therapists in upholding their clients' dignity and rights, ensuring that EMDR therapy is carried out with the highest level of integrity and professionalism.

Working with vulnerable populations creates unique challenges and opportunities for EMDR therapy. Tailoring the approach to meet the specific needs of these groups demonstrates not only EMDR's versatility but also its ability to promote healing and resilience in the face of profound adversity. Finally, EMDR therapy is critical in addressing the deep-seated traumas experienced by vulnerable populations, demonstrating the importance of ethical and cultural considerations in its practice.

CONCLUSION

Reflecting on the journey through the comprehensive exploration of Eye Movement Desensitization and Reprocessing (EMDR) therapy presented in this book, it's clear how profound and wide-reaching the impact of EMDR can be. From its roots in treating PTSD to its applications across a spectrum of psychological conditions, the versatility and efficacy of EMDR therapy are undeniable. Each chapter has tried to give you a full picture of this powerful therapy tool by talking about everything from the basic ideas and research behind EMDR to how it is used in therapy, how to become a therapist, how to supervise therapists, and how important it is to think about ethics and culture.

As the author, my hope is that this book not only serves as a resource for those new to EMDR but also enriches the practice of experienced therapists. The journey through the structured phases of EMDR, its adaptability to diverse client needs, and the emphasis on continuous professional development underscore the dynamic nature of this therapy. Moreover, the exploration of EMDR's application with vulnerable populations highlights its potential to foster healing and resilience in even the most challenging circumstances.

I invite you, the reader, to share your thoughts and reflections on this book by leaving a review on Amazon. Your feedback is incredibly important to me, not only as a measure of the book's impact but also as a way to engage in a broader conversation about EMDR therapy. Whether you are a practitioner, a client, or simply someone interested in the field of psychotherapy, your insights and experiences can contribute significantly to the ongoing dialogue surrounding EMDR and its place in mental health care.

Thank you for accompanying me on this exploration of EMDR therapy. It is my sincere hope that the knowledge shared within these pages inspires and supports you, whether in your professional practice or personal journey toward healing and growth. Your review on Amazon would be greatly appreciated and would help others discover the transformative power of EMDR therapy.

BOOK 7

SOMATIC
PSYCHOTHERAPY

INTRODUCTION

In the pulsating heart of human experience, where mind and body intertwine in a continuous dialogue, somatic psychotherapy emerges as a bridge between the individual's inner and outer worlds. This book, "Somatic Psychotherapy," arises from the desire to explore and deepen this dialogue, offering a comprehensive guide to the theory and practice of one of the most innovative forms of therapy.

Somatic psychotherapy, with its roots firmly planted in the disciplines of psychology, medicine, and Eastern body practices, represents a holistic approach to healing. It goes beyond the traditional mind-body paradigm, inviting us to consider the body not only as a mere instrument or vehicle of human experience but as an active participant and co-creator of our psychological and emotional reality.

This book aims to serve both mental health professionals and those approaching the concept of somatic psychotherapy for the first time. Through a historical overview, exploration of key theories and techniques, and presentation of case studies and research, we aim to provide a solid and accessible understanding of how somatic can be integrated into therapeutic work.

Somatic psychotherapy offers unique tools for addressing trauma, anxiety, depression, and many other disorders, promoting well-being through the recognition and appreciation of the body in its entirety. This book is an invitation to explore these possibilities, to discover how somatic work can enrich therapeutic practice, and, above all, to recognize the transformative power of deep listening to our bodies.

With the hope that "Somatic Psychotherapy" can serve as a beacon for those navigating the sometimes-turbulent waters of healing and well-being, I invite you to embark on this journey with me. Through the following pages, we can together discover how the integration of mind, body, and spirit can open new pathways to emotional freedom and personal fulfillment.

CHAPTER ONE

DEFINITION AND ORIGINS OF SOMATIC PSYCHOTHERAPY

Somatic psychotherapy resides at the intersection of mind, body, and spirit, offering a holistic approach to healing that recognizes and values the inseparable link between physical and psychological well-being. This chapter lays the groundwork for understanding somatic psychotherapy, exploring its definition, key principles, and historical evolution. Through this journey, we aim to build a solid understanding of how the body can become a gateway to profound self-understanding and emotional experience.

Somatic psychotherapy, with its roots in ancient wisdom and modern scientific discoveries, invites us to reconsider the role of the body in our emotional and psychological lives. This chapter introduces readers to the foundational concepts that form the basis of somatic psychotherapy, laying the groundwork for a deeper exploration of its applications and techniques in subsequent chapters.

Definition and Principles

Somatic psychotherapy is based on the premise that the body and mind are inherently connected and that this connection plays a crucial role in mental health and the healing process. Unlike traditional therapeutic approaches that tend to focus exclusively on the cognitive and behavioral aspects, somatic psychotherapy integrates the body into therapeutic practice, valuing physical sensations, movements, and bodily energy as key components of the human experience.

Definition

Somatic psychotherapy is a therapeutic approach that incorporates body awareness and body techniques to explore and address psychological issues. Using techniques such as mindful breathing, movement, therapeutic touch, and sensory awareness, somatic psychotherapy seeks to unlock, and release accumulated physical and emotional tensions, promoting healing and holistic well-being.

Key Principles

- *Mind-Body Interconnection:* At the core of somatic psychotherapy is the belief that mind, and body are not only connected but also mutually influence each other. Emotions and thoughts can manifest through sensations and changes in the body, just as physical conditions can affect mental and emotional states.

- *Body Wisdom:* This principle acknowledges that the body possesses intrinsic wisdom and a capacity for self-healing. Listening to and interpreting the body's signals can provide deep insights into emotional and psychological issues.

- *Experience-Oriented Process:* Somatic psychotherapy focuses on the present experience of the body rather than purely cognitive interpretations or analyses. This approach enables clients to directly experience shifts and changes in bodily awareness, facilitating deeper healing processes.

- *Integration:* A fundamental goal of somatic psychotherapy is to integrate physical, emotional, and cognitive experiences, promoting a sense of unity and coherence within the self. This integration helps individuals feel more whole, connected, and at peace with themselves.

- *Empowerment and Self-Healing:* Somatic psychotherapy aims to empower the individual, providing tools and techniques to support self-healing and self-regulation. This approach promotes personal empowerment and resilience.

The Mind-Body Connection

The relationship between the mind and body has been a subject of study, debate, and reflection since antiquity, evolving through various philosophical, medical, and psychological paradigms. Somatic psychotherapy, rooted in contemporary understanding of this connection, deepens the dialogue between the physical and emotional dimensions of being, revealing how each influence and shapes the other in a continuous cycle of interaction and feedback.

Biological and Neuroscientific Foundations

Recent discoveries in neuroscience have significantly enriched our understanding of the mind-body connection, demonstrating that emotions and thoughts are not isolated phenomena in the mind but rather experiences that involve specific bodily activations. Research has highlighted, for example, how areas of the brain involved in emotional regulation, such as the amygdala and prefrontal cortex, are actively connected to the autonomic nervous system, influencing bodily functions such as heart rate, breathing, and muscle tension.

These findings underscore the importance of considering the body not only as a passive recipient of stimuli or a container for the mind but as an active participant in the emotional and cognitive process. Somatic psychotherapy utilizes this understanding as a basis for techniques aimed at restoring balance and promoting healing through awareness and modulation of bodily responses.

Body Memory

A key concept in somatic psychotherapy is that of body memory: the idea that the body retains a trace of lived experiences, including traumas and stresses, in the form of muscular tensions, altered breathing patterns, and postures. These bodily "memories" can influence our behavior, emotions, and thought patterns in often unconscious ways, leading to automatic responses that may be dysfunctional or limiting.

Through mindful exploration of these body memories, somatic psychotherapy seeks to free individuals from old patterns and promote new possibilities for being and acting in the world. Somatic work, therefore, aims not only at resolving specific psychological disorders but also at releasing bodily tensions and blocks that may limit an individual's ability to live fully and authentically.

Integration and healing

Somatic psychotherapy sees the integration of mind, body, and spirit as fundamental to healing. This does not simply mean acknowledging the presence of a mind-body connection but actively working to harmonize and align these dimensions of being. Through practices that increase body awareness, such as meditation, mindful movement, and deep breathing, individuals can learn to tune into their physical and emotional needs, promoting a sense of well-being and integrity.

This integration enables not only greater self-regulation and resilience in the face of stress and trauma but also deepening interpersonal relationships and increased openness to richer and

SOMATIC PSYCHOTHERAPY

more meaningful life experiences. The mind-body connection, therefore, becomes not only a field of healing but also of personal transformation and growth.

The recognition and exploration of the mind-body connection in somatic psychotherapy offer a powerful path to understanding and healing. Through the integration of techniques that foster awareness and regulation of bodily experiences, somatic psychotherapy opens new avenues for addressing psychological disorders, promoting health and wellness, and supporting a fuller and more authentic life experience.

Historical Overview

The history of somatic psychotherapy spans across different cultures and epochs, reflecting humanity's long quest to understand and heal the relationship between mind and body. This subsection traces a path through key moments and influential figures that have contributed to the formation and development of somatic psychotherapy as we know it today.

Ancient Roots

The concept of the interconnectedness between mind and body is not new. Ancient medical practices, such as Ayurveda in India and traditional Chinese medicine, have always recognized and treated the individual in holistic terms, considering the balance of physical, emotional, and spiritual aspects fundamental to health. These traditions have emphasized the importance of techniques such as meditation, mindful movement (e.g., yoga, tai chi), and breathwork to maintain or restore this balance.

The Influence of Psychoanalysis

Sigmund Freud's psychoanalysis, which dates to the early 20th century, popularized the notion that unconscious mental processes, including those originating from childhood traumas, can affect behavior and mental health. Wilhelm Reich, a student of Freud, extended these ideas by proposing that emotional repressions could manifest as physical tensions, a concept he termed "muscular armor." Reich is considered one of the founding fathers of somatic psychotherapy for his pioneering work in exploring the link between emotional and bodily states.

Twentieth-Century Evolution

Throughout the 20th century, interest in the mind-body connection continued to grow, leading to the development of various schools of thought and therapeutic practices that emphasize the importance of the body in psychological healing. Figures such as Alexander Lowen, creator of bioenergetics, and Moshe Feldenkrais, founder of the Feldenkrais Method, introduced techniques that utilize movement and body awareness to address emotional and psychological blocks.

Somatic Psychotherapy Today

Today, somatic psychotherapy encompasses a wide range of approaches and techniques, all with the common goal of integrating body and mind in the therapeutic process. Approaches such as Sensorimotor Psychotherapy, developed by Pat Ogden, and the work of Peter Levine on Somatic Experiencing focus on resolving trauma through regulating physiological responses and increasing body awareness.

The most recent findings in neuroscience, developmental psychology, and trauma studies continue to influence somatic psychotherapy. The growing evidence of the effectiveness of these approaches in treating a wide range of psychological disorders has led to a broader recognition of their importance and utility in therapeutic practice.

CHAPTER TWO

KEY THEORIES IN SOMATIC PSYCHOTHERAPY
Wilhelm Reich and character analysis

Wilhelm Reich, one of Freud's most innovative disciples, left an indelible mark on somatic psychotherapy through his theory of character analysis and the concept of muscular armor. Reich believed that psychological defenses manifested not only at the behavioral or psychological level but also in the body in the form of chronic muscular tensions. This section explores Reich's contribution, outlining how his ideas laid the groundwork for the integration of somatic into therapeutic practice.

The Concept of Muscular Armor
Reich introduced the concept of "muscular armor" to describe how emotional repressions and psychological conflicts crystallize in the body, leading to energetic blocks and chronic muscular tensions. According to Reich, these tensions serve as a defense mechanism to contain anxiety and prevent the expression of painful or socially unacceptable emotions. However, while muscular armor may offer temporary protection, in the long run, it inhibits the natural flow of life energy (which Reich called "orgone"), leading to both psychological and physical dysfunctions.

Character Analysis
Reich's character analysis was an extension of psychoanalysis aimed at understanding and modifying deeply rooted behavioral patterns that form an individual's "character structure." Reich believed that these character structures developed early in life in response to childhood experiences and traumas and were expressed both psychologically and bodily. Through character analysis, Reich sought to free the individual from the chains of old emotional wounds, facilitating a freer and more authentic expression of the self.

Techniques and Applications

Reich developed a series of techniques to work with muscular armor, including breathing exercises, massages, and other body practices, with the aim of releasing physical tensions and, consequently, freeing repressed emotions. This somatic therapeutic approach aimed not only to resolve psychological symptoms but also to promote overall well-being, increasing the capacity for pleasure and emotional connection.

Impact and Legacy

Reich's theories and practices profoundly influenced the development of somatic psychotherapy, inspiring subsequent generations of therapists to further explore the role of the body in the therapeutic process. Although some of his ideas and methods have been subject to controversy and criticism, Reich's contribution to understanding the mind-body connection and clinical practice remains fundamental. His emphasis on integrating psychological analysis and bodywork has paved new paths in mental health care, underscoring the importance of a holistic approach to healing.

Wilhelm Reich and character analysis represent a pivotal moment in the history of somatic psychotherapy. His pioneering view of the body as a field of psychological expression and healing laid the foundation for therapeutic approaches that recognize the inseparable interconnection between our emotional life and our physical being. As we proceed, we will see how these principles have been adapted and expanded in subsequent somatic theories and practices, bearing witness to Reich's enduring legacy in the field of mental health.

Bioenergetics by Alexander Lowen

Alexander Lowen, a psychiatrist, and analyst was a student of Wilhelm Reich and developed bioenergetics to understand and treat psychological tensions through the body. Bioenergetics is based on the belief that the body and mind are functionally identical; what happens in the mind reflects what happens in the body, and vice versa. This section examines Lowen's contribution to somatic psychotherapy, highlighting the theory, techniques, and impact of bioenergetics.

Foundations of Bioenergetics

Bioenergetics is based on the idea that every emotional experience has a corresponding manifestation in the body in the form of muscle tension or energy. These tensions can become chronic, leading to what Lowen described as a decrease in vitality and pleasure in life. Bioenergetic work aims to identify and release these tensions to restore the natural flow of life energy, thus promoting emotional and physical health.

Bioenergetic Techniques

Bioenergetic techniques include exercises aimed at increasing awareness of one's body and releasing accumulated tensions. These can range from deep breathing exercises, stretching, and movements that stimulate specific areas of the body to more direct techniques such as working on voice and emotional expression through the body. Lowen emphasized the importance of grounding as a source of energy and stability, encouraging practices that connect the individual to the support and strength of the earth through the feet and legs.

The Role of the Bioenergetic Therapist
The bioenergetic therapist works collaboratively with the client to identify areas of tension and energy blocks in the body. Through careful observation and guiding the client through specific exercises, the therapist helps to explore and release these tensions. This process not only alleviates physical symptoms but can also lead to significant insights regarding underlying emotional issues, thus facilitating psychological healing.

Impact and Legacy of Bioenergetics
Bioenergetics has had a significant impact on the field of somatic psychotherapy, extending and deepening the understanding of the mind-body connection. Its emphasis on bodywork as a tool to access and transform emotional experiences has influenced many other somatic approaches. Bioenergetics continues to be practiced and taught worldwide, testifying to its effectiveness and the importance of bodywork in psychological therapy.

Alexander Lowen's Bioenergetics also stands as a significant pillar in somatic psychotherapy, offering a powerful methodology for exploring and healing the relationship between body and mind. Through his work, Lowen gave people practical tools to release their full potential and promote integration while easing physical and emotional tensions.

Stanley Keleman's Body Psychology
Stanley Keleman, a pioneer in the field of somatic psychotherapy, developed somatic psychology as an approach that emphasizes the role of bodily structure and formative processes in shaping psychological and emotional experiences. Through his work, Keleman explored how the body organizes itself in response to life experiences, creating patterns of behavior and emotional reactions that are visible in the body's form and movement. This section examines the theory, practices, and impact of somatic psychology in the field of somatic psychotherapy.

Foundations of Somatic Psychology
Keleman conceives of the body as a sequence of organized forms that develop over time in response to life experiences. These shapes, or "body patterns," are not static; rather, they are constantly changing because of interactions with the outside world, interpersonal relationships, and

emotional experiences. Somatic psychology is concerned with how these patterns influence and are influenced by the psyche, providing a framework for understanding the individual.

Techniques of Somatic Psychology

Techniques of somatic psychology focus on exploring and modulating the body's formative processes. This may include work with breathing, movement, posture, and touch to help individuals become more aware of their body patterns and how these patterns influence their emotional and psychological well-being. Keleman emphasizes the importance of "self-formation," a process through which individuals learn to consciously influence their bodily organization to promote health and psychological adaptation.

The Self-Formation Approach

Self-formation is a key concept in somatic psychology, involving the individual's ability to actively participate in their own emotional and bodily evolution. Through self-formation practices, individuals can learn to modulate their muscle tension, breathing, and movements, thereby influencing their emotional and psychological states. This process enables greater autonomy and agency in self-regulation and the management of stress and trauma.

Impact and Legacy of Somatic Psychology

Somatic psychology has had a profound impact on somatic psychotherapy, expanding the understanding of the link between body and psyche. Keleman's work has inspired therapists and practitioners worldwide, offering a model for integrating bodywork into psychotherapeutic practice. His emphasis on self-formation and the ability to actively modulate one's bodily experience have provided valuable tools for personal well-being and psychological growth.

Stanley Keleman's Somatic Psychology, like the contributions in previous topics, represents a significant contribution to the field of somatic psychotherapy, offering a unique perspective on the dynamic interaction between body and mind. Through understanding and modulating body patterns, somatic psychology provides powerful avenues for healing and psychological integration, emphasizing the importance of bodily awareness and self-formation on the path to health and well-being.

CHAPTER THREE

OPTIMIZING MUSCLE HEALTH THROUGH SOMATIC PRACTICES

Muscular discomfort is a complex issue that stems from our natural protective instincts, which are deeply rooted in our bodies. These muscles contract when we experience physical trauma or prolonged stress, acting as a defense mechanism to prevent further injury. However, if left unaddressed, this temporary shield can transform into chronic tightness and persistent pain.

To understand the origins of muscle tightness and pain, it is essential to recognize the signs of muscular tightness, such as reduced mobility, stiffness upon awakening, or a persistent, dull ache. Recognizing these signs leads to uncovering their roots, which are often complex and highly individualized. Some triggers may be acute injuries, such as sprains or muscle tears, where the body immobilizes the injured area to foster healing. Without proper treatment and rehabilitation, these muscles may remain contracted, evolving into chronic pain and tightness.

For others, the origins may be less overt, involving factors like repetitive strain, poor posture, or emotional stress. Repetitive strain injuries, born from the continuous use of specific muscle groups, are often observed in individuals with certain jobs or hobbies, leading to microtears and inflammation. Poor posture, whether in sitting or standing, imposes undue strain on muscles and joints, causing certain muscles to tighten in compensation, leading to discomfort. Emotional stress can also physically manifest, particularly in the neck, shoulders, and back, as muscles tense in response to psychological distress.

Comprehensive treatment plans should consider physical, emotional, and lifestyle elements. By addressing these various aspects, individuals can embark on a journey toward relieving their discomfort, culminating in improved mobility, diminished pain, and enhanced overall health.

Temporary relief from muscle pain and discomfort is often sought through massages, chiropractic adjustments, and other forms of physical therapy. However, these treatments often do not address the underlying habitual nature of muscle contraction and tension that leads to chronic pain and dysfunction. The short-term effectiveness of common treatments is limited, as muscles may revert to their tensed state soon after the therapy session, particularly if the underlying cause of tension, such as poor posture or repetitive stress, is not corrected.

Muscle habituation is a condition where muscles remain in a state of contraction due to repeated use, stress, or injury. This state is intertwined with the nervous system's control of muscles and is influenced by neuromuscular patterns, sensory motor amnesia (SMA), stress, and emotional factors. To overcome these limitations, it is crucial to address the habitual nature of muscle contraction through several key strategies:

1. Awareness and education: Becoming aware of one's own body and the pattern of tension is the first step. Somatic education focuses on increasing body awareness, allowing individuals to recognize and alter their habitual patterns.

2. Consistent practice: Changing neuromuscular patterns requires consistent practice and re-education. Somatic exercises designed to retrain the nervous system and muscular control offer a way to gradually replace old patterns with new, more functional ones.

3. Addressing emotional stress: Understanding the link between emotional stress and physical tension is vital. Techniques that address both the psychological and physical aspects of stress can lead to more comprehensive and lasting relief.

4. Integrative approaches: Combining somatic practices with other treatments can provide a more holistic and effective approach to managing and preventing muscle tension.

In summary, temporary relief measures can provide immediate comfort, but they fall short of addressing the habitual muscle contraction that often underlies chronic pain and dysfunction. Re-education is a pathway back to optimal health and functionality and entails retraining the brain to reconnect with and regain control over these 'forgotten' muscle groups. A key strategy for addressing SMA involves targeted movement exercises focusing on the affected muscles, which are less about strength or endurance but more about gentle, deliberate movements designed to rekindle the mind-body connection.

Central to SMA re-education is the concept of pandiculation, which

SOMATIC PSYCHOTHERAPY

involves conscious muscle contraction and a slow, controlled release, in contrast to passive muscle stretching. This technique resembles a natural yawn, where the body first tightens and then gradually relaxes.

Treatment approaches like Hanna Somatics or the Feldenkrais method involve specific movements to counteract SMA, fostering greater bodily awareness and refined muscle control. The re-education process also involves unlearning—releasing harmful postural habits, movement patterns, and emotional responses contributing to SMA.

In overcoming SMA, patience and consistency are vital. The body requires time to adjust and adopt new functional patterns. Regular practice of somatic exercises and a mindful approach to daily activities can gradually lead to significant improvements, paving the way for a harmonious and pain-free bodily experience.

Somatic practices are deeply rooted in the connection between the physical and psychological aspects of our being, offering a spectrum of benefits that transcend mere pain relief. These practices focus on the internal experience of movement and sensation, bringing about a myriad of life-enhancing benefits.

1. Enhanced Flexibility: The first and often most immediately noticeable benefit of somatic practices is the enhancement of flexibility. This is not just a domain for athletes seeking a wide range of motion but is essential for anyone aiming for a healthy, active lifestyle. Through their gentle, controlled exercises that focus on the internal experience of movement, they encourage muscular relaxation, leading to increased ease and range of motion. This improvement in flexibility is vital for injury prevention, supports healthy aging, and elevates functionality in daily activities.

2. Improved Posture: In our contemporary world, poor posture has become a common ailment. Somatic practices delve into the underlying causes of poor posture, guiding the body to release chronic muscle contractions and embrace healthier postural habits. This newfound postural awareness often leads to decreased discomfort in areas like the back, neck, and joints. Furthermore, improved posture enhances breathing, circulation, and overall appearance, fostering a sense of confidence and well-being.

3. Fluid Movement: The grace and ease of movement, often admired in dancers and athletes, are beneficial for everyone. Somatic practices enhance movement quality by developing body awareness, coordination, and control. This heightened awareness and intention in movement often unveil a new level of harmony and efficiency, transforming everyday activities into smoother, more pleasurable experiences.

4. Effective Pain Management: Chronic pain, a prevalent issue, can

SOMATIC PSYCHOTHERAPY

significantly diminish life quality. Somatic practices present a non-invasive, medication-free approach to managing and often alleviating pain. By addressing the neuromuscular patterns at the root of pain, these practices enable individuals to foster a supportive and functional relationship with their bodies. Many find substantial relief from chronic discomfort as they learn to release tension and move in natural, pain-free ways.

5. Emotional and psychological Well-being: The benefits of somatic practices extend into the emotional and psychological spheres. As individuals forge a deeper connection with their bodies, they often experience enhanced mental and emotional health. The introspective focus on physical sensations can be meditative and calming, reducing stress and anxiety levels. Moreover, gaining control over one's body and reducing pain can lead to feelings of empowerment and elevated self-esteem, fostering a more positive life perspective.

Somatic techniques have a unique impact on our physical and mental health, focusing on the internal experience of movement and sensation. They offer transformative tools for those seeking pain relief, improved physical abilities, or a deeper sense of mental and emotional equilibrium.

CHAPTER FOUR

THE FUNDAMENTALS AND EXERCISES OF SOMATICS

In exploring the essence of somatic exercises, we find ourselves considering the fundamental concept of pandiculation, a process far more intricate than mere muscle stretching. This natural, instinctual act, often observed in both animals and humans upon waking or after periods of inactivity, serves a purpose beyond the simple. It resets muscle length and tension, releasing accumulated stress and priming muscles for efficient movement. Unlike passive stretching, pandiculation engages muscles actively, fostering neuromuscular re-education about their optimal functioning.

The Three-Stage Process: Contracting, Lengthening, and Relaxing

Pandiculation is a choreographed, three-stage process intricately designed to recalibrate muscle tension and length.

In the initial stage, the focus is on intentionally contracting the already tight muscle group. This further contraction sends a potent signal to the brain, acknowledging the muscle's current state and priming it for change. This stage is pivotal, as it enhances the muscle's proprioceptive feedback, setting the groundwork for effective release.

The second stage involves a deliberate and slow lengthening of the muscle beyond the typical range achieved in passive stretching. This phase allows muscle fibers to elongate, fostering improved flexibility and circulation. It also encourages the brain to recognize the muscle's full potential range, challenging ingrained patterns of movement and tension.

The concluding stage is complete relaxation. After the active contraction and lengthening, allowing the muscle to fully relax helps the nervous system recalibrate and accept this new state as the muscle's 'normal' tension. This phase is crucial in solidifying the changes induced during the exercise and establishing a new baseline for muscle function and length.

Immediate Effects and Long-Term Benefits

The immediate aftermath of pandiculation often brings a palpable sense of release and enhanced mobility in the targeted muscle groups. Practitioners typically report reduced muscular tension, an increased range of motion, and a deep sense of relaxation following a pandiculation session. These immediate outcomes contribute to more balanced and efficient body posture and movement.

The long-term advantages of regular pandiculation practice are profound. Over time, these exercises can affect enduring alterations in muscle contraction and relaxation patterns, fostering a more harmonious and pain-free bodily existence. Pandiculation helps keep chronic tension from coming back by constantly challenging and renewing the neuromuscular system's patterns. It also improves overall somatic awareness and control. It stands as an indispensable element in the somatic toolkit, offering a proactive means to preserve and elevate bodily health and functionality.

Body Awareness Techniques

Establishing Connection with the Body

How do we reflect the connection between mind and body, especially in the wake of trauma? "Body Awareness Techniques," a critical component of our series, introduces methods integral to somatic therapy, focusing on re-establishing this vital connection. These techniques advocate for a heightened awareness of bodily sensations, movements, and one's overall relationship with the physical self. This reconnection is the initial step towards identifying areas of tension, misalignment, or imbalance. It encompasses a range of exercises that encourage individuals to become acutely attuned to their bodies, often leading to revelations about movement patterns, stress points, and avenues for change. This increased awareness is key to pinpointing the origins of discomfort or pain and laying the groundwork for targeted somatic exercises.

Coordinative Arm and Leg Movements

Coordinative movements, particularly those involving arms and legs, are designed to sharpen body awareness and enhance neuromuscular coordination. One foundational exercise, for instance, involves lying on the back with knees bent, feet flat, and arms extended. Participants then engage in slow, synchronized movements, rolling their arms in opposite directions while gently twisting their knees and heads. This not only fosters awareness of limb interconnectivity but also encourages the central nervous system to undertake more complex, coordinated tasks. Such movements aim to disrupt habitual patterns and introduce a diverse range of motion, heightening one's attunement to their body's capabilities and limitations and encouraging movement with greater efficiency and grace. The deliberate, mindful nature of these exercises ensures every movement is fully experienced, fostering a deeper comprehension of the body's mechanics and the synergy between its various parts.

Enhancing Sensory Perception
The goal of enhancing sensory perception is to fine-tune the body's ability to perceive and respond to both internal and external stimuli. This involves exercises that amplify sensitivity to touch, proprioception, and kinesthetic awareness. Techniques may include concentrated attention on different body parts, exploring nuances of touch and pressure, or engaging in movements that demand balance and precision. Through these practices, individuals learn to detect subtler aspects of sensation and movement, leading to heightened body awareness and control.

By regularly partaking in sensory enhancement exercises, individuals cultivate a more nuanced sense of their body's spatial occupation, movement, and responsiveness to various forms of touch and movement. This not only contributes to enhanced bodily control and ease but also nurtures a more profound and appreciative relationship with one's physical being. Enhanced sensory perception forms an essential component of somatic practices, as it underpins the ability to early detect imbalances and apply appropriate somatic techniques to restore harmony and well-being.

Focusing on Specific Areas

Lower Back: Alleviating Common Pains Addressing the lower back is crucial in somatic practices due to the widespread occurrence of lower back pain. Specific exercises target this area to alleviate pain, improve flexibility, and strengthen the muscles around the spine. A typical exercise might involve lying flat on the back, legs extended, then performing gentle twisting motions or pelvic tilts to engage and release the lower back's deep muscles. These movements aid in loosening tight muscles, correcting imbalances, and promoting better alignment, which is key to alleviating lower back pain. The aim is not merely pain relief but to reeducate the muscles into healthier, sustainable movement and relaxation patterns.

Right and Left Back: Achieving Symmetry and Balance Focusing on both sides of the back is vital for overall symmetry and balance. Imbalances between the right and left sides can lead to postural issues and reduced mobility. Exercises targeting these areas often involve lateral stretches, twists, or bends, encouraging both sides of the back to function harmoniously. By doing so, these exercises help equalize muscle strength and flexibility on both sides, fostering a more balanced and functional back. This bilateral focus benefits not just the back but the entire body's alignment and symmetry.

Spinal Freedom: Enhancing Spinal Health Fostering spinal health is foundational in somatic practices, given the spine's crucial role in overall body function and movement. Exercises aimed at 'Spinal Freedom' seek to increase flexibility, fluidity, and range of motion in the spine. They may include arching, curling, twisting, and elongating movements, promoting each vertebra's independent movement. Such practices help decompress the spine, relieve tension, and encourage a more dynamic and adaptable spinal column.

These exercises are conducted with meticulous attention to the sequence and quality of movement, ensuring the spine is engaged gently and effectively. The emphasis is on smooth, flowing movements that respect the body's natural boundaries while gently extending its capabilities. Regular practice of these spinal exercises can lead to reduced stiffness, diminished pain, and an overall sense of ease and mobility in everyday activities.

Extending Flexibility and Movement

Hamstrings: Beyond Basic Stretches
How do we extend flexibility and movement in our bodies, particularly in areas like the hamstrings, which are pivotal for our mobility and posture? In our exploration of somatic practices, we discover that beyond basic stretches, there's a world of deliberate exercises that engage the hamstrings more holistically and effectively. These exercises often integrate stretching with contracting and releasing movements, fostering a deeper understanding and control of these muscles. Techniques may include seated or standing stretches that not only elongate the hamstrings but also engage surrounding muscles and joints, ensuring a comprehensive range of motion and flexibility. The goal is to move beyond mere temporary elongation toward sustained, functional flexibility that supports everyday activities and reduces the risk of injury.

Side Stretch: Lateral Flexibility
Lateral flexibility is often neglected in traditional exercise routines. In somatic practice, side stretches focus on the muscles and connective tissues running along the body's side, enhancing breathing, posture, and movement. Techniques may involve standing or seated stretches with one arm lifted and the body gently bending to the opposite side. These stretches benefit not only the muscles but also the intercostal spaces between the ribs, promoting expansive and relaxed breathing. Regular practice of these stretches can lead to a more graceful and fluid range of motion, especially in activities requiring side bending and twisting.

Thighs: Deepening the Stretch

The thighs, comprising several key muscle groups, are essential for standing, walking, and moving efficiently. Somatic practices offer varied exercises that target these muscles comprehensively, delving beyond superficial stretching to deeply engage and educate the muscles. This might include seated or standing exercises focusing on extending, contracting, and releasing the thigh muscles mindfully. Special attention is paid to how the thighs interact with the rest of the body, ensuring that, as they are stretched and strengthened, they do so in a way that supports overall bodily alignment and functionality. These practices ensure that the thighs are not just flexible but also strong and supportive, contributing to a more stable and agile body.

Specialized Focus Exercises

Neck and Shoulder: Releasing Tension

The neck and shoulders, common sites for stress and tension, often suffer from stiffness, pain, and limited mobility. Somatic exercises for these areas involve gentle, controlled movements to encourage muscle relaxation and lengthening. Through lifting, rotating, and stretching movements, these exercises aim to release accumulated tension, restore natural alignment, and improve nutrient and oxygen flow to the tissues. Performed slowly and mindfully, these movements allow the brain to recalibrate its perception of tension and relaxation. Regular practice can significantly reduce the frequency and intensity of neck and shoulder discomfort, leading to a more relaxed posture and an overall sense of well-being.

Comprehensive Range of Motion: Integrating Different Body Parts

Achieving holistic improvement in movement and flexibility requires viewing the body as an integrated system. Somatic exercises for a comprehensive range of motion involve sequences engaging multiple body parts in a fluid, coordinated manner, such as combined spinal twists, hip rotations, and arm stretches. The goal is to improve the functional interplay between different muscle groups, ensuring movement is efficient, graceful, and balanced. As individuals master these comprehensive exercises, they often notice improvements not only in targeted areas but also in overall coordination, balance, and ease of movement.

Personalizing Somatic Practices for Individual Needs

While general principles and exercises exist in somatic practices, the most effective approach is tailored to everyone's unique body and specific needs. Personalization might involve modifying exercises for injuries, focusing on tension or weakness areas, or aligning practices with personal goals. This bespoke approach ensures the practices are safe, comfortable, and maximally beneficial, possibly involving collaboration with a somatic practitioner for personalized exercise development. As the individual's body changes, so can the exercises, making somatic practices an increasingly effective tool for physical well-being.

CHAPTER FIVE

UNDERSTANDING
SOMATIC SYMPTOMS

Understanding the distinction between somatic symptoms and somatic disorders is crucial not only for mental and physical health professionals but also for individuals seeking to comprehend their own experiences of illness or distress. This differentiation is critical for formulating accurate diagnoses, planning effective treatments, and providing the right support to those in need.

Somatic symptoms refer to physical manifestations that an individual may perceive, such as pain, fatigue, or gastrointestinal disturbances, which do not have an immediately identifiable medical cause. These symptoms are real and can significantly impact a person's quality of life, influencing their ability to perform daily activities, emotional well-being, and social relationships. It is important to note that the presence of somatic symptoms does not necessarily imply a psychological origin; however, they can be influenced by psychological factors such as stress, anxiety, and depression.

On the other hand, somatic disorders, previously known as somatoform disorders, are characterized by excessive concern about physical symptoms suggesting a medical condition but which cannot be fully explained by a medical diagnosis after thorough examination. These disorders include a variety of conditions such as somatization disorder, conversion disorder, persistent pain disorder (previously known as somatoform pain disorder), and illness anxiety disorder (formerly known as hypochondriasis). In these conditions, physical symptoms are accompanied by significant levels of distress and concern, which can lead to frequent medical visits, tests, and procedures, often without significant relief.

The main distinction between somatic symptoms and somatic disorders lies in the role played by health anxiety and excessive concern in somatic disorders, compared to the possible lack of a clear psychological origin in somatic symptoms. While somatic symptoms may be an isolated expression of discomfort, somatic disorders represent a more complex pattern of experiences and behaviors related to the perception of one's physical health.

In addressing somatic symptoms, the approach can vary significantly depending on the presumed underlying cause or contributing factors. Strategies may include pain management, relaxation techniques, physical therapy, and, in some cases, pharmacological interventions. The goal is to alleviate physical symptoms by improving the quality of life.

For somatic disorders, treatment requires a more integrated approach that addresses both the physical and psychological aspects of the condition. Psychotherapy, particularly cognitive-behavioral therapy, has been shown to be effective in modifying dysfunctional thoughts and behaviors related to health anxiety. Interventions may also include patient education on symptom management and strategies to reduce the frequency of unnecessary medical visits.

Understanding the distinction between somatic symptoms and somatic disorders is vital for directing individuals toward the most appropriate treatment pathway. While both experiences involve the perception of physical discomfort, their origins, implications, and management strategies differ significantly. Effectively addressing these conditions requires a holistic approach that considers the complexity of the interaction between mind and body as well as the need for personalized treatments that respond to the specific needs of everyone.

Types and Manifestations of Somatic Symptoms

The concept of somatic symptoms encompasses a wide range of physical manifestations that can significantly impact an individual's life. These manifestations vary greatly in terms of intensity, duration, and origin, requiring personalized attention to fully understand their impact on a person's well-being. Among the various types, chronic pain emerges as one of the most pervasive and challenging experiences, deserving of in-depth analysis.

Chronic Pain

Chronic pain is defined as pain that persists beyond the normal healing period, typically considered to be over three months. This type of pain can range from mild to debilitating and may be present in different areas of the body, manifesting in various forms such as musculoskeletal, neuropathic, or visceral pain. Unlike acute pain, which serves as an alarm system for the body, chronic pain often lacks an evident biological function and can become a standalone health condition.

Characteristics of Chronic Pain

Chronic pain is characterized by its persistence and its profound ability to influence an individual's quality of life. Reduced mobility, difficulty performing daily tasks, sleep disturbances, and changes in mood, including anxiety and depression, are some of the effects of chronic pain. The pervasive nature of chronic pain means it can affect not only physical but also emotional and social health, leading to a vicious cycle of pain and psychological distress that can be challenging to break.

Origins and Contributing Factors

The causes of chronic pain are diverse and often complex. They may include underlying medical conditions such as arthritis, diabetes, or autoimmune diseases, but they can also arise without an identifiable medical cause. In many cases, chronic pain results from a combination of physical, psychological, and environmental factors. Stress, past traumas, and lifestyle factors like physical inactivity can all contribute to the development and maintenance of chronic pain.

Management and Treatment

Managing chronic pain requires a holistic, multidisciplinary approach that may include pharmacotherapy, physical therapy, psychotherapy, and lifestyle modifications. Somatic psychotherapy offers valuable tools for addressing chronic pain, helping individuals understand and modify the relationship between their pain experiences and their emotional and behavioral responses to it. Techniques such as body awareness, meditation, and mindful movement can help reduce pain intensity, improve functionality, and enhance quality of life.

Chronic pain represents one of the major challenges in the field of somatic health, requiring a comprehensive and personalized approach to treatment. Understanding its manifestations, origins, and effective management strategies is crucial to supporting individuals affected by this debilitating condition. Somatic psychotherapy emerges as a crucial component of this multidisciplinary approach, offering hope and relief to those living with chronic pain.

Fatigue and sleep disorders

Fatigue and sleep disorders are two of the most common somatic manifestations that significantly influence individuals' health and overall well-being. These conditions, often interconnected, can stem from a wide range of underlying causes, including physical, psychological, and environmental factors. Their management and understanding require a holistic approach that considers the interaction between body and mind.

Chronic Fatigue

Chronic fatigue goes beyond the normal tiredness resulting from physical exertion or lack of sleep. It is a persistent condition of exhaustion that does not improve with rest and can significantly limit a person's ability to perform daily activities. The causes can be multifaceted, including medical conditions such as chronic fatigue syndrome (CFS), sleep disorders, depression, anxiety, and prolonged stress. Other somatic symptoms like muscle pain and weakness are frequently present with chronic fatigue, which can make diagnosis and treatment more challenging.

Sleep Disorders

Sleep disorders, such as insomnia, sleep apnea, and circadian rhythm disorder, affect the ability to fall asleep or stay asleep and the quality of sleep itself. These disorders can have a profound impact on mood, cognitive performance, physical health, and overall quality of life. The causes of sleep disorders can vary from anxiety and stress to underlying medical conditions, stimulant substance use, or environmental factors such as noise or poor sleep hygiene.

Integrated Management of Fatigue and Sleep Disorders

The approach to treating fatigue and sleep disorders must be personalized and may require collaboration among specialists from various fields, including general medicine, psychology, physical therapy, and nutrition. Managing these conditions may include strategies such as regulating sleep schedules, regular physical exercise, relaxation, and mindfulness techniques, and, in some cases, pharmacological interventions.

Somatic psychotherapy offers valuable tools for exploring and modifying how fatigue and sleep disorders manifest in the body. Through body awareness and movement, individuals can learn to recognize and manage tensions and stress patterns contributing to their condition. This approach can also help identify and modify lifestyle habits that perpetuate cycles of fatigue and sleep disorders, promoting self-care practices that support quality sleep and optimal energy levels during the day.

Fatigue and sleep disorders are complex somatic symptoms that require holistic attention to an individual's health. Understanding their causes and seeking effective management strategies are essential for improving the quality of life for those affected. Somatic psychotherapy, with its focus on mind-body integration, emerges as a promising therapeutic approach, offering new perspectives and tools to address these pervasive challenges.

Gastrointestinal and cardiovascular symptoms

Somatic symptoms can manifest in various areas of the body, affecting various systems and organs. Among these, gastrointestinal and cardiovascular symptoms are particularly significant due to their frequent association with stress responses and emotional conditions. Understanding these manifestations requires a holistic approach that considers not only the physical aspect but also the psychological and environmental impact on an individual's health.

Gastrointestinal Symptoms

Somatic gastrointestinal disorders can range from mild symptoms such as bloating and abdominal discomfort to more severe conditions such as irritable bowel syndrome (IBS) and gastritis. These symptoms often intensify during periods of stress or anxiety, suggesting a close connection between the nervous system and the gastrointestinal tract, also known as the brain-gut axis. Gastrointestinal manifestations can significantly compromise quality of life, affecting eating habits, sleep, and daily activities.

Effective management of somatic gastrointestinal symptoms includes identifying and modifying stress factors, adopting a balanced diet, and, in some cases, using medication to alleviate symptoms. Psychotherapy, particularly cognitive-behavioral therapy, and somatic psychotherapy, can offer valuable tools for managing the anxiety and stress that often accompany these disorders, promoting relaxation and body awareness strategies that help mitigate the emotional impact of symptoms.

Cardiovascular Symptoms

Somatic cardiovascular symptoms, such as rapid heartbeat (tachycardia), chest pain, and palpitations, can be particularly alarming for those experiencing them, often leading to concerns about their heart health. Although these symptoms may sometimes indicate underlying medical conditions, they are not uncommonly influenced by or exacerbated by psychological factors such as anxiety, stress, and depression.

The approach to treating somatic cardiovascular symptoms requires a comprehensive medical assessment to rule out organic causes. Subsequently, strategies such as regular physical exercise, deep breathing and relaxation techniques, and psychotherapy can be helpful in managing stress and reducing the frequency and intensity of symptoms. Somatic psychotherapy can help individuals develop greater awareness of the connections between their emotions and physical manifestations, offering personalized paths to relaxation and psychophysical well-being.

Both gastrointestinal and cardiovascular symptoms illustrate the complexity of the interaction between mind and body. Recognizing and treating these symptoms requires a multidisciplinary approach that considers the individual's physical, emotional, and psychological health. Somatic psychotherapy, with its focus on integrating mind, body, and spirit, offers a unique and powerful perspective for addressing these symptoms, promoting self-management strategies that can significantly improve quality of life.

SOMATIC PSYCHOTHERAPY

CHAPTER SIX

SOMATIC PSYCHOTHERAPIES

In the vast field of somatic psychotherapies, a fundamental question arises: How does our bodily experience shape our psychological well-being? This group of therapeutic approaches recognizes the body's important role in our mental and emotional health. Based on the premise that emotional, psychological, and mental distress frequently manifests physically, they imply that true healing requires not only engaging the mind but also the body.

The evolution of somatic psychotherapy stems from a deeper understanding of the inseparable and reciprocal relationship between mind and body. This approach melds body-focused techniques with traditional psychotherapeutic practices, fostering holistic healing. It is particularly resonant for individuals who have endured trauma, chronic stress, or those in pursuit of profound, transformative change.

By tuning into the body's sensations, movements, and posture, somatic psychotherapies strive to unlock, and release accumulated tension, alleviate physical discomfort, and confront unresolved trauma. Practitioners of this approach maintain that altering physical patterns can catalyze changes in emotional and psychological patterns, leading to significant shifts in an individual's life experience.

This approach underscores the interconnectedness of our physical and mental states, highlighting the body as a pivotal landscape for healing and transformation. In this light, somatic psychotherapy offers a path to understanding and working through the psyche and engaging directly and meaningfully with the human self, facilitating a journey toward comprehensive well-being.

In the realm of psychotherapy, a groundbreaking and nuanced approach emerges right-brain psychotherapy. This form of therapeutic intervention ventures deep into the intricate interplay between the mind and body, with a particular emphasis on the significant role of the brain's right hemisphere. It is anchored in the understanding that our emotional lives, intuition, creativity, and the processing of nonverbal cues are deeply rooted in this part of the brain. This approach seeks to engage the right hemisphere's capabilities to confront and heal emotional and psychological distress, often entrenched in nonverbal and unconscious patterns.

The most recent advancements in neuroscience have informed psychotherapy, which acknowledges a fundamental division of labor within the brain. While the left hemisphere excels in tasks like logical reasoning, language processing, and analytical thinking, the right hemisphere offers a realm where emotional and experiential data are processed in a more global, holistic manner. It is within the right hemisphere that our emotional experiences are woven together and where the subtle nonverbal cues of our existence—facial expressions, tones of voice, and body language—are interpreted and understood.

Thus, this therapy employs techniques specifically designed to stimulate the right brain. These methods enable individuals to tap into deep-seated feelings and memories, realms that might remain obscured in more traditional, left-brain-dominated verbal therapies. Through right-brain psychotherapy, individuals can access and integrate these profound emotional experiences, fostering a journey of healing that is as comprehensive as it is transformative.

The benefits of right-brain psychotherapy include deep emotional healing, enhanced body awareness, reduced physical tension, and improved nonverbal communication. This approach offers comprehensive benefits that address the multifaceted nature of the human experience. It acknowledges and leverages the right hemisphere's powerful role in emotional processing, body awareness, and nonverbal communication. By doing so, it facilitates a deep, holistic healing process that can transform not just the mind but the entire being, leading to a more integrated, aware, and fulfilling life.

Exploring the different techniques and approaches in somatic psychotherapy delves into a rich and varied landscape of practices aimed at promoting holistic well-being. This therapeutic approach integrates body and mind, recognizing that emotional and mental issues are often stored and reflected in the body. Through techniques like body scanning, breathwork, movement therapy, and touch, individuals can connect with their bodily experience in profound and meaningful ways, paving the way for increased resilience, emotional regulation, and overall well-being.

The Genco Method Somatic Release offers an innovative approach to healing, incorporating mindful breathing, visualization, and conscious cellular interaction. This practice guides individuals through a journey of inner exploration, allowing them to access internal resources and facilitate transformation and healing.

In conclusion, this exploration of somatic psychotherapies, right-brain psychotherapy, and the Genco Method Somatic Release underscores the depth and breadth of healing models available to those seeking holistic well-being. It is a tribute to the profound interconnectedness of mind, body, and spirit and the unlimited potential for growth, transformation, and healing that resides within each of us. As we continue our journey of self-discovery and healing, we can embrace the wisdom of our bodies, the insights of our minds, and the power of our spirits to create lives of purpose, vitality, and joy.

CHAPTER SEVEN

PERSONAL STORIES

This chapter introduces us to the deeply personal narratives of those who have embarked on a journey through the realms of somatic psychotherapy. Beyond mere accounts of healing, these stories are emotionally charged testimonies that reflect the transformative essence of somatic therapy. Through these narratives, we immerse ourselves in a wide range of human experiences, from the dark valleys of trauma and the suffocating grips of anxiety to the relentless struggle with chronic pain and the enigmatic reality of somatic disorders. Each tale mirrors an individual's journey through their physical and emotional realms, guided by the principles and practices of somatic psychotherapy.

The Rebirth of Michael: A Journey from Darkness to Light

Michael's tale commences in a quaint town nestled amidst rolling hills, where the picturesque landscape starkly contrasts the shadows that cloaked his childhood. He had grown up in a home where abuse was constant, so every day was a struggle for his emotional survival. Both physical and emotional maltreatment left profound scars on Michael, unseen to the naked eye but deeply etched into the fabric of his soul and body.

Upon reaching adulthood, Michael made the move to the city, determined to leave his past behind. He entered the field of social work because of a strong desire to help those who had gone through similar struggles. However, despite achieving professional milestones, the specters of his past continued to haunt him, manifesting in panic attacks, insomnia, and a perpetual muscular tension that seemed to enwrap him like a second skin.

The pivotal moment for Michael arrived following a particularly arduous session of verbal therapy, during which his therapist suggested delving into somatic psychotherapy. Initially skeptical, the notion that his body could harbor the key to unlocking emotional pain felt foreign. Yet, spurred on by his yearning for solace, he decided to give it a chance.

Michael's voyage through somatic psychotherapy commenced with the gradual but steady realization of the concealed tensions within his body. Under the guidance of his therapist, he learned to discern and articulate the physical sensations associated with his traumatic memories. This process of bodily introspection marked the initial stride toward emancipating himself from the shackles of his past.

As the sessions progressed, Michael delved deeper into exploring his trauma through movement and breath. He unearthed those certain somatic exercises evoked intense emotions. Rather than stifling them as he had done in the past, he learned to allow them to course through him. This practice of bodily mindfulness and acceptance became integral to his healing journey.

The zenith of his odyssey occurred during a session in which, through guided movement, Michael succeeded in unburdening himself of a profound emotional tension that had been suppressed for years. It was a cathartic experience, heralding the dawn of his emotional renaissance.

Today, Michael feels as though he has finally seized control of his life. Though the trauma remains indelible, it no longer exerts the same grip over him. Armed with strategies to manage panic attacks and muscular tension, he finds solace in breath and mindful movement. Somatic psychotherapy has bestowed upon him resilience and hope, empowering him to gaze toward the future with optimism.

Michael now resides with a newfound awareness of himself and his body. Somatic healing has taught him that pain can be transmuted and that every breath can propel him toward liberation. He shares his narrative to inspire others grappling with their own traumas, underscoring the possibility of emerging from the depths of despair stronger, more cognizant, and imbued with vitality.

Michael's chronicle serves as a poignant reminder of the inherent healing potency of the mind-body connection and the capacity to triumph over even the most profound adversities, rediscovering serenity, and joy in life.

Marta's Journey Towards Light: A Story of Healing and Transformation

Marta, a young and talented programmer, found joy in creating and solving complex digital puzzles. Her life was an intricate tapestry of professional success and intellectual challenges, yet it lacked balance. She started to experience chronic back pain because of spending long hours in front of a bright screen. Initially attributing the discomfort to poor posture or occasional strain, over time, the pain became a constant shadow that overshadowed her life, hindering not only work but also moments of relaxation and restful sleep.

Marta's quest for relief from her chronic pain led her to explore various therapies and remedies, but it was the discovery of somatic psychotherapy that marked the beginning of true change. This approach, which views the body not only as the receiver of pain but also as the key to understanding and resolving emotional and physical issues, opened a new dimension of self-healing for Marta.

Marta approached somatic psychotherapy with openness and curiosity, and an experienced therapist helped her look past the physical symptom of pain to investigate its deeper causes. She soon realized that the long hours in static positions were not the sole cause of her discomfort; accumulated stress, tight deadlines, and pressure to maintain high work performance were manifesting in her body as tension and pain.

With dedication, Marta began practicing body awareness exercises, learning to tune into her body's sensations and listen to the messages they sent her. She discovered that muscle relaxation and mindful breathing not only alleviated her pain but also offered moments of peace and inner calm, rare in her hectic life.

As she integrated these practices into her daily routine, Marta noticed changes not only in her physical well-being but also in her work life. She began taking regular breaks, practicing stretching exercises, and adjusting her workspace to promote better posture. These small but significant adjustments translated into a reduction in pain and an increase in her concentration and productivity.

The most notable transformation, however, occurred in how Marta perceived herself and her work. Somatic psychotherapy taught her the importance of balance between mind and body and helped her recognize and manage stress in healthier ways. This newfound awareness led her to reconsider her priorities, seeking greater balance between her professional and personal lives.

Today, Marta lives by a new life philosophy. Chronic pain no longer dominates her days; she has found harmony and well-being by integrating somatic psychotherapy into her lifestyle. She shares her story to inspire others to recognize the importance of listening to their bodies and adopting a holistic approach to health.

Marta's story is a powerful reminder of the transformative impact somatic psychotherapy can have. Hers is a testimony to how, through listening to the body and practicing mindfulness, it is possible not only to alleviate physical pain but also to rediscover the joy of living fully, both in work and in personal life.

Sara's Dance Against Anxiety: A Journey of Transformation

SOMATIC PSYCHOTHERAPY

Sara lived for dance, finding in movement not just a profession but a true calling, a way to express what words could not convey. Her life seemed to dance to the rhythm of uninterrupted music, between dance lessons, performances, and the continuous search for new choreographies that could tell stories in a unique and touching way. However, the anxiety simmering beneath the surface transformed these expressions of freedom into moments of profound discomfort.

Sara's anxiety wasn't just an overbearing presence in her daily life; it was like a shadow that obscured her art, seeping into her performances and making every movement a battle against fear. Physical symptoms like palpitations and difficulty breathing were as debilitating as the anxiety itself, trapping her free spirit in a body that seemed to betray her at the most critical moments.

The journey toward healing began when Sara, driven by the desperation to find a solution, turned to somatic psychotherapy. This approach, which placed the body at the center to understand and address anxiety, offered her new hope. Her therapist, an expert in the link between movement and emotional well-being, guided her on a journey of self-discovery that would far exceed her expectations.

The first revelation for Sara was gaining greater body awareness. By learning to tune into her body's sensations during dance, she discovered how anxiety altered her perception of movement, turning what was once pure joy into a source of stress. This awareness led her to reconsider her approach to dance, no longer just as a performance but as an intimate dialogue with herself.

Through specific somatic psychotherapy exercises, Sara began to explore new ways of moving, incorporating deep breathing techniques and muscle relaxation into her dance routines. These tools gradually transformed her artistic practice into a powerful healing ritual, a moment to reconnect with her body and mind in a judgment-free context.

The real breakthrough occurred when Sara began using movement to express and rework the emotions fueling her anxiety. Dance became a channel through which she could release accumulated tensions, a bodily language that allowed her to converse with the hidden parts of herself. Every step, every gesture, became a word in this inner dialogue, helping her understand and accept her emotions rather than fear them.

Over time, Sara rediscovered joy in dance, finding a balance between artistic expression and personal well-being. Anxiety, though not completely gone, had lost its paralyzing power. Sara had learned to dance with her fears, transforming them into movements of strength and resilience.

Today, Sara has not only regained her passion for dance but has also expanded her role as a teacher, incorporating elements of somatic psychotherapy into her classes. Her story has become an encouragement for her students and for all those struggling with anxiety, demonstrating that it is possible to find a way out through mindful movement and connection with one's body.

Sara's transformation celebrates not only overcoming anxiety but also rediscovering herself through dance. It's a journey that illuminates the healing power of bodily expression, offering hope and inspiration to those seeking to reconnect with their essence in a world that too often pulls us away from our center.

In conclusion, the journeys of Michael, Marta, and Sara highlight the transformative power of somatic psychotherapy in addressing various challenges and obstacles in life.

Michael's story illustrates how somatic therapy enabled him to confront and overcome the deep-seated trauma from his past, ultimately allowing him to regain control of his life and find resilience and hope for the future.

Marta's journey showcases how somatic therapy helped her to alleviate chronic pain and rediscover balance and well-being in her life, leading to a newfound harmony between her professional pursuits and personal fulfillment.

Sara's experience demonstrates how somatic therapy empowered her to confront anxiety and reconnect with herself through dance, transforming fear into strength and resilience, and ultimately rediscovering joy and passion in her art.

These stories collectively underscore the potential benefits of somatic psychotherapy for readers, emphasizing its capacity to facilitate healing, promote self-awareness, and foster holistic well-being. Whether confronting trauma, chronic pain, or anxiety, somatic therapy offers readers a pathway towards healing, self-discovery, and a renewed sense of vitality and purpose in life.

CONCLUSION

In wrapping up our journey through the realms of somatic psychotherapy, I extend my deepest gratitude to you, the reader, for accompanying me on this enlightening exploration of the intricate connection between mind and body. Your engagement and curiosity have enriched our collective understanding and deepened our appreciation for the transformative potential of somatic healing.

I am immensely thankful for the opportunity to share this knowledge with you, from the foundational definitions and origins to the key theories that underpin somatic psychotherapy. Your openness to new ideas and willingness to explore the depths of your own somatic experiences have been truly inspiring.

As we conclude this book, I invite you to reflect on the insights gained and the practices encountered throughout our journey. May these teachings continue to resonate within you, guiding you toward greater awareness, resilience, and vitality in your life.

I would be deeply honored if you could take a moment to share your thoughts and experiences by leaving a review on Amazon. Your feedback not only helps others discover the value of this book but also contributes to the ongoing conversation around somatic healing and psychotherapy.

Once again, thank you for your presence and participation in this exploration. May the wisdom of somatic psychotherapy continue to inspire and empower you on your journey towards holistic well-being.

Conclusion of the
"CBT + DBT + ACT Workbook"
Collection

Dear Valued Reader,

As we approach the conclusion of our journey together through the "CBT + DBT + ACT Workbook," I want to take a moment to extend my heartfelt gratitude to you. Your commitment to walking this path of self-discovery and healing is not only brave but profoundly impactful. It has been my honor and privilege to guide you through the complexities of Cognitive Behavioral Therapy, Dialectical Behavior Therapy, and Acceptance and Commitment Therapy, sharing strategies and insights that I hope have been transformative for your mental health and well-being.

The process of writing and compiling these therapies into a single workbook was driven by a deep desire to offer a comprehensive tool that could serve as a beacon of hope and a source of practical guidance. Your decision to embark on this journey with me is a testament to your strength and your dedication to personal growth. I am truly humbled by your trust in this work and in me as your guide.

As we part ways, I encourage you to continue applying the practices and reflections you've encountered in these pages to your daily life. Remember, the path to healing and personal growth is ongoing, and each step you take is a testament to your resilience and courage.

I would be incredibly grateful if you could take a few moments to share your experience with the workbook on Amazon. Your feedback not only helps others find this resource but also supports me in creating more work that can aid in the journey of healing and self-discovery. Whether it's a thought on what resonated with you, how you've applied the techniques, or any transformations you've noticed, your review is invaluable.

Thank you once again for allowing me to be a part of your journey. Remember, the strides you've made and the insights you've gained are just the beginning. May you continue to grow, heal, and thrive in all aspects of your life.

With deepest gratitude and warmest wishes for your continued journey,

Emily Jefferson